Secrets & Lives

Mary Loudon was born in Oxfordshire in November 1966. She is the author of two highly acclaimed books, *Unveiled: Nuns Talking*, which was a bestseller in the UK and Australia, and *Revelations: The Clergy Questioned*. She has won two awards from the Society of Authors and one from *Cosmopolitan* magazine, and two poetry prizes. She has written and broadcast widely, contributed to the book *Mind Readings, Writer's Journeys Through Mental States*, and is a regular book critic for *The Times*. She lives in Wales and London with her husband, Andrew St George, a crisis consultant and author, and their daughter.

'Sharp, poignant, tragic or comic short stories, told in the interviewees' words without direct intervention from the author ... [They offer] a powerful sense of the sheer wonder and private eccentricity of human life ... All the stories are readable and some are remarkably intense, [with] Dostoyevskian power'

Brian Appleyard, *Sunday Times*

'[These] accounts of blighted lives and ruined businesses are sober, unrancorous and fair-minded to a fault ... Brutal transitions are countered by an equally powerful sense of continuity. A poignant picture of change.'

Hilary Spurling, *Daily Telegraph*

'This book reveals the intimacies and indiscretions of life behind garden walls and net curtains in a way seldom, if ever, associated with the sedately average English heart, pulsing reticence, moderation, stability and other supposedly age-old virtues ... Sins, anti-social behaviour, criminal acts, jealousies, infidelities, disenchantments, moments of madness, despair and pathos are all unearthed where they had been buried by prudence and propriety ... A remarkably uncensored portrait. Confessions ... that undermine widely held myths about Middle England.

Evening Standard

'Where's your sense of community now? Read Loudon's subtle and insightful collage of interviews and you realise that it still lives on. Loudon wrote of her anger as a teenager at hearing Margaret Thatcher say that there's no such thing as society. It's a sweet, neat form of revenge to show, as she does here, that there is.'

The Scotsman

'A picture of the far-from-average individuals to be found in any average English town ... the pieces do not betray the toil that must have gone into getting them on to the page. The subjects come imperceptibly into focus as they speak of loss, suffering, betrayal, fortitude and big ideas ... A retort to metropolitan snipes at small-town provincialism.'

Times Educational Supplement

Secrets & Lives

Middle England Revealed

Mary Loudon

PAN BOOKS

For my husband, Andrew St George.
Best friend, light of my life.

First published 2000 by Macmillan

This edition published 2001 by Pan Books
an imprint of Macmillan Publishers Ltd
25 Eccleston Place, London SW1W 9NF
Basingstoke and Oxford
Associated companies throughout the world
www.macmillan.com

ISBN 0 330 36865 6

1 3 5 7 9 8 6 4 2

A CIP catalogue record for this book is available from
the British Library.

Typeset by SetSystems Ltd, Saffron Walden, Essex
Printed and bound in Great Britain by
Mackays of Chatham plc, Chatham, Kent

Contents

Contents

'We know our places here, we mingle not
One in another's sphere, but all move orderly
In our own orbs; yet we are all concentrics.'
— *Ben Jonson*

Mary Loudon

From Estate Agents to Muslims
via the Old Berkshire Hunt

When I was nineteen, Margaret Thatcher announced that there was no such thing as society, and I felt passionately that she was wrong. That infamous remark of hers lies alongside the many reasons why I wrote this book, although it has nothing whatever to do with what has finally appeared on its pages.

I grew up in Wantage, a medium-sized market town which sits at the foot of the Oxfordshire Downs, several miles before Oxfordshire meets Berkshire and stops being fairly serious countryside; before woods, downland and swooping fields of wheat and barley shrink further back from the M4, and an already struggling landscape is reduced to mock-Georgian housing estates buffeted by motorways, industrial units and small, scruffy fields fit only for clusters of grazing horses.

This book is not about Wantage, but as Wantage is where the people whose stories make up its pages live, or have lived at some time, it's perhaps useful to know just a little bit about the place itself. Wantage is a medieval town whose social and economic progress through the centuries can be identified by many things but perhaps most obviously by the variety of its architecture. There's some good medieval (what remains of it), a little Georgian and Queen Anne, and a colossal amount of Victorian, heavy with the certainties of the age.

The local stone is a sort of yellowish grey, much duller and less attention-seeking than Cotswold stone, the local brick, terracotta. Even towards the end of the twentieth century, which has contributed to small English towns little of aesthetic value and much that is downright ugly, Wantage, by no means chocolate-box pretty, is still pleasing to look at.

During my lifetime, Wantage has undergone the same sorts of changes as small towns all over England. The market square was once filled with local butchers, bakers, tobacconists, newsagents, grocers, fruiterers, fishmongers, ironmongers and jewellers, all of which have since been usurped by charity shops, estate agents, building societies and chain stores like Blockbuster Video and WH Smith. Many traders, whose businesses were generations old, fought bravely into the eighties but with little success. By the end of that sorry decade, they'd either gone bust or slunk from the square and into the side streets, taking over premises from other businesses crippled by the double blows of competition and relocation. Meanwhile, beyond the square, executive housing estates have encroached upon the green belt that once separated the town from its nearest neighbour; rural buildings have been converted into luxury homes beyond the financial reach of most local people; and some remaining areas of outstanding natural beauty, large private gardens, orchards and old allotments have been sold to property developers.

It is easy to feel sentimental or angry, or both, about these changes. After all, Wantage was once the commercial centre for twenty-five outlying villages. It had two flour mills, an engineering works, a dairy, a foundry and a railway station. At the turn of the century it supported over sixty shops and a flourishing market. One flour mill survives, but the railway station was closed and the poetically named Elm Farm Dairy was taken over by Unigate. The travelling market still comes twice a week but local beef, lamb, poultry, eggs, cheese and domestic goods have been replaced by stalls selling Indian T-shirts, Filipino basketwork, discounted sweets and towels from Taiwan. Fruit, flowers and vegetables remain but are imported from Spain, Chile and South Africa.

Secrets & Lives

With the economic reshaping of small towns during the eighties came obvious attendant social change. While life for many within the town remained relatively unchanged, and the poorest sections of the community felt no improvement whatever in their general living and employment conditions, more and more commuters, mainly from London, poured into Wantage and its surrounding villages. Waitrose arrived and the Co-op departed. Ford Cortinas were superseded by Mini Metros, which gave way to Vauxhall Astras, which were replaced by four-wheel drives and Mercedes. House prices rose, wine bars opened and the local prep school thrived for the first time in years. There were traffic jams over the Downs when the point-to-point or sheepdog trials took place, and the church was full for Midnight Mass on Christmas Eve, as swelling numbers of people confirmed themselves as custodians of thoroughly respectable English rural traditions. Eventually, of course, the bubble burst. House prices slumped; the wine bars closed; shop premises emptied once again, and this time remained empty; and people started to talk openly about their depression and marital difficulties.

Despite all this, despite the effect of Thatcher's skewed vision of Britain, and the devastating and permanent ramifications of her social and economic policies upon individuals and families, something fundamental about the nature of Wantage appears to have remained intact. When I walk around the town now, it looks much as it ever did, largely because lives are being lived in it as they always were. People are still being born, going to school, getting married and dying there. And while every individual life has its joys and tragedies, on a community level nothing more remarkable than this steady human turnover is happening in the town today. Certainly nothing very dramatic happened there when I was growing up. There was plenty of outrage on the front of the local paper: there was infidelity and petty crime and some ongoing local feuds; there were several minor business scams, some entertaining racing scandals and one tragic domestic murder. Probably the highlight of my teenage years was when Wantage was clearly confused in the minds of some overzealous TV researchers with somewhere else, and thus became the subject of a TV documentary on rural violence. The researchers doubtless believed – or wished to believe – that Wantage, being not so far from Reading, which had a fairly established reputation for violent city centre thuggery, must also suffer from marauding gangs of youths who got their kicks from sticking six-inch nails into the flesh of policemen and two fingers up at the magistrates who sentenced them.

The film-makers, once they arrived, had a tough time. They managed to get footage of a seventeen-year-old girl swearing aimlessly outside a pub; they found a shopping trolley dumped in the local stream and a disgruntled member of the public to grumble about it; they interviewed a group of inebriated boys who pointed out, quite accurately, that weekly brawls had always been a part of life because as far as they were concerned there was bugger-all else to do on Friday and Saturday nights. Best of all, they managed to track down a couple of bemused police officers who, when asked in pressing tones if they felt threatened on the beat on a Friday night, turned vaguely towards the camera and laughed in disbelief.

Over the years, I have maintained strong links with Wantage, despite moving away. My chief attachment to it is personal, emotional; it is my family home and I am still deeply attached to it. The road I walked up to primary school is the road I walked down with my husband on our wedding day. It is also the road which marks, quite literally, the final departure of local inhabitants; the road along which I have watched the snaking away of several friends' funeral hearses. I have also always liked the lack of anonymity of the place. I like the fact that it's hard to walk around the market square without running into someone you know, though it can be irksome if all you're there for is a postage stamp. In fact, the market square was precisely where I secured quite a lot of the interviews for this book: I remember swapping telephone numbers with a woman I'd been trying to track down for months, outside the shoe shop. Four or five people made arrangements with me in the supermarket, one at the taxi rank, two in the swimming-pool changing rooms, one in the churchyard, and one at the dentist.

Personal feelings apart, Wantage intrigues me as a writer; not as a place but for what it symbolizes. For while the town has always been prosperous by national standards, it nevertheless contains within its boundaries pronounced economic disparity and social diversity. Between the town's picturesque centre and its pretty surrounding villages are the housing estates where most of the local population lives. Yet to increasingly ill-informed sections of the media, with its bludgeoning approach to most things non-metropolitan, towns like Wantage are quintessential Middle England because they supposedly represent a distant life of cottages, rose-filled gardens, home-made jam and safety.

Although Middle England, as a term, has never been properly defined, it is generally used pejoratively, and understood to mean whatever the user wishes. Middle England, middle class, middlebrow, middle income, middle of the road: Middle England appears most often to mean a vague kind of middling privilege, almost always of a soft southern kind. Middle England may not be on the map, but it is recognizably green-welly land, where people go to church and vote Tory; it's a culture of cricket and Range Rovers and Sunday lunches; where a guilty collective social conscience keeps those who live there mindful of the ills of the rough-tough country beyond, although they are relieved to have as little as possible to do with their urban counterparts.

This of course is a ridiculous cliché. Middle England is a place, and a disposition, as bleak for some as it is privileged for others; as loathed as much as it is loved; as progressive as it is steeped in nostalgia. All the same, I love clichés. As a writer, they give you something to work against. Having written previously about nuns and clergy, two groups of people about whom many people have strong but often inaccurate notions, I hoped that a collection of life-stories of those living in an ordinary English market town might offer a strong corrective to the myth of harvest-festival cosiness and rural bliss, whilst simultaneously reinforcing some of the more enduring aspects of contemporary English life. I wasn't remotely interested in local history: I simply wanted to find out about Middle England – an England, as it happens, of extremes and opposites — and I chose to do this by investigating the inhabitants of the place I knew best because it was the most direct way to the heart of the matter.

While Wantage is not demographically or economically representative of everywhere else, the concerns of the people who live there are. Wantage is not the post-industrial north, it's not the suburbs, and it's no more Bolton than it is Penzance; but fractured families, drug-taking teenagers, confused thirtysomethings, cheating spouses, the decent, the hard-working, the snobbish, the contented, the envious, the lonely, the unemployed, the ambitious, the violent, and the bereaved are everywhere. For me, the fascination lies in discovering how the infinite variety of people who make up the backbone of provincial England reflect something of our national character, fears, hopes and desires. Geographically speaking, Wantage may not be just anywhere, but humanly, it is.

When I left school, and effectively left Wantage, I travelled fairly extensively, went to university, and then took up my backpack once more upon leaving, and went to work in Calcutta, India. Like many twenty-two-year-old backpackers, I was running away from a relationship, but I was also discarding everything else that I felt at the time to be stifling about life in England: its climate, its codes, its expectations, its cynicism, its fumbling inability to express itself except in clichés; worst, most pernicious of all, its class system. And despite the irony of working in a country with more than just a few relics of the British Empire to show for itself, it is probably no accident that I embarked straight away on a long and cheerful relationship with an Australian man, upon whom all the dark subtleties and elephant traps of English social intercourse were entirely lost.

I don't know why I so hated the English class system, but I did and I do. Apart from being bullied at school and beaten up for being posh when I was a child, it's never otherwise been personally detrimental to me. My background was a privileged one: it was financially prosperous, educationally rich, emotionally stable, and full of fun. I was brought up to believe that I was lovable and I was encouraged to do the things that I enjoyed. But I was also brought up with a strong sense of other people's value in the world, a value that didn't depend upon background or education, that didn't, in fact, depend upon anything in particular, and it's probably the most useful thing I learnt. It has left me with a terrific anger at the way in which we English pigeonhole and label one another; at the petty — and not so petty — social injustices we still mete out to those not like ourselves; at the way in which our voices, our dress, our names, our education, our colour and our occupations say almost nothing about the people we are, but betray, to those who still believe in such crude means of deciphering, enough details for them to decide what we are like.

This doesn't mean I do not have my own opinions about the way other people operate: there were certainly plenty I had to put aside in the course of my work, which were at odds with those of the people I interviewed. I loathe fox-hunting. I think building on greenfield sites should be banned, that all individual farm subsidies should be stopped and grants paid instead to trained custodians of the land before the UK's entire wildlife goes to hell for good. I uphold individual choice but I don't believe that public schools and private medical care are healthy for a society which purports to be egalitarian. I think English society is badly polluted by snobbery, racism and ageism, and I become dogmatic when confronted with them. I have little time for the established Church. I think company cars should be banned. I believe children should be taught how to think, not how to remember. But so what? Most of the time my views don't even interest me all that much, and anyway many of them may change with greater age and experience. While my own feelings about an issue or idea inform my work, I hope that they do not prey upon someone else's. I write books as a way of exploring questions that I have, and finding out about people I don't know, and not in order to prove to myself something that I already believe.

All this does, however, raise the question of objectivity. Listening to people and writing stories is not a science. I can only present people as I see them, and I have only one pair of eyes. As for what I see, and hear, I generally believe most things that people tell me, but even if I have some doubt I don't think it matters, because I believe that everything somebody tells me tells me something about them, and *that's* what's interesting. The biggest challenge to me is to present it as purely as possible while making it readable, to distil without deceiving. I nearly clobbered the person who said to me once, 'Sounds piss-easy what you do, interviewing people and writing it out.' Well, there are certainly many far less enjoyable ways to make a living, but as for verbatim transference from tape to paper – if only. This book is one hundred and fifty thousand words long. The original material I had at my disposal was over two million words long, and knowing what and when to cut, although instinctive, is a slow process with no logical explanation. A sculptor was asked by a friend, as he worked on a large marble elephant: 'How do you know, when faced with a lump of marble, where to start?' The sculptor replied: 'I just chip away the bits that aren't the elephant.' While every word and every sentence of every story in this book is true to its narrator, in terms of structure it is true only to me, the author. If a story is recognizably an elephant, it is nevertheless my elephant: in that sense alone each story is mine, for my sensibility and my response to each person is embedded in its shape, for better or worse.

However, to keep some check on where the narrator stops and the author begins, I always offer people I work with right of veto over the final story. It seems to me the only morally proper way to proceed if you are working with the most intimate fabric of people's lives, and truly only fair. Possibly, though I can't be sure, because the offer alone affords them some degree of trust they almost never ask for anything to be changed; and while this keeps my life easy, it has a more important long-term aim, which is for mutual personal harmony in years to come, long after this book has been forgotten.

As for the people themselves, while many of those whose stories make up this collection have achieved great success in their lives, none of them is famous, or indeed infamous. We are living in the bizarre age of the celebrity, very often a complete nonentity who has managed to hitch a ride with the media despite an astonishing lack of talent or substance. There are no celebrities in this book, because the whole notion of celebrity is insidious, with its implication that the only lives worth reporting and aspiring to are those which contain money, and a very limited type of social access and glamour, as their main ingredients. And while it would be naive and romantic to suggest that anonymity or 'ordinariness' — a term I dislike intensely — necessarily breed humility (they don't), it's probably fair to say that those who do not have an image of who they are reflected in the national press are less dependent for their self-knowledge upon a view of themselves that extends beyond their own social circle.

It's also worth bearing in mind that while most of the stories in this collection cover pretty specific experiences of life, for each person's story there might have been dozens of others. A tragic event, say, doesn't make for a tragic life overall; neither does most suffering or regret last for a whole lifetime. Since this book was completed, the lives of everyone contained within it have changed, some for the better and some not, though few of them dramatically. The stories that appear here as portions of ampler truths are necessarily limited by time and circumstance. Though I would hope to have captured something essential of each person, there are infinitely more angles to any individual than I could possibly secure in just one story.

This book is not social history and it's not analysis. The closest analogy I can produce is to say that all I've done in writing is to take a series of photographs. The chief differences are that when trying to capture your subject in writing, you have more dimensions to play with and more details available to you: you are able to produce in one portrait more variations of light, dark and shadow than the laws of physics ever allow a photographer in just one photograph. This does not mean that writing is a superior medium, it means that it is less subject to regulations outside itself, and thus the writer is furnished with greater latitude than the photographer. Having said that, the process is similar in lots of ways. Stories, like photographs, are often attempts to capture in one particular moment something much more general and universally recognizable than the individual subject itself.

In the end, I wrote this book for myself because there were things I wanted to explore. There are writers who say they couldn't live without writing, as an abstract form of activity, and I always wonder what on earth they are talking about. I couldn't live happily without my husband, or regular swimming, but given the chance I can go blissfully for weeks without writing because, for me, writing is a response to life, not life itself, and it only has meaning when I have something I want passionately to investigate. This book is a response to the many different questions I had, and still have, about the way other people cope with life and death. It's also a rejection, if you like, of the ways in which we English usually approach one another: tentatively, cautiously, almost always with suspicion.

When Margaret Thatcher said, 'If a man finds himself a passenger on a bus having attained the age of twenty-six, he can account himself a failure in life,' she meant it. She actually believed that to be using public transport rather than driving a privately owned car was proof of a severe personal deficiency. She was a victim of that most contemptible of English weaknesses: the inability to see past the most superficial totems of success or failure to the person beyond. But because Thatcher is sadly not the only one, because all English people, however unconsciously we might do so, find it almost impossible to meet other English people without mentally placing them socially, the men and women in this book appear with nothing to show for themselves except their names. A great deal more becomes apparent from their stories, but at least the choice of what to present of themselves is all their own. I have no illusions whatever about the power of the written word to change anyone, but if, in my moments of private reverie, I dream of anything, it is this: that this book may be a place where one person can meet another absolutely head-on, at least without initial prejudice, fear or assumptions; a place where background, profession and standing are subordinate to humanity in its many rich and complex forms.

Graham Douglas

Cutting It Big

As a child, I used to brush it off. People used to say, 'Who's your mum?' and I used to say, 'I haven't got a mother, I've never had a mother.' It obviously cut very deep but I didn't realize it at the time. The split between my mum and my dad was very bitter and I think the only way for them to cope with it was to have absolutely no contact whatsoever.

My dad came down south in a turmoil. He just wanted to get out of Newcastle, get away, and that's what he did. He literally got on the train and came down here and found work at a warehouse, and moved me and my brother down south straightaway, the following week. It was a massive upheaval. Incredible. My mum and everything to do with her, I just shut it out. I had to, to live with it. I had no contact with my mother from the age of eleven up until I was twenty-four.

My nan and granddad eventually came down from Newcastle. And my nan, as far as she was concerned, it was like everything to do with my mother was bad. Although my dad didn't really put her down too much, my nan was so anti I was always under the impression that my mum didn't love us. 'She doesn't love you because she doesn't contact you; she doesn't write to you; she doesn't send you cards.' And she didn't, but I don't really know what the reason was behind that, whether things were being blocked and weren't being given to us. I've since been reunited with my mum and it was very emotional, it was a turning point in my life, to be honest, a bit like Cilla Black's programme *Surprise! Surprise!*, though not quite as bad as that.

It was important to be reunited with my mum but she didn't have a lot to say that could help me. Because it was such a terribly bitter split it seems she welcomed the breathing space. She says it's not because she didn't love us, it was just the only way to do it. My dad fought for our custody and it was just the way it happened. I'd never do it to any of my children if I'm fortunate enough to have children, you should always allow them to have contact with both their parents, it's not healthy not to. She met someone else not long after they'd split up and she had another boy, he's seventeen now, at sixth form. She's now split up with that chap and is with another man, who she's married recently, and I sincerely hope, for her sake, that she's going to find a bit of peace and happiness in her life now.

My mother's a typical Geordie and I think that's half the problem. I find it difficult to relate to her, particularly with so much of a gap between us in those years. When I left my mother I was a child, and now I'm an adult, I'm a professional, it's a different world. She let go a young boy and a young professional man comes back with his flash car, earning good money, with a southern accent: she must find it very difficult as well. She's quite tough, quite hard, on the exterior because life's not that easy up there at times, there's a lot of unemployment. She's very no nonsense, no fuss, no frills. I love her, and I love going back to see her but we don't have a great deal in common apart from the fact that she's my mum and I'm her son. Clearly you can't make up for that lost time.

I was always very confident, very cocky, very arrogant with women from very young, and I think a lot of it was to do with my mother and the fact that I had a nasty attitude towards women. I didn't want to hurt them, not physically, but it was a sort of one-upmanship: no one's going to get to me, I'm cool and hard. This was repeated many times in my relationships from quite a young age. Then I met Jane at sixth form and that was a fundamental change for me. It was the most serious relationship that I had. I was with Jane for seven years and after we split up I started to get very unhappy. I got quite depressed and didn't know what it was all about and I had to go to a doctor. I was on antidepressants. I was twenty-four and at a very low ebb.

Around the time Jane and I split up, I met my mother again for the first time. I think my dad, discovering that I was obviously very unhappy, thought that maybe this was an opportune time for me and my mum to get back together. I was very emotional but I didn't feel like there was as much coming from the other side. My mum's a different person from me in many respects. She still loves me but we're different people, and I had a lot of therapy at the time to help me face that because I was very unhappy, very depressed. I've slowly pulled myself out of it, with my career and my work being the guiding light really. Through the trials and tribulations that's what kept me going, kept me focused. But there were some pretty awful times when I thought I was never going to pull through it.

I never thought I'd have a proper relationship again. After Jane I met one or two women but the problem was I didn't really like myself, and if you don't like yourself, if you're not happy about yourself, you can't give yourself to somebody else and you can't love somebody else. So there was a lot of soul-searching to be done, a lot of building to be done, and I'm hopefully just about there now. The job's going great and life's pretty good, apart from the fact that I met this woman, Melanie, nine months ago, and I think it's the deepest I've ever felt for anybody, and she's gone to Scotland for four years and I know in my heart of hearts it's over.

Part of my problem when I was young was I used to drink too much and it made me aggressive, got me into trouble. I probably turned the traumas of my childhood into aggression when I was older. I've been through some great therapy though, fantastic. A lot of the medical profession pooh-pooh alternative therapy because it's not medical, is it, it's a bit quirky, but I had hypnotherapy and it was quite good. They take you back to your childhood and I discovered through digging into my childhood emotions that my family's break-up had had a major impact on me. Although my parents split up when I was eleven I was pulled between them for about three or four years before that, so during one or two sessions I was that little boy again and an awful lot of hurt came out. That was the idea, to get you to see this pain and experience it again and then move on. It's not like Paul McKenna, where you don't remember a thing you've done; you're still aware of everything that's going on around you and when you wake up you still remember everything. I've not really had a problem since. We all have ups and downs, life is like that, but now I'm able to deal with the downs as well as the ups. Generally I'm quite an enthusiastic and get-up-and-go sort of person, so it was quite a shock to be diagnosed as suffering from depression at twenty-four, wondering why have I got this big black feeling inside me?

I have been feeling pretty low lately, having lost Melanie to university. I've been feeling as if I needed a little bit of divine help, so I've been to church once or twice. I've always felt a little bit of a pull spiritually, and we all have our own views on it, but I've needed it lately and it's helped a lot. I couldn't believe I could feel so much for somebody after everything I'd been through, and then for it to go: I didn't realize how strong I was going to feel after she had gone. We had a bit of a bust-up about six weeks ago, when I sent her packing. It was basically because I got very jealous of a work colleague of hers when she went on some do, and it's never been the same since. It was such awful timing because she was here and we were living together, it was awful, awful timing, and I just couldn't understand why I'd let myself do that. I think it was a defence mechanism from being so hurt during my life. I think I was thinking, I'd better get my rejection in first before she goes off to university and decides that it's not right. And now I feel stupid because I shouldn't have let it happen: it was misplaced, the jealousy.

It goes back a long way, this defensiveness. As a teenager I always felt under pressure. I was a very good footballer. After school I was playing at Oxford United and I had trials for various professional clubs, but all of it was lived through the eyes of my dad and he used to put an awful lot of pressure on me to train and get fit. He was desperate for me to be a professional footballer. I know we all want the best for our kids but it was too much and he'd be the first to admit it now because he's remarried with young children again and he's much more mellow. If he hadn't put so much pressure on me I might possibly have been a professional footballer because I certainly had the talent to do it. There are players playing now who I watch and think, Yeah, I could have done that. But at that crucial time everything he wanted me to do I wouldn't do.

Perhaps subconsciously I blamed him for my mum and him splitting up. It was a difficult life at home. I used to have to do all the washing and ironing for us, all the cooking. I used to have to come home and clean the house, iron, wash, at the age of fourteen. No one knew at school. At school I was the hard guy. I used to piss off everybody: I had a little bit of a Geordie chip on my shoulder, to say the least. I was never in deep trouble but I was always on the edge of it. I've been in quite a few brawls, quite a few fights, nothing major. I never made it on to that ITV documentary, *The Shire Wars*, about rural violence. But some of the people I used to go around with clearly were quite nasty; one or two ended up in prison. When I think about it now it's really sad.

The teachers always punished but they never asked me why I was behaving so badly. Teachers don't, do they? I've discovered in my job, going through everything I've gone through, if you can relate to people's emotions it's far more rewarding. I get so much business just because I listen to people and I'm sincere and I've got some sort of empathy with them. But I've only been able to do that because I've been through a lot of pain myself and I understand it now, whereas before I couldn't. I reckon a lot of teachers don't have that ability, it's either inside you or it's not. People like the PE teachers, you'd get a cuff round the ear, not a question. I think I've been quite successful in what I do and I'll hopefully be a lot more successful, but I come across some teachers now who won't even give me the time of day, it's obvious that they're slightly jealous of what I've achieved. I get that feeling because when I walk past them in the street they won't even say hello to me. You know how you try to get a hello out of somebody because you know them, and they just look straight through you? It's awful, isn't it.

I've discovered I am quite an emotional, sensitive person. My problem is that I haven't discovered it in my mother, which after all the pain I've gone through I would have liked to have discovered; or at least I haven't discovered it in a way that makes sense to me. I did try ever so hard but it didn't seem to quite gel, you know. Maybe she feels exactly the same. Now our relationship seems very superficial and I find it difficult to talk to her about anything. We have a few sentences and then there's silence. She's a different animal altogether. She views life in a different way: 'Therapists? Depression? Give yourself a kick up the bum.' I suspect deep down she thinks I'm weak.

Up in Newcastle, from the age of six or seven, we used to run round the streets fighting. We used to have street fights, gang fights with other kids: it was all about territory and who you didn't like, that was my upbringing. My mum and dad were teenagers. My mum was nineteen by the time she'd had us, my dad was twenty; all he was interested in was going out to have a few beers. They weren't worried about where me and my brother were. We've both turned out really well, if you think about it. My brother has done exceptionally well. He's a PE teacher and he's also a rugby coach for Worcester, he's well into his sport. After his PE degree he did his Masters in Sports Psychology. It's very trendy now, Sports Psychology, every team or sportsman's got a psychologist to get the best performance out of them. A psychologist! Twenty years ago you'd get a kick up the bum: 'What do you want a psychologist for? Give yourself a clip round the ear!'

My brother's married with three children and I'm very envious of him, in a way. It's obvious that I've suffered a lot more than he has because otherwise I would have settled down in a relationship happily with children by the age of thirty, and I haven't. I didn't realize how lonely I was until I met Melanie. So I'm envious of my brother because he's got what, on the face of it, seems like the perfect marriage. I suppose no marriage is perfect. Grass can always look greener on the other side, and I suppose in another way I'm not that bothered because I meet so many of my friends who are in relationships and they're obviously not happy. I go out to so many clients who are splitting up, every day, and you need to be a bit of a counsellor to deal with that. Like I was saying earlier, it's good if you can empathize with people and this is where I think a lot of estate agents go wrong, because they're so aloof and so brash, they forget that it's a person's life that you're dealing with. They forget that selling houses is all about life and life's experiences, that it's a people business, totally, selling houses.

Melanie used to work for me. I employed her as a weekender when she was at college. We've had similar experiences, because I got the impression she had a very unhappy childhood, but she comes from completely the opposite end of the social spectrum to me, her dad's a very, very successful businessman. Though there was nothing there when I first employed her, by Christmas we'd got friendly and then the office party happened. I fought it for a long time because I was her boss but it just grew and grew.

She was twenty and I was thirty. She was thinking of going to St Andrews University, so I took her up to Scotland to suss the place out and we had the most romantic time. We stayed in the Golf Course Hotel overlooking the beach, and she met the English tutor there, and everything just felt so right. I was there backing her and supporting her and we were living here together as a happy couple and then all of a sudden she's gone and I'm very sad, to be honest. I miss her. I've lost something. I feel I need her here and I know there's a part of her that would have loved to have been here for me. But she wants to get a career, and I support that. I could almost say she's the right person for me but at the wrong time, if that makes sense.

I'm at a very sore point at the moment. It was so unconditional and so magical, it caught me so unawares. I told her the other day on the phone, I said, 'Mels, you just loved me to death. I've never felt loved like that before.' I've been carrying on on my own for years now, thinking I don't need anybody, but I discovered I do. Now she's got this life where everything's new and exciting, and I have the same life, minus her.

Basically it was just one big holiday at school, and I realized I needed to get my act together. I went back to do a couple of 'O' levels at sixth form, and I got the English but not the Biology. I also did an alternative qualification called Certificate of Extended Education, some Mickey Mouse qualification, and why I ever did it I don't know.

I realized I wasn't an academic, so I decided to go out into the workplace. I got a job as an administrator at Rutherford Lab up near Harwell for a couple of years. That got me into the general ways of working life but it was so mundane and so boring: you could plod along for seven or eight hours and not really get a lot out of it, or you could bust a gut and still not get a lot out of it. These Civil Service places are like that, it doesn't matter what you do. So I thought, What do I want? I want to be a salesman. And I applied to insurance companies and estate agents and I ended up joining an estate agency.

I discovered I had a real flair for estate agency. I was so keen to learn, so willing to get on and do it, I found I had a real edge. I was actually a manager of my own office within three years, by the time I was twenty-two. I was electric as far as selling houses was concerned. I think I was different because I was a bit more sincere whereas a lot of estate agents just seem to be out to make a quick buck, they're terribly pompous and arrogant. The biggest philosophy is not to think of your pocket at the end of the day but to think of your client's needs, and sometimes that means you might give advice that isn't necessarily to the benefit of the company. You might say, 'That house isn't right for you,' or 'That flat isn't right for you,' and people then recommend you, and this is where you can be successful. That's the philosophy I've practised for about eight or nine years now.

I've been in the Wantage office five years now and I think I'm the top agent in the town by *miles*, although I'm sure the other estate agents wouldn't agree. But some of the estate agents have been in this town for twenty, thirty years, and I feel I've taken over the mantle of them in some ways. If only I could be master of all areas of the market, but you can't. In an ideal world I'd have a company with departments which would deal with every sector of the market. I have a cross-section of property from £40,000 to £300,000 as we speak, I've got a lovely cross-section, and I think I win over business because of a slightly different approach. I'm professional, I know my stuff, but there's also the human element to it as well. I think I've added a different dimension and I think the way we do it is unique. People like it. People say, 'They're so nice in your office, they're so interested in you and that's a change.'

When people find out that you're an estate agent, no matter what thing you go to that's social, they always want to talk to you. 'What's mine worth?' 'Come and value mine.' Property's always topical, isn't it. The other thing I love is the competitiveness of it. In my football when I was a young lad I used to love being the best out there on the pitch, I knew I was really good at something when I was playing football, better than everybody else. It's the same being an estate agent. I've got to be the best. Call it insecurity, call it what you want, but I've got to be better than everybody else, and I will be. It's not so much the name above the door. To be honest, I don't look at it as 'Adkin', anyway: it *is* 'Graham Douglas Estate Agents' already. I've doubled the business in that office in five years. There are thirteen Adkin offices and mine's one of the top ones. At the Regional Managers' meetings our office was, 'Pah! Wantage!' and now all of a sudden it's a buzz; we were the jokers and now we're the tops. I've turned it right around. It was a bit of a homecoming really for the sort of person I was. It was a bit scary coming back to this town to get respectability after the way I behaved when I was young.

These days I've got some really good mates, but I've moved on from the mates I had at school, I have a different type of friend now. I don't think any of them know the depths to which I went down, or the traumas. They knew what was going on but I couldn't discuss it. I think men find it difficult to discuss those types of things with other men because it's not the culture, is it, it's not a manly thing, is it, to share with each other. It's funny, Saturday night I met up with some mates: Dave, another chap called Gavin, and another lad called Paul. And we were all sat round this table and two of them, Dave and Paul, have just come out of university as mature students, just finished their degrees, haven't got a proper job. Gavin's a trainee accountant. And we went round the table, we did this round robin, and we said to each other: 'Well, are you happy? What's your life doing, and how happy are you, and where do you think it's going?' And not one of us was actually happy. I'm unhappy about Melanie but I suppose out of all of us I was probably the most settled in my career and where I thought I was going.

Then again, it doesn't mean anything unless you've got someone who's special to you, and that's what I thought I had. But I mean, all the guys, Dave and Paul, they've done their degrees but they're still doing the wrong things. They're going out and getting drunk every night and pulling women, and ending up in bed with women they don't even want to be with, but they're just like, 'Oh all right, we'll have another beer,' you know, 'Fuck it. We'll have another drink. Who cares?' You know? And it'll hit them one day.

Having said that, I think men do look at themselves an awful lot more, emotionally, than they've ever done. I'm a nineties man and perhaps that's what it's about. But women seem to want you to be everything and that can be confusing, and I'm not sure men know what they want either now. I mean, take Melanie: she's young and she's a student and she's everything that I thought I wouldn't find attractive because I thought I'd be more likely to go for a thrusting career girl, a merchant banker or something in London, estate agent, whatever, and she's the total opposite. When she did some summer jobs before university started, one of them was working for an executive property search company and this was what caused our bust-up. I got very jealous of this fifty-five-year-old man who she ended up in the pub with, one of her bosses. I got very insecure about the whole thing because he had come from a wealthy background and he drives around in a big Range Rover, and I just lost it, lost it because of this bloody fifty-five-year-old bloke. And Melanie turned around to me and she said, 'You think you want this thrusting career girl,' because I'd been pushing her to get her degree, get a career, everything; and she said, 'But you don't really want it, do you? You think you want a woman in a career but you're not really sure, are you, whether that's what you really want?' And, yeah, we men are confused. We don't really know what we want. We think we should want a career woman but we're not sure we do.

When I felt as if I was more in control than Melanie, I used to say to her, 'Perhaps it's just one of those moments in time, Mels, you know, we love each other, it's great, everything's fantastic about it, but maybe it's just that we're meant to meet and push each other off in different directions.' After all, she inspired me quite a lot in my work, to have the dreams that I've got. I always had them, but she brought them more to the surface. And in many ways that was what held Jane and I together because, OK, Jane and I fell in love and everything, but what sustained it in the latter years, when we were more like brother and sister, was the fact that I actually fell in love with her parents and the stability as much as her, because my whole upbringing was totally unstable and here were some people who believed in me. I mean, mine was an awful family background and I just fell in love with her parents. It was great. They used to talk at the dinner table on a Sunday, and debate, and it was all so different from what I'd ever been used to.

I've tried to stay friends with Jane but it's always difficult. I mean, she's now married to somebody else. She rings me up occasionally, which is quite nice, to just catch up, but I'm very careful not to ring her because I wouldn't want to give the wrong impression, do you know what I mean? I found it hard when she got married, to be perfectly honest, because the relationship represented family and stability. It was everything that I always wanted as a child and all of a sudden it was gone, and I think this is why I had this big depression. Massive. This is why I needed the therapy.

Jane was good for me. She put me on the straight and narrow.

Nobody thought that I was going to go anywhere but Jane's parents always used to say I was the son they always wanted, and they helped me when I got my first job, and then when I went into estate agency, and they've tracked my career ever since and they always call in to see me. It was really ironic actually, because the Adkin Christmas party when Melanie and I got together, it was in the Bear Hotel, we had a big party, there was about forty of us, and at the other end of the room there was a little party and Jane's mum and dad were there. I know Wantage is a small place but for them to be in that room at the time when I met Melanie, who is the person that I have felt the most for since I split up with Jane, it is incredible really. Weird.

I had a man the other day, he'd been a bank manager here for twenty years, lovely chap, got lots to talk about, very upright, very, very sturdy, very honest man, and I made an effort to adjust to his way of thinking and his approach. You've got to be a chameleon in this job. It's like acting, you go out and play a part: but I go back to what I was saying earlier about being sincere. Every person that comes into my office, I am interested in. Some estate agents are totally out of touch with people and emotions and what life is all about now, and there are plenty of wide boys around in the business, plenty of white-sock estate agents. People tell us about them: they say, 'What are these people on? We went in and they didn't even look at us.' But you can be too pushy too, and that's the wrong approach as well. It's finding a happy medium, finding the balance.

I am not saying there isn't room for tradition but if people think I'm vulgar, a bit of a maverick, or an upstart, because I think differently, that's not right. I just enjoy making people happy. Honestly I do, because there is an awful lot of unhappiness in our business and there is nothing better than when someone comes in and says, 'Thanks very much,' because you do a good job ninety-nine per cent of the time but there's not that many people come in and say thank you. I've had bottles and cards, which is lovely, but it's probably not more than ten per cent of our clients come in and do that. It's not to say they don't mean to, they've just got so many other things on their mind it doesn't occur to them to thank the estate agent. After all, moving house can change your life. Like people splitting up, that's trauma, that's difficult. I don't like that, it makes me sad, because they do share an awful lot with you and maybe that's my trade secret, that I listen. The other day I had this lady, she was getting divorced and she was really upset, so we sat down and had a cup of tea and a long chat and I think after that it was easier for her to talk about selling the marital home. I wasn't just some salesman to her, you see. I cared about how she felt.

We sell an average of two hundred or more houses a year in this office, that's fifteen to twenty a month. There are six agents in the town and I don't suppose you will ever lose the old-school-tie situation where clearly people who've got houses worth £300-, £400-, £500,000 will go to agents like Knight Frank, or Savill's, or John D. Wood, because they're perceived as selling that sort of house, and it's wheels within wheels, they've probably all gone to the same schools. I've had the opportunity of selling two or three houses in the £500- to £750,000 bracket and every time we've been more successful than your Knight Franks or whatever because we've gone at it with a bit more keenness and efficiency. But I'd like to retain as wide a market as possible, and if you go too expensive you won't be able to do it. We could change our image completely and go more upmarket and have lots of leather-bound furniture in the office but we may well cut off the hand that feeds us if we do.

I'd welcome any house and any client. Personally, I'm as comfort-able dealing with a one-bedroomed flat as I am dealing with a lovely £300,000 house that I sold in East Hendred the other day. I enjoy them for so many different reasons. Young first-time buyers, I get so inspired because they get so excited: a new house, it's their kingdom, it's everything to them. But a lot of agents tend to look down on people with small properties. Maybe it's age, but if there came a point when I felt that I couldn't go out and look at yet another house on a housing estate I'd step away from it and get one of my younger members of staff to do it.

Everybody seems to want to move here. Wantage is a lovely town and it's so attractive for anybody wanting to come out of London, plus more computer technology means more people can work from home. There are going to be more and more mothers who work from home and more and more businesses run from home. That's why the prices are so high. Look at my house: a two-bedroomed semi for £75,000. It's a blooming box. Prices have risen by twenty per cent in the last twelve months. Eighteen months ago, your average first-time buyer round here could afford to buy a three-bedroomed semi at £65,000. That same three-bedroomed semi is now £80,000. Now, have their salaries gone up that much in that time? No.

In the recession, when prices were twenty-five per cent lower, the one- and two-bedroomed flats and the two-bedroomed houses, nobody could sell those. It's taken us ten years to recover what we lost in the recession, which is really scary. I guess what everybody aspires to is the roses above the door, a two- or three-bedroomed cottage, perhaps in the sort of £80,000 to £120,000 bracket, which is what you'd have to pay for it here. And nobody ever wants development, though it always seems to be the people who complain that the town isn't a thrusting commercial enterprise are the ones who complain about new development.

I dealt with a property called the Old Post House in West Hanney, which borders the church, and the vicar objected to the development of plots in the back garden. This was a big old period house, you've got the church here and the Post House here, both on the green. Well, the two owners of the Post House had a big scrapyard in the back garden, they'd been running it for years on about an acre of land, and we tried and tried to get planning permission to put two houses in the back garden and couldn't, the planners wouldn't allow it. I approve of planning but planning can be very corrupt; it's not always about what you know, it's about who you know, and a lot of the reasons for it being turned down were never really disclosed, but the fact that one of the local neighbours was related to a politican — well, you get the picture.

You can understand the other people's argument: there's this lovely period house next door, and there's this scrapyard, and now they're trying to get planning permission to put two houses in the garden. I think, also, people are still recovering from the ruthless attitude of the eighties where it was profit, profit, profit at all costs, and they're suspicious of development. I'm a Tory kid: I grew up knowing nothing different. I've never known a Labour government before now and I like the approach of the new Labour Party, they've adjusted it to appeal more to changing people, changing values. Nobody goes into business for charity but in the eighties it was almost at the expense of everything else. Estate agency was disgusting in the eighties: it was yuppies and Porsches and power lunches and that was all it was about; your Golf GTis, your flash cars. I think we've come full circle in the industry, and I hope it has been led by people like me who are trying to take it back to a more personal thing again and away from the Porsches and the white-sock lads. If you can be professional yet enthusiastic, you'll break down all those social barriers.

I considered a couple of years ago setting up in Newcastle, in fact I was offered quite a good job, but I feel more southern than northern now. I don't feel like a Geordie now. I feel like this is where I belong. I feel more settled down here, I guess. Most of my life now is attached to my work and all my success has been based around continuity and a little bit of stability, and the best office I've ever had is in Wantage. I've been in four offices, so I've done the whole of south Oxfordshire, and I know it all like the back of my hand. I have business aspirations far greater than Wantage and I know I could run a company that could have successful offices in every town, but Wantage means the most to me. It's where I spent a lot of my young life and where I'm quite well known, and it's the most successful town, so it seems like a good place to start and a good place to settle.

Wantage will never be much more than it is now. It's human nature, everybody wants everything to be better than it is, but Wantage is small. It's a very pretty town, it's a friendly town, it's like any other town, really: a lot of people know other people's business, which is more often bad than good. I think we as a town are probably a little bit closed in on ourselves. As a businessman I've been invited into the Chamber of Commerce, and Rotary, but I haven't joined because I find they're a bit more roll-your-trouser-legs-up than anything else, so I tend to sit back. Perhaps it's selfish. Perhaps I should be more involved, but they just don't appeal to me.

A lot of people from my school days and my sixth-form days, all they wanted to do was to get away from Wantage. It's quite funny, it's almost like a disease, all they wanted to do was escape. My old friend Anna Blunt is a classic example, really. Anna is very funny about Wantage, she's got a real chip on her shoulder about it. She hates it. She thinks it's a very small town and small-minded, and that's not true. But when you're young you always think you've got to go somewhere else to cut it big.

Sue Cobham

Horse and Hound

Thursday is Harmony in the Home day. John Barton 'King of the Garden' comes and I spend all day gardening with him and it's fun alive, I really look forward to it. John is an old friend of ours, who used to be a farm manager and now runs a grounds maintenance service. I met him again when he was mucking out a friend's stable and he gave me his card. He has about three or four clients and we're one of the lucky ones because we get one whole 'John' day a week, and that's completely changed my life because I was struggling with this garden. Although my husband Ralph's very keen on gardening, he works abroad so much that he can do very little. He's also not the world's greatest mechanic: I suppose he could mow the lawn but I'd have to give him a serious lesson first. Ralph plants things whereas I do destruction: mowing, pruning, poisoning, weeding, chopping and cutting.

John chose Thursday as my lovely cleaning lady, Angie, comes that day. I thought, Let's have everybody on Thursday, it'll be such fun; and it is. We have tea breaks at two-hour intervals, and I always make a cake, so a day that could be quite a slog is no slog at all, we enjoy ourselves out of sight and it's brilliant. I never agree to do anything else on a Thursday now. Harmony in the Home is also a weedy joke I share with a chum of mine, because to her and me, what does 'HH' stand for usually? *Horse and Hound.* Now Ralph and I can keep on top of the garden and grounds. I've been out in the garden all day today and I haven't been lonely, and I'm not exhausted, because John does all the really tiring bits and I help him. Lots of things you can't do by yourself. You can't put a gatepost in by yourself. Like many things in life, gardening's better done in teams, even if they're only teams of two.

Teamwork is my *favourite* subject. I never stop banging on about it. If somebody else isn't depending on you, why get out of bed? Also, you get to know people when you *do* something with them in a way that's completely different from those whom you only know socially: there's something very ecstatic about running something with some-body, even if it's only a local jumble sale or cleaning the church. I'm the 'Queen of the Church Cleaners'. Twice a year we all descend on the church and clean it furiously and drink millions of cups of coffee, and lots of people have said they enjoy it that way. Any physical teamwork, like riding a horse, or dancing with somebody, or acting in a play, is amazing. I have a friend who, some years ago, rowed in a Greek trireme. Researchers discovered, by reading a whole lot of Greek scrolls they dug up somewhere, how to build a trireme with three banks of oars. Well, these chaps built it and assembled a team of a hundred and fifty people, and they all went out to Greece for a fortnight: 'Let's get this thing rowing!' Could they do it? No. They were going mad and getting their oars tied in a knot, and everyone was getting in a rage, until after about three or four days one of the rowers said, 'I think we should take the rhythm from the *middle* bank of oars rather than the top one.' So they tried that and bingo! They did it! They shot off across the Aegean like Derby winners. My friend said that to be acting in unison with a hundred and forty-nine other people was the most thrilling experience he'd ever had, physical, mental and spiritual.

I was always in a team. I'm one of those people who *loved* boarding school; I joined in furiously, played every available sport. Wizard fun! Nowadays it's very unfashionable to like school but I enjoyed myself out of sight. My team now is the horsey club; the Pony Club and the local hunt. Most of my friends here are connected with the horsey world because around here if you want to make friends you need to make friends within a club. Anywhere which is technically in reach of London operates completely differently from somewhere which is not, because people can import their own friends here, and they do. Nobody needs to be mates with the people who live nearby because they can have their own friends down from London. Still, Wantage is the most *brilliantly* friendly place. I hadn't been here a week before the lady in the paper shop was greeting me: 'Hello, Mrs Cobham, I've got your *Horse and Hound*.' Actually, we couldn't afford the *Horse and Hound* then, we took the weekly *Guardian* in those far-off days. Quite hard work, the weekly *Guardian*, and no racing pages either.

When the ponies that my children rode were of a suitable size for it, I used to help with Riding for the Disabled every week and it was frightfully rewarding. Later, I helped with an adult class, seeing, ten years on, riders whom I'd known in their schooldays. I noted that the riding of most students was probably about the same as when they were children, and quite wrongly I thought, 'What's the point of this? They're not getting any better.' And that was so arrogant of me. I mean, am I getting better at riding? No. I'm probably far worse than I was at eighteen. But does that stop me riding? No. I do it because I like it. Well, *they* do it because they like it. The important thing is that it brings joy to their lives and to those of their carers. A huge number of carers say, 'They're so happy after their riding lesson, they'll be easy to handle for three days afterwards.' It's an input of joy. The fact that they're not getting any better at riding is absolutely irrelevant. It helps them to make friends with people whom they don't already know, because they have to relate to the helpers. In some cases, I also think it helps with their speech, because some who don't speak very well, or very much, may talk to the pony because they're so interested and excited by it.

I feel tremendously strongly about riding and I feel tremendously strongly about countryside sports, as does Ralph. I hunt with the Old Berkshire Hunt because I have this quaint, old-fashioned approach to life, which is that you hunt where you live, you use the village shop if you've got one, you send your children to local primary schools, and you go to the parish church, whether or not you like it, because that's *your* church and if you don't support it, who will? Some people like to hunt with other more fashionable packs of hounds but I think you should support the local scene.

The Old Berks hunts Monday, Wednesday, Saturday. But unless you've got unlimited time and money you wouldn't go out three days a week. Most really keen people will do one day a week. Not all hunts are fox hunts either. There are deer hunts, hare hunts, and now mink hunts: the otter hounds, which aren't allowed to hunt otters any more, now hunt mink, which are the most appalling pests. When a mink comes along the whole riverbank dies. They kill all the water voles and water rats, and they're there because 'animal lovers' let them out of mink farms because they thought it was so much nicer for the mink to live in freedom. It probably is nicer for those of the mink which survive, but it's jolly bad news for a whole lot of other wildlife.

Obviously it's possible to hunt in different ways. It's possible to control fox numbers without hounds. There are huge parts of this country where foxes aren't hunted because the terrain isn't suitable, and there people go out and shoot them instead. And that's fine if they're a brilliant shot and there's nothing else in the way, but you can never be certain you're going to kill it, and the kind of death that follows wounding by gunshot is appalling, it's gangrene; so controlling foxes with hounds is much the best way because there's no wounding. The fox either goes free or it's killed, and it's jolly quick. Everybody says it's torn apart alive. It is not. Let's get this completely clear. Hounds do not tear foxes apart alive. The first hound grabs the fox behind the ears and breaks its neck. Anybody who tells you a hound tears entrails out of a live fox's tummy is wrong because no hound wants to be bitten. This is a very primitive thing: any predator species wants to *kill* its prey, it doesn't want the prey turning round and biting it. Whereas species like jackals go for the jugular and bring their prey down from the throat side, the foxhound does it from the top and breaks the neck.

The paradoxical thing about blood sports is that the sportsman loves his quarry and in order to pursue it he's hugely knowledgeable about it. There are guys out there, terrier men and earth-stoppers, who probably don't do a huge amount of reading and writing but they know where every single fox-earth is. They are amazingly knowledgeable about the habits of a fox: they know where the litters are in spring; they know the movements of the fox; they know how many foxes that particular part of the country can support. Often, even if hounds don't kill a fox, by dispersing the fox population pressure is taken off one area. If fox litters are not dispersed, the area where the cubs are born will soon become short of food. Then hens are going to be killed as mine have been: bang, gone, the whole lot killed, none taken for food, just heads off, bodies strewn all over the orchard. It must be such fun chasing hens, I guess foxes just get in the mood. Hens make a huge fuss, they can't really fly, they're not very fast. Brilliant fun if you're a fox.

People who hunt the fox are not only knowledgeable about the habit of the fox but also about the countryside and habitat. There would be so many fewer woodlands and hedgerows in this country if it wasn't for countryside sports. And every piece of habitat that's suitable for wild mammals, such as the fox, has huge pluses for birds and insects and smaller mammals, like weasels and field mice. If hunting with hounds was banned, I should think, within five years, the fox would be extinct. It would just be shot to blazes because there would be nobody interested in conserving it. 'Why conserve it? It's vermin, let's get rid of it.' And who's going to eat the rabbits if there are no foxes? We're absolutely knocked over with rabbits in this area. Once you start getting your oar into the food chain, the whole balance is upset.

A lot of landowners keep shooting habitat because they like going shooting, or fox habitat because they like hunting. A lot of them don't do either but benefit hugely from the activity of the hunt in the case of fallen stock. Until the BSE scare, the fallen stock service was free to farmers; now it costs a small donation. If you have a sheep, a cow, a pig or a horse that has died, you ring up the kennels at the hunt headquarters and they come and take it away. Try asking the knacker-man to come at six o'clock on Saturday evening: forget it! And when he *does* come, there'll be a huge bill.

With hunting, there's a sensible chain. The hunt removes the animal and the hounds get to eat the flesh. When our foal died in the field the kennels took it away, the flesh was fed to the hounds, sensible recycling. The takeaway service is worth many thousands of pounds in convenience to stock owners, so any stock farmer wants to keep on good terms with the local hunt for that if no other reason. And in the more isolated regions of the country, like the West Country, hunting is a social life. Once people get too old to drive their cars after dark, then the pub, the whist drive, the pie-and-peas supper are closed to them. But there's this lovely, jolly club open to them: meet a chum or two, see the hounds move off, see them draw a couple of covers, and then off to the boozer and home in time for tea. They've had a lovely walk in the countryside, they've seen their friends, they've enjoyed a unique spectacle, and if that goes, how are country people going to see their friends in the winter? People say that side of country sports is exaggerated but it's true.

I feel very strongly about people who are not prepared to listen to reasoned debate, and the strident anti-blood sports movement doesn't want to listen to reasoned debate. Somebody's got to control fox numbers, and the impression that hunting with hounds makes on fox numbers is minimal, anyway. *Nobody* will win if hunting is banned. Masses of jobs would be lost, masses of hounds and horses would be lost and masses of good countryside management would be lost. We used to see quite a bit of the anti-hunt activists, although hunt saboteurs prefer things like the Boxing Day meet. Where my son Hugo lives in West Sussex, the hunt saboteurs are frightfully keen and come out every single time. I believe that, nation-wide, saboteurs are now doing fewer small hits and targeting some high-profile hunts like the Beaufort with massed forces. They send everybody down in vans and really go for it. It is appalling. They hit people over the head with baseball bats and try to pull people, often elderly followers, off their horses. If that happened in a football crowd those guys would be in prison. With the Old Berks I've seen and heard them luring hounds on to the railway line, where they've been run over by trains, all in the name of kindness to animals.

They are a most unpleasant bunch of people. Their language is unreal. Their whole approach is completely negative: their main hate is people sitting on horses, whom they perceive to be arrogant. They're not seriously knowledgeable about animals in any way. But if there was a war on, those guys would be winning VCs because they're completely fearless and extremely aggressive. They're nearly always quite young, very angry, both men and women. Five earrings in the ears. They're guys that like a fight, they think nothing of swinging a baseball bat at a car with a child sitting in a child seat, or throwing acid in faces. One group of antis drove a van straight at a terrier man; he was sitting in his van with his elbow half out of the window and his arm was smashed to smithereens.

Antis don't want to talk to us about hunting. Forget it. A reasoned debate? Forget it. Their normal conversation is, 'You blanking, blanking, blanking scum.' Hunt followers are directed not to speak to saboteurs but to send for the police, who usually manage to remove them. There is now an offence called aggravated trespass, which enables people to be moved off property or land if they're threatening to interfere with or stop a legal activity. One day, of course, hunting may not be a legal activity, but if hunting were banned, I would still do it. I would definitely go to prison, without a stagger. It's going to be crowded in the prisons, too, because a lot of people think like I do, and where are they going to put us all?

I very much hope that the Government will take this whole confrontation out of the political arena because it shouldn't be there. It's not an issue. The sorrows of the world are so much more important. People are suffering, and dying, and jobless, and ill, and being killed in Eastern Europe. We shouldn't give a moment to the field sports debate. We shouldn't be wasting time on something which is working and has worked well for years. We should spend our time trying to make the world a better place because the world's in a loony old state.

Colin Stimpson

Dancing, Not Speaking

Lardy cake. Fruit cake. Doughnuts. Sponges. Jap cakes. We used to have jam tarts, custard slices, custard tarts. Custard tarts've gone out of fashion now. Apple tarts. Little sponge cakes. Sponge dips, Viennese, Swiss rolls, macaroons. Battenbergs. There was Congress tarts, Eccles cakes, Banbury cakes. Banburys are very similar to Eccles cakes, but they comes to two points at the end. They were nice warm. Banburys we used to do on a Monday but the Banbury cake's just gone right out the window now. There was all the puff-pastry side. We had cream horns, apple turnovers, apple strudels. Cream slices, jam puffs. We did meringues. Cor, it was an enormous amount when I think about it. And on Fridays and Saturdays we did cakes with fresh cream. The rest of the time it was confectioner's cream.

The bread was the thing what brought people in. We did roughly seven hundred and seventy large white loaves every week. The smalls was one thousand and fifty. Nutty cob, about a hundred and fifty. Hovis we used to do two hundred and thirty a week. Hovis loaves, all you add is yeast. Everything else is put in there, even salt is in it. All you have to do is add the yeast and the water. I baked bread for forty-odd years. When I left school, I wasn't going in for baking, I was trying to go in the Post Office. But there was two of us went for the Post Office job, and whoever didn't get it went for the baking job. I didn't get the Post Office so I went for the baking.

We often go down the town now, and people stop us and say, 'I wish you was still going.' I say if they'd have patronized us when we was here, we'd have still been here. But I think the recession does make people go to places like Waitrose. How can we compete with somebody who's charging half the price for a loaf than we are? I know ours was a better loaf, I've never tasted a loaf yet to touch ours, but when you think of people with families, that's it. They were buying these rubbishy old cakes, but it was for the family and it was a lot cheaper, so we was hit. When they opened Tesco's away from the town, we was finally killed off. If Tesco's had brought the trade into Wantage it would have been different, but we used to have a Tesco's bus come into Wantage to take the customers out. There was nothing we could do about it. And it used to annoy me something terrible, because the bus used to come in right past our shop, pick people up, and you'd say, 'Look, they're taking our customers away, literally from outside our door.'

Sometimes people would come in, like after they'd been to Tesco's, and they'd just get one loaf from you, and that's all they'd have, and you can't trade like that. It's impossible. Before, we used to have queues everywhere. Ours used to block the entrance to the shop next door. Today you can walk round this town and there's nobody about. It really sickens me. I tried, tried many a time, to work a way to keep people in the town, but it didn't work out. To think of the amount of shops we had in those days, compared to what there is today; and we was one of the first to go, we was. I went to see Dennis, the gentleman's outfitter three doors down, and he says, 'I ought to tell you that I'm packing up.' And I said, 'Well, so am I.' And we was two quality shops.

We blamed ourselves, really. We blamed ourselves, something we were doing wrong. That's the feeling you get when the recession comes on. And so we said, 'Well, the only answer is to get out and cut our losses.' The woman who took over from us, she desperately wanted the business, and she was over the moon with it, but within two years she'd gone bust. People was going bust everywhere. We didn't. We got out, paid everything off, we didn't have a thing left. We didn't go bankrupt, this is the one thing we tried to avoid, because we didn't want that on our conscience, but to be honest, today most people don't give a damn. I know someone who has been bankrupt three times. He starts up the next day under a new name, and no one can get the money he owes them off of him. It's one of those laws that should be stopped, because there's a lot of people done out of money because of that. We could have had a bank balance put away somewhere, thousands of pounds, but it would've been on our conscience, so Margaret went back into the nursery school, and I went into the wholesale bakery business. It don't compare with what we done before: it's all sealed stuff now, that's what people want, for vending machines and petrol stations.

Everybody who was employed at the time accepted it, except one, and that was a bloke who'd been with me for some twenty-odd years. And from that day to this they've never spoken to us, his family. We've heard through the grapevine they wanted us to go bankrupt so that they could get redundancy. When I sold the business I had an offer of about £2,000 on top of what I sold it for, but they said they wouldn't keep the staff on; so I took a lower cut, so that they'd keep the staff on. And that bloke still won't even speak to us today.

The wife of this bloke, she'll literally walk the other side of the road if we're on the pavement. And one day, this was only about a month ago, we was coming out the car park of Waitrose and I said to Margaret, 'I'm going to get a paper over the road,' so I crossed over the road and Margaret stayed on that side. This woman, she walked round, didn't she, and she stopped dead as soon as she see both of us on two different sides. It doesn't bother us, really. It's just the fact is, I used to give him two big bonuses every year, one at the summer and one at Christmas. Didn't have to, I just done it, you know, because he was the bloke who could literally take over if I was on holiday or anything. But no, they won't speak to us now, and a couple of times we've been to a New Year's Eve dance and they've been there, and to be on the same dance floor as them, that was putting me off of the evening.

Mandy Payne

Staying on the Bus

I've brought a collection of photos from some of the films and things that I've done, and I thought it would be fun to show you what they are.

That's a hairstyle that I had done in the film *An Ideal Husband*. I was just an extra in it but it was great fun. There's me looking really miserable. And there's me with two very sexy men. The one on the left was as gay as a daisy. I wanted him to be my partner in the ballroom scene because I liked the look of him, but they wouldn't let me have him, they gave me this old duffer here instead, which I was really insulted by.

I got a lot of stick for this next photo, because I'm really flat-chested. The wardrobe lady put this corset on me, under the ballgown, and it didn't really make any difference. She said, 'Is that all you've got?' and I said, 'Well, yes,' and she said, 'It won't do, it won't do. Wadding! Bring me some wadding!' So they put all this wadding in and it still didn't make much difference, so she said, 'Shoot her from the back,' and they did. I was really miffed. They painted my hair, too, with a palette of paints, to make it sort of gingery. I couldn't understand why they didn't just stick a wig on, because it took about three hours every morning to curl it and just for a film extra that was an awful lot of trouble to go to. I hate the term 'extra', actually; I prefer to call it 'background artist'.

That's me in prison. I've been in prison lots of times, which is a bit of a worry. I've been in *Touching Evil*, and I've been in *The Bill* many times, always as an inmate. It's great fun. I love doing those sorts of parts. I've got an agent, I've got my Equity card, and I really want to start getting speaking parts, but it's so difficult. That's why I'm going away in September, to drama school in Harlech. I'm going to learn the ropes and find a way in.

That's me in *Cider with Rosie*. That's me in the latest *James Bond*. And that's me in the Gambia with a crocodile. Really silly thing to do: I climbed into a crocodile enclosure. Wouldn't do it again. But I love crocodiles, I'm fascinated by them, and I haven't got a zoom lens on my camera and I wanted to get close, so I climbed in. I touched the crocodile and he was lovely, but unfortunately two other ones started coming towards me quite quickly and I just froze. Legs turned to jelly. Eventually I came to my senses and scrambled out of there quick. And that last photo there: that one's me with blonde hair, doing a dance in a fashion show.

When I was at school I was extremely shy, incredibly shy. I didn't really speak to anybody, I always had my head down, and I always did exactly what I was told. My parents are really into classical music, so my two brothers and I all learnt instruments. Tim, the eldest, is a professional clarinet player, and I did what I was told and learnt the clarinet. But my passion is pop music and soul and what I really wanted to do was play the saxophone, because I desperately wanted to play in bands. My father couldn't understand it. He kept saying, 'It'll be a phase, it'll be a phase,' and I said, 'It won't. I'm going to do it.' So I saved up the money and got one, got a sax, and just took to it, straightaway from the word go.

When I first started playing the saxophone, I tried to join a swing band in Oxford. I couldn't really read the music that well but I could play by ear, and from the heart, which I feel is where music is anyway. But because I couldn't read the music they took the mickey out of me at the audition, they basically laughed me out of the place. So as I went home I thought, OK, there's a weakness, I'm going to put it right. I rang the leader the next day and said, 'I'm going to come back. Just give me a few weeks and I'll get this together.' And I sat at home and I read every piece of music I could find, and just learnt it and learnt and learnt it. I never went out. I stayed in and I just played and played and played. Then I went back, and I could see the people there thinking, Oh God, she's back. And I said, 'Right, where do we start?' and I ended up pretty much getting a lead position in the band, much to some of the people's dislike.

That was a good experience, being laughed at by that swing band, because afterwards I thought, If anybody knocks me I'm going to come back at them: I'm never going to be knocked again because I had all this at school. At school I was bullied for years, until I finally got sick of it and decided to learn kung fu, and after that nobody bothered me. So after joining the band, whenever my brother Tim was home I'd have a little bit of sax tuition. He taught me all the classical side of things, which made me a good reader, and I got through all the Royal Schools exams, right through to Grade Eight, and got distinctions and merits on everything. It took about five years and I just got better and better and better.

Ever since I left school I'd had fairly normal jobs, mainly general shop work, and I absolutely hated them. I also worked at the Dairy, or the Dreary as I call it, and I thought, I have to change this, I have to get out. So in between the jobs, I played with the swing band, and I saved up and bought other instruments, and now I've got a tenor, two altos and a soprano sax. Beautiful. All Selmers. The best, the very best. Then I began to get my own things together. I started a band with a friend, Paul, called The Soul Devotion, and I've formed two others since: Safe Sax, and The Red Hot Horny Section. My dad said, 'You can't call it that!' I said, 'I can.' I played sax for that one, and I was the lead singer as well. I did very well out of the bands. I travelled up and down the country, playing gigs in pubs and clubs, and it was great fun, great money. I also had a couple of duos and they were very successful too, and because I don't drive, because I never have enough money to keep a car going, I was always on buses at night, or staying at somebody's house, sleeping on a floor somewhere, but I loved it. It suited me fine. I like my life unpredictable.

A few years ago, I started teaching the sax so I could give up the shop jobs and just play and teach music. My parents have been really good, because I've set up a music room at their house, and I've got pupils from eight years old to seventy-six years old and they're all lovely. Wantage has been very useful for me because I've built things up from here. I worked at a local radio station in Oxford, doing bulletins, because I decided I want to get into acting. I've joined local amateur groups, I've taught music here, and everything I've done it's been possible here, it's been on this doorstep, so I haven't needed to go anywhere as yet. Now, I do. All my life I've been in Wantage or thereabouts, and I'm perfectly happy to go away. I don't like Wantage that much, to be honest. I like city life, I like the business of things happening all the time. Now I've got my Equity card, I've got absolutely no ties, and I want to get away and do something.

So many people say I'm a dreamer and it won't happen; that I won't make it, won't get into acting. But I will do it. Everything I've said I'm going to do, I've done, and I've never been more determined in my life. I think you make your own luck, and if you're determined enough, and you work hard enough, it will happen. I've already gone to great lengths. My front teeth are glass, I had to pay nearly £1,000 to have them done, so that they'd look OK for television. I've had hair extensions when I've thought I'll probably get more parts in period dramas if I have long hair. Now I'm saving up for cosmetic surgery. I hate the way I look. I actually went as far as seeing a surgeon in Oxford, and that was expensive, it was about £85 just to see him for twenty minutes. He said he'd never met anybody so informed, because I went in there telling him what he was going to do. I want my nose adjusted, and I'll probably get some lines and things done at the same time. It sounds really vain but I've never particularly liked my appearance; and also, I had a particularly rotten boyfriend a few years ago, who hit me, and I feel that he's changed my nose, because that's where I got beaten, so I'd quite like to change it to basically wipe that out. And I'm going to. I've got a separate savings account that money is going into, and when I get the money together, I'll do it. Then it'll be my nose again, and not his. But I'm not doing it because of him, I'm doing it for me. It's for me, definitely.

I've had various boyfriends but I can't think of anything worse than marriage. I know my parents are really disappointed but I don't care. It doesn't appeal to me. My parents are always saying, 'Clock's ticking away. What about children?' I don't want children at the moment. I never have. I don't have one maternal bone in my body, which is probably really awful. There's a terrible pressure; terrible pressure, even from my friends. They say, 'Children: what's going to happen?' 'We wish you'd meet someone nice and settle down.' It really is constant. If you don't want marriage and children you're made to feel as if you haven't grown up yet: 'She's going through a phase.' Well, if I'm going through a phase, it's been a very long phase.

Sometimes people say, 'Well, are you gay?' 'No.' 'So why aren't you married?' Why should I be? You shouldn't have to do it just because society says that you should. Even my mother says, 'Oh, isn't it sad that you haven't found the right one.' My parents have been saying that since I was eighteen. All my relatives, every Christmas they come over and say, 'Not married yet?' 'Nope.' That's probably terribly selfish of me, but every partner I've had has basically had a problem with me going off and doing gigs and fashion shows. Anything that comes up, I'm there, I'm doing it, and they don't like it. Well, tough. Nobody is going to ever stop me doing what I want to do again. I'd like to, later on in life, maybe adopt or foster children that need homes, if I'm financially stable and perhaps with a chap. At the moment I'm happy going in my own direction.

There was one chap that I was with for ten years, and he was lovely. He was the only one that was OK, really; all the others were just a complete waste of space. But, deep inside, I probably deliberately chose chaps that were wrong for me so that I wouldn't be side-tracked by love, because I don't want anything getting in my way. And maybe I am a dreamer a bit, but I think you have to be to do what you want.

Normality just doesn't appeal: being married; two point two children; getting up and going to work at the same time every day; coming home. Scary. It's definitely not me. It's variety I want. I've got so much pent-up energy, and so much that I want to do, and perhaps I want to prove people wrong; you know, all the people that bullied me at school, and all the people that laughed at me that day when I went into that hall and tried to play the saxophone and didn't play it very well. So everything I say I'm going to do, I make sure that I do it well, and I try as hard as I can.

There's a programme called *Stars In Their Eyes* on telly, I don't know if you've ever seen it. I applied for that once and I got to the top hundred people out of forty-five thousand applicants. I was really pleased about that. But again, people were so negative. They'd say, 'What are you *doing*?' and I'd say, 'It's *fun*. It's something *different*. Why not?' I am a bit eccentric, I suppose, but I know I'm going in the right direction, I know that I'm doing the right thing, and I know that I'm going to succeed, in whatever way. I'm not saying I'm going to be a big film star, although I'd love to be. But if I'm not, so what? I've had a go. As far as I'm concerned I'm successful now, because I'm earning money from doing something that I like doing. I work for myself, teaching and playing music, so that's successful, isn't it? But people tend not to see it that way and that makes me angry.

I was with a chap for three years who hated me doing my music, was very threatened by it, and I gave everything up because of him. Such a foolish thing to do, because I was in the first band I'd started, The Soul Devotion, and it was a real success, people absolutely adored it and followed us everywhere. I was emotionally very, very ill because of that chap. I think *he* was ill, actually, I think he had a real problem. He put me down. He was always saying, 'People don't like you. All this stuff you're doing is totally wrong,' and he used to push me about a bit. He was insanely jealous if I looked at another chap. He wasn't the one that did this to my nose, the one before him did this, but this chap was really worse in a way, because it was more emotional, more saying awful things, and my confidence just went straight down the pan.

I started making myself sick. I got thinner and thinner. I was very thin at the time anyway, but he would say, 'You're fat, you're too fat,' and the more somebody tells you that, the more you believe them. He'd say, 'You're not attractive. Nobody likes you. You'll never have anybody else.' I can see now that it was actually his insecurity, but because you stop going out, and you stop seeing your friends, it builds up more and more and more and more, and in the end I became suicidal and needed help. I remember playing him a beautiful classical piece on the saxophone because I wanted to impress him, and he just said, 'That's crap. You can't play.' And I know that I played it really well. I can play, and I'm good.

I got away from him in the end. I just moved. I became very frightened of him, so I gave my notice at my lodgings in Wantage and moved to a friend's house in a village outside, and I house-sat for her for six months. I just disappeared. That's how I got out of it. I started playing the saxophone again, built up my lessons, and went from there. I fought back in tiny steps but it took me ages to rebuild my confidence. Being bullied by him was like being bullied at school, it was like falling from the top to the bottom again. But the anger of it's done me good. It's been a learning curve.

I wrote him a letter the other day. I thought, I have to let this go; so I wrote and said, 'I'm moving on with my life and I'm very happy, and I wish you the best of luck, but if I see you in the street I'm not going to be your friend. If I see you in the street, I'll walk past you and hold my head up. I'm not frightened of anybody now.' And I really felt great, because it was three years of being an emotional wreck, three years of hell, sheer hell. But it's part of the path I'm going on, I think, because it won't happen again. I was doing a James Bond film last month, and I thought, If he could see me now; nobody's going to stop me now.

I've let it go now, the baggage from that time. I thought, Yeah, move on: learn from it but don't take it with you. It's taught me lessons. I've come back a stronger person, more determined. I'm going to be OK, I'm going to get on, but I think those two bad relationships affected me in quite a big way, in that I've been burnt, and I suppose I'm a little bit wary of chaps now.

After that last dreadful relationship, I went through a phase of having real thrills with exploring the sex side of things. I met this other chap on a film set, Patrick, who lived in London, and he was absolutely stunning. He was a male model, and I had no confidence, so I thought, What's he interested in me for? I'm unattractive. But he totally built me up and we really hit it off. We went to London, and we went to all these sex parties and did all sorts of things, and I had a great time. We used to go to this regular party on a boat, and there were people there from teachers to magistrates to bikers, and it was just fantastic. You know, no inhibitions at all. And that really did me good. I just thought, Yeah, this is great: I can happily walk around this boat naked. No shyness whatsoever. Good fun.

When I went to London, Patrick and I had the most outrageous fun, and it was brilliant, it was just this great adventure every time. When he came to stay with me it was awful. He was a real bore. I think he was from quite a wealthy family, whereas I'm not, and he was like, 'Oh, darl., can you just pop out and get me some wine? And I want it to be the best type. Don't just get any.' I'd cook him a meal and it would be, 'Oh, darl., that's white bread. I don't have white bread, I have brown,' and he got worse and worse and worse. And then one day I went out to do a saxophone lesson, and I came back early because my lesson hadn't turned up, and I got in, heard a noise in the bedroom, opened the bedroom door, and there was this woman – this image of a woman – in my dress, a long dress, high heels, made up beautifully. And he said, 'Hi! I'm Patricia. Meet the other side of me.' And I said, 'Take those clothes off. Please, just take those clothes off.' Later we had a good chat, and I said, 'I'm really glad to have met the other side of you, but you have been a real bore this week, with the brown bread and all that, so I'm quite happy for us not do this any more,' and he was fine about it.

He wasn't right for me because he was so picky but he did me a great favour. I mean, I've done it all now. If anyone asked me if I'd explored my sexuality to the full I'd say yes, I most definitely have. It was so *interesting* to go to parties where you happily take your clothes off because everybody else does, or you might wear a bit of leather or something, and walk about, quite relaxed, and talk to anyone. You get such a cross-section of nice, interesting people, and I remember telling a couple of my friends about this and the reaction was shock, horror, don't tell us any more! But it really wasn't a bad thing to do, it was very interesting. The atmosphere was like, 'Hey, live and let live, it's a free world.' It was free and easy and there was nothing too outrageous going on, but if there was, you didn't have to watch.

Before that, I'd been completely restrained for three years with somebody who knocked me and knocked me and knocked me. I wasn't allowed to look at anybody. If we went out, I had to look at the floor. Afterwards I thought, Sod it, I'm going to do completely what I want now, and I did, I really went to the other end of the scale, and it was fantastic. It did me the world of good and I've no qualms about it at all. No skeletons in my closet. It was great fun, it was something that helped at the time, but if I do get into another relationship, I don't have to do that again: anything I do would be done out of love.

I'm now completely on my own and I've never been happier. Occasionally the loneliness cuts in, but I do crave my own space and I think living with somebody would be hard: hard for them. I would be difficult to live with. I'm not saying that I'll never settle down but at the moment the time's not right. Until I get everything out of my system and go to drama school I cannot have any distractions, and I just feel that that's what a relationship would be. There was a chap that I really did like, and got quite attached to recently, but he's gone to Australia for a year. So what I've done is, because I'm changing my name to a stage name, I've taken his name because I liked and respected him. So instead of being Mandy Payne I'm going to be Amanda King. I just thought he was nice, and I thought: Amanda King? Yes, it works really well.

I think I'm still sort of finding who I am. There's lots of me. There's the theatrical, mad, completely insane side. There's the caring side. I worked for a while as a carer with mentally handicapped people, and I really got into that and would love to do more. There's the travelling side: I've done an awful lot of travelling with my mother, and that I really enjoyed. I've been all over: Hong Kong, Singapore, Thailand, Malaysia, India, the Caribbean, Egypt. Loads of places. America. It means I never have any money but I have a brilliant time. So there's a lot of different pieces of me, and I know there's more.

There are lots of times when my parents have said, 'What are you *doing*? Why are you playing in bands?' But I needed to. I needed to do that, because being on stage, singing, acting, performing, it's building up confidence. We did a great gig in Reading. I had to front a band, and Hot Chocolate were playing there as well, and it was brilliant, I really loved it. I got the audience going, and that's an act. You turn into somebody else when you get on the stage, and I like the opportunity to be somebody else. That's not because I'm unhappy with who I am, because I like who I am. I think I've done OK. But I like playing other parts.

Having had some very, very bad times, I intend to live every day to the absolute limit. There's so much to do and I've got so many goals: radio, play reading, any film part, TV, even behind the scenes, just to *do* it. And I write stories as well, I'm always writing stories, quite dramatic, way-out stuff, serial killers and that sort of thing, but I love it. I'm constantly practising accents at home, constantly trying to get things right, constantly trying to get as much experience as I can, because I want those acting parts in films or television, anything as long as it's speaking, and I'm going to do it. I'm going to find a way in because I won't let anyone stop me.

If the acting doesn't work out, I can always fall back on teaching, and going out and doing a few gigs in pubs, but I'm determined that it will work out. People in the business can be really patronizing if you've worked as an extra but I'm not going to let that get in my way. The last time I was on *The Bill*, they had these two buses to take actors and extras around different parts of the set. They had a red bus for actors and a blue bus for extras, and I was told by the lady in charge to get on the red bus, so I did, and this actress was on the bus. She only had a tiny speaking part but she saw me and she said, 'Get off!' I said, 'Sorry?' She said, 'You're on the wrong bus. You're an extra.' I said, 'I'm a person.' She said, 'No you're not, you're an extra.' I said, 'I'm a person and I'm staying on this bus.' So she got off and complained. I stayed put. There was no way I was getting off that bus.

Sem Seaborne

Bitten by the Bug

Everybody gets a different blend of things from the Morris but you've got to be bitten by the bug. For me, the music is number one because it's beautiful music, and it's music from the same sources which has inspired great composers like Benjamin Britten, Vaughan Williams, William Walton, Butterworth and Grainger. The music is wonderful, and it's a joy to play, and I've been playing it since I was eighteen and I don't tire of playing it.

Number two is the feeling that you're participating in keeping a bit of history alive, which is four or five hundred years old, and maintaining a tradition, and I feel strongly that society needs to have those sort of traditions. A society without history and tradition is shallow. And no names, no pack drill, but if you've been to the States you'll know what I mean. It's what makes being English, to have history and tradition. I mean, there are plenty of people who are not a bit interested in Morris dancing but they like to know it's there. It's a bit like cricket. You don't have to go and watch it but its being there is part of being English.

The third thing for me is the camaraderie which comes out of the Morris, this blokeish thing, this need the sexes have to spend time with their own sex groups; and to go Morris dancing as a group is the same sort of feeling you get playing in a cricket team, or a football team. It's probably the ultimate form of team bonding, and that's a major part of the enjoyment. For other people, that priority order would be different. I know people who only go because they like dancing. They don't care much about the camaraderie, don't stay in the pub afterwards, and don't drink much, if at all. Equally, I know people who don't dance, pretend to play the fiddle a bit, but largely they're there to drink beer.

For the purists, Morris dancing is an entirely male occupation. There's certainly historical evidence that women have got involved at various times, but by and large the Morris, as it was danced in the borders of Herefordshire, Shropshire, Gloucestershire and Oxfordshire, was a male pastime. We're about twenty men and we're called the Icknield Way Morris Dancers. We have a complete age span. We have a young lad of seventeen, who's been dancing with us for ten years. We've got a son of one of the dancers who's just ten years old. Our oldest member is seventy: he learnt to dance the Morris when he was up at Cambridge as a young man and he's still going strong. Most of us, I would say, are in our late forties.

We have a complete span across social levels as well. Morris dancing is quite unique in that way. It's better than any management-training course I've been on because it cuts across social strata. At one time we had seven Ph.D.s in the team. We had the commanding officer of an RAF base, we had the secretary of one of the Science and Engineering Research Council committees, but we also had a forester, a labourer, a guy who worked in a factory, and they're all brought to a level because the labourer is possibly a better dancer than the RAF commanding officer. You're in a melting pot. Frequently you go off doing things at weekends, where you're living fairly close together in an intimate situation and it's more than just Morris dancing. I understand that if you're an uninformed member of the public you can look at a bunch of guys waving handkerchiefs about and think, What nonsense. But that's probably just the tip of the iceberg in terms of what people get out of it.

Morris dancing is a great thing to debunk but that's part of the

English character, isn't it. As a nation, we are great at being self-critical. The Germans, the Romanians, the Portuguese, they love their folk traditions. You won't meet a German or a Portuguese who would insult their folk traditions in the way that the Morris gets hammered in this country. But it's not just the Morris which gets attacked. It's in the English character to try and knock what we're good at. We knock our cricket team, we knock our football team, it's in our nature, as an island race, to do this. As Morris dancers, we live with it. If you were a sensitive person, you wouldn't be Morris dancing on the streets.

When Morris dancing was discovered as a folk culture, by a man called Cecil Sharp in the late nineteenth century, people tried to explain it as something pagan; the peasants worshipping the ancient elements and all this sort of stuff. But it's largely nonsense, all that. The serious researchers have shown quite clearly that there was nothing that resembled Morris dancing before the mid-1400s. Then quite abruptly, from about 1490 onwards, there's loads of stuff in the records. If there was anything that resembled it before then, it would be clearly evidenced somewhere because mankind communicates by visual art. You only have to look at cave paintings to know that: if man has got a message, it goes up on the wall.

So, from being a court entertainment in the late fifteenth century, the dances spread down the Thames Valley, which was the main communication route during the fifteenth and sixteenth centuries, as part of the Whitsun sports. There they evolved as village variations of what was possibly just one Morris dance. The Morris dance then became part of the Whitsun games, and because when Christianity came it was much easier to superimpose Christian holidays upon the old pagan or Roman holidays, people decided that the Morris must have some connection with pagan ceremonies, but that's nonsense. The Morris was danced at Whitsun because that was the main holiday. The connection with fertility is quite fictional but it's colourful to suggest it. Lots of Morris teams will refer to their dances as being descended from fertility rites but mostly it's bunk.

When Cecil Sharp did his research there were only about four or five villages left in Oxfordshire where they were still able to Morris dance. But he then went touring on his bicycle, interviewing people in the villages around Oxfordshire who had been dancers in their younger days, and because he was a musician he was able to put down some notation and tunes which allowed the dances to be re-created from about twenty villages.

The traditional village dances are all handkerchief dances. The stick dances didn't get introduced until maybe the late 1700s and probably had a military connection. Here in Wantage we do a mixture of the handkerchief and the stick dances but the bells are always there; it's the one singular thing which defines Morris dancing, the presence of bells on legs. Costume has always been important. In the beginning, Morris costumes were expensive and lavish and made of Flemish silk, but as the Morris got into the hands of ordinary village people they didn't have that much money to throw away on costumes, so they ended up with what was typically the costume regarded for summer sports, which was whites, and then they used shoulder ribbons, rosettes and baldricks – which are the crossed ribbons across the chest – to add colour and ornamentation.

The dances and the tunes are very hard to disentangle from each other. Some of the tunes would have been common country dance tunes, or tunes taken from *The Beggar's Opera*, or *Orpheus*. There's a tune called 'The Quaker', which is a tune used for a side-step dance, so the dance is called 'The Quaker' or 'The Side-Step Dance'. But then there's something called a corner dance, and there are two or three tunes for that, one of which is called 'Banbury Bill'. There's a dance which involves a lot of stepping back, which is known as 'Step Back' or 'Old Molly Oxford'. There's a dance called 'The Ring of Bells', which we do because it's very popular with the public. It uses sixteen sticks, and the tune for that, if you trace it back from a musicological point of view, was the same tune used for a folk song called 'Farewell Manchester'; and before that it was known as 'Felton's Gavotte', because it was written by a Reverend Felton in the 1700s.

The tunes are often very similar because when popular opera tunes got into the hands of the common people who couldn't read music, they passed them on by ear, and the tunes got slightly changed each time. There are about thirteen different versions of a dance called 'Trunkles', and Mike Heaney from the Bodleian Library, who's an absolute genius with this stuff, has tried to find out where the word 'trunkles' comes from. He's taken all these different tunes, all called 'Trunkles', and he's put them through a computer to try and find a common tune. And he's actually come up with the possible explanation that it comes from a country dance named after Shakespeare's character Trinculo, with a dance called 'Trinculo's Reel', and he's postulating that Trinculo became corrupted to Trunkles.

There's no evidence of any traditional dances in Wantage, so we dance dances from other Oxfordshire villages, such as Headington, Bampton, Leafield, Stanton Harcourt and Ducklington. It makes it more interesting for us, because there are a lot of different styles in that combination. We do eight different village traditions, which is about twenty-five dances, whereas if you dance, say, for Abingdon Traditional Morris Dancers, you only do dances from Abingdon, and that's a very singular sort of style. They struggle more, I think, to maintain their teams because there's not such variety.

The Bampton dances are nice and relaxed, and our team likes dancing the Bampton style; it flows easily, you don't have to be too energetic. Dances from Bucknell are extremely energetic and fast, and when I was Foreman a few years ago I stopped us doing them because we looked so puffed and unfit, we couldn't do justice to them. Adderbury dances are fairly steady, we don't get puffed or over-exhausted doing those. And we're just about clinging on to Ducklington, which is about half way between Bucknell and Adderbury. Because of my interest in all things historical, I researched a lot of dances thoroughly. People say of me, 'When Sem gets into a subject, he has to research the hell out of it.' That's the academic streak in me, of course, which annoys lots of people.

We practise every Wednesday night during the closed season, which is from mid-September until the first of May. We train new dancers and it's a social gathering; it finishes about a quarter to ten, and we go down the pub. There's a lot of après-Morris in Icknield Way, and the après-Morris is very important to me. A lot of teams just go home but Icknield Way is a very social club: we like to go down the pub and sing and play music, and each week we go to a different pub on a four-week rotating cycle. The traditional teams, the Bampton guys for example, don't practise during the winter at all. They start practising after Easter so that they're ready for Whit Monday, and they dance two or three times during the summer and that's it. You might say that Morris dancing at its best, the ultimate, is Bampton, because that's the real thing, undiluted, undiverted for hundreds of years. At the other end of the scale, you've got teams who travel to Hong Kong, Japan, New York, regularly, and they're doing it because they enjoy it. But what's Morris dancing? It's what you want to make it. You can make it what they do at Bampton or you can travel the world.

As teams go, I think Icknield Way is as close to a traditional side as you'll get. It's fiercely male only. We work hard at the particular dances. There's a lot of self-criticism. I think we've got a sense of what's good, and we try to achieve it, even though we're all getting older and can't get off the ground as far. We're pretty organized. The Squire is the main man of the team, and the Squire determines what is going to be danced, and who will dance it. The Foreman is the man who runs the practice evenings and tries to drill everybody to a standard in each particular dance, so we might have two or three Foremen at any one time, and each Foreman might have a speciality village tradition to look after. Because I've researched Stanton Harcourt quite a bit, I tend to look after that tradition. There is a Chief Musician (which is me), there is a Stickman, who tries to produce some good quality sticks. That's not as easy as it sounds. They have to be the right sort of wood, normally hazel, otherwise they'll snap. And there's a Bagman, who looks after the diary arrangements and the money.

On average, we're dancing out once a week between the first of

May and the middle of September, and possibly every other weekend at a local fête, or somebody's wedding, or somebody's birthday. This weekend we were down in Yateley, in Hampshire, on a day organized by Yateley Morris Men, where they invited a dozen sides along. The following day was the Newbury Show, where we were being paid to perform for visitors to the show. But in our heyday in the late 1980s, we had ninety-six invitations to dance in one year, and we turned out fifty-two times. As most of that was in the summer, that was twice a week. We had a big enough team to do that then: we once put out two teams in two different locations.

The team's relationship with the town is stronger now than it has been in the past. The team used to spend more time dancing in other places than it did in Wantage, and some used to say Wantage didn't deserve a team because the town wasn't interested and it didn't support us. But I think I've managed to change things in that respect, by getting us involved in other events in Wantage. We've been visiting local pubs more than we used to, and I've been instrumental in trying to get the Wantage Festival of Arts going, and incorporating Morris activities in the Festival. We arranged a national meeting of the Morris Ring, in Wantage, to coincide with the Festival's grand finale. We took over the marketplace and there were about a hundred and forty men in total. They came up from Cornwall, they came down from Durham, they came from everywhere, so it was a wonderful display and that opened a few eyes locally.

The wives' relationship with the team is generally one of tolerance. I think quite a few of the wives get frustrated that they don't see their husbands as much as they would like during the summer when the grass needs cutting, or the house needs painting. We do have a Ladies' Night once a year, where the ladies are invited to a meal at a local pub. But for those men who get a hard time from their wives, they'll either give up Morris dancing or they'll get a divorce, and both things have happened. Some people, they get the bug a bit too strongly, and it can lead to domestic disputes, shall we say.

Morris dancing is one of those things which is very difficult to give up if you've got the bug. Historically, it really should be about young guys doing athletic things and showing how gracefully they can caper and leap and dance when they're at a peak of fitness. But if you saw a photograph of a typical Morris man today, it would be an oldish guy with a beard, looking like a garden gnome, and I have difficulty with that image because I don't want to give it up but I don't actually think it's the right thing for a bunch of rickety old men to be dancing.

I think that's one of the things that gets to people. I think it gets to them that this bunch of guys who are dancing are chartered accountants and solicitors, and people think they should be rustic types doing this bucolic activity. There's a wonderful story of how Cecil Sharp cycled out to Eynsham, and these old boys trooped in out of the fields, with their boots all covered in mud; it was November time and they looked really miserable. But then one of the guys played a mouth organ and they started dancing, and Sharp describes how their cares and worries and dejection just fell away from them. Now, you only have to update that a hundred years by saying, 'Well, here's a guy, these days he's got to throw away his laptop and his briefcase and take his jacket off, and he's the same guy, he's just doing a different job.' We don't work in the fields any longer. We have to work in offices or laboratories, or whatever. But the point is that when we get together, we get away from the cares of the world, the things that we have to grapple with on a daily basis. It's escapism.

I'm a chemist and I sit on European committees as part of my job: I'm the Chairman of a European committee and I really believe in Europeanization. I'd go the whole way, I'd have a Federation of European States. And that's an odd thing for somebody who believes in English tradition to say, but I don't think it does anything at all to devalue local traditions. You don't have to lose the Morris by becoming European. I tend to regard the centre of civilization as being somewhere within a fifty-mile radius of Oxford but the English are more accustomed to travelling around Europe now and we're becoming less xenophobic.

Sometimes French colleagues say to me, 'The English stood up against Hitler, they stood up against world oppression when they were almost alone in the world. How does a country like that, and a country that produces Elgar and Dickens and Thomas Hardy and Shakespeare, also produce the *Sun*, the *Daily Star* and the *Sunday Sport?*' I say to them: 'Sure, we've got the *Sunday Sport* and all that that means. We've also got the *Guardian*, the *Daily Telegraph*, the *Observer*, and *The Times*.' There's more cultural diversity here than in much of Europe, and that's something else which is part of being English, the diversity our society has *because* of our colonial interests. You go to Denmark, it's a very pure country. They're all Danish, and they all look Danish because there are few immigrants and it's all very bland. It's a monolithic culture, it's too pure. They don't have the colourful aspects we have in England with Notting Hill Gate, and Indian restaurants, and Chinatown. Those things are part of being English too.

Generally speaking, Morris dancers are very traditional, nationalistic types: you know, English beer must be sold in a pint, English currency must have the Queen's head on it. But the more people from the professional classes dance the Morris, the more that will change. I don't want to give the impression that I'm a typical Morris dancer.

Pamela Elder

Kate

Kate was an amazingly relaxed person but she had an awful time when we moved here. She was sixteen and about to start her 'A' levels. The sixth form at that stage was all about self-motivation and I said to the teachers, 'I think Kate needs a bit of help here,' because she was so laid back. She was bright but if she could get away with doing nothing then she would do nothing. She'd lots of other good things here too, she was suddenly meeting blokes, and when the teachers said to me, 'We expect her at that age to motivate herself,' I thought, Hey, come on, it's a bit young. It was a very liberal, middle-class view of education. If she didn't get an essay in, it was her problem and I disagreed with that, knowing my child as I did. Also, we'd lived in Spain and Kate was so good at Spanish she wanted to do it at 'A' level but the school didn't do it. I'll never forget it: they said, 'Can she do history?' I said, '*History*?! This country's education is *obsessed* with history. She doesn't *want* to do history, she wants to do *Spanish*. Three hundred million people speak Spanish.' So she left after a year and went to Oxford FE College to do Spanish, French and English, and then she got in to London University to read Spanish and she really blossomed. She was having the best time of her life.

Kate died at the end of her first year at university, in the June. She stepped off a bus as it was starting to go and obviously lost her footing and fell. Whether the brain-stem death was caused by the fall or the three cars that subsequently went over her, we don't know. None of them stopped. Looking back, you know, I kept thinking, You teach your children how to cross the road, you teach them to say please and thank you, you teach them everything you can think of but you don't teach them how to step off a bus. You always look back and say, 'What could I have done?' But nobody, I don't think *anybody* ever says, 'Be very careful when you are stepping off a bus.'

Afterwards, we had several phone calls from the local press saying, 'Aren't you mad about hit-and-run drivers?' I said, 'Well, no.' Of *course* it's tragic, hit-and-run drivers, but I tried to look at the other side of the argument. She was dressed all in black that night, as she liked to do, and the wonderful man who was a mini-cab driver who *did* finally stop, we met him at the hospital and he said he finally realized that it was somebody lying in the road because he saw blonde hair but at first he thought it was a bin bag, a black bin bag. Now, it's the Finchley Road, midnight, dark, there's something dark in the road. They probably didn't see her. Maybe they didn't. And I know some people can put all the anger and energy that comes from a sudden death like that into something positive but I did *not* want to do that and the family didn't want to do that, we didn't want a campaign on hit-and-run drivers, it wasn't right.

However, when it came to the bus conductor that was much more difficult, because we had witnesses who said they desperately told him to stop the bus and he wouldn't. He said in the evidence, 'Flipping student, probably had a few to drink,' and one woman said, 'If you want to bring a civil action, I will be your witness.' She was so angry that he wouldn't stop. When the case came up, he came to the inquest and in the end he was fined £100. When I met him I could have gone for the jugular. His solicitor kept him well away from us as if I was going to attack him, and I certainly felt I could have done, but what would I have achieved? I wouldn't have got Kate back. And maybe yes he should have stopped the bus; and maybe, looking back, I should have taken out a civil action; that may be something I'm still a bit ambivalent about. But at the time I didn't want to, it didn't feel right, we as a family didn't want to, and I think you've got to go with your instincts at the time.

The other thing that is important to say is that Kate had been very impressed that her dad had carried a donor card, so we felt strongly that her body should be used for ... But again you run into clichés and expectations. You have people saying, 'You'll feel marvellous because you've given life to somebody else.' We felt *flattened*. Flattened. All I could think was, Every one of her organs was perfect, why haven't I got her? Why isn't she alive? Her heart, her lungs, her corneas, her kidneys: all I could think was, If they're all perfect, why isn't she still here? So I would still do it, we as a family would still do it, because it has given somebody life, but *don't* assume that it's going to make you feel wonderful, because it didn't for us; *don't* give me this crap about feeling marvellous. If you get a bit of comfort from it, great. Any comfort you can get is important. But it didn't comfort us, not one of us.

They say there are stages you'll work through. For crying out loud, you can't *order* emotions! Grief is unique, it's completely individual, you can't put people's behaviour into a theory, you can't impose thoughts and feelings; you can't! And people are very quick to throw you into counselling or on to some kind of antidepressant. I didn't want either. In the end I tried both because I felt maybe I should but I was off both very quickly because it wasn't right for me. If it works for someone, lovely. Think of Dunblane. They sent a whole team of counsellors in and they didn't want them. People closed their curtains. And why shouldn't they? If I want to be closed, if I want to hold my grief to myself, I will do. It doesn't make me a dysfunctional human being. You see, I've been challenged so much by people on this. Even fairly recently somebody said to me, 'You're not letting go of Kate, that's the problem.' And I would argue, 'I don't *need* to let go of her: I am coping; I'm out there doing what I want; my life is great.' Yes of course there will be black days. I'll go up to the cemetery and cry and chat with Kate. Often we go up to the cemetery together, her sisters and I, we say, 'Come on, Kate, if anybody can get us through this, you can.' And why not? If you feel the need to do it, do it.

I recently read some research papers written by a man called Tony Walter, from Reading University, who'd lost his father and his girlfriend to cancer, and he asked: 'What are the magical properties of letting go?' For him it was important to continue talking about those people. And honestly, reading that was like a beacon. I thought, Thank God, nine years later somebody's saying what I feel. So if you need counselling it should be there; if you need antidepressants for a bit, yes; if you need to go to Compassionate Friends or CRUSE, yes; if you want to throw yourself into work, which is what I did, busy busy busy busy, so I wouldn't have to think about Kate's death, yes. That was right for me at the time, so let's be much more open to the fact that grief is quite unique and everybody's experience is different. I'll miss Kate until the day I die. There's never going to be a time when I don't think, She might have been married by now, I might have had a grandchild. But I think what people fear is that you are still too absorbed, and that absorption in the deceased is not allowing you to move forward into new relationships and new things, even though that's patently not true.

It's quite difficult to say how it affected me and Tom. We didn't talk very much, none of us, not even myself and the girls. Myself and the girls, we could talk if necessary but we'd more likely go up to the cemetery and have a good cry together, or we'd say, 'I just feel rough today.' Sometimes they'd find I was crying and we'd just have a big hug and cry. Tom didn't talk at all but then he doesn't talk about things, he is much more of an introvert, and he found talking about Kate extraordinarily difficult. He and I'd go to the cemetery together, we'd always be very close physically, we'd just sit there or we'd hold hands, and sometimes I wanted Tom to talk but you can't force things like that. He would listen to music. The funeral for Kate was very, very special because we took over the church and took our hi-fi down and we played everything from Mozart to Dire Straits, and he spent ages on that, Tom did. It was recorded to perfection.

I do remember one critical time I was crying on the bed and Tom came up and I said, 'I can't go on. I don't want to go on. I can't go on.' Floods of tears. And he very carefully and gradually got me out of that, not with many words, it was very much the gestures, not the verbal stuff. Tom's relationship with Kate had been strained for years, although it was improving in the year before she died. We had had big rows because she seemed to be going wild, and as parents you worry. She came home with the most dreadful men. One particular one was dreadful, we thought he was an awful influence on her. He was actually a very gentle person but we didn't know him: that was the top and bottom of it, looking back we didn't know him, so we thought he was dreadful because he wasn't at her intellectual standard. And Tom, he was coming to grips with his daughters' growing up, having their own sexual partners. She was the first one and he was finding that very hard. He still does. He will admit he doesn't like any of the boyfriends they bring in, none of them are ever any good, not to him. And Kate was so flamboyant, with the make-up and the cigarettes. She was like, Here I am, I'm alive! 'Live for the day,' she always used to say, and Tom found that very hard to come to terms with. They clashed very strongly at times. I tried to be much more reasonable about the boyfriend than Tom, but she was bright and she was gorgeous and he couldn't see what she was going for this man for. Like a lot of parents who didn't take any time to find out what he was like, we just dismissed him.

The other awful thing is how trivial things change your whole life. The weekend Kate died I'd got my parents here and Kate rang me up and I said, 'Kate, you couldn't stay on another couple of days, could you, with your friends up in London, so that Mum and Dad can have your bedroom upstairs?' 'Oh yes,' she said, 'Don't worry,' and of course she never came back. And you look back and think, How can such a trivial thing change our whole lives? The *resentment* I felt towards my stepmother ... But then again, if your number is up, your number's up. Tom had a horrendous crash on the Newbury to Wantage road a few years earlier, he just lost it and turned the car over, his BMW was flat as a pancake. How he got out we'll never know. He squeezed out through a window and he just had a broken collarbone and the odd bruised rib. Everybody looked at that car and said, 'Well, he's a goner,' but he wasn't. Kate steps off a bus. I do think that when your time has come, that's it. It's not a religious sense I have. I'm not in the least bit religious and the vicar who came here straight afterwards, not the present vicar, obviously thought he was being helpful but he was dreadful. He didn't know what to say, we didn't know what to say. I suppose he felt he ought to come out of duty but he didn't know us at all. He said, 'I'll say a prayer for you.' That wasn't helpful. It didn't mean anything to us.

Kate always wanted everything with style. If she had been married she would have wanted the best – the church, the white wedding, the Rolls – so she had to be buried in style. We got an outside vicar in who Kate had known and he was marvellous. I said, 'We never go near the church, we don't actually believe in it, but I feel this is right for Kate,' and he was great. Thomas Hardy had a thing about fate and there's something I can't explain but I felt something similar. Kate wasn't going to make it. Tom did. She didn't.

When I was going through that phase of terrible, terrible grief it didn't matter that I had three other children who needed help and support and bringing up. Tom was an absolute rock but I just didn't want to go on without Kate. I found a lot of the things you read about the bereaved are true. You read that people will cross the road so as not to talk to you because they're embarrassed and they don't know what to say, and they do. It's very hurtful. You don't want that at all. I remember going down Priory Road and somebody who I knew said, 'Oh, are you out and about already?' and I was speechless. What was I meant to do? I had children to feed. They don't mean to be unkind but it is, it is, and all this 'time will heal' stuff, and 'your three other children' stuff, all that is not helpful. And people saying, 'I *do* understand what you're going through.' *Nobody* does unless they have lost a child. Not a husband, not a mother, a *child*. I honestly believe people want to be kind but they don't know what to do and they don't know what to say.

The worst thing was trying desperately never to mention Kate's name. There's you desperate to talk about her because it was important to talk about her and you just want someone to listen, you want to be able to bring her into the conversation, and the most negative thing was finding people don't want you to do it. They're frightened of bringing up the subject and yet if you bring it up yourself, which I tended to do, they can't handle it. You'd hear them sometimes: 'What am I going to say now? Why is she talking about her?' That, I would say, was the worst. My work colleagues were fine. One or two were very good at just giving me a squeeze, or if I was up front giving a session and they could see that perhaps I was not coping, they could step in beautifully and take over the session, which I thought was very good and very sensitive. I'm a health consultant and I work with companies like Remploy and Oxford City Council on stress management and stress awareness, so sometimes it was appropriate to explain myself. I sometimes just said, 'I am a mother and I have lost my daughter, and I have my rough patches,' but I had to be careful when to judge whether that was OK, and I could only say that because my work colleagues were so great.

Apart from working, reading other people's experiences about how shitty life can be was very helpful. I've got loads of quotes that made sense: C. S. Lewis's *A Grief Observed*; Susan Hill. Diana Lamplugh said that a family is like a circle and when one member disappears the circle is broken and becomes smaller. I needed to validate my experience of grief and reading helped me do that. A lot of parents must say this, that my daughter's life must count for something. You're looking for some sort of meaning, some sort of comfort in meaning. Diana Lamplugh has thrown herself into a campaign, marvellous; there's Mrs Lawrence, the murdered headmaster's wife; the Dunblane Snowdrop Appeal. Those are ways of validating their experience.

Our way was the annual Kate Elder Lecture at London University. It was their suggestion, which was lovely, and every year they get a famous Hispanist to come over and talk about Spanish literature and now it's packed with students, none of whom knew Kate, but it doesn't matter, they are getting the best speaker on something that they are studying and that's good. Every year we have a Kate Elder prizewinner who I always meet and write to, and it's the best first-year Spanish student. As a family, we've all loved that. Making your child's life count for something is desperately important but you have to find your own way. Diana Lamplugh said to me, 'Pam, I've nobody, I've nothing,' and I know how important it is sometimes to pop up to the cemetery and have a chat.

I depended on Kate an awful lot because of the gap between her and the three others. She was so good when the triplets were born: she was five years old and she never had a single jealous tantrum. If I was having problems with the triplets I would say, 'Kate, come on, what are we going to do?' After she had gone up to university we got even closer. I could meet her without thinking, Who the hell is she going out with? Is she coming in at night? All that changed, so I could pop up to London and have a glass of wine, you know, a laugh and a giggle, go and see a daft film and lust after Kevin Costner or whoever it was at the time. That last year was lovely. A lot of people say I idolized her, and I did really because I never thought I would have this lovely blonde child who was perfect. The paediatrician told us when she was about two, 'She's a bit special, this child.' All those things come back to you when you have lost her. And I did think she was a bit special. The triplets are and I love them just as much, but after Kate I had three miscarriages and I thought we'd never have any more and I treasured her as a result.

The other critical factor was my own mother. I didn't find out enough from my father before he died but my own mother left us at six months. She was having an affair with another man, and whether she abandoned me, or whether my father stopped her from seeing me, I never knew. Certainly in 1942 men didn't usually get custody but my father did and I had no connection with my mother ever again. Then he remarried, to my stepmother, and we didn't get on well, but then looking back, poor soul, it's bad enough getting on with your own children, never mind bringing up somebody else's. When I had Kate, it was this *instant* love affair. We've all heard parents say this. The bonding was immediate. This child, I adored her from the word go and I thought, 'How could anybody give up this?' It brought me right back to my own mother. How could anybody do that?

Kate was special, she was special in my life. I often said she was the best thing that happened to me and I shouldn't have been saying things like that really because I was saying it to Tom and rejecting him in a way, but it had been so powerful, the emotions. My life could have been over when I lost her. I felt it was over. I just couldn't understand why I had to lose her, and everybody who's lost a child would say the same, I'm sure. Her of all people: my first-born who was so much wanted, who I thought might be my only one. I remember she was very bashed when she was born. It was a forceps delivery and she was badly bruised from the forceps. After the accident she was on life support and Tom and I both said, 'She's just how she was when she was born. Lovely big cheeks.' And her face: her face wasn't harmed at all but there were these tears of blood because of what was happening in her head, and we kept wiping them away and I kept thinking, She can come through this, I can nurse her, I've always been keen on nursing, I can nurse her, I can bring her through. And of course we couldn't but at the time nobody explained what brain-stem death was. These consultants are brilliant but they talk to you in their brusque way and I didn't know what they were telling me, I wanted them to put it in simple terms.

Although we agreed to donate Kate's organs it was handled very badly. I had to demand after a year to know what happened. Was the operation successful? And then there was the police. We had to go to the police because it was a sudden death and as we sat there the policeman came out with this question: 'Was Kate trying to commit suicide?' Well, I was fit to kill him! I babbled, I said she'd just finished the first year, she'd passed the first exams, she was in love, she was happy ... and Tom very calmly knew how to deal with it. But you should be warned about a question like that. Tom took over and explained that that was not the case. That's where his strengths were, coming in at the right moment with the calmness, because I was distraught. Christ, my lovely daughter wasn't committing suicide at all! Christ! I was very angry then. I was angry about all sorts of things. I was angry with people who hadn't lost children, and I thought wicked thoughts, particularly if I saw somebody dreadfully disabled or a child who had no hope of any quality of life. I thought, Why not them? Kate had everything. Why not them? I don't like saying it. It's a pretty awful thing to admit.

The girls coped differently. Alex was the one that when I read some of her poems I realized she was suicidal. The other two have said that they spent a lot of time keeping Alex on track, pulling her through. She eventually did go to counselling because she was having nightmares for two or three years or more, the poor lamb was really suffering. She wrote poems and her writing really helped her. It helped me too. I wrote a journal for Kate that I've got upstairs. I would talk through the past and I would talk to her about the present, and I kept that going for quite a long time. And you can see the resolution in Alex's poems when she finally says, 'I can smile again because I've got Kate inside, and everybody who meets me knows that they've got to understand about Kate before they can really get to know me,' and she puts that very well, very well. I feel the same way.

However, when I started to write something for inclusion in a book on grief I had such rows with Nancy. 'I don't want to do it! Why the fuck have you got us involved in this? I don't want to go back over this. *You* got into this, *you* do it!' We had a real battle. Anyway, bless her, she did get involved and what's come out of it is that she was having a tough time with Kate, she said their relationship was awful that year before she died. Alex says that Kate had seen that Nancy was going a bit the same way she had, mucking up on the exams, going a bit wild with the pubs and the cigarettes. Kate had put that behind her and was working hard, so when she saw Nancy they clashed. Nancy said, 'I didn't get on with Kate, we hadn't spoken civilly for months,' so it was very tough on her, though she's worked through it since.

I would say Kate is reintegrated into my life now. Often with the girls, we've looked up and seen it's a lovely bright sunny day and we think of her as bright and sunny because she was like that, with the blonde hair, and we think, I wonder if she is looking down on us? She is still there for me. I have a relationship with her. And being here is important because of Kate. Wantage is where Kate is.

Her death has given me a different perspective. The trivia that I used to get upset about is no longer that important, but that's about getting things more into perspective, it isn't about my personality changing. At least now I do feel able to deal with bereaved people. I feel as if I have got much more empathy, much more understanding, and I'm not as dismissive as I could be. I found it quite hard with the triplets not to be overprotective and I had to fight with myself to let them do their own things. I had to let them get on buses. I couldn't teach them to drive, that was something I couldn't do. I only lost it once when Helen rang me from Ecuador and said, 'Right, Mum, I'm off to Colombia, I'm back-packing.' I thought, Drugs! Not her taking them, but drugs in her knapsack. I said, 'Oh, Helen, I really don't want you to do that. Have you thought about this?' and Alex said, 'You've got to let her. She knows.' Helen was on the phone saying, 'Oh, Mum, you'd see things differently if you were here, stop fussing,' and I couldn't cope with it and I slammed down the phone and I yelled at Alex and she flew out the door and we had a great rumpus of a row, and then I came back and thought, No, Pamela, come on, come on. That was the only time it burst out. Otherwise I've managed to allow them to do their own thing. I can't hang on to them just because I've lost Kate.

Henry Robinson

Onward, Christian Soldiers

It was 1925. I travelled all day and at a quarter to four I got off the train at Wantage Road station. I knew nothing at all about Wantage: all that appealed to me when I applied for the post was that it was a Church of England school and it was all boys. I got off the train and I looked around and I thought, Where the Dickens have I landed? I couldn't see the town anywhere. The stationmaster said, 'You're better off on that old tram or you've got a two-and-a-half-mile walk in front of you.' I was one of the last persons who went on the Wantage tram. That was on a Wednesday and the tram ceased on the Saturday.

As I got off the tram a ginger-headed lad met me and he said, 'I've been sent to conduct you to the school.' So I went round and I met the headmaster, Harry Gregory: wonderful, *wonderful* headmaster, but this was about four o'clock and he kept me there until half-past six, giving me all the details of what would be expected of me. He was a workaholic. *Nothing* stood in the way of his school and he expected the same from his staff. I was taken to my lodgings and I started in the school the next morning.

There were a hundred and forty boys, aged seven to fifteen. The school was terribly run down. There was one big long room and three classes were being taught in that room: the headmaster was in the middle, I was at one end and someone by the name of Blackwell, who has gone long ago, was at the other. Then there was a very tiny room for the boys who came up from the infant school. There was a terrific apex in that building, I dare say about twenty feet high, so lessons had to be arranged so that one wasn't doing oral work while the others were doing written work.

There was no provision whatsoever for the staff – no staffroom at all. And let me describe to you the toilets, a delicate subject possibly. There was one seat for the boys, one cast-iron basin, with cold water of course, and a stand-urinal. Nothing for staff. Mr Gregory said, 'If ever you have an emergency, you must slip across the road to Tom Sims the upholsterer, he'll understand.' The heating was terrible too. You needed to teach in an overcoat during the winter. The school was heated by a large water boiler, of the sort they used in foundries. It was in the middle of the large classroom and the headmaster, of course, sat with his back to it. It was solid fuel, and when it was fed, shovels went in and smoke came out and filled the blessed room, and we put up with it until 1928 when the Church decided to build a new school on a new site.

I can only describe the new school as five boxes stood on ends, but it was luxury because the boys had a cloakroom and five washbasins, the staff had a small staffroom, one toilet, and one handbasin, porcelain, marvellous, and the school opened on 19 July 1928. I hadn't expected to stick it that far. After one term with Mr Harry Gregory it got a little bit too much for me. My landlady said to me, 'I shall have to raise your weekly fee, you are using so much gas.' I was marking books till after two and three o'clock in the morning, so I paid her a shilling a week more, which was considerable in those days. When I went home after one term I said to my father, 'I shall never stick it there, I shall give in my notice for the end of the current school year.' It was drive, drive, drive all the time by Harry Gregory, and not only his staff, he really drove the boys. 'Well,' my father said, 'have a little common sense, finish your year and see how you're fixed then.' I finished that year and by then I felt a loyalty to a man who had dedicated himself to teaching. I dedicated myself to Harry Gregory and Wantage. We had a wonderful understanding after that.

Being a church school, the day started off with prayers, a hymn and six verses of Psalm 100, 'Oh come let us sing unto the Lord.' Then there was religious instruction for three-quarters of an hour. When I became Headmaster I had the impression that the boys liked to choose the hymns. Now, what is the hymn that invariably they chose? 'Onward, Christian Soldiers'! And they sung it with wonderful gusto. Yes, I should say three-quarters of the boys who had the pleasure of choosing a hymn chose 'Onward, Christian Soldiers'. We were also expected at church on Ash Wednesday, then each Wednesday through Lent and on Maundy Thursday, when we always had a sung mass, sung with great gusto. We broke up on Maundy Thursday but the invitation still went out for boys to attend the church on Good Friday, and do you know, about eighty per cent turned up after we had broken up for the holidays.

Punctuality had to be kept religiously. When I got to school there was always a crowd of boys waiting to get into it. They were brought up to the saying, 'Punctuality is the politeness of princes,' and they observed it. When I took over the Headship I was at school by a quarter past eight, the staff were supposed to be there by half-past eight and the morning started for the boys at a quarter to nine. They lined up in the playground or, if there was inclement weather, in the long corridor inside. There was an inspection. Cleanliness? Hair done this morning? Cleaned your boots this morning? And if there was anything amiss with these boys they were sent for a ticking off by the headmaster. It paid dividends. They expected to be well turned out and of course it was expected of the staff too. The headmaster wore a suit and black shoes and the staff didn't go about in jeans and open-necked shirts.

On one occasion we were breaking up for the summer holidays and one of the masters said, 'Mr Robinson, when I come back you'll find a change in my appearance.' I said, 'What would that be?' He said, 'I'm going to grow a beard.' I said, 'If that's it, it's against my advice and against my wishes, so we shall have to make a decision when you come back.' But when he came back there was no beard. He said, 'I've thought about you a lot: I wouldn't displease you in any way.' Good lad.

One term, two new boys came. They were good loyal lads, but the long-hair cult was coming in and I said on no account would I have a boy with long hair in my school. One of these lads, I said to him, 'I want to see you in my room before you go home on Friday afternoon.' 'Yes, sir.' 'Now look here,' I said, 'if you come on Monday morning without having your hair cut I shall send you back home until you get it cut.' That was Friday. Monday morning he was waiting at my door: 'How is this, sir?' I said, 'That's good. You've done what I wanted you to do.' The Tuesday afterwards we were going into church, and his mother came up to me and said, 'Mr Robinson! I want you!' Cor, I thought, I've got to play it cool, because she was a character, I can tell you. So I went slowly down. 'Yes, what can I do for you? I've got to get back into church, make it brief.' She said, 'I want to shake your hand and say on behalf of my husband and myself how much we admire what you have done.'

You see, discipline was absolutely stonewall and parents and children alike understood that. I had to keep my buttons polished because I had sons of all the headmasters in the town at the school. They were sent to me because there was never any tomfoolery at all. When a boy started talking to me his first address was 'Headmaster' and his second was 'sir'. All the members of staff were 'sir' too; there was no messing about with Christian names. Parents learned to understand the set-up of the school, and parental interference was absolutely nil. That was my system and it worked.

Parents pulled together with the school too: homework in those days always consisted of the three Rs, reading, writing and arithmetic, as well as rural studies and spelling. The three Rs are the thing but they don't teach them properly these days. And any boy who had homework, he took a note home and it was signed by the parent to say that they would supervise him. As a result, I didn't have any problems with the boys, none at all. I had only one occasion of truancy. One day I looked down the register and said, 'Where is Smith?' Quite a problem boy at times but turned out all right. One boy said, 'He's gone over to Letcombe, sir, to the racing stables.' I said to my deputy, 'Take my class!' I got in my car and I went tearing over to Letcombe and Smith was halfway to the racing stables. 'SMITH! GET IN MY CAR!' 'Yes, sir, I'm sorry, sir.' He didn't play truant again.

In fact, Wantage never had a more loyal lot of boys. By the time I was Head the school was so popular it became overcrowded with boys from the villages: at one time there were forty to a class. Two boys came in from Fawley, the Bracey boys came from Woolley Park, Thompson came from Farnborough, lots came from Hanney and how many came in from Hendred I wouldn't know. They were wonderful, the village boys: they came in on their bikes, they walked, they jogged, and I never knew them to be late. The same going home: in a band; well behaved; marvellous. They were a grand lot of boys.

I was helped by the school's relationship with the police. In 1939 I was called for military service but I had had a very serious operation and I couldn't serve. I was so disappointed when the doctor told me that, that very evening I went down to the police station and joined the Special Police. I knew the Chief Constable of Berkshire through shooting associations, and he made me Wantage Divisional Officer. All through the war there were Special Constables manning every railway bridge and every level crossing, and I had Specials to look after as far as thirty miles away. The police then went out of the way to help the school. I had the Superintendent's son, two sons of the Chief Inspector, two sons of the Sergeant from Hendred, and I would only have to say I wanted someone to referee a football match and half a dozen off-duty policemen would volunteer. When we had school parties they would come and give a hand. On a school outing I always insisted that a policeman went with the boys on the coach, and the boys really enjoyed it: it taught them to respect the police in the street. When they saw a policeman in the street they didn't run around the corner to get out of his way, they went and had a word with him.

I'd have given my life for those boys. But when the first comprehensive was to be built, there was talk of girls coming to the school. The

Director of Education was a very good friend of mine and he kept me well informed of the whys and wherefores of what was going to happen at the school, but I could see only problems. There were outside boys' toilets, five seats and the urinal, open, and there was no provision that could have been made for girls. I didn't like it. It was 1966 and there was chaos. They wanted me to stay but we had a very strict code of discipline which everybody seemed to admire, and having taught boys all my life I could not think of a little girl standing there and me giving her a good ticking off. It would have been most unfair of me to have stayed, so I just saw things through and then I left. I couldn't have stayed. I wouldn't have been able to.

It's over thirty years since I retired now and well over seventy years since I came to Wantage. There was gas lighting then, and all the utilities belonged to the town: the water, the gas, the electricity. If you wanted a policeman after midnight you usually found him at the gasworks, with the manager down there, making toast and cooking sausages on a shovel. The water was gravity-fed from just below the old workhouse, where Gandolfo has got his training stables now. They had their own chapel at the workhouse, and their own cemetery: at Christmas we always took a party of boys up to entertain the residents.

I moved into my house in 1936. It was raw fields when I came in and every stick and stone I put into it. I've got a lot of grounds at the back but the problem now is my sight; my wife died ten years ago and I can't do what I should do. I did manage to fill my greenhouse with tomato plants a week ago but that's about as far as I can go. I haven't been able to read a newspaper for over six years, and I enjoyed shooting; for years I was booked all the way through the season by various farmers, but I gave it up before I shot somebody by accident. My son Terry came in last evening: he and his wife look after all my business and I wanted him to fill in some cheques. Like I said, I can't see to read. I attempt a signature on the cheques but one or two have been sent back recently. In my wastepaper bin there, there are two torn up because I made a frightful mess of them.

I went to the eye hospital in Oxford and I didn't get anywhere with them, so I went to see Dr Ambler here in Wantage, he is very good, but he said, 'Henry, you've got to resign yourself.' I said, 'Well, that's what you say. Do you mind if I have a second opinion?' and he said, 'Of course not.' I went to the Acland, a private hospital in Oxford. We were there one and a half hours and the consultant said, 'No, nothing can be done for you.' Terry sat through the whole thing and he said, 'Look here, Dad, you've got to accept it.' So that was it. I resigned myself to it. It makes things very heavy for me because I was an avid reader and now there's very little I can do all day, so I sit here and I look out of this big window. I can see a car go past because it's moving and I can at times see people come to the door. It's a great handicap but then you'd expect me to be worn out by this time. I've had my day.

Winifred Pope

Lifeblood

It was all bare. Blackboards and chalk. Nothing on the walls by the children. The previous head teacher, Henry Robinson, had already left: the girls came that term and I think he couldn't face girls after all those years of boys only. I didn't know anything about the school but I looked around and I thought, Hmm, I could do something here. I thought it would be a challenge. I just had that feeling.

I expected to stay about five years. Those five years turned into five times five because there always seemed something else you could do in the place. I certainly was never bored. We had some super times and marvellous staff and children. And when I was in hospital recently an old pupil came to see me and he said, which thrilled me: 'The best days of our life were when we were at the junior school.' He said, 'We reminisce about it of an evening and we nearly roll on the floor with laughter at all the things we did, and all the laughs we had. It was wonderful.' So I said, 'Well, that's a terrific thing to say,' because as a head teacher that's what you want it to be; a happy time as well as a time for learning. I think if children aren't happy they don't learn. They don't do as well as when they're contented.

I realized when I came to Wantage that some of the children were extremely bright and they wanted an enormous amount demanded of them, so I taught full-time myself to begin with, which was what I loved doing. I've always felt that you've got to give a lot of time to children who have learning difficulties, but I think you've equally got to make sure that bright children aren't idling along, that they're stretched and they make the most of their potential. I certainly think, going back a generation, a lot of potential was wasted, particularly when the theory was that education mattered for boys but not so much for girls. I mean, when I first came here, there really weren't any suitable books for the children to read. They were *Salute the Empire* sorts of things, you know, chaps in long shorts and hats saluting the flag. In the store room there was brown paper and string and that was all. The county was very good, they gave me extra money to start buying things, but books were not a priority before we arrived: I think it had been very much talk-and-chalk up to that time.

We got the school sorted in the fullness of time. With children, you've got to do things properly from the beginning. When I had infants, I taught them to join up their writing almost from the word go, and I used a structured reading scheme with phonics from the beginning too. When you teach, the greatest thing of all is the relationship between teacher and child, because if a child gets on with his teacher he'll learn anything. He'll write, he'll read. Having first-hand experience helps too. When you look at things it's easier to be able to write about them afterwards, so I took the children out a lot, to see things. And in order to be able to write, you've got to be able to converse, you've got to have a vocabulary, and you've got to learn that, haven't you, so the children and I used to talk a lot. I learned over time that teaching is all down to personal relationships. I mean, I couldn't not get on with a child because it wasn't fair to that child. You've got to find a point of contact. And if you work hard enough you always find there's something. We naturally, all of us, like one person more than another, but as a teacher you must be scrupulously fair; fair to boys and girls. You've got to see that both of them have exactly the same opportunities, and if one group does something, then the other must do it. It must be fair and it must be *seen* to be fair.

Personal relationships take time. They take time to grow. I think the main thing is always to be very positive and rejoice over what children do. You praise them and eulogize something they've done well, make a real scene about it. You've got to be quite dramatic, in a way. You can be very pleased about good things, and then you can be very sorrowful about bad things. Sometimes you have to do it with your tongue in your cheek, but you can't let them know that, because you teach children by boosting their morale and appealing to their better nature, and also by saying to them that you know they can do something; because then they believe you, and they try it, and they *can* do it.

You've also got to judge everybody according to their strengths. I mean, I know that some people are always going to be better than others, say, at maths, but if that person is doing as well as they can, well, that's super, isn't it. And I think you've got to make people see that everybody's got something to give, therefore everybody matters. One thing I could never stand was if one child laughed at another's mistake or misfortune. That used to make me very angry, because I think that's very demeaning and demoralizing. I never did it and I would never have them do it. I always said, 'We're a community, and we support each other,' and you hope that's what they're going to do through life, isn't it. It's so easy to make people feel under-confident and that their efforts are no good. Nobody is brilliant at everything but I wanted everybody to feel that they were valued in the community; and they responded, they were nice with each other. I remember somebody once said to me, 'Oh, I am sorry for you. You've got so-and-so coming to your school and he's as thick as two planks and a real nuisance.' 'Oh,' I said. 'Well, thank you. That's very encouraging.' And he wasn't Einstein, you know, but he was a nice child and very responsible. I used to ask him to keep an eye on the class if I had to go out of the room, and he was absolutely marvellous.

I'm interested in children, I like children, and I don't really think that children are all that different from adults. You can talk to them in much the same way. I know there are times, probably with your own, when you give them a smack and say, 'That's enough,' but you can't do that in school now. We used to be able to. We once had a child, a very, very difficult boy, though he came out OK. It's very sad, actually, it's terrible, he died last year. He had a heart attack at thirty-two. In fact, he shared my birthday. Anyway, one playtime he was out in the playground and he got a nettle, and he had a whale of a time, he went round nettling all the girls. So of course they all came shooting to me: 'Oh, Miss Pope, Miss Pope, Philip's nettling us.' I said, 'Yes, I can see he is.' So I went and got a nettle, and I went up behind Philip and I nettled his leg: oh and he let out such a howl! I said to him, 'Now, Philip, you know what it's like, don't you.' I didn't say any more to him but he didn't do it again. You couldn't do that now; you'd be had up. But Philip didn't bear any malice and he took the point. Sometimes, it doesn't do any harm to do that sort of thing to children. Often it saves a lot of time and energy.

Mind you, I always say of children who are difficult that there's no point in getting hot under the collar with them: you've got to try and get them to open out and find out what's going wrong underneath, what's causing it all, and that is a time-consuming job. With some of them, it's knowing the signs. And if other teachers saw the signs coming up, sometimes they would send the children to me and I'd find them something to do, or we'd have a chat. I can remember one boy who had a filthy temper, particularly when he was playing football. Playtime was a hazard. And I said, 'Well, we've got to do something about it because you can't go to secondary school like this, it's going to make life so difficult.' And together he and I came up with the idea that when he knew he was getting excited, he'd roll off the pitch and run all round the field until he got himself under control, and then go back. And he worked on that and he wasn't successful every time but he virtually overcame it; and I thought that was terrific because he certainly got in a real paddy before.

To get people like that to open up, they've got to trust you and have confidence in you. What influences you most when you're at school? A contact with a teacher, probably. And a lot that you do afterwards has been influenced by a teacher, hasn't it. That's what school's all about, interaction between children and teachers, and if you share a few jokes, all the better. We always seemed to have a lot to laugh about. I felt it was a priority to know the children, and to know the families, and to know when families are going through difficult times which will repercuss on the child. And every year, with a new intake, I kept on asking names until I knew who they were because really I was the only person in the school who *could* know everybody's name. It's vital to know people's names, so that you get to know them, and when things arise, you know how they tick.

I also wanted the children to realize that you might not agree with somebody else but you didn't have to fall out about it. You've got to try to teach children to learn to respect other people's views, and to disagree but still remain friends. We often invited people in from outside to talk at assemblies, about other ways of life, or other cultures, and I would always say to children, 'If you think somebody else's way of life is odd, remember that ours probably seems just as odd to them.'

If you teach children about respecting difference, and you pick on what is good and nurture it, that way you teach them moral values. Moral values are the lasting things that prepare you for life, so you aspire to make them more open-minded, because they can be very prejudiced, children, by what they see and hear on television, and what their parents say. We also tried to share people's achievements, the things they'd done outside school. If they'd had a stall in their garage for Save the Children, and raised £20 and had a letter back, I'd read that out after assembly. Or I'd say if they'd done a tap dance exam or something; all the time trying to widen people's horizons, all the time trying to open doors for people.

Now that paperwork has multiplied so much for teachers I don't know what will happen. So many of my colleagues are now counting the days to when they retire. They can't get out quick enough, because the workload is so ridiculous, and they're so harassed and strained. That's what is so sad. I was very fortunate that I enjoyed it to the end. I still think it's far more important having time to converse with your children than doing a whole lot of paperwork. Paperwork takes time from when you can be with children. I always used to say to parents, 'If there's any problem, come to school at any time,' and that's getting increasingly difficult now. That's very worrying, because I don't see how you can run a school if you haven't got that contact with them. Teachers are going to get more removed from contact with children and families, and for me that's the lifeblood.

Terina Cox

Proud

I had this pain going down my arm all the time, it really really hurt. I couldn't move, couldn't drive, couldn't do anything, so I went to the doctor's and he said to me, 'Can you do me a urine sample?' I said, 'I've only got a pain in my arm, what's the problem?' I was thinking *major* problems. So when he walked back in the room and said, 'I'm pleased to tell you you are nineteen weeks pregnant,' I nearly died on the spot. I said, 'You're joking!' He said, 'No, you're nineteen weeks pregnant,' and I burst into tears. I didn't know what to say. I never went home for a week, I thought my dad was going to kill me.

I was eighteen. But I was taking precautions and my boyfriend, I'd been with him for five years, since I was thirteen, so it was like God, shock, horror, this isn't supposed to happen. Because me and my friend Jenny, we were meant to be going off to America together. We were going to be nannies in America and then this bombshell. I couldn't believe it. Everything was still normal, I was still regular as clockwork, this is what I couldn't understand: I was taking the Pill. Well, from that day my life changed completely.

I was living at home with my mum and dad and the one thing my dad always said to us girls was don't ever bring trouble home: well, you know what that means when your dad says that. My sister was married by then and living nine miles away, so I went to her and she was the first person I told. She phoned my mum. My mum hit the roof. So I said that was it, I wouldn't come home, I would stay with Vivian until I found myself somewhere to live. My dad took the phone off my mum and he said to me, 'You get your bloody arse home here now and don't be so stupid.' I said, 'But you always said if we bring trouble home that's the end of it.' He said, 'Get home now and don't talk so stupid, your home is here.'

So I got home and Mum wasn't very happy and she got on the phone to the doctor; she wanted to know if I could have a termination. The doctor said, 'Ask Terina if she wants one,' and I said, 'No bloody way, I'm not aborting a baby, not at nineteen weeks, that's killing a child and I'm not doing that.' I said, 'He or she wasn't planned but he or she is mine, it's growing inside me now, it's part of me, so I will look after it the best way possible.' Oh, there were lots of rows, how was I going to do this and that, and then Nathan was born and my mum completely changed. She wanted me to give her Nathan and me to carry on and live my life but I said, 'No, I've had him, he's my son.' He was five weeks early, and slightly jaundiced too, and they took him away to put in an incubator. I fed him every hour. The nurses never done it, I did it, and even though I never held him until he was four days old, when I did it was so natural.

I could not believe that this little thing was mine. He was tiny, absolutely dinky, all legs. When you deliver that baby and the baby is put straight on you, there is nothing in this world that can ever help you explain that feeling to anybody. I was determined that no one would ever take my son away from me and they never did.

I moved out of home when he was three months old. I spent six months in a homeless hostel and I got my first home when he was nine months old. I was on my own after that. I have never asked my family for help. My mum has looked after my children three times for me, and my eldest is twelve, so I've done it all myself and I'm very proud of what they are.

Nathan's dad, he wanted to be with me but I didn't want to be with him. We had grown apart. Then I did a stupid thing. Nathan was just over nine months old and I married his father. Everybody kept saying to me, 'You've got his child, you've got to marry his father, you shouldn't be a single parent.' So I thought, Fine, I'll go along with society, I'll marry him. It lasted two weeks and it took me two years to get divorced, so what was the point? Nathan still sees his father and we get on really well now, we just didn't then. We got divorced in the January, he married in the April and I married in the November.

David and I had been seeing one another on and off for about three years prior to me marrying him. My other sons, Luke and Harry, belong to me and David but I didn't marry David until Luke was six months old: I wasn't going to commit myself again just because I had a baby. In the first five years we had some really bad moments. I have actually packed my stuff and gone to walk out and leave him with the kids, that's how bad things have got at times, and he just never ever let me go. I'm glad he didn't. I would never change anything now. They all give me grief, God do they give me grief, and the dog is a boy as well so I'm well and truly outnumbered. But the love that I get from all four of them you could never wish for in a million years.

I would never turn the clocks back. My family are my life and I never thought I would be like that. I just thought it was going to be me on my own, sorting the rest of my life out, doing my own thing, and it isn't. Every single one of them is so affectionate. They are no angels, far from it, but they are proper little boys and you can't knock them for that. Nathan is twelve, Luke is eight, and Harry is six.

That's my husband in that picture with them, my David. He's my toyboy, he's four years younger than me. He's a builder. David has always had a crew cut and he used to wear big Dr Marten boots; he was one of those who did it his way and not your way, basically. He was always in trouble at school too, like me. He used to be in the same class as Ian Ockwell, who was a right tearaway, they were good friends: David used to call Ian 'Ocky' and Ian used to call David 'Pigsy'. Anyway, one day, Ian stabbed David in the hand with a fork in a cookery lesson. David was banging the wooden spoons on Ocky's head, using his head as a drum, and Ocky said, 'If you do that to me once more, Pigsy, I'm gonna stab you with this fork.' So David done it again and Ocky turned round and stabbed him straight through the hand with the fork. David had to go to the hospital and have his hand stitched.

Ocky lives over there now, that house across the road. And when the weather's nice we all sit out the front and have a natter about the old schooldays and things that went on and some of the things that we can remember. And we wonder: how the hell did we ever get away with them?

With me, bad behaviour was always frustration. When I was at Miss Pope's school my hair was quite long and one day this other kid, Andrew Matkin, he came up behind me and put this plasticine in my hair. I turned round and shouted at him, and the teacher had a go at me, and then she come up behind me with a big pair of scissors to cut my hair and I flipped. I went for Andrew and hit him, and as the teacher came running towards me, I can remember it as plain as day, I picked the table up and threw it at her. I was only ten years old but I was quite big. I said, 'I hate you, you fat old bag. You're not cutting my hair.' And I threw an absolute mental fit. I was trying to grow my hair down to my waist. I wanted to look like my auntie.

Then I ran away. I ran out of the school, went and sat up the park for the rest of the day and went home as normal so my mum wouldn't know anything. But Miss Pope had been on to my mum and my mum had been waiting for me to come home. 'Have a good day at school, did you?' she asked, and I said yes, but as I still had the plasticine in my hair I told her what had happened. She said, 'I know. Miss Pope's been looking everywhere for you.' I got upset then. I didn't mean to worry Miss Pope. I was just so angry, I didn't think. I burst into tears and had to have all my hair cut off short right there and then. I could have killed Andrew Matkin.

When I went to school the next day, Miss Pope and I, we sat for about an hour talking, and at the end she gave me a big hug. This is one of the many incidents that happened at school and yet Miss Pope, when I went back the next day, she sat and talked to me. I love that woman to pieces. She made a big impression in my life, very, very big impression. She was the only one that took time out to listen to me. I think when you are slightly creative and you struggle to express yourself nobody really wants to listen to you, they tend to think you are just being a pain in the butt and push you to one side; and every time I tried to express myself I found myself getting into trouble, but Miss Pope always used to listen to me. She said, 'Terina, just come and talk to me,' and that's exactly what I used to do. We had this rapport that I have never had with anybody else before or since. She hit me in the heart and you never forget that. I think she is one in a million. Never ever have I found another teacher to compare to her. I remember thinking that day, If only I'd gone to her yesterday, none of this would probably have happened.

I wanted to stay at Miss Pope's school for ever. My first day at secondary school I cried. I hated it, I was absolutely petrified. I was shaking from head to toe because I was so nervous. The place was massive and I was used to being where everybody knew me and I knew everybody else, and where the teachers were friendly. That first morning I met two teachers, Mr Hollings and Mr Eaton. They asked my sister to take me down to meet them and I thought it was to be introduced and say hello and make me feel welcome at the school. So I went down to see Mr Hollings and Mr Eaton and they took one look at me and said, 'Oh no, not another Saveall,' which was my name before I got married, and from that day on I was branded because of my sister's behaviour at school. From that very first day I was picked on.

There wasn't one teacher that had time for me at secondary school. The worst was a vicar who taught there once. He called me a slut and a slag and a whore and a tart one day. I was having an argument with somebody as we walked past the lollipop lady, and she started to have a go at me. I said, 'Don't have a go at me, you're nothing but an old bag,' and he came up behind me and hissed, 'And you're nothing but a little tart and a slut and a whore.' I went home and told my mum what he had said and my mum flew down the school. I thought she was going to kill him. He was absolutely gobsmacked, and then as my mum walked away he said, 'Well, she *is* nothing but a tart.' Oh, dear. My mum went straight in to see the headmaster and gave him what for. I never spoke to that teacher again. Even to this day when I see him I just look the other way. I saw him a little while ago and just looked at him as much as to say, 'Go away. I'm older now. Just leave me alone.' And he stared at me and then he turned around and walked off. I don't believe he's a real Christian. I think he hides himself behind that cloak. He wants shooting.

I made one friend at that school, but I can't even remember her name. Anyway, her and me, we had this row, just a silly little tiff that you have as you are getting to know people. Well, somebody decided that they were going to cut her coat up with a pair of scissors, and they put the scissors in my schoolbag. So I got the blame for that and I was absolutely devastated. They suspended me from school.

My mum got me back into school and then I started going out with this boy called Nicholas Parry. Oh, I was smitten by him, I absolutely idolized him, until this new girl moved into the second year and began seeing him behind my back. I remember her name was Mandy. I said, 'Oi, I want a word with you,' and when she came over to me I punched her straight in the face. I said, 'He's mine, leave him alone,' and this instant black eye showed up. I got hooked up by the deputy head for that. He picked me up by my shirt from behind and out the door I went and I was on a warning then.

It was one thing after another. A girl called Cheryl Saunders, me and her were really good buddies at school. We used to get on really well and we had a fall-out one day and her sister decided that she was going to have a go at me about it, she started getting gobby with me. So I said, 'Just go away, it's nothing to do with you,' but she got her finger and started poking me in the shoulder and I said to her, 'Don't poke me,' and she said, 'Yeah? What you gonna do about it?' So I dropped my bag and punched her straight in the face. I said, '*That's* what I'm gonna do about it.' But that deputy head, he was standing right behind me. And that was it, I was out. I was expelled. I was taken to the headmaster and he said, 'Terina, I'm expelling you. I don't want you back in this school.' I said, 'Fine. You can stick your fucking school right up your fucking backside.'

My mum was pulling her hair out. It took six months to get me back into school. They were going to send me to St Mary's for day release and I said there was no way I was going on day release, not with all those snobby girls. They tried to get me into Segsbury School: Segsbury wouldn't take me. I had a headshrinker. I went to a child psychiatrist to find out why I was losing my temper. I told her what she could do as well.

Then my luck changed. I was friends with this nice girl, Bridget Duncan, from Miss Pope's. Bridget's mum and dad were nice to me and her mum showed me how to do lace-making. I loved it, I thought it was a lovely thing to do. Anyway, Bridget's dad, Mr Duncan, was the headmaster of another secondary school in town, Icknield School, and he knew me. He knew me as me and he said, 'We'll take Terina, no problem.'

I never ever got into trouble there. I was fine from the day I started. It was there I met up with Jenny and we just clicked straightaway, me and Jenny did. Jenny knew nobody there. She was from the Children's Home, and once I knew her I just didn't want to get involved with anybody else. I didn't want anybody on my back causing me problems and we got on so well that we stuck together.

Jenny was having a bad time and if I wasn't down at the home with her, she was at my house with me. Wherever she was I was, and wherever I was she was. That's how my school life went at Icknield School until the end of the fifth year. I'm ever so ashamed to tell you this next bit, really I am. We had this student teacher come down from London: she had just finished all her training and because she had been teaching in London she thought she was this real hard case. She thought she had been teaching the roughest of the rough. She arrived at the school and she introduced herself to us and said, 'Before any of you think about giving me trouble, I will tell you now I have been teaching in London and you children from the country could never compare with the children from London.' So we thought, Oh yeah?

We had a few lessons with her and this one particular day I couldn't be bothered to do my homework the night before, so I sat in the lesson doing it, as I knew she was only going to read to us anyway. Well, the class was a bit rowdy. This teacher's desk was in front of mine and I was sat doing my homework and she was trying to get everybody to be quiet. She says, 'If you'll all be quiet, I can get on and read.' And somebody at the back mutters, 'If you shut up *yourself* you could get on and read.' She looked at me and said, 'What did you say?' I said, 'I never said nothing.' She said, 'Yes, you did.' I said, 'I did not.' She got a bit hysterical, 'You did, you did!' I thought to myself, Calm down, Terina, but she kept on at me and I said, 'Are you calling me a liar?' 'Yes.' So I got a bit closer and said again, 'Are you calling me a liar?' She said, 'Yes, and what are you going to do about it?' So at that I jumped over the table, grabbed her by the hair, pulled her away from the blackboard so I didn't hit the blackboard and punched the living daylights out of her.

It was awful. There was this blood pouring everywhere and she was screaming and screaming as she ran down the corridor. The class went completely silent. I just sat back down calmly and carried on with my homework. Then Mr Duncan walked in. He said, 'Terina, can I have a word with you please?' And when I said, 'Why?' he said, 'I think you know why.'

I went and sat in his office and my mum appeared and he said to my mum, 'I've got no option but to suspend Terina.' He said to me, 'Terina, I don't want to do this. You know how much we think of you' – meaning his family – 'but why on earth did you do it?' When I told him why he said, 'I'm sorry, I've still got no option.' We got a letter to say that I was expelled and a week later I went to work full-time. That was the week I was meant to do my exams and what they didn't tell me was that I could have had a home tutor and done all my exams at home. I desperately wanted to do my art exam and I never done any exams at all in the end.

It was such a waste because even though I'm not the most intelligent of people, I always got on and done my work. I never ever skived school, never. I loved every day at school, apart from those earlier days when people backed me into the corner, because whenever I'm in a corner I have to fight back. I really regret doing what I did to that teacher but she called me a liar and I'm not a liar. I might be a lot of things but I am not a liar, and there was no way I was going to take the blame for something I hadn't said. I knew I was right and this is what I always say: 'I never ever argue with anybody unless I know I'm right.'

Obviously as I've got older I've got calmer. I don't do things like that any more. The only time I fire up is when anybody has a go at my children, and there are a few up here who do; stupid women who will eff and blind at your children instead of coming to you and saying that they have a problem with them. I broke somebody's drive gates the other week. I heard this woman screaming and shouting at my Luke in the garden, fucking this and fucking that at him she was, and all of a sudden I heard my Luke say, 'But I didn't do it!' and that was it: I was gone from Dawn's garden straight round into this Tracy's garden, except I couldn't get in, her drive gates were locked. So I took a few steps backward and swung them open and broke them off the hinges. I said, 'You ever talk to my children like that again and I'm gonna kill you.' I was raging, absolutely raging, and my Luke was stood there with tears in his eyes and I was thinking, You *don't* speak to my children like that: you can have a go at me like it but not them.

I've always stood by them. I've always backed them up because if I can't nobody else can. The one thing I made sure I did when Nathan went to Icknield School was talk to the school, because there are some teachers that were there when I was there, and I did lay it on the line that I did not want my son treated badly for what I did. I didn't want him judged by my past behaviour. That happened to me at school, being a Saveall, having a bad name, not having a chance to prove anything different, and it's absolutely unfair on a child.

After I got kicked out of school, I wanted to get away from Wantage. I wanted to just go, I had had enough. I was very, very badly labelled and I needed to get out, I needed to go away and find myself, which I did, and I came back a better person.

I had a friend from school called Sarah, and her family moved away from Wantage when she was thirteen. I'd kept in touch with Sarah and when I got expelled the final time I went to live with them for a while. She and her mum and her sister were all working at Chessington Zoo on the funfair, and me and Sarah both got a job. I worked the Gallopers, the old-fashioned horses that go round and round, and I absolutely loved it. I was me, I was free. I was still planning to go to America with Jenny, we wanted to be nannies over there and travel the world, but when I came back to Wantage I fell pregnant with Nathan. Sarah's mother and father got divorced shortly afterwards. Sarah's mum went off with the man from Chessington Zoo, the bloke that was running the place, and they've got a place in Tenerife now.

I lived in Wantage for a while but when David and I got married we moved to West Sussex. We were there five years until I realized I needed to come back here. It was partly triggered off by my friend Melanie Johnson, who lives down the road here. I've known Melanie all my life. I remember her and me having a fight on the school playground at Miss Pope's, and she ripped all the buttons off my new school blouse, but me and her have always got on. Well, Melanie's little boy, Shane, had leukaemia and died. It's tragic. And her husband left her when Shane became very ill, and they are now divorced.

Shane was seven when he died. He has to have been one of the happiest-go-lucky children you ever met. Even through his leukaemia he was always laughing, always joking. Even at his most illest he was a lovely little boy. There was a point when there was nobody who could give bone marrow, and I saw Melanie in the town one day and she had me in tears, and I said to her, 'Look, I'll have a blood test done, if you need me and if I'm compatible then he can have the whole lot if he wants it, as long as it makes him better.' And she said, 'Terina, there are so many people that have said that.' He was one of these children that just had this aura around him: he just glowed and he never, ever complained. And you only had to touch him with your fingertips and he bruised.

It will be two years this December that he died now. It's not long, but like Melanie says, she has got to carry on, she's got two girls and a little boy, Dean, who is younger than Shane. When I first found out that Shane had got leukaemia it was one of the key turning points in my life. I said to David, 'We have to move back to Wantage. Not for Shane because he's got leukaemia, but because it's home.' It's when I realized that all my friends were here and my life was here. It's what brought me back. I remember Melanie being pregnant with Shane and the day Shane was born. I remember the day she had her eldest one, Kerry. All those things were part of my life and it's very difficult to turn away from that. I think maybe I feel it even more because I never had any of that when I was younger, it was always, 'Oh, that's Terina Saveall, we'll push her to the side, she's the bad girl, we don't want to know her.'

You see, the thing about this town is there's a part of my life, like with Miss Pope, that's always there. People are always there. There is only one person that I will never see again and that's my friend Jenny. I miss her so much. I would love to bump into her again, even though I know I never will. She's in my heart anyway, and that's where she stays. But I know that if I walk around the town I bump into my friends from school who are still here, and that means a lot to me. I feel I belong. People who know me know I was not just that rough girl from down the road, I was me, I was a person, and that went a long way with me. With Mr and Mrs Duncan I was a person, I wasn't some troublemaking little cow. And when I was treated like a person I acted like a person. But when I was treated like a troublemaker I was a troublemaker. And when there are people who've been good to you in a place, you don't want to leave it. Why would you go and start again where no one knows you?

I feel that I'm a better person for all that I've experienced anyway. Even with my tattoos and my hair – I've had my hair shaved, I've had it pink and yellow and blonde and red and blue, you name it, I've done

Mary Loudon

it – I can still get on with people. I mean, I have worked for some snobby people, cleaning their houses, but I found that I have always hit it off with them because I am me. There are plenty of people round here that I know that try to be something they're not. I've got a friend called Caroline who won't speak to me now, she's bought her own house and she's totally up herself whereas I am quite happy living in my council house, pottering around, doing my own thing with my kids.

In fact, it's really only outsiders that come into Wantage that don't know me who I get grief from. All right, I've got tattoos up my legs, on my arms, on my back, but that's how I express myself. I had my first tattoo done when I was eighteen. It was a little boxer: it's here, with Nathan's name underneath. My most recent one's an elfin. It doesn't hurt, it's better than sex any day of the week. Honestly, you have to experience it just to know what it's about. I had it done because I was curious. It's like all this body piercing stuff that everybody's having done, I thought, I wonder if that hurts? So out of curiosity, and it cost me twenty quid, I had my belly button done, just to see whether or not it hurt and how it was done. Well, it didn't hurt and I took it out a week later.

They numb you with a spray and they get these pliers, pinch your belly button up, mark it with a pen both sides, keep it pinched with the pliers, and use this great big needle thing to push the ring through and put the little ball in the ring, and then that's it, it's done. I thought there was a lot more to it than that. A friend of mine has both her nipples pierced: the thought of it makes me cringe but she says she likes it. Another friend's been done down below. She said it's brilliant, and her feller's been done too: the Prince Albert, they call it. She says her sex life is out of this world now.

Jenny's mother and father lived away from Wantage and she was put into a home because they said she was difficult to cope with. Jenny wasn't, all Jenny wanted was a bit of love. But her mother was a sore woman; she was not that nice, and her father was not that nice either. They give her a dog's life. So Jenny was very quiet, and because she was so quiet they thought she was a problem. They couldn't see that if taking money off your parents or stealing from a shop or chucking your bedroom upside down means you're going to get some sort of attention, whether it's a slap or whether it's the cuddle that you want, it is better than nothing.

So Jenny was put into the Children's Home and she had it rough. She spent most of her time at my place and if we weren't at my place then we were down the home together. We had our lives set out: off to America, travelling, freedom. We had to get the money together to do this, and while we were trying to do that, bang, I found out I was pregnant with Nathan, which meant I couldn't go. Jenny decided she was going to go and make a life in Swindon, so off she went to Swindon, and I had Nathan and was in the hostel. We kept in touch for a while but then she just disappeared without a word. I found out later that she had gone to America after all. She wanted to do what we were going to do together.

Jenny wasn't as strong-willed as I was, she could be moulded to how you wanted her. In America, she got in with what she thought were really nice people. It was a cult, but they became like a family to her and she thought it was brilliant. I can't remember exactly where it was. I was told, but I blacked it all out after I heard what happened to her. Anyway, she got very involved with these people and then she came back to England for a visit. She didn't know I was in Wantage again. Nobody told me she was over, and nobody told her that I'd moved back here, so I never got to see her. When I found out, I was really upset. I so wanted to see her: it was something I had been really waiting for. I heard she was mixed up with this cult, that she'd gone all religious, and I panicked. I asked everybody for her address but nobody had it. I wanted to write to her but I got no response from anybody. No answers to any questions.

Then a few months later I was stood in the pub with my husband and some other people, and a friend of ours, Andrea, she walked into the pub and said to me, 'Terina, have you seen my mum?' and I said, 'No. Why?' She said, 'She's got something to tell you about Jenny.'

Andrea's mum, Rose, worked at the Children's Home. I said, 'What's that, then?' Andrea said, 'Only that she's been found dead in America and that they used her as a sacrifice.' And this is how she told me: she just blurted it out. I was hysterical. Two days later I found out from the people at the Home that Jenny had been found dead at the side of a road and they thought that she had been hit by a car. But then they had opened a murder investigation when they discovered her heart had been cut out. My whole body went down into my feet when I heard that. I could never explain that feeling to anybody. I asked what had happened to Jenny's body and they said they were going to try and get her back to England. I asked them to let me know when they had.

Anyway, for some unknown reason, I think it was funds, they didn't do it. Rose explained it to me and I said, 'Look, Rose, if I can raise enough money to get the body back, can we have it buried over here?' Apparently yes that was fine. So I tried to do a collection with everybody who went to school with her because it was very, very important to me. And do you know, practically nobody gave me any money. They just didn't want to know, almost like they were embarrassed. So now she is in an unmarked grave in America.

I just wish I could find her. I would like to be able to put flowers on her grave. I would like her to know that I care enough to do that. She was a big part of my life that was taken away, she was so lovely, she had a big impact on me. And to think that those people were supposed to have cared about her, they were supposed to look after her. It was nearly six years ago now and I still can't get over it. It still hurts. Jenny went away and away went her life.

She really wanted to make something of her life too. She came from nothing. She was abused physically, she was abused mentally. Being a parent myself, I cannot understand how people can do that to their children. That's why I would love dearly to help children that are abused mentally and physically, that have no life. When my children are older I would like to go into fostering, to do something for those children. I thought about working with Social Services but my one disadvantage is if I see a child hurting then I hurt, and if they cry, I cry, and although it's a good thing, it's also a very difficult thing. So I can't do it at this moment, I'd be too involved. Maybe ten years down the line, ten years maturer. I'm maturer now than at twenty. I'll be maturer still at forty.

Jenny, to me she was just beautiful. We were always together, always. She was more of a sister to me than my sister has ever been or ever will be and that's exactly how we were: we were soulmates and I feel I let her down. I still feel really gutted. I can't talk about her without crying because it hurts so much. What I'll never come to terms with is the fact that there was nobody to care for Jenny even after she died. So to me, society sucks, I'm afraid. Everybody says that I was the rebellious one up against society and that I should conform to society's ways. But why the hell should I? At least I *care*, which is more than I can say about a lot of arseholes out there – excuse the expression. If I could have done something more I *would*. I would not have just stood back as if that's it, over and done with, forget it. A lot of people look at me and think I'm a hard nut and a cow but I know I'm more emotional than a lot of people. At least I can cry. At least I can show somebody that I love them. I'm not frightened of that.

I didn't have the best of upbringings. My mum and dad didn't have it easy. My dad was a long-distance lorry driver, my mum used to work in the International supermarket. She was wonderful, she was always there for us. My dad was never there because he was always in the lorry. I never remember my dad giving me a cuddle. I can always remember my dad shouting at me and giving me what for. I can remember my mum trying to share her love amongst Russell, Vivian, me and Darren, which she found very difficult because for a week at a time it would be her coping with us alone and my dad would be away. I remember my mum having to make ends meet. She would make cuddly toys and clothes for kids. She did anything she could, and I thank her for that. But my dad was quite hard on us and I hated him for it at the time. I used to think, God, you're so horrible, you never give us anything. Now I certainly appreciate everything I've got because we work hard, me and David; we work hard to make sure our children have everything they need. We went skint to make sure that they had their ponies. The other day they were being a bit sassy and David said to them, 'How many children do you know that have got a pony each?' And they all said, 'None.' He said, 'There you go, you want to remember that. You want to remember that we do everything we can for you.' We don't give them loads of pocket money. We don't say, 'Yes, you can have what you want when you want.' It's not good for them. They are taught their manners, they know their Ps and Qs.

That to me is quite important because a lot of my friends with children, they think they're posh because they have bought their own houses and they have their brand-new motors and they can give their children these PlayStations and £1,000 mountain bikes, and yet their children are absolute little monsters. They're horrible, they're rude, they're ignorant. At least mine are polite, they are kind and caring, they are not conceited. I'm proud of what they are. They are lovely kids and I'm not saying that just because they are mine. Sometimes I feel really guilty because there are kids at school wearing £70 trainers, and mine go off to school with £20 shoes, but I just don't believe that it should be given to a child on a plate. They have to learn morals, they have to learn right from wrong, they have to learn the value of things.

I'm thirty-one this year, but I'm still learning. It never stops. I'm still learning about being a mum. There has to be so much love and so much caring otherwise you end up with a rebel on your hands. I was a rebel but I always had a purpose to what I was doing: I was usually trying to say something that I didn't know how to express. Growing up, I have learnt how to explain myself, and it's not my mum's fault but all I ever heard my dad do was shout and I think that didn't help.

I try not to shout at my kids. Of course I do sometimes, but you teach children by being loving, not by being angry. Like anything, you only realize how precious they are when you think you might lose them. Harry has been wrapped in cotton wool for years because he died on us three times as a baby. We have gone to hell and back with that child, so we never told him off until he was about three years old. When he was born the valve muscle at the top of his stomach, the one that closes when you eat, it wasn't closing, and that was causing projectile vomiting. Food would shoot up through this valve and straight out. Well, we kept going to the doctors, and they kept saying there was nothing wrong with him, and were we overfeeding him? I wasn't overfeeding him.

Anyway, he stopped breathing once after this projectile vomiting, he was like a rag-doll. I took him straight to the doctor and the doctor said he would be fine, give him a little while, and we weren't happy with that. By this time, he was all limp and grey. He looked awful, all blue around his mouth, so we took him straight to Casualty ourselves and we went through one hell of a traumatic time there. We had a student examine Harry. He examined him everywhere and then he said to us, well, he wanted to know if we had abused Harry sexually. You can imagine what I was like. I was distraught because my baby had stopped breathing and he asked me that! I think he took one look at us and decided that because I've got tattoos, and David's got tattoos, we were dirt. At the time I had my head shaved too. Now, I'm not an everyday Joe but that doctor probably wouldn't have asked everybody that question.

Anyway, they couldn't find nothing wrong with Harry. The second time it happened the doctor came out and he was fantastic, he got the ambulance straightaway. I was working behind the bar at the Wheatsheaf pub in Hendred and I had a phone call to say, 'Whatever you do, don't panic, but Harry stopped breathing and he's on his way to hospital.' I was panicking so much I nearly killed myself coming around the bends, I had to talk to myself to calm down. 'Calm down, calm down,' I kept saying to myself. I met the ambulance as it was coming out of Wantage Hospital on its way to the Oxford hospital. The ambulance drivers were friends of ours so they were hanging on for me to get there, and I jumped into the back of the ambulance.

He was in for a week. They done tests, they couldn't find anything wrong; so they done intense tests and they still couldn't find anything wrong. He was projectile vomiting still, but he hadn't done it in front of anybody, so they gave him the barium feed and it came straight back up. This was when they noticed the valve muscle at the top of his stomach and they said it was nothing to worry about, that it would get better as he got older.

Well, blow me, we brought him home, he wasn't out of hospital for seven hours when it happened all over again. But this time it was more severe. David gave him mouth-to-mouth resuscitation. The doctor phoned for the ambulance before he had even got to us. By this time Harry was stone cold, his veins had all collapsed, he had had a rush of fluid round his brain and his fontanelle was up an inch or so with the fluid. He was six months old at the time.

We got him to the hospital. We had to stop along the way and I had him wrapped in blankets, I had him over the heater in the ambulance. His heart rate and everything had gone down. They slowed the ambulance along the way, we were crawling, we must have been doing about five miles an hour. The ambulance driver was talking to the ambulance man in the back, and he was monitoring him, and I didn't understand anything that was going on. I could hear the radio going, I could hear the doctors talking, I could hear them saying about the Casualty entrance. It was all confused in my head. We got to the Casualty entrance, I stood up with Harry in my arms in the blankets, and the doors opened and suddenly the doorway was filled with all these nurses and doctors, and Harry was grabbed out of my arms and he was gone: I didn't even step off the first step out of the ambulance.

I was put in this tiny little room, and nobody explained nothing to me. I was completely on my own because David was at home with the other two, and I remember just sitting there. I couldn't hear him cry, I couldn't hear anything, nobody came and explained anything to me, and I felt as if I was in the same situation as I was back in school. I lost my temper. I tried to get in to see Harry and they wouldn't let me through. But as they pushed the door open I could see my baby just laid there; arms and legs, no movement, no nappy, his eyes were closed. I thought he was dead. This nurse pushed me back out of the way and I said, 'Hold on! That's my baby in there. If he's dead I want to be with him. If he's alive I want to be with him,' and the nurse said I

couldn't because the doctors were doing tests on him and I couldn't be
in there getting in the way. She pushed me back out of the way and I
lost it, just flipped my lid, I punched her and she went flying back
through the door. But to this day I can still see him laying there, this
tiny, tiny little body. He was so small, and he was grey and blue around
his nose, his mouth was blue-black, it was awful. And this other nurse
put her arm around me and walked me out of the room and said,
'Everything will be fine. We will get him sorted out and everything will
be fine.'

They got him sorted out and brought him up to the ward and he
was there for a week. They couldn't get the drip in his arms, his hands
were black and blue. They tried under his arms, they tried everywhere
on him, he was like a pin-cushion. He had beautiful curly hair, it was
blond-white, and in the end they shaved his hair on one side to put the
drip in his head, and it didn't go in, so they shaved the other side, my
beautiful boy, and that's where it ended up being. They had this cap
thing bandaged around the drip; he had an oxygen machine at the top
of his bed to the right-hand side; he was on a mat so if he stopped
breathing they would know; they had this monitor wrapped around
him too, and down at the bottom of the bed there was another
machine. The door had to be kept open all the time for these alarms
to go off so that they could hear. It was an absolute nightmare. I have
never seen anything like it. I cried and cried because I thought that was
it, I thought he was gone, I thought there was no way he was going to
come through. But he did.

The only thing they could put it down to was Sudden Infant
Death Syndrome. I said, 'What's that?' The consultant said, 'It's cot
death.' I was all confused. I said, 'He wasn't in a cot,' and she said, 'I
know. It's just a name we've got for it.' So for two years, as you can
imagine, I never slept. We had Harry in a Moses basket by the bed,
and I used to sit up and watch him all night to make sure he was
breathing. The doctors and health visitors here were absolutely fantastic. They were trying to get a monitor put on him so that I could sleep
at night, so that if he stopped breathing an alarm would go off. I was

talking to the health visitor in the corridor at the health centre one day, and we didn't know there was anybody listening to our conversation, and she said she didn't know where to get this monitor, but she'd try and find out. They were very expensive, she said. That afternoon, I had a phone call, 'Terina, we've got you a monitor, somebody's donated it to you, some lady whose child has had the same problem.' I thought that was fantastic, brilliant.

I was walking through the town one day and a lady stopped me and said, 'How is your son now?' and I said, 'He's fine, thank you. We had somebody donate a monitor,' and she said, 'Yes, that was me, that's why I was asking. I wanted to know if he was OK.' I said, 'Oh, thank you, but how is your baby?' And she said, 'He died.' Oh, God, you couldn't console me. I cried and cried and cried, and this woman said to me, 'Oh, please don't cry,' and I said, 'But your son's died, you've given me your monitor.' I just didn't know what to say to the woman, I felt so gutted for her. To give my son a chance, and I had never met her from Adam. I think that was one of the nicest things that anybody has ever done for me around here because without her we could have lost him.

David's and my marriage went through a lot of problems after that. For the first five years of our marriage, we went through hell and back, we really did. The first five years of marriage are difficult anyway. You can live with somebody for ten years but being married to them is different, whatever people say to the contrary. For the first five years of marriage, you learn so much more about them, and there are things that you didn't know that you thought you knew. But we communicate, which is the most important thing in a marriage. We have been married eight years this year, and for the last three years it's all gone nicely and according to plan. Harry's fighting fit. Nothing ever drags him down.

My mum and dad have been married thirty-six years this year, and they've had their problems, God they have, but they're still together. My dad is a different person these days. He used to be so hard. Two weeks ago, for the first time in I can't remember how many years, he gave me a cuddle. He was all achy, he was moaning because he's lost a lot of weight and he's been ill, and I said to him, 'Give us a cuddle, Dad.' He said, 'What do I want to give you a cuddle for?' I said, 'Because I want one.' That cuddle was for about five minutes. As he's getting older he is taking more to me. As a child he never really took that much to me, I don't know why, perhaps because we were very much alike. Now I could spend all day every day with my dad, we get on really well.

Two years ago I lost three stone in weight and I went down to a size fourteen. We were going to my brother's daughter's christening and my dad said to David, 'Cor, what bird you got on your arm now? I'll tell Terina when I see her.' And I said, 'It *is* me, you silly old sod,' and he said, 'You don't half look good today.' That goes a long way with me. It sticks with me for a long time because my dad never used to say anything nice about me.

One thing that I have to say because I was so proud: he said to my sister, 'I'm really proud of Terina,' and Vivian said, 'Why?' And he said, 'Because she has given me three healthy grandsons.' Vivian said, 'Well, I've given you two grandchildren,' and he said, 'Yes, but you have daughters. Terina's got three boys and they will be good grandsons when they are older. I'm chuffed to pieces.' She got all upset about this, Vivian did. So I said, 'Well, look at it this way, Vivian. That is the one and only time Dad has ever said he's proud of me, isn't it?'

Robert Macdonald

All That

I've been extremely lucky to know where I fitted in in life. My business is a six-generation, father-to-son, family business. I would have felt it would have been a great breach of family trust if I hadn't gone into the firm and I suppose in a sense my life was mapped out from the start, and my life career's been not so desperately different from my father's or my grandfather's. I hope my son would see it in rather the same way. I've very much enjoyed working in a private family business and not having to run a publicly quoted company. I've been a director of publicly quoted companies, and it's very satisfactory in a private company not having the journalists and the fund managers sniping at you about returns the whole time. The strength of a private business is you can take a very long-term view, and you can invest in something which you know there's not the slightest chance of it showing a proper return for ten years, say. You try and keep the dividends reasonably low, so you can plough the cash that's generated back into the business, hopefully grow successful, provide employment, and provide a fascinating job for the next generation.

Of course, things have become much easier over the last five to ten years, because top tax rates on unearned income have gone down to 40 per cent, instead of being 98 per cent. And 'unearned income', as far as I was concerned, was dividends from the firm. This was something that the old Labour government eventually understood well. There was a stage during the Wilson–Healey era when they were absolutely determined to destroy the power of anyone running a private business, whether it was first-, second-, third-, fourth- or fifth-generation, and handing it on to their children, because that was hereditary privilege and therefore a bad thing; and the taxation system was geared to make that quite impossible. And then that began to change, thanks to the work of various people in the private-company sector who pointed out that private companies (if you include the self-employed and farmers), compared with public limited companies, employ over 50 per cent of all the people in this country, discounting the government sector. They also pointed out that in this country the number of small companies being set up and surviving into the next generation was a tiny fraction of what it was in America and elsewhere.

Gradually that point has been appreciated, so that if you don't take the money out of a company it is possible to maintain it. Before, the only way you used to be able to pay inheritance tax was from selling three-quarters of the business to provide the cash. Though the success rate won't be very high, now it is perfectly possible for an entrepreneurial, hard-working individual to build up a successful business in this country. If he's got a little furniture factory or something, he should now be able to hand it on. It's a great strength, I think, continuity. For nearly two hundred years, our business has gone through all sorts of upsets and near disasters, and bankruptcies, and we're going through a difficult period at present. It sounds very pompous, but one tries, in those circumstances, to keep faith with one's forebears and do what's expected of one. I would also like to think we're handing on a business which has a reputation for integrity, because frankly, a lot of business doesn't have great depth of integrity.

We still run the firm much as we always have done. Much of its business is overseas: we employ local people wherever we are and we also have a substantial expatriate management cadre; people from British universities who very often want to work abroad because their parents had been in the Foreign Office or one of the big overseas companies. They work alongside their overseas equivalents and then retire from overseas aged fifty-five. We've never changed the retirement age: it goes back to the old thing a century ago that by the age of fifty-five you were riddled with malaria and gin, so you had to come back to Britain, but it still suits some nowadays. People can build up quite a lot of capital by the time they're fifty-five, and then they're young enough still to get another job on return to this country. At least, that is the theory.

Of course, there are terrible lists which come out, which study our sort of business and say the owners are fantastically rich and all that sort of thing. It isn't quite like that. It's rather like owning a very large estate because I would never, over my dead body, I would never sell any of our firm's shares. Through my life, my ambition has been to pass them down to the next generation, and that means that spare cash goes towards transfer tax and other imposts. I think every generation has always been brought up to believe that the shares are a trust: they provide a job, and an interesting job, but they're not something to sell and then go and live in the South of France. If they were, the parent company would have gone public a long time ago.

So while the *Sunday Times Richest* list, or whatever it's called, is of course a lot of nonsense, it's completely altered my life, unfortunately. My secretary tells me I get over two thousand personal letters a year now, on thicker and thicker writing paper, which I have to deal with, so it takes an hour a day, easily, out of my life. There's one come in this morning which I have to pay attention to. And of course the trouble is, you either say no, and we obviously have a committee that looks at these things, or you say yes, and if you *do* do something there's always a real danger that it's counterproductive because people think, 'Oh God, he's got a million quid or more and all he's given is five thousand pounds. Mean!' So it's unsettling. Letters from students are easiest to handle, because if they are clearly an interesting and deserving case that's the sort of place where five hundred pounds makes a hell of a difference. It's much more difficult when it's a Cabinet Minister or a London hospital.

I consider myself extremely lucky. I had what I suppose is archetypally considered an upper-class upbringing, namely Eton, Brigade of Guards, Oxford; all that. I was lucky to have been brought up during the War in a big house, bigger than this one, with eight children including cousins, and we all ran around freely, and if you wanted to go to the cinema you had to bicycle five miles, so it was a proper country life. On the other hand, my mother, who came from good Quaker stock, would have felt very, very strongly that privilege meant responsibility, a very deep responsibility, duty; and I think I probably feel that quite deeply. My mother believed – and we always used to try and explain to her that it wasn't terribly easy nowadays to follow that principle – that of your income you saved a third, you spent a third, and you gave a third to charity. And we'd say, 'That's absolutely fine, but, Mum, when you're paying rather a lot of tax that's the equivalent nowadays.' And she'd say, 'No, no, you save a third, you spend a third . . .'

I was also brought up by both my parents to believe that if you have privilege you've got obligations. I'm chairman of a national charity, which dispenses around £15 million a year. I think that's worthwhile. I haven't done very much locally. Sally was the president of a local organization. I was a churchwarden for some years but I had too many other distractions to give the role enough attention. Also, I do not have enormously strong religious faith, and much though I respect our local vicar and find church services, particularly evensong, a comfort, I was not sure I should continue, though somebody has to do it in a village like this. If people think I can help in things, then I will try and find time to do so. On the other hand, I hope one is not regarded in an old-fashioned Lord of the Manor way.

Class is a very difficult thing. For my generation, I think the two years' National Service was terrifically formative and very good. It was a great bond across all classes. And of course, contrary to what the outside world thinks, the real toffs, which I don't consider myself to be, are much less class-conscious than an awful lot of other people. I was very amused by that list that they've brought out now, of eight social classes, where Princess Margaret came in the eighth and lowest category because she's an unemployed woman, on her own, and temporarily disabled.

I don't think about it very often, but I think, surely, the class structure in this country has broken down. It's always been extremely open and upwardly mobile, actually, this country, much more so than almost anywhere else. Much more so than somewhere like Australia, for example, contrary to what people think. Australia is really quite snobbish. What has certainly changed here, in terms of employment, are the jobs that people do. There are young men in the village here – gardeners, foresters, grooms, domestic servants – married, with a wife working locally, maybe with two cars and very much leading what my parents would have considered, for want of a better word, a middle-class life, which is excellent and wonderful, and I don't consider that odd. But fifty years ago it would have been odd, for example, that the chap who was digging the vegetable patch was like that. What I'm saying is, I think there are more and more people of that sort.

I'm a little bit atypical, I think, for someone of my background, because during the most impressionable time of my life, which in my case was arguably between the ages of twenty-five and thirty, I was right outside of traditional English class structure because I was working overseas. I think I would be much more class-conscious than I am if I had, directly after leaving university, become a London stockbroker, say; but working with all sorts of different people of different backgrounds and nationalities I hope made me a little bit less conscious of all that. But maybe I'm wrong that class structure has disappeared: maybe everyone is acutely conscious of where they fit and want to fit one rung higher up.

Funnily enough, I had this conversation with a senior politician once, talking about social self and privileged upbringings. Somebody else who was there said to him, 'Well, actually you had a far more privileged upbringing, although your father was working-class, than Winston Churchill did, who had a broken home, who was unstable and would never have known quite where he fitted in; whereas your father became a local councillor, highly respected in his community.' As a small boy, he saw people deferring to his parents. I thought it was quite an interesting point. It's like if you were Arthur Scargill's son, you'd possibly be much more sure of your position than the Duke's younger son, with split parents and no role.

Around here, there are manor houses every couple of miles along the Downs, so although you've got people whose family have lived here for three or four generations or more, who would be regarded, and would see themselves, quite rightly, very much as the old-style squire, there are also quite a lot of people like me, from other areas. There are people I've known at school and university, and in business, who live in largeish houses around here, so we're not completely cut off. I don't know how people regard me locally but I would hope that we're not regarded as people just living in a little world, in an ivory tower of our own, never seeing anyone or not participating, but to some extent I have to admit that's true. I'm not terribly sociable locally. I don't go down to the pub every Saturday and Sunday. But that's because I work in London, travel for several months of the year, and I like to relax when at home.

One of the things which would bring one into a lot of social contact round here, but which I don't participate in, is the life of the horse. I was brought up with horses. My father had been a cavalry instructor when he was in the army at the end of the First War, and he was a beautiful rider, a very skilful rider. When I was young, I was made to ride a Shetland pony, bareback, with a sixpence between each knee and the side of the pony, and my arms stretched out in front of me with two bantam's eggs in my hands so I'd learn not to clutch the reins. If one didn't break the eggs, one was allowed to keep the sixpences. So the horse and hunting was a very central part of life but I didn't enjoy it. I've got nothing against hunting but I don't actually like riding. I shoot a bit, but I don't enjoy it now as much as I did.

I do have an interest in flying aeroplanes. I've got a little grass strip just up the top there. I've always loved flying. I did it in the University Air Squadron originally, and then what was called the Auxiliary Air

Force, weekend flying. I've always loved the beauty of flight, I think it's a wonderful thing. But also, curiously, as a pilot it's very relaxing because you can't think about anything else. You've got to concentrate on what you're doing. You know, I suspect that the whole thing of class is easier to cope with if there is some activity one is deeply involved in. Round here, if you're deeply involved in racing, it's much easier: racing is a surprisingly classless thing. I find racing the most boring business in the world, but it is a good breaker-down of social barriers. But flying is also completely classless. There's absolutely no feeling in the flying world about all that social stuff. In the flying world what matters is whether you can fly the aeroplane or not.

Terry Fraser

The Destroyer's Legacy

Sometimes I think it's been the worst move I've made, to come back to this country. Since I came back here I've had six jobs, mostly in sales and public relations, and every company I've worked with has gone bust. They close, or the receivers walk in on them. And maybe I've been unlucky; unemployment is not so noticeable down in this area. But in the Midlands, and up to the north, and Scotland, you had areas which centred around the shipyards, mining, steelworks, whole towns were built on them, and all the other businesses fed off them. Take the main core away, and they all collapsed.

Under Maggie Thatcher, it was one of the worst times this country has gone through. She did away with a lot of manufacturing industry, construction industry, and I'm not talking about house building, I'm talking about factory building, office building. Massive debts all over the show. The coal mines went, the shipyards went, and there was nothing to replace them. The Tories just cleared those industries, but that was people's livelihoods. You can't demolish whole areas and then expect people to survive, because you've destroyed everything. And the Tories reckoned industry was costing us too much, but it costs us a lot more in paying unemployment and redundancies. It costs us billions more.

What do you do with all those hundreds of thousands of people that were depending on those industries? The Tories didn't care at all. Not only did they not care, but they went about things the way that Hitler went about clearing up the Jews, Poles and various other nationals: anybody that wasn't his ideal, he wiped them out, and the Tories did that to people in their way. It was a scorched-earth policy, and that's what Margaret Thatcher was using.

Margaret Thatcher brought in an element of greed: me first and you last. She destroyed the National Health Service, she destroyed education, she destroyed the idea of caring for other people. She knew about saving money and making a profit: she didn't know anything about caring. Closing the mental institutions, and putting those people out into the care of society, it's failed miserably. Many of those people have ended up in prisons and they shouldn't have. It's things like that that Thatcher did. I really thought she was evil. I called her 'Hitler'. And Tebbit was her bloody Himmler. They were Fascists, there's no two ways about it. I don't care what anybody says: nobody can convince me any different. Self, self, self, that's what she was, and that's why I cannot understand why some people still think she was good. A lot of Tories don't now, but it's taken them a long time, and a lot of people's lives have been destroyed. The Tories crushed people, and some people couldn't get up again. She destroyed the fabric of this country.

Now there's a whole generation, two generations, and some of them have never worked, never had the chance. There's been no training for them. When I left school, you picked out the type of career you wanted, in my case engineering, and you went for training or you got apprenticeships; then suddenly, these were no longer available because companies didn't do training any more, because they'd all been cut to the bone. So the Government put these schemes together which were meant to keep people out of the dole queue: I ran one for four years when I got back from South Africa and I couldn't get an engineering job. And some of these people never really got back to feeling that they were worth something.

Since I came back to this country, I've been made redundant ... do you know, I've lost count. Five times? First, I ran that Government Community Programme I mentioned: it was set up to make the unemployment figures look better, not to really help people, though I tried to. Then I worked for myself, had my own building company going, had people working for me when I needed them. And then I had to give it up, I had a disablement which was affecting me. I've got spondylitis. It's after years of being a construction engineer, there's years' worth of damage in the arm: I've been trapped underground a few times in mines, in floods, and in a flood you're thrown about. I was trapped in rock falls. I've had various injuries over the years; you get them. So this arm is in pain most of the time, and the neck gets it too. And when you apply for jobs and put down on your medical form that you've got spondylitis, companies don't want to know you.

The first time redundancy happened to me I went straight into another company. That lasted about two months. Then I went to another one and I was out after three weeks, it was closed down. The next one lasted six months. I was getting a bit bothered then. I thought, Blimey, am I a Jonah or something? What's happening? When I was working in South Africa, I was in development engineering for the brewery Bass Charringtons, and sometimes I was in charge of three hundred people. After that, I was doing temporary work here and there. That was 1984 and that was a bad time. Maggie was in full swing, and if you were unemployed she was always cutting down on the unemployment money. If the wife worked, as mine did, it was cut even more.

I did anything. I was doing sales, painting, driving jobs, anything to get some money coming in. The recession hit me badly, very badly. I owned a house in England years ago but I sold that in the seventies, and when I came back in 1981 property prices were crazy, and I'd no funds left after my building company ended. And I suppose, as you get a bit older, you don't pick up quite the same.

After a while, I thought, This is no bloody use. So I started again on my own, commission-only sales in the building trade. I organize jobs for people, builders and customers, and that's how I've carried on ever since, though I'm not supposed to be working at the moment, because of this spondylitis. Sometimes I'm in real agony with it. It affects the back as well as the arm, and I keep a stick in the car, in case I need a stick. I fitted a kitchen cupboard for an old lady the other day and I can hardly move now.

When I'm at home, if I'm not working I always like to do something with my time, whatever it is. I'll always find something else to do. You've got to give back in society: you've got to give, that's what it's all about. That's why I joined the town council. I've done ten years on Wantage Town Council, I've been a district councillor for the last eight, and town mayor for nearly two. I've always been interested in politics and I wanted to try and change the place for the better.

I always get involved with where I am. When I was in South Africa I was involved with the Scouts: I was a Group Scoutmaster and Acting District Commissioner. I ran the Pipe Band for the high school. I was a Reserve in the South African Police Force. That was good, it was not like the picture you get painted at all. Whites were quite happy to work alongside the blacks equally, and vice versa, and there's been much more amalgamation over the years since. I've got black and white friends. It didn't bother me. When people say to me, 'South African police are hard, they treat the blacks terrible,' I always say to them, 'You've got to remember that fifty per cent of the police force is black,' and the important thing was there were black officers as well. My boss was black, and I'm not talking about since Mandela took over, I'm talking about the seventies. He was in charge and we saluted him, and he was 'sir' to us. Yeah, apartheid is wrong, but there were parts of South Africa that were freer then than you'd think from the Press over here.

So me being on the council here, and being the mayor, I suppose you could say it's similar: it's me getting involved. I'm nearly at the end of my second mayoral year now. It ends in May. That's election time again and I will relinquish the seat of power, so to speak, and breathe a sigh of relief. It's heavy going, you know. It depends what you put into it, and how you do the job, but as mayor you are legally responsible for the council: if the council end up in court, you are the one that stands in the dock. You're the first port of call for complaints, but sometimes for a pat on the back as well, from the public at large. You act as PR for the town. You have a duty to bring together various town organizations and see they're all treated as fairly as possible. And some organizations that have never been recognized are recognized now, and that has been the biggest personal achievement I feel as mayor.

Then there are mayoral events, like the Town Mayor's Carol Concert, and the Town Mayor's Ball, but we have strange rules. Any losses made on those events, the mayor has to pay for them, not the council. Now, to me, that's wrong. I get an allowance, it was £1,500 this year, but that's to pay for my petrol, or phone calls, stationery, whatever, that I do from home. It has to cover other things too. When I go to open fêtes and go round all the stalls, there's raffles, all sorts, and you can't walk past and do nothing. I also go to lots of AGMs. I go to the Red Cross, Children in Need, NSPCC, because they ask the mayor to come. If you don't go their funds are reduced, because when they send out their letters to various companies, if the companies see a dignitary has not turned up to an AGM, they don't support them financially. They say, 'If the mayor is not interested in it, why should we be?' So I always try to turn up to as many as I can to help them.

I took the mayorship on at a difficult time for me personally, and I took it on to make sure I could still do something. I said to myself, 'Yes, I'll go for it.' Now I want to clear the decks and get myself sorted. I'm always here for others at the moment, you know? Now I need money for myself, I need money coming in. I need a job that I can do. I know I've got this thing here with my arm but there's plenty of jobs I can do. I've looked after the town, I've got to look after myself now. I've put everything into being mayor. It's replaced a lot of what I was doing when I had a job.

If you're the mayor, people don't realize what your life is like. To be redundant, and to be short of cash, which is what I am now, is difficult. But people see me walking around town and most of them won't believe I need a job. I've seen jobs advertised, and they say, 'You don't want that. Give over!' They think I'm joking. I say, 'No, I'd like it,' and they won't take me serious. People have the impression that if you're a mayor you're doing OK. They say to me, 'You look like a mayor. The last one didn't. But you look like a mayor when you're walking around. You look like somebody.' Well, I might look like somebody.

John Tighe

Nasty Possibilities

I came back here from London because I knew I had to get out of banking. I was bored out of my mind. It was the work, it was just terribly mundane. And obviously I was in the privileged position of being on a post-graduate management programme, but it just wasn't for me. I'd sit there at work wishing I was back at my desk reading things and studying. The prospect of thirty or forty years at something like working in a bank: appalling! I could feel my brain atrophying.

I started working at the sports centre in Wantage three days after I left the bank in London, and I spent a few months just working at the centre and saving some money up. That's when I made my decision to go for the writing, because I knew it was something I'd got to do. Writing's something I think I've always had an aptitude for, but it's not something I used to see as a career. To be honest, I was never really quite sure what I wanted to do, apart from join the air force, but when I applied, although I got right to the end of the selection process I didn't get in.

The novel's in the fairly early stages at the moment. I'm coming towards the end of my initial research. When I started writing it, I didn't know what sort of time frame I was going to be looking at, not having done it before. The closest I got was writing my Master's thesis up in Cambridge, which was twenty-five thousand words, but that's academic work, and that's slightly different. So I started with some themes which I thought I'd like to deal with. The things that interest me are connected with modern-day Europe and political integration, or otherwise, and the impact that the European Union is having on politics and life in this country.

I'm a Conservative. I wasn't too happy with the last Conservative government, as a lot of people weren't, but most of my views would fit in with Conservative Party views. I think Conservatism has taken a bit of a rap over the last few years because it's become associated very much with Thatcherism, which is not quite the same thing. I think people now see Conservatism as Thatcherism, they think the two are the one and the same, and if you call yourself Conservative people think you're going to be running around shutting everything down, and worrying about accountancy, and that doesn't necessarily fit with more traditional Conservatism. Conservatism is about preserving communities, but if you run everything on the basis of what's efficient, that's not necessarily what's best for the country or for the communities that are involved. That's where Thatcherism departed from a more traditional Conservatism. But because of what went on during the eighties and the early nineties, people think if you're a Conservative you're a heartless chap.

I would say that Conservatism comes down to individual responsibility and a degree of self-reliance. What upsets me is people blaming others, or the state, for things not going right for them. OK, I'm not saying there aren't people in unfortunate circumstances, but I don't like the nanny state as a whole. I think there's too much governmental interference as to what goes on in people's lives. And obviously, now there's European intervention, and that's what my novel's about. I don't think we're about to plunge into a third world war, but I think we're heading for a lot of tension, a lot of disaffected electorates who feel it doesn't matter who they vote for, whether they're in France, Germany or here, and who feel that everything is being run from abroad. Personally, I think that's going to lead to a lot of civil strife, possibly to civil wars.

I'm implacably opposed to Federalism, quite vehemently so, for a number of reasons. First of all, I think the whole system as it exists is profoundly undemocratic. I recognize that democracy is not a perfect system, but the notion that towards three hundred and fifty million people from, at the moment, fifteen different nations, or states, can all live under an almost identical framework, I think is a nonsense. Obviously, my primary concern is this country, but it can be the same for other countries as well. The legislation coming out of Brussels just can't represent that diversity of people. It also emasculates national parliaments because if legislation that goes through Parliament conflicts with any European legislation, sooner or later it will get struck off the statute books, because the European Court of Justice has made it quite plain that it's there to harmonize legislation throughout the Community. Then we will end up with a situation where it doesn't matter who we elect because there'll be very little that they can actually do. I think, to a lot of people, that's not manifest at the moment, but as time goes on it will become more and more obvious.

There is so much all-encompassing interference from Brussels in just about every facet of what goes on in our lives, from fishing to agriculture to labour relations, justice, home affairs. There are moves to co-ordinate an EU foreign policy, and even a defence policy, and these sorts of EU policies have been likened to a ratchet effect, which is, you can go forwards with a process but the EU will never let you go backwards. Once you've devolved something to the EU, once you've given something away, it's gone, that's it. It just marches on, involving more and more areas of life, and yet federal states have a habit of breaking up after a while. There are so many examples of federalism going wrong: Yugoslavia, the Soviet Union; Canada's got a lot of tension.

What got me writing my novel is that I was struck by the fact that there is a lot of literature dealing with different aspects of the European situation, both for and against, but there are a tremendous number of misconceptions about Europe, partly because of the pro-European propaganda that's being generated by the Commission. There's millions of pounds going into the propaganda, and it's being disseminated through schools and various projects where they have to display a European flag otherwise they don't get funding, that sort of thing. And there are lies, damn lies and statistics, and people come out with all sorts of reasons why we couldn't possibly survive outside the European Union. The favourite seems to be the trade figures, you know, that half our trade is with Europe and we'd all lose our jobs. Of course it's rhetoric, but it's also absolute nonsense!

First of all, if we changed our relationship with Europe we wouldn't stop trading with one another. They want our products, and vice versa, and they're not going to stop trading with us out of malice. Going beyond that, eighty per cent of the trade that goes on in this country is within the UK economy. Only twenty per cent of it is import/export, and about fifty per cent of that goes to the European Union. So that leaves you with ninety per cent which is either domestic or elsewhere in the world. That's an example of propaganda. People are told all sorts of scare stories about what will happen if we don't immerse ourselves in Europe, and when they've got the Prime Minister or the Chancellor feeding this stuff, you can forgive them for being confused. So I thought, well, these books that warn of what's going on, they tend to preach to the converted. I thought if I can come up with a novel, a thriller, which is the sort of book which is going to have a much wider readership, then perhaps I can bring some of these issues to the attention of a wider audience.

So for the last three months I've been part-time at the sports centre, and when I've not been there, I've been downstairs, writing. I spent some time up in the library at Cambridge, researching things that have been going on in Germany and Eastern Europe and the former Soviet Union, trying to look for events and potential catalysts that would allow me to build a thriller round them. And my starting point is a post-monetary union situation, so it would be set ahead a few years, early twenty-first century, that sort of time, where countries don't have control over the interest rates and the exchange rates, and fiscal transfers are limited; where you've got language and cultural problems, i.e. where people can't move freely from one country to the next in the way you could if you were a US citizen, with a largely homogeneous culture and a common language and so on.

This is my starting point: a situation of civil unrest. Because if you combine economic problems with a democratic deficit, then you've got a recipe for extremist parties becoming more and more successful. I mean, already in Germany there are nearly five million unemployed people, which is approaching the levels of the early 1930s, with the rise of Hitler. France, I think something like eleven or twelve per cent of the workforce is unemployed. Spain, it's about twenty per cent at the moment; and this is because they've been working to meet the criteria to go into European economic and monetary union, you know, cutting back on public spending, having artificial exchange rates.

I'm looking at the possible after-effects of all this. I'm looking at a possible resurgence in nationalism. I'm looking at a situation where you could end up with a pact for the twenty-first century, like the Soviet–German Molotov–Ribbentrop pact, and that might seem quite a long way from the European Union but some kind of tacit division of Eastern Europe is what I believe to be a possible outcome of it. I've been looking at various authors, and how they've dealt with thriller writing and international politics. I enjoy Tom Clancy. He deals with international politics as well as the military side. Frederick Forsyth is another good one. So hopefully what I'll have at the end of it is a novel which will stand as a thriller in its own right, which is not too far-fetched, which will be constructed in a way which makes it plausible. It just happens that since I started my research, Russia has collapsed, so there's all sorts of nasty possibilities. I think I'm going to end up writing something which is not beyond the realms of possibility.

Andrea Belcher

Curl Up and Dye

I didn't want it to be like the normal salons, I wanted it to feel like home. I wanted everybody to come in and to feel at ease, so if they're running behind, they don't feel all het up. Apparently, or so I've been told by numerous customers, my salon's like the film *Steel Magnolias*. I've only ever seen it the once but there's Dolly Parton and Julia Roberts in this back room having coffee the whole time and this is what my salon's meant to be like, ever so relaxed. I've got proper coffee, and a big toy box out the back so the children can play with the toys while their mums are having their hair cut. But I do get very cross with my members of staff if it's not a professional image portrayed either. I want it to be a relaxed atmosphere, you know, if a customer wants to have a portion of chips in here, they can do whatever they want as long as they're happy. But I will not have my members of staff being disrespectful to customers and joining in, eating a portion of chips with them. Even though it's a relaxed atmosphere for the customers, I still want customers to have respect when they come through that door.

Because I'm so relaxed in here, it's very hard to get the right balance from the staff. My sister's superb. If there is such a thing as people being indispensable, then she is close to the mark. She came to work for me purely as my nanny and my receptionist-cum-everything else, because I was pregnant with Connor when we opened. She's now decided she loves hairdressing. She's twenty-four and I've just entered her for the National Trainee Award because she is good. The customers get ever so upset when I shampoo them now. 'Do you have to do it? Can't your sister do it?' She's brilliant. Some staff, they've not been what I've wanted, or they've totally got the wrong impression of how I am as a person. I mean, I had one member of staff, she smoked the whole time in here and I said, 'This is a non-smoking salon. I think you're taking the mickey slightly.' Or she'd come in the salon and eat her sandwiches. And I'm like, 'No, no, no, no, that's what the staffroom's for. You do not eat in the salon.' One, for health and safety reasons; two, it's not very hygienic; and three, it's not a bloody cafeteria where you can sit down at any point and have your packed lunch. But she made that mistake because I'm so relaxed.

One thing I have learnt, you cannot be a boss and a friend, I'm afraid. When I first opened, I tried to be everybody's friend and it just backfired all the time. I had people turn up fifteen, twenty minutes late, with no apology. So I won't go out socializing with any member of staff. I do with my sister, but not much, because it's very difficult to detach yourself from family business and work business. But I'd run a couple of salons before I opened Curl Up And Dye, and had people underneath me, so I more or less knew how you treat people in respect of getting the best of work done without stepping on their toes. And I've been self-employed for nine years, so I knew how the Inland Revenue worked, though it's a totally different ball game when you've got employees. I'm working a lot of hours, and it's as hard as I expected it to be, but that's the emotional strain you've got at the back of your head the whole time: you've got to keep an eye on the stock coming in; you've got to keep an eye on the money; and also, you have to answer for everything. So when things go wrong, which I don't believe in, but when they do, everybody expects you to be perfect. I think that's what I found really hard.

Luckily, the bank gave me a small business loan. Most of the other things, like decor-wise, was stuff that came out of our own pockets. My partner, Glen, his dad got a lot of things on trade. But you're probably talking about £10,000 all in all to set it up, so a lot of money went into it that we haven't actually had the chance to get back yet, because it's still the first year of trading. I don't know what the accounts are doing, because my accountant's still got the books, but I don't think it's made much of a profit. It's probably broke even.

I'd be lying if I said it was a bed of roses, because it flaming hasn't! Glen and I have found it hard, in the respect that I was earning good money before and then I went to nothing. Not only did we plough all our money into the shop, but I didn't actually have a wage up until three months ago, and my wages before were anything from £300 to £500 a week, depending on how many days and how many hours I worked. Going from that to nothing has been a real struggle. Now my wage is only £100 a week, so it's still a big difference, but I'm hoping, in five years' time, that I'll be able to sit back and put it all down as good experience and go on to my next venture. The house isn't tied up in the salon, so that's good. I know most businesses tie up their properties but I didn't want to do that.

Because Glen's self-employed, and he's a builder, it's made it a lot harder. I'm sure if he worked full-time as an employed person it would be a different kettle of fish altogether, because you'd get holiday and sick pay, but this year the building trade's been awful and it's been constant fights at home because there's been no money. It's hard when you're both self-employed: it's best when somebody has somebody else to fall back on. Mind you, I've always said that the morning I wake up and say, 'I've had enough,' that's the day I get out of hairdressing, because if you haven't got your heart in hairdressing you're not going to give the best performances on your cuts. And I love hairdressing, I really do. My interest in it came, really, from my auntie. She always did our hair as children, and whenever I was asked what I wanted to be when I grew up, it was always a hairdresser. I was just fascinated by it. Mum said the first cut I ever did was on my sister's hair when I was seven. I cut her fringe right to the hairline.

Cutting is still my favourite part of the job. I love cutting, and I love barbering; I do like my men's work. I'm not so keen on perms because each perm looks the same as the next perm really, it can either be loose or tight, or it can be big curls or little small curls. But colouring is a different ball game altogether. Colouring can look so dramatic, and it can look so natural, or so bright. And because I've now had thirteen years of hairdressing, I can look at a picture in a magazine and analyse it to a customer's head. I won't give anything to anyone if I think it's going to not suit them, or they haven't got the hair type, or basically it's just going to look awful. And I'm very hot on consultations if you're not a hundred per cent sure. Don't start and then halfway through think, Christ, what the hell am I doing? That's one thing I also stipulate with the staff members. You must be a hundred per cent sure what that customer wants before you even attempt to wash their hair, because I've seen so many stand-up rows between customers and stylists when the customers have not got what they wanted. And as far as I'm concerned, they're paying for something, so they should be getting the best deal and the best service, regardless of how cheap or how expensive a product is.

When I trained in hairdressing, it was bloody hard to get qualified, and then for six, seven, eight years, you could be anybody, it didn't matter. But now it's done a U-turn again and it does matter. Salons now require exams to an advanced hairdressing level and you have to have over two years' experience, although it all depends on the individual how quickly they learn. It depends how committed they are, and how quick they pick up things; you know, the simplest of things, like holding scissors and a comb in your hand at the same time. The actual technique of hairdressing is getting better and better. The technical work side is more into colours now, more the natural colour base, more lowlights than highlights. Structure-wise, it's a lot of cutting. Before, it didn't matter how rubbish the cut was as long as the blow-dry looked good at the end of it, whereas now the cutting has to be a hundred per cent precise and the blow-dries aren't important.

I've worked in loads of different salons: Reflections, Rowleys, Toppers, Visions and Guys. They all had a different type of customer, so when I came here I left the range of customers I wanted to attract open. I do only one regular shampoo-and-set now, and that's not because I don't want to do any shampoo-and-sets but most of my customers are young generation, lots of mums with children, from my age to about fifty, and they don't go for shampoo-and-sets, they want cuts and styling. I do a lot of gents as well — last night, I did four — and my sister does a lot more teenagers than me. I think they can relate to her because they think that she's a lot younger than me, even though she's only four years younger. But because she's not married, with no children, it's a different kettle of fish. As soon as you say to a teenager 'married with children', it's like, 'You're obviously a frump, then.'

When you become a salon owner you step into a different world. To me, I'm just Andrea that works in a hairdressers, but I do get treated differently, which is so wrong; like when I go to my daughter Jamie-Louise's nursery. She's been to a private nursery since she was six months old, and it's a different ball game now, I have different people speaking to me now because I'm a salon owner. I think it's so wrong I just disregard them. I'll give them the time of day, purely because I would like them to be a customer in my salon, but that's it. It's so wrong that before they wouldn't speak to me because I was only a hairdresser and not good enough for them. Money talks and it shouldn't.

A lot of people wouldn't speak to me because I was divorced as well. Quite a few people threw stones because I got divorced from Jamie-Louise's father when she was just two. It's not so important to them now; as far as they're concerned, they class Glen as my husband, and I have another child with him, and it's wiped out the fact that I was divorced. But for eighteen months a lot of them didn't speak to me. Quite a few of my girlfriends found I was a threat to them and their partner, which I just found unbelievable, to be honest; friends that I'd been friends with for donkeys' years, and all of a sudden the phone calls got less and less. Now I see one or two of them just occasionally. You find out who your friends really are when you get divorced.

Now my trouble is, everybody assumes you must be married if

you're a couple. Like, a prime example, we went away this weekend and Glen was called Mr Belcher, which I found quite funny but Glen obviously didn't because that's my ex-husband's surname. Or I was called Mrs Puffitt, which is Glen's name, because they assumed I was his wife. And as soon as they discover you're not married, it's like, 'Oh right, OK,' and they don't know what to say to you, they get very embarrassed, whereas I don't really care, to be honest. It's just a common factor of life now, living together. Yeah, divorces are made too easy nowadays but there's also a lot more harder work to a marriage now than what there used to be, because nowadays women have to work, unless the husband is on a massive amount of money, which isn't the case usually.

I was married to Michael at twenty-two and I had Jamie-Louise when I was twenty-three, so I was ever so young. I was with Michael since I was seventeen, so I was with him a long time, and getting divorced was very painful, I didn't cope with it very well. I shut myself off from everybody. I detached myself from my family and my friends, from everything, because people don't know what to say to you. And so many people say they know how you feel when they don't know how you feel, so it was easier to detach myself from them all. There's still ever so much of a stigma about divorce. My mum's family, which are a big unit locally, couldn't cope and still don't cope, and it's been three years down the line and they still don't speak to me like they used to. The arms don't go open now. Rather than people greeting me with hugs and kisses it's just, 'How are you?' and that's it, which is very hard and very upsetting but you do learn to cope with it. That's the main reason why I could live away from here now, because of getting divorced and being isolated from my friends and family: it makes you realize that people aren't as important as you thought they were.

You become a different person at the end of a divorce. Sitting with a total stranger, going through every dirty piece of underwear, with solicitors: you're fighting over the same thing, mud-raking the whole time, it's just awful. I felt that I was a nobody afterwards. I felt that I didn't own the name Belcher any more, but I couldn't go back to being Andrea Alexander because I had left that behind as well. So for a while I felt, Who am I? As for getting married again, I was adamant that I'd never get married again. One day, perhaps, I will. Marriages are meant to be for life and they're not. But then life isn't for life; you have to live for each day rather than plan too far ahead. That's another thing that you find when you get divorced, that you can't plan to the end of the year; you plan to the end of the month, maximum. And you never rely on anybody, you become very independent, because you've been let down and you refuse to be let down any more.

I had the opportunity, five years ago, to open up a salon, before I had my daughter. And hairdressing-wise, I was as capable then as I'm capable now of opening up a salon. But emotionally, there was something missing in my life. I hadn't had enough experience. Two years after being divorced, this came up, I was ready to take it. I think the emotional strain of the divorce and being able to detach myself, like I was saying, being the boss and being Andrea, playing different roles, meant that I was capable of doing it professionally. Getting divorced gave me the experience of playing different roles in order to cope, because as far as I'm concerned, I'm quite a few different Andreas. I'm the Andrea my dad needs, as a daughter to care for him, because he's ill. I'm the Andrea to Glen. I'm Mummy to Jamie and Connor. I'm Andrea to my employees up here, I'm Andrea to my customers that have known me for years. I'm loads of different people. So there's lots of positive things have come out of my divorce.

The only negative thing that still hurts, even now, are the lies that Michael done. That still hurts. And the fact that I'll always have to share my daughter. I was asked, the other day, would I let her go to live with her dad, if she persisted? Well, I'd have to, because I'd lose her otherwise. But having to share a child the whole time is horrible. It still hurts, every other weekend when she stays with her dad on a Saturday night, allowing another woman to look after my daughter. It's only for twenty-four hours but allowing somebody else to look after my daughter who hasn't got a clue who she is, that still hurts, and that's three years down the line. Michael's partner's a nice person and I get on quite well with her now, but that's for the sake of Jamie-Louise, not for the sake of anyone else. As soon as they get in the car after a weekend, I'm almost spitting and cursing to Glen as they leave. And it's hard answering questions to Jamie-Louise the whole time. Like we went away this weekend and she made me feel a right floozy, because she kept saying to everybody about Glen, 'That's my mum's boyfriend.' In fact, at one point she said, 'That's my mummy's lover and that's my mummy's lover's child.' Thanks, Jamie-Louise! Thank you very much. I said, 'I think you forgot to tell them that Glen is your step-dad, and he and I are actually living together, and we've got a salon together.' Glen's my best friend and he looks after me and gives me advice, and that's how I always thought marriage should be.

I think one reason why my marriage failed is because of what happened to my dad. My dad is another area of my life that's always been a struggle because for the last nine years I've basically looked after him. He had an industrial accident nine years ago and he didn't get proper compensation, and I gave up work to help look after him. He fell down the inside of one of the cooling towers at Didcot Power Station. That's when I became self-employed, so I could be flexible to take him in and out of hospital. But he had a stroke two and a half years ago, and he's only fifty-nine, and he's been poorly ever since and permanently in hospital in Oxford.

My dad was always the one who had the answers whereas my mum's not a worldly woman at all, bless her. Mum can't drive, and Mum's got four children, but it was relied on me to take them backwards and forwards to hospital every day, to visit Dad. I suppose I'm the one who always said, 'Oh, I'll do it, it's not a problem.' I think my marriage suffered because when the phone rang I always ran to my mum and dad's aid, and that's another area where I've now become a different person because my parents aren't number one priorities now. My children are number one priorities, and Glen is. But I've had to detach myself again and it has been hard. Now I refuse to do all the driving and I can go in and see my dad because I want to, not because

Mary Loudon

I'm feeling I have to take somebody in to see him. I'm still going in every night but it's different. It's been a big change for me. It was very hard for me to open this salon and detach myself from my mum and my dad but I had to do it. I had to say, 'Right, this is where my life begins again.'

Peter Stevenson

Millstones and Dog Beds

I had the opportunity to go to New York, in the army, doing cipher work, and I came to the conclusion that that would drive me mad. Nothing else appealed to me, so I came back here and started growing things. I had a £500 loan from my family that I was told I should do what I liked with, as long as I paid it back. I put it into a greenhouse, and for two or three years I had no money whatsoever coming in, except the odd half-crown from my grandfather when he came over to visit. That was very useful, went a long way; almost a couple of gallons for the motorbike.

One weekend, we had a lot of gladioli left over and Mr Honeychurch who worked here suggested we put a stall down town and see if we couldn't sell them. So we took a stall down the town on the Saturday morning, my brother John used the car to run up and down three or four times, and we sold £4-worth of flowers in the morning, for a one and sixpence toll on the stall. We decided that that was quite a feasible way of getting rid of the produce from up here, and after eighteen months or so we started doing Witney market, then Abingdon market, and in the end we were doing thirteen markets a week.

When we first started off we were growing carnations, geraniums, fuchsias, tomatoes and cucumbers, and other flowers by the season. Tomatoes and cucumbers we haven't grown now for probably twenty-five years. It's cheaper to buy them than it is to grow them. I don't think there is a tomato industry left in this country now, it's nearly all imported. Then, when people began to want more variety, and to make up the quantity, we started buying flowers from Covent Garden, then we started dealing with Holland in 1960, for bulbs. Now we're using the Dutch and Danish markets nearly as much as we used to use Covent Garden. The world has got that much bigger, or smaller, whichever it is. In the past you had your carnations, chrysanths, daffodils, tulips, freesias and anemones, and they were all grown over here. Lots of flowers are imported now. They're Israeli, South African, Colombian. They fly them in on temperature-controlled planes to London from Africa almost as quick as it takes for me to drive up to Covent Garden and back.

Everything is much more mechanized now. Even on the growing side, everything is done on a production-line basis rather than the old-fashioned way where you'd take your cuttings and wait for a couple of months for them to root, and then pot them and grow them. Now you stick your cuttings in pots and sell them six weeks later because the temperature control is much better. The days are gone when you used to have to get your coke in from the local gasworks, and then go down to the boilerhouse on a cold night and find that because it's been raining hard it's all flooded, and the fire's out, so you'd have to pump the water out and start again. Most of our plants are grown with gas overhead heating now whereas before we were buying anthracite by the lorry-load.

Everybody's favourite flower was the carnation at one time, that or freesias. Then the spray carnations came in and became popular, and flower-arranging ideas changed. You went through the more eccentric type of flower arranging then, with a log and just two odd flowers, though that never actually came down to these parts. It was the big towns that wanted modern arranging, it never really caught on in the country areas. People like to think it has but the flowers that sell best are still the standard mixed bouquets. If you send some of the modern arrangements out, people come back to you and say, 'Well, it's very nice, but where's the flowers?'

The flowers themselves change with the times. Roses have changed completely in their style. They used to be a summer flower. Now they're all year round and you get roses on three-foot stems, whereas in the old days you were lucky if you got much more than nine inches. Spray roses came in, spray roses went back out. People want the bigger, single blooms again and they like a fairly big firm head on the top. One customer at our Newbury market, every week she used to have a bunch of garnet roses, and if there was a week went by when I couldn't get the garnet roses there was tears on the stall over it. That was every Saturday morning for seventeen, eighteen years. People get very set in their ways with flowers. There's other people that have come in every Christmas and want yellow roses; they've probably had them for the last twenty years, because they had yellow roses on their wedding day and they've had them for every special occasion since. A lot of the older people still want the same flowers as when they got married, and it gets increasingly difficult to get some of the varieties.

We hardly sell trees any more. Five years ago we were selling a lot more trees than we are now. Everyone's gone into bushes and shrubs and smaller things because everybody has much smaller gardens. The people with bigger gardens have had them longer, and they've got more mature trees which they're not having to replace so often. When we had the big winds five years ago, and the big trees went, yes, there was a lot of sales then to replace them, but most people don't want trees. If they do, it's always the same one: flowering cherry. Flowering cherries are the most popular small tree by far. Apple trees are very steady but nothing like what they used to be. This week we actually had somebody plant an orchard up, round their house, with thirty trees in. I can't remember the last time somebody came in and wanted thirty trees to plant an orchard up: it must be ten years ago. These days, it's an apple tree, a plum tree or a flowering cherry, and that's all they can get room for.

It's not a big site for the amount that we do. It was one acre when we started and there was just Mother and myself. Now there are about thirty-nine staff, which is less than we had, we did get up to nearly sixty four years ago. There's twenty-odd employed at our other garden centre at Heathrow and we were up to thirty-three here when we were doing a bit more growing, but as we've started to buy in more plants we've cut the staff down.

My sons have come into the business as they've left school, or they've gone to work other places and then come back here. My eldest son, Richard, has worked for me all except for one week of his life, and I think he's thoroughly enjoyed it. Philip went away to university, went to work as a chartered accountant down at Bristol, and then decided he wanted to come back and work in the business. Ian's at our shop in Heathrow.

Philip has bought the house next door at the bottom of the garden, which I bought just to stop anyone else that's going to give me problems going in next to us. Richard lives at the back next to Granny, in my Auntie Queen's old house. I now live along the bridle path, and I've got the ground opposite it, where we have the tunnels that we use as a nursery. We've got six and a half acres altogether and it's just about enough for what we want. We don't use it all at the moment, some of it's down to pasture. Richard hasn't got such a big garden as what Auntie Queen had, because we took a little bit of that off for growing. Then we bought Joe Jordan's bungalow, which we enlarged the car park with. And then we bought number seventeen, which Philip's now living in. Then we bought Staple Cottage about three years ago and that finally cleared all the other people out from next to us, and we kept the garden of that.

The backbone of the business has always been cut flowers and the make-up work – wreaths and bouquets – but the make-up side seems to be changing a lot. I mean, where you used to have a funeral with, perhaps, seventy wreaths, at anything from £2 to £5, now a funeral that would have had seventy probably only has five or six wreaths, and they're much more expensive. That old thing of everybody, neighbours, friends sending flowers has gone. Now it's family only. It's like it's not such a community thing any more, a funeral.

Lilies are no longer a popular flower for funerals: people have roses now. You'll find that they will very often stipulate no lilies for funerals. They'd rather have them for weddings. Carnations are popular for funerals, and freesias: that's because it tends to be the flowers that the people theirselves would have liked, and it's the older generation that's dying out. In the old days there wasn't so much choice. Your spring funerals then were daffodils: now you don't hardly use a daffodil, they don't last long enough. Nowadays people want something that's going to last ten days on the grave.

This week, we sent about fifteen funeral wreaths out on Monday, twenty out on Tuesday, we sent three out today, we're sending five out tomorrow, and another seven or eight are being picked up on Friday. That's about fifty a week and that's about average. They cost anything from £10 to £150, if you're having a large coffin spray. The family often wants just one wreath, but if people send their own they tend to spend around £50 apiece.

And then there's all the other bouquets and arrangements. I suppose we send out about ten of those a day, seven days a week, so that's a total of a hundred and twenty arrangements of some sort each week, and then there'll be extra ones that people collect from here. And weddings. We do for weddings all the time. We used to cope with about five or six weddings on a really busy weekend but now we don't like doing more than three, particularly if they want us to do table arrangements and churches, because there's only five people doing the arrangements, and it's a great pressure, especially when you've got all your normal customers coming in as well.

There's also the special occasions, like anniversaries and new babies and retirements. There's the big days throughout the year: Valentine's Day is going up, Mothering Sunday is levelling out, Father's Day has never taken off; you might get ten or twelve bunches asked for, no more. For Valentine's, most people just come in and pick up a rose, but we usually have three people delivering on Valentine's Day, and it's almost always a dozen red roses. The people who will spend £40 or £50 on a dozen red roses, you just can't believe! And it's not always the people that you think have got the money to spend that do it.

Fashions change and you've got to move with the times to be able to afford to carry on, and what a lot of people might call marketing is a gut feeling. You get asked for something, and if you get asked twice for it, then there must be somebody looking for it. So you get it in, and if it doesn't go, drop it. Mind you, some of the stonework out there has been around for seven or eight years; things like the old millstones. We bought two of those. The first one we earnt about £300 on selling it. The next one sat here for six years.

At the moment, the pet trade is one of the biggest outlets we've got. Ten years ago I wouldn't have dreamt of selling a lot of pet food. But now, everybody has their pets, and they look after them better, and they have beds for their pets. Ten years ago you would never have thought of buying a bed for the dog and a blanket to go in there. You'd put a cushion down in the corner, and you'd forget it, wouldn't you. But now we sell a hundred dog beds a year. And you've got to cater for all different sizes, so we've got seven different sizes out there, and then the cushions, and then the blankets. And in the past, people wouldn't have bought dog food. If you hadn't got something left over from dinner to feed the dog with, it would go without. We must have well over ten thousand different items to choose from on our pets side now: food, beds, toys, vitamins, collars, leads, cages, aquariums. It's nothing for people to have gerbils and mice and rats and some goldfish as well these days. Before, if you'd got a family dog, that was it.

Perhaps it's something to do with the fact that England's not so countrified as it was. You used to go out and see the animals outside. Now you don't so much, so people are bringing the animals into the house to be able to experience them. And I think where people used to go for a country walk to see the countryside, they're now bringing the countryside into their own homes, and if they can't buy a tree, or a shrub, they buy a pot plant. They come here every weekend and load up their cars. I think more people go to garden centres on a Sunday than go to church now.

It means a lot to me that this is a family business. If it wasn't, I would have probably been gone out of it a long time ago. But there's someone coming on after me and that gives you something to work for. It's when you see your grandchildren out there: they're probably just in the way but it gives me an awful lot of pleasure to see them help do the make-up work, though the staff don't always appreciate them. I'm absolutely a hundred per cent sure that Thomas'll follow into it. But there's seven grandchildren altogether and if seven of them come into the business they've got problems, haven't they.

Our first full year in business our turnover was £535. The second year, we doubled it to £1,100. Now it's about £3.5 million. We work seven days a week. We're not at home much. We hardly ever go on holiday. My wife goes on holidays, with her sister. She's been to Hong Kong, Italy, on safari in Kenya. It doesn't interest me at all. I'm quite happy to go down to our bungalow on the south coast, watch the sea come in, go for a swim, go out in the boat, and come back and sit there. It's right opposite Cowes Harbour and you see all the racing going on. As far as I'm concerned, I would rather go down there for a fortnight than I would go abroad for a month.

John Salter

In Transition

My first parish, St Paul's, Tottenham, in London, was a Victorian parish and the church building had been demolished. On the site a block of flats had been built, which incorporated a worship area, so the altar was at one end of the church, and there was a bar and social club at the other, which I thought was heaven, really, because you could go straight from Mass into the bar. The curate's flat was part of the block of flats, as was the parish priest's accommodation, and there was a church primary school adjacent. The liturgy and the theological expression was entirely my own there, so I was blissfully happy.

At the end of that time, I felt that I ought to go somewhere that was very different; if you like, in a missionary context. So I elected to go to an outer-city estate on the outskirts of Birmingham. It was a square mile with thirty-four tower blocks and all the kinds of problems that the *Faith In The City* report highlighted, and it was an incredible place to be and work. The tradition of the parish was evangelical, and there was only one celebration of Mass with any singing once a month. I gave it ten and a half years, and in that time we moved into a Catholic liturgical expression. I taught the Catholic faith, as I understand it, within the Church of England, and when I left the congregation had to produce a profile of what they wanted in their new priest, and the first sentence read, 'We want a Catholic priest.' I felt that was a tremendous affirmation that those ten and a half years had been well spent.

The word 'Catholic' is often misunderstood in Anglicanism. Another phrase that's used is 'High Church', and 'High Church' and 'Catholic' to most people mean dressing up and bells and smells. And insofar as dressing up and bells and smells are holistic – that is, they take into account all the sorts of things that stimulate us as human beings – then yes, they are Catholic; but I would never say that that was the essence of what I mean by Catholicism. Catholicism, in my view, is about our understanding and our vision of God, and our understanding and vision of His creation and its redemption. However, one ought to be able to present the Christian faith in a way that embraces the variety of traditions, so I strive, in my style, to hold together both the formality of Catholic ritual with an openness that makes people feel at ease.

During my time in Birmingham I had felt that I would like to go next to one of those tractarian Catholic parishes which had got a glorious history, very much like the parish in which I grew up in Swindon, to see if I could move people forward, because quite clearly the Catholic faith is alive within the Anglican Church; as a movement it has always looked to what Rome was doing. Of course, things had changed in Wantage over the years. The vicarage, for example, was now a small house in the grounds of the former vicarage. The town had clearly expanded, and the church buildings needed a lot of work done. I think I was also expecting priestly life to be a lot easier coming to a place that hadn't got the social pressures of an inner city or outer estate, and I began to realize that there were different pressures here but they were equally as intense.

Having embraced that now, things have got easier. But looking back over seven years here, you do become aware of insularity and a powerful resistance to change, and yet at the same time there's a tremendous amount of creative good going on. If one reads *What's On In Wantage*, I'm just amazed at the opportunities for leisure and activity that there are. I don't think I've ever been in a place where that is true.

And I was talking recently to a bereaved wife, and she described this as a place with a village mentality, and she said so in a very positive way. She was talking about the intimacy and the homeliness, and that when there is a crisis everyone pulls together because it's small enough for people to know each other. I would want to echo that. I know I wear a uniform, so therefore I'm recognized, but there are vast numbers of people who will stop and speak to me, and greet me very warmly: because the town is small enough they know me and therefore trust me.

That's very different to working on an outer-city estate, where the Church has moved to the margins of society, and is perhaps tolerated but quite often there is hostility. And I suppose, through my interests, I meet people here who have absolutely nothing to do with the Church. It's not unusual for bikers to turn up here, because I ride a motorbike. In fact, somebody turned up on Monday afternoon and hopped off his motorbike and came and had a cup of tea. And when there's been a tragedy or a death in the biker community, they've sought to draw me in, to be involved in it. Now, there is the opening of a door because at one level it's leisure for me, and yet through that leisure I can build bridges between the Church and a community which is not normally associated as being part of the Church.

This is very important, because Catholicism talks about the whole of a person, not just the religious dimension. In 1847, a priest called Butler came to Wantage, and he transformed not only the church life here but the life of the town. Butler sought an excellence in worship, and beauty in the church building, but he was also passionate about education, so he founded schools. He was keen on establishing a religious community, and he did that within two years of arriving here, and that community of nuns still continues. He built a church for the town workhouse; he was involved in providing drains and housing in the town. Now that, if you like, sets the agenda for me. What I see as my role is, in fact, continuing that tradition of Butler; of excellence in worship and dealing with the spiritual dimension of life but also being caught up in other aspects of life. The big difference between Butler and myself is that in thirty-four years he had fifty curates and a convent full of nuns, and whilst I rejoice in the past, I am committed, passionately, to developing the ministry of lay people because it's the church community that must do the work that was the work of priests and nuns in the past.

That's a vision, if you like, and an ideal. I think I'm a person of ideals, but I realize that an ideal is something you work towards. There isn't anything that's *given* about it. In my world of dreams I would want the parish to be in a particular way, but I realize that one is operating within reality, and so I know I need to keep in balance the things that frustrate and drive me mad alongside those things which are positive and creative. Butler's population in Wantage was three thousand, and the population now is eleven thousand and growing, so we can never be the Church in the way that it was a hundred and fifty years ago. But we can still be as vibrant and exciting and reaching outward as they were at that time. And whilst I am definite in my Catholic views and in my expression of them, in a market town I'm very aware that we draw together people from every shade of Anglicanism. We also have in the congregation people from other denominations, and you have to take seriously the way that you relate to people who are not only of other parts of the Christian family, but also of other parts of the human family, and it's been important for me to actually reflect on that. I would want to argue that it is right for me to do that from within the conviction of my own position; nevertheless, it is possible to build bridges between Christians and people of other faiths, and of course between Christians and people of no faith at all.

One of the things about Catholicism is that it is community orientated: it thinks in terms of community, which it calls 'the Church', whereas non-Catholicism tends to be individualistic, so that individuals are allowed to make their own decisions over and against the Church, and while I would say that individuals can hold opinions, it should be done within the context of the Church. These days, there is variety from which people can choose, and also the *expectation* that you can choose, whereas I would want to say that spirituality can be a searching, but in that process, and quite often before someone has found something, people do need to change direction, or change attitude, so that the searching actually becomes an acceptance and an obedience.

I'll try and find another way of putting it. There are times when, as a priest, I'm very aware that I do things because of my obedience to my ordination when I would prefer to be doing other things. Searching is so often the individual's quest for *fulfilment*, and my reading of the Christian Gospel is that fulfilment never actually comes until we are obedient to God's will for us. I'm powerfully influenced by Benedictine spirituality. I make my retreat in a Benedictine monastery for a week each year but I also try and go for a day each month. With Benedictinism, the vows are to obedience, stability and the conversion of life, and that makes a great deal of sense to me, because stability means holding on, remaining where you are, sometimes feeling a desert experience, and yet remaining in the desert in order to grow. That growth is the conversion of life that Benedict talks about. Stability is brought about through obedience, and Christians do live under a discipline; the earliest word for Christians was 'disciples', and it's through that obedience that fulfilment and freedom come. If one seeks to be obedient, fulfilment is the gift that goes with it.

All this is very close to the marriage vows. And yet in the society of which we are part, you come across people who have got multiple partners, or who move from one relationship to another. Spirituality is not about centring life upon oneself. Christian spirituality is about centring one's life upon God, and we do that through the community, which is His Church, of which we are part. So it's much more an outward-reaching than an inward-seeking thing, and that is absolutely true in relationships; that in marriage one is always seeking the good of one's partner, not the good of oneself, and yet seeking the good of one's partner brings fulfilment and enrichment to one's own life.

I see a great deal of pain in broken relationships; not just the adults that are involved in it, but what the children have to carry. Now of course one's got to accept that if there is total breakdown then that must be recognized, but it seems that the definition of total breakdown is so much easier to what it was considered to be some years ago. One can divorce more quickly than one can marry, these days, which is not as I would want it to be: nevertheless, through mistakes, and through crises and disaster, can blossom creativity, and people who are in those contexts need to be affirmed and lifted up, and I would hope that that's something that I would be involved with. When there is a breakdown in a relationship, it's the last time that you should be talking about ideals, or hammering people with moral absolutes, because what people need is to be in touch with what they feel deep down.

I'm fairly definite and strong in the position I hold about marriage, and in some sense, perhaps I'm too absolute. I won't remarry people who've been previously married to someone who is still alive. And the reason I won't do it is because I will not put myself in the position of making a judgement about previous relationships and the relationship they're in. But that's not to say that I don't think the Church itself needs to do something about it. At the moment, I either feel I have to say no to everyone, or yes to everyone. My present practice is a compromise. I suggest that the couple goes to the registry office to register their marriage in law but then come to church to dedicate those vows in the presence of God, and we offer prayers, and the kind of service that we offer is not second best, it is equal to what we do when we celebrate marriage in church. I would never want a couple to feel that we were downgrading the level of their commitment, and when handled with sensitivity and compassion and care, people respond to that, and they don't see that in any way there is a judgement being made.

I also wouldn't work alongside a woman priest. I wouldn't want to do it because one of us would have to preside at the Eucharist, and if I didn't recognize that she was a priest then you can begin to see the complications. What I would want to say, and people never really understand this, is that my opposition is not on the grounds of sexism. It's not because a person is a woman and not a man. My anxiety is that the Anglican Church, which claims to be part of the universal

Church, has gone in a direction which neither the Roman Church nor the Eastern Church is prepared to go, and that troubles me because this question of authority for a Catholic is linked to what's called the 'consensus fidelium', the consensus of all the faithful people. Now, I recognize that it's very difficult to make decisions when the Church is divided, and the Church is divided. But it troubles me greatly, as someone who embraces Catholicism within the Church of England, that I find myself caught in that divide, in that tension. I can produce an argument, a Catholic argument, for the ordination of women as priests, and that may be the argument that ultimately persuades the whole Christian world, but we haven't reached that point yet.

In the parish, there's a substantial majority that are in favour but there is a significant minority who are not. There is pain either way. That's why I say living with the tension is not easy. Sister Barbara Noreen from the convent works in the parish; I have two lay pastorates, one that works in the hospital, and one that deals with the bereaved, and I have no problem with women priests coming to preach. I have no problem with women in the deaconate, and that is because there were women who were deacons – but not priests – in the early Church. If, ultimately, the ordination of women is what the whole Church is going to do, I do not have a problem. It's not a problem at all. All I want to emphasize is that Anglicanism is a tiny part of the Christian family, and whilst my views in the Church of England may be eccentric, set in the context of the wider Church my views are entirely central.

Some people have argued that the equality of women is a moral issue. I would want to say that ordination is not about equality, it's a completely different game. On moral issues, I think it is possible to take a stand. I can give you an example of that, on the whole area of relationships between the same gender. Once you've accepted that sex is part of that whole that comes together to express relationship and love, it seems to me it's quite acceptable to say that that kind of depth in a relationship between two men, or two women, should be recognized, affirmed and cherished. To say that in the present climate is very contentious, and the question thrown back at me might be, would I proceed to a Service of Blessing of two men, say? Having stated the argument, I would still err on the side of caution because I would not wish to do something because *I* wanted to do it. I am a priest of the Church, and it's only when there is quite clearly a consensus in that area that I would feel happy about proceeding, but I think it is a different issue from the ordination of women. It's a moral issue, and it's about relationships, where I think there can be a change.

When talking about these issues, some people make the distinction between Christianity and the Church. I wouldn't do that, because for me they are one. St Paul talks about the Church as a body, and describes Christ as its head, so the organic unity of the Church is a very powerful idea. There would never have been a distinction between Church and Christianity in the first thousand years of the Church. That takes us back to individualism: people find it much easier to talk about Christianity when they want to talk about individuals making a faith commitment to Christ than they would in terms of being part of the baptized community. Doctrine expresses faith in an intellectual way, but faith is expressed in all sorts of other ways as well: it's expressed through prayer, it's expressed through fellowship, and I see my essential role as in the context of the gathered church, the people who meet Sunday by Sunday, and day by day, to celebrate the Sacraments and to feed on the presence of Christ together. But it's not an exclusive club. There is a sense in which it's a springboard for bouncing out into the wider community, which is both Wantage and, indeed, a global community.

I don't get depressed by people who don't come to church because I think we're in an age of liberation that we haven't known since Christianity was established in this country. People are not in any way coerced into church, and if you look at the history it wasn't that long ago that nobody had a position of any social importance if they were not baptized and a communicant. It wasn't that long ago that you had to be baptized in order to get into Parliament. Now there is a total freedom in response to God, and I actually welcome that freedom. I would anyway want to say that we should be in service to a wider community. People turn to the Church for all sorts of reasons, and providing we respond to them by being honest, and by being real, then I think we can start to open doors and allow them to ask us questions; not for us to give them answers but for us to work with them about where the answers might be. That is a hopeful thing, because it means that people actually want to ask questions about faith, and they want to express that faith, and they want to worship. So churches may be growing smaller but I think they're growing stronger, and that, I would say, is very positive.

As a curate in Tottenham, I found it fascinating to have within the parish a Brahmin priest and his wife, who had read astrology in Delhi, and who read palms. It was absolutely fascinating to find where there was convergence in what we said and thought, and where there was divergence. And I was recently in Reading, and paid a visit to the synagogue in the centre, and found the rabbi's tour of the synagogue absolutely fascinating. And when I offered to cover my head, because I know that was a way of being sensitive to where they are, he said he was quite happy for me to go into the synagogue with him as I was. And I really felt there was a desire to come together, and to go as far as we could together, whilst recognizing our distinctness. We're in a transition phase, our society is coming to terms with being multicultural and multi-faith, and while I would want to speak about God in a Christian context, I am open to what other faiths are saying, and genuinely seek to see where we do converge.

The biggest difficulty for Christians, certainly for those of us who have positions of responsibility, is the confrontation with apathy. People's lives are now so organized and busy that the space left for God and spirituality appears to be ever-shrinking. I'm very aware that, even in my own lifetime, going to church was actually part of entertainment, and people point to *The Forsyte Saga* as being one of the signs of the end of that: people were watching the television, so evening worship collapsed. Here in Wantage you get the person who commutes backwards and forwards to London, who doesn't come to church. But when a child is born, they will come because they want to celebrate the birth, although their view of baptism may not be the view that the Church has of baptism. At a later stage, we come into contact with them through school, or it'll be a moment of joy when a wedding comes along, or a moment of grief when someone dies. Those sorts of things draw me into a relationship with individuals and with families around the community.

There are other ways in which I get involved. People have this sort of establishment view of where the vicar fits in, so there are all sorts of social functions, some of which have a ritual character, such as Battle of Britain Sunday, and others which are simply dinners, to which I'm invited because I am this establishment vicar figure. There is also the natural blossoming of friendship. I do love the people here, and the place. I came here shortly after being married, and my second child was actually born in this house, so leave-taking will be very hard. But trying to move this parish forward has proved a lot tougher than I thought it was going to be. In the outer-city estate in Birmingham, it was possible to achieve things much more quickly because the population was constantly moving. In a sense, I was a stable factor by being there ten years: most of the schools had two to three head teachers in that same passage of time, so for me to be creative and constructive and build was a lot easier than it is here. To achieve what I want to achieve here, my timescale is much longer, because people are very set in their ways, and I am reconciled to that.

People say this is a middle-class town. It's not: my impression is that it's a predominantly working-class town but the middle classes are very visible and very vocal. One of the things that's been quite special for me here is to see the congregation expand and change so that people who wouldn't have come to church before are now joining the church community, and feeling part of it. It's also been wonderful to see the renewal and restoration of the church building, but I don't want it all to stop there. My hope is that the building will become much more accessible to the community around. Someone said to me a year ago that they were anxious, with all these new things going on in the church building, that it would cease to be a church. I assured them that it will continue to be a church but I am aware that what we mean by 'church' is changing. We're currently planning for a millennium New Year's Eve party in the parish church, which will begin with worship at eight and then move into a shared supper and games and dancing, and ultimately, celebrating the new millennium at midnight. We can do that because we now have a building with toilets, with kitchen facilities, with space to be social as well as to meet for worship, and all under the one roof. At one level, it's a restoration to what a church building was like in the Middle Ages. My dream for the future is that we can draw all sorts of people into that building for all sorts of reasons, without it losing its dignity, its sense of mystery, and its prayerfulness.

Michael Foster

Guessing the Weather

Cats. Cat food is *huge*. Cats first, in front of dog food. Pet food by the ton. And they do a lot of baking here, the country folk: we sell a lot of flour. That's your elderly, coming in on the buses from the villages in the middle of the week. Milk and bread sell most of all, which tells me that we're a convenience store and it's the basics that count. We sell a lot of fruit and vegetables, which is surprising, because we're in a fruit-growing area. Healthy living, I suppose. Fish. Cigarettes. Cheese.

We have sixteen thousand transactions a week but then we're a small branch. Waitrose in Bath has over forty thousand transactions a week. Of course, Bath is much bigger and they don't spend very much in Bath, it's mostly basket trade: still, forty thousand transactions, that's a lot of basket trade. Here, we have a third trolley trade, which is the families spending their £40 to £100 a week. A third is elderly folk, and they don't go to Sainsbury's because it's a bit of a trek out of the town centre. And then there's a lot of the pop-ins, the schoolkids with their sandwiches and their Coke, the office workers at lunchtime. It's hard money, taking small amounts. You've got to man the checkouts, and when people come in, because it's their meeting place and they have a nice little chat in the gangway, you've got to hang about until they are ready. What every store likes is people to fill up big trolley loads because that's easy money but some stores are going crazy and opening twenty-four hours a day. They're frequented by customers at three o'clock in the morning. Married women get up at six to do the family shop while the husband's still at home with the kids. I hope that doesn't become popular because I don't want to trade twenty-four hours a day.

If you want to earn more dosh, then you have to run a bigger store. This is one of the smaller Waitrose stores in the country. Go to Stroud, *then* you can have a shopping experience. Twenty-five thousand square feet, it's superb. Here, we can't have a patisserie, we haven't got a fish counter, we have limited assortments on most of the other products. We don't do china and glass and kitchen utensils, or newspapers and magazines, though we do do flowers. Salisbury, too, that's a shopping experience. There they do radio and television, china, glass, towels, haberdashery, and petrol as well. In Salisbury, they're stocking something like thirty thousand different products. Here we stock about twelve thousand. I want to cater for everybody that walks in off the street but in less than nine thousand square feet it's difficult.

More difficult is guessing what the customer preferences are going to be, and what the weather's going to be like. Today, we're planning the orders for Easter. What's the weather going to be like for Easter? If it's warm, then it'll be salads. If it's salads, we don't want to order root vegetables and potatoes, and we don't want to order roasting beef or mince; we want to order steaks and chicken drumsticks because people start having barbecues at Easter. We don't want to order whole turkeys or whole chicken, we want to order ham and coleslaw. So we order more ham and coleslaw, and the weather changes, and there's a freshness code on the food, and if the deadline comes it's reduced or destroyed. The weather's such a pain in the neck I do often think of having a bar out in the Canaries instead, but you want to go to the Canaries to enjoy it; you don't want to work, you want someone else to run the bar. See, there are my girls out there, sitting with their papers spread out wherever they can find room, to do their ordering, and all they're thinking about is the weather.

We try very hard to get it right because wastage affects your profit margins. I get my knuckles rapped if we have too much wastage: that's known and unknown wastage, so it has to cater for the thieves as well, or for our bad practices, like if we reduce something and forget to record it. If you're clever with your ordering, and you're lucky with the weather, then you can achieve less than three per cent wastage. Some branches, they have an arrangement with the Salvation Army, where if a product's on its sell-by date, they come and collect it. We're keen to look at that as well because we now get Landfill Tax. Anything that we write off, we have to pay £10 a ton for destroying it: your carrots that go mushy, your potatoes that have started to go green, your cabbage that goes yellow; nothing you can do with those. Meat, if you can get something for it, better to do that than throw it in the bin. The last resort is always to sell reduced-price food to the partners.

That was one of the reasons I went into this job, because people have always got to eat. When money's tight, when the mortgage repayments are high, the interest rates are up, people downtrade, so the luxury items, the extras, the nice-to-haves, they don't have. They go back to the basics, the simple food and vegetables. You stop selling your fillet steaks, your rump steaks, your roasting beef. People do away with roast dinners and go for the cheaper cuts, or just the mince or sausages. Booze sales drop. But overall it doesn't make as much difference as you'd think.

BSE, now *that* affected sales. It *really* affected sales when it was at its height. Each time a new scare came out, people wouldn't buy beef. Then when it was half price they stocked their freezers with as much as they could get. That is the absolute truth. As soon as it got its red 'Reduced' sticker on it, then it didn't make a blind bit of difference. Tells you a lot about the public. And each time somebody else came out with something new, you could tell because your meat cabinet was sitting there untouched: so your labels come out, and you start whacking the price down, and when the customers know it's going to be half price then it's loaded in the trolleys.

The one thing that really affected trade was a few years ago. The council put in a new flood-relief scheme, and at the same time the district council decided to improve the relief road at the back here. They took away about a third of the town car park, and then they came into our car park and started spreading out from us, and that virtually destroyed the town over a three-month period because the traffic lights and the roadworks were horrendous. Car parking in Wantage is pretty appalling anyway. And on the local radio it kept advertising, 'Avoid Wantage, because of the roadworks.' That was a terrible planning exercise by somebody. So many small businesses went down. We survived but it cost us a lot of money over three months. A lot of the smaller, individual, family-owned businesses really struggled and then went under; and there was no recompense, there was no way they could sue or claim for loss of sales, it's too difficult an exercise. And you look around town now and what are we? We're banks, building societies, estate agents and charity shops.

Everybody, my old boss, my new boss, my colleagues in London, said it would be a big change for me out here. I used to come out this way fishing, years ago. But it was no big deal except, perhaps, with the pace of life, because here everything can happen tomorrow. In London, it happened yesterday. Everybody lived and drove at breakneck speed. Now it takes me twenty minutes to come to work, and the sun's up, and the drive is over the fields.

My mother used to work in a fruit and veg shop at the top of our road, and I used to go and help when I was about ten. It seems crazy but there was something about working with the people, and filling shelves, that I enjoyed. And when a shop opened in Dunstable in 1966, my father came home on the Friday night and said, 'There's a weekend job for you going in the local paper. You want to write off and apply.' They were recruiting weekend assistants, as we do now. There were two hundred and fifty applicants and they selected twenty-four of us, and that's how I started. Don't ask me what I enjoy about it because I'm not sure, apart from the fact that every day is a new challenge, there's always something different. I like the public, because I spend a lot of the time on the floor, so you get to know all your regular customers. Go to a Tesco or a Sainsbury's, you rarely see the manager on the floor. Waitrose believe in the customer contact, so if Mrs So and So can't find her cheese or her biscuits or her squash, the partners take her to the fixture: that's a trademark of our business.

Waitrose has always been perceived as expensive. There is a Sainsbury's in the town now. All the supermarkets do shopping-basket tests, where we look at the top three hundred lines – Heinz Baked Beans, Kellogg's Cornflakes, whatever – and adjust our prices to ensure that we meet the competition price. And repeatedly, *repeatedly*, we come out £4 or £5 a week cheaper. We don't sell Mickey Mouse brands but we offer better value. And unlike some companies, we don't operate a two- or three-tier pricing structure where, if we were in the town on our own, we would raise our prices. We won't do that because we believe in honest and truthful shopping.

Some of my colleagues and I, we sometimes say that we're not paid as much as we're worth. I'm the store manager but I'm also the father figure for the people in the branch. In department stores, there's a person called a registrar, who's independent of management, that the rank and file can go to if they feel the management are being unreasonable. But we don't have a registrar on site here, we don't have a medical sister on site, we don't have a staff and training manager on site, so I'm all of that rolled in. On the other hand, one of the greatest benefits of working for the company is that the previous chairman set up a 'long-leave' scheme, so when you've done twenty-five years in the business you can have six months' paid leave off, and that's for everybody; management, rank and file, the trolley man.

I had my long leave last year. You think it ought to be something momentous. Everybody says you've got to do something worthwhile to make it a real memory. But I've got two young children, seven and five, and in this job you see the children for half an hour in the morning and the same at night and you miss them growing up. I've got a twenty-one-year-old daughter from my first marriage, and I missed her childhood, and I regret that. So I made a conscious decision that I would spend six months with the kids, and we had most of the summer in the Canaries and then when term started I cycled to school with them every day and came home to have breakfast with my wife. It makes you realize that family life is important, that there is something else outside work. Coming back: like a new job.

Actually, I do know what I like about this job. People watch. I pride myself a great deal on knowing about people. When you work with the public it's a real eye-opener, you get to know all their little habits. People are funny creatures. You get the same people coming in at ten to nine on a Friday night, even though we shut at nine. Sunday afternoon, there's several always come in at quarter to four even though we shut at four; and it's not because we have all the reduced goods there to attract them, because you reduce them earlier, to get rid. People are very strange.

Take Saturday mornings. Saturday morning is something completely different. Saturday morning you get a particular type of customer. They're the very regular, standing out there at twenty past eight, impatient. We smile when we go to open the doors at half-past eight because it's your same faces always there, and as you open the door somebody rushes into the wine because he's *always* first and he's going to make sure he's there. And somebody else scoots off to the deli because he wants to be served first. And if the weather's really hot that affects shopping patterns as well because people want to get the shopping over and done with, so they're here along with the regulars, champing at the bit at half-past eight. Well, that upsets the normal Saturday regulars, doesn't it, because there's all these other people; there's a queue at the deli and they don't like that one bit. I watch them in amusement.

We pride ourselves here on providing a service for everybody. We do get a lot of the green wellies, and we get a lot of the horsey brigade, and they spend lots of dosh, so that's very good, although the nasty ones are really bloody awful. Talk to you as though you're worse than something on the bottom of their shoe, feel that they can say anything and show no respect for you whatsoever. I always think it may be something to do with their personal life, and here is an opportunity to come and vent their anger, because they exaggerate so much.

I'll look for a larger branch sooner or later, because each year, whatever job you're in, you think, What's going to drive me forward this year? There is only so much you can do in one branch. Training new staff is always a challenge and it's got its good points, this place. The girl that was murdered in Wantage recently, a relation of hers works here. That tragic car accident a while back. What terrible things to have to come to terms with. What traumatic things. But although there's a hundred and thirty people work here, it's one big family, and that's something that I've always said, that this is a family shop and everybody ought to be committed and working for one another so when there's a tragedy everybody is supportive and rallying round, although they also know when to give someone a bit of space. It's the one thing that makes our company stand head and shoulders above others, the fact that we're all partners in the business. I use that term every now and again, 'We are all partners in the business,' because it does make a real difference, and being somewhere small makes even more. It makes this a very good place to work.

I learnt a lot when I came here. They say there are four key things that are supposed to cause the most stress in your life: you change your wife, your house, your job, you move. I did all that and I changed my boss as well, all at the same time. My first wife's solicitor, he was an absolute so and so. He had the stone as well as the blood and everything else. I remember one day getting a letter from my solicitor, and I just thought, God, no more, no more. And I took a can of beer and said, 'I'm going to go to the bottom of the garden and sit there for a while.' And I sat there for about half an hour and I thought about my life. And from that time on, I've accepted that you get two sorts of problems; the problems that you can do something about and the problems you can't. The problems you can, then get off your butt and do something about them. The problems that you can't, put out of your head. So when people come to me with their problems, I get them to analyse them. 'What can you deal with? What can't you? If you can do something, go away and do something. If you can't, just for God's sake stop worrying about it.'

When I was getting divorced, my boss used to say, 'I don't know how you cope.' But you have to, don't you. So when I read about people that have committed suicide, I wonder, Can things get that bad? Can they? All the trauma that they leave behind as well, it's bad. I just can't believe how people can get that low. It must be terrible. Not that it's ever happened to me. Me, when I'm low, tomorrow's another day. The sun'll come up in the morning. You have to latch on to the good things in life. That was what I did that day when I went to the bottom of the garden, I focused on the good things. And we have a mini-situation like that in the store every year after Christmas, because in the run-up to Christmas everybody gets excited, and it's busy and everybody's pulling together, and it's all great fun; and then after Christmas it's a great anti-climax, nobody's got any money, the weather's horrible, everybody's worn out, doom and gloom, and somebody has to go out and raise the heads of all the troops. Somebody has to go out there and say, 'It'll be different next week. It'll be different tomorrow. I guarantee the sun'll come up in the morning.'

Joanna Castle

Dear Farmer Giles the Wicked

My whole life I wanted to farm the farm in Cornwall. My mother was a farmer in Cornwall, and she was left the farm by her father. She left me a cottage in Cornwall, which is wonderful to go to, and I still have it to this day. I remember her saying to me, 'You won't forget which is your home.' I was desperately homesick when I first came up here.

At seventeen, I went to Lackham Farm Institute. There were only five girls and about a hundred men. We did all sorts of things like bee-keeping, home-made sausages, chopping up a pig, pickle-making, and those skills I never lost. After that, I went on to Seale-Hayne agricultural college in Devon, and specialized in dairying. I met David at Seale-Hayne. Didn't have a lot to do with him because I wanted to go home and farm, but I used to play tennis doubles with him because he was very fair and didn't poach: he just let you miss the ball. After Seale-Hayne, I went back home and farmed for three very happy years with my sister, who had been to Oxford University and got a degree in Agriculture, but then she got married and I got married to David. The farm in Cornwall was no longer possible.

The day David and I were married, my father-in-law, Bertie, made me a partner in this farm, and they let me go on wearing my Wellington boots ever since. In 1963 that was quite revolutionary. Even being a woman farmer in Cornwall you were very much a second-rate citizen. I remember taking a young heifer into Liskeard Market and hearing us both described as 'well bagged up and breeched down'; getting poked with the farmers' sticks as you went round. You were a bit of a laugh, so you really had to work hard to establish yourself.

Occasionally it goes against you. For years I did all the educational farm walks here. We had a tie-in with Reading University, so I did quite a lot of adult education. I had some farmers come from Pakistan. They arrived in a minibus, in their traditional garb, and I could see by their faces they weren't at all pleased to see me. The first question the leader asked me was, 'Madam, is your husband ill?' I said, 'No, he's fine, but I do the farm walks.' I had to work very hard with that group to prove I did know what I was talking about, and I had to leave the room while they prayed to Mecca. And at the end I put out my hand to shake hands, to be told, 'We don't touch another man's woman.' They then explained to me that although they accepted me they thought it was completely wrong, and in their country the women would be revered and kept in the home. The thing that really tickled me pink, and I didn't tell them, was what David was doing that afternoon: a slide show for the Mothers' Union. I thought that would completely blow their minds.

The Ethiopians, they wanted to know about women in farming. The first question I was asked was, 'What is your age?' I said, 'Well, you never ask a woman that, for a start.' The next question was, 'Who gave you the power?' What on earth can you say? I said, 'It's my own right. I am an educated woman. I am perfectly entitled to be a partner in this farm.' I enjoyed those visits: you have a chance to talk at all sorts of levels and it's made me question myself. I took a group of Chinese farmers over to where the girls were helping David to do the silage, and I was asked, 'How do you get your daughters to work on the farm?' I said, 'Well, it's easy. I pay them,' and the reply was, 'You pay *girls*?' The Indians have got it a bit better: it's the men who talk but it's the women who look after the cattle.

For a while I was very interested in cattle-breeding with blonde Aquitaines and Limousins. Once, I took four beautiful bulls up to the

Carlisle bull sales, and David and I had a good system going; I was taking them in the ring one at a time, and he was bringing the next one to the ring and taking the other one away. We got round to the last one, and there were an awful lot of people there, and we missed each other, so I had to take my bull back and tie it up, and David brought the last bull in because I didn't have time to get back round to fetch it. The bidding on that bull was very, very slow and it only just met its reserved price. Afterwards, the farmer came round to see us and I said to him, 'Oh my, you've got a cheap bull.' 'No,' he said, 'I haven't.' He said, 'It's the one you couldn't handle, your husband had to bring it in, it's obviously bad-tempered.' It wasn't. I'd brought all those bulls on at home and looked after them. I used to train them to walk behind the Land Rover.

When David and I came here in 1963, we had to make a decision how we were going to farm this farm with David's father Bertie as well. This was basically an arable farm and Bertie had somewhere round three hundred acres. We're now up to five hundred and sixty acres, which is a medium-sized farm for this part of the world. Bertie didn't ever want to farm animals, he was a machinery-orientated man, an arable man, although the amazing thing with Bertie was he always looked ahead and he never ever stopped learning. I can remember him going to night classes to do welding, and once, I'd just finished calving a heifer, I said to Bertie, 'Cor! Come and see what I've done!' and he said, 'Girl, come and see what *I've* done!' He'd been welding a metal waste-paper basket.

David and I decided to go in for beef cattle because it made economic sense. You've got to appreciate all our land is good land and we can grow wheat on it, so whatever else you do with it has to equal a crop of wheat. We knew that dairy herds had always got excess calves and we bought those to rear as beef cattle. In the good old days, it was the Hereford–Frisian. Latterly, it was Limousin or Charolais or Simmental. People asked me why I had the continental breeds. I would have loved to go back to the Hereford–Frisian but we could only rear here what we could sell. People don't want to eat fat and the continentals have far less fat in their meat than the good old Hereford and Aberdeen Angus. Years ago, in this country, we used carthorses a lot for ploughing. On the Continent, they used oxen and draught cattle, and so those cattle tended to produce a lot of muscling. It's terribly sad, when the British used to breed the finest livestock of all times, and it's desperate on the veterinary side too, now; there's no research going into things like calf pneumonia because there's no money in it.

We used to have well over five hundred head of cattle a year to look after. Each animal would stay with us for eighteen months. I would buy in two hundred new baby calves from the dairy herds every autumn and they were bucket-reared here. We also used to go to Wales in October, to the suckler sales, to buy older calves. Sucklers were cows that lived on the Welsh hills. They would have a calf, and the calf would stay with it right the way through spring and summer, be weaned in the autumn, and then we would buy and truck home between a hundred and twenty and a hundred and sixty of them each year when they were about six months old. This meant that in the winter we'd have three groups of calves: the new, unweaned calves we'd bought, the same ones that were a year older, and the Welsh sucklers. Fortunately, I had an absolutely super woman to help me. It was a fantastic relationship and I couldn't have done it without her. We weaned, we de-horned, we neutered, we administered medicine, we did literally everything ourselves. Five hundred cattle a day, twice a day, day in, day out, for thirty-four years. Our lives revolved round it, and so did the children's. We didn't have summer holidays. The first time we ever had Christmas off the farm was last year, the year I stopped rearing calves.

We had an awful lot to compensate. We had space, and we made our beef pay and our harvest pay. We had some fairly good years, there's no denying it. We employed people too. When David and I were first here with Bertie, we had Gordon, Freddie, Jim and Stan, all full-time, plus the lady I worked with, and any agriculture students. Gordon stayed right on until last year. He started off as a boy of eight here, under David's grandfather, leading the carthorses. He's never gone out of Wantage, never done anything else, never been anywhere. He was just 'Kent' in the farm book, and he would line up against the kitchen wall every week, and the workers' wages would be put in a bowl, and his name would be entered in the book, and he would touch his cap and say, 'Yes, sir, no, sir, three bags full, sir.' But things have changed and Gordon has actually become one of our best friends now, a wonderful friend. His loyalty to this family's been amazing. We rejoice at his happy happenings, and he rejoices and grieves with us. And he's Gordon, he's not 'Kent'. It's been like a social revolution. That Gordon's equal doesn't even come into it. Of course he is. He's Gordon and we are friends.

Now labour has changed. The image of the farmworker is still this chap with a straw drooling out of his mouth, and in the past where it was true that we mopped up a lot of people that were happy to work on the farm, and we could usefully use, now we can't. Every year, one of us is on some Agricultural Training Board course, whether it's electric fencing, or safety on the fork-lift truck; and nowadays, if you're going to employ somebody, you've got to ask to see all his certificates otherwise you're stuffed for insurance. Now we're into the era of contract and just using labour when you need it. We don't have full-time staff and this year we sold our combine harvester. It's cheaper to pay contractors when you need it, and there's quite a lot of money tied up in a combine. A new one's maybe £100,000, and for here you'd only use it three weeks of the year.

The combine's very sophisticated now. It gives you a printout of every field, the yields you're getting as you go along. It's like the drill which our son, Ralph, uses with his tractor: that will tell you where the phosphate is, and the potash, and the nitrogen, and it'll put on exactly what you need. Having come from Cornwall, which, let's face it, was behind in agriculture, where I used to sit on a stool and hand-milk South Devon cows with the most dreadful-shaped teats you've ever seen, my hands still ache from it, into oval-shaped buckets; and Teign Alice, who was really bad-tempered, used to get her foot in the bucket; and there was April, who couldn't bear me whistling ... And I've come from that to five hundred head of cattle and computerized combines. It's a huge new ball game. It's like what I was saying about Gordon: amazing revolutions have come into the farming community and they've been reflected in every aspect of our lives.

I pay compliments to Bertie and David on this, because they were both very far-thinking. They've been able to see things and develop them, and that's the way I think we've managed to survive, by David looking ahead. David's also very keen on conservation. He's planted two extra miles of hedges on this farm, and thousands and thousands of trees. We always used to joke that when we had children he used to plant a wood for them. One of the things that amuses me is how David's father would have looked at conservation. Bertie's idea of conservation was to get rid of rabbits. They ate his crops. The lambing people, the last thing they wanted was magpies or foxes. In the war, farmers were getting rid of gorse. David has a great love for trees and hedgerows: instead of having a stone epitaph when we die he would rather leave hedges and trees; he feels very strongly about that. But it's complicated. In the conservation areas of the farm you're welcoming squirrels and other animals. Outside the conservation areas, you're waging war.

Over this farm, because we've got all sorts of different soil types we've tried to make corridors of conservation, so instead of just taking ten acres, fencing it off, boom boom, that's it, we have little areas: a hedgeway, a ditch, a pond, a stream, a coppice, a bank. That, to me, is really enriching a farm; not only whatever wildlife is there but also the scenic beauty of it. Look at our Downs, these rolling Downs. You don't find stone walls up there, you don't find oak trees growing, but you will find cowslips and harebells and hawthorn trees. There's such diversity and that's what the huge excitement is, but there has to be balance. I am fully aware that you have to control rabbits. There has got to be a badger cull. And while I rejoice to see a vixen with her cubs, it's the most wonderful sight, on the other hand, when she eats my geese ... well, maybe I should have kept them in a bit better.

I do feel nature needs controlling. I am a food producer and I am in conflict with nature. I make my living from the land: I have got to be prepared to keep a control because of the job I do. I deplore factory farming, where you're tipping in fertilizer sprays, chemicals: on the other hand, I'm not an organic farmer. I'm sure organic farming is not sustainable at the end of the day. If you go in for organic farming you need more land because you're going to have more wastage, it's a fact of life. Where's that land going to come from? It's going to come from the areas that are supporting wildlife now. And certainly the Third World countries can no more support organic farming than the man in the moon. It really amuses me listening to those people that will eat pulses and beans and all the rest: do they know how many sprays are on them? Do they know how many sprays are actually on their coffee beans? That's one of the things that I find very difficult about people who scream conservation, I do think they've got double standards.

Always in life, and especially in farming, you've got to try and keep a balance of things. People's concepts of sprays, for example, are still sort of total kill, because in the early days there was only DDT, which annihilated everything, and is still used tremendously in the Third World. Well, they've got very sophisticated now, pesticides. You can spray and kill exactly what you want to kill. You can kill your aphids and leave your ladybirds and your bees alone. You can kill for specific weeds. Some sprays now, once the chemicals are in the plant, that's it, end of conversation; those sprays don't leave residues in the land, so you haven't got this horrible blanket effect. I'm a great believer in trying to choose the middle road. If you can avoid using sprays, economically you're better off, so if you're a good farmer you practise crop rotation. If you know what you're doing, you can apply basic principles and modern technology at the same time.

People have a lot of ideas about the countryside. They think it's idyllic and quiet, and then they move into it and there's no street lights, and the cows smell, and the cockerels crow. But it's no good you as a farmer saying that you were there first; it doesn't wash. I've already lost one of my cockerels. There was a little note left beside him: 'The next one will go as well.' The cockerel I have now is called Lavender and he has a very little crow. Pathetic, isn't it. Health and safety rules haven't helped anybody either. Everything about farms is seen as dangerous. In the past, children were allowed to stroke the sheep that were here. Now the only sheep's wool they're allowed to touch is a fleece that I've washed and spun-dried. Children used to be able to pat the cows. Now they can't. It's awful. To be able to touch, to see, to smell, is all part of it. I've been among livestock all my life. I've reared children, I've looked after old people, and it's about being sensible. My work clothes, they stay in the outhouse.

Everything comes down to common sense but it's extraordinary, isn't it, how the farmer has changed from being dear Farmer Giles to being somebody wicked who poisons the land, whose animals you've got to let out from behind bars. I started doing farm walks here because I felt terribly strongly that people should know where their food came from, and we, as farmers, should be open. I think you are entitled to come and look at the farm, to tell me whether you like the way I'm rearing calves. It's a two-way thing for people to understand the problems in food producing. It's gone wrong because people have endowed animals with human feelings. Farmers, even the bad ones, will look after their animals, because if they don't it's not economic. That's the bottom line. When I take schoolchildren into the calf-house it's, 'Oh, aren't they lovely,' and 'Oh, I want to take one home,' and I say, 'OK, you can take one home. Before you take it home, what does an animal need? It needs stockmanship, and food, and water, and space.' And you start them thinking: cows are not pets.

The cow out there in that field, her name's Becca and I've done her a huge disservice, I've humanized her. Now I can't go in the field with her because she's dangerous. She thinks I'm her mother and she wants to show her love by licking me and nuzzling me, treating me just like an animal. She's three-quarters of a ton: how can I stop her knocking me over? I've had cracked ribs off her; other people she's fine with. But the animal that will hurt you is the one that's lost its fear of you, so now there's always a fence between us. I kept Becca because she was so good on the farm walks, and so wonderful with children, but animals really should live in herds with their instincts intact. To humanize an animal takes away a lot from it.

When I started working with the schools, I wanted children to understand that about animals. I also wanted children to understand about crops and whether we use modern technology; and if we overuse modern technology, like factory farming, whether organic farming is sustainable, and whether your mum is going to buy cheap white eggs, or whether she's going to buy the free-range. I say to the children, 'OK, here are my chickens. I don't let them out first thing in the morning.' 'Why?' 'Well, I wait till they've laid their eggs, because if I let them out, do you know where they're going to lay their eggs?' 'No.' 'Well, they're going to lay their eggs on the dung heap because it's warm. But do you know that eggs are porous? So are you going to eat my free-range eggs that I've picked off the dung heap?' That's a real-world scenario, and for years I've been chipping away at the idea that farms are those glamorized places you see in storybooks.

You take children out to look at nature. You look at a molehill. They say, 'Is that all?' You see, they need David Bellamy actually going down the molehill and talking as if he's the mole. They've got used to nature on television. The other problem is, people don't walk today, most people hardly ever leave their cars. So many of the local schoolkids I talk to have never actually been up on the Downs at all, so although they're aware of it, in another sense they're completely and utterly blind: blind to the fact that grasses have flowers; that if you look under a piece of rotted wood, there's all sorts of incredible things there; that if you want to see a mole, you've got to sit and sit and sit and sit, and *wait* to see it. Nature on television, it's so easy, isn't it. The fox cubs are lovely and the badgers are lovely. And the kids wear their 'Save the Environment' sweatshirts, and yet they've lost the whole point of the environment because they don't understand it.

I think we farmers feel dreadfully threatened by that sort of thing. You've only got to switch on the television and even the kids' programmes are all about animal rescue. I usually switch the television off. If I see that mad cow on the news fall over once more, that poor animal, I'm going to scream. And you only ever see the loading of cattle lorries on television where an animal has slipped. We trucked cattle home, at six months of age, every year for years and years and years, and the worst we ever had was one bruised hip, because those cattle drovers knew what they were doing, knew how to pack them in and load them. There are people who complain about calf exports yet they don't realize that a cow has to have a calf to produce milk, and has to have a calf every *year* to be economic. That's my biggest argument against everybody who shouts and screams about calf exports, and I agree calves shouldn't be exported, I agree there shouldn't be veal calves, and OK, there's vegetarianism, but they're shutting their eyes, those people, they're not seeing the whole equation. Where do they think those calves come from? We have all these surplus calves because we drink milk. If you don't want export calves you shouldn't drink milk.

This is the sort of argument I have with children. They say, 'Oh, these calves, they've got to leave their mummies at four days old.' Yeah, they do, and they perhaps shout that night. And the next morning, when I arrive with a nice bucket of milk, they start shouting for that. OK, you leave the calf with its mum for six or nine months on your Welsh hills, and if daddy bull is still around, and you're not careful, they're quite likely to be unmarried mums. And mum and the calf when they are parted at nine months, the bonding has taken place fully and she and the calf are heartbroken. So what do you want me, as a farmer, to do? Leave the calf somewhere it may die giving birth because it's not big enough? Take it away at four days? Take it away at six months?

That's the thing with farming, it's not black and white, it's grey, and that's what's so interesting about it all. I can understand, though, how the public feel resentful of us. It horrifies me when I look at the accounts, to see the government handouts we get, be it subsidies, or area payments, or education grants, but we actually *can't* survive without them, and that's desperately worrying and upsetting. The Government's got us where they want us, and you begin to do things that attract subsidies because that's the only thing you can do. Take set-aside land, for instance. Every year it's laid down how much of our arable land has to be set aside, and in order to get our subsidy we can't grow an arable crop on that land. But it doesn't do wildlife a favour at all, because if the land is left for so many months the wildlife might move in, but then you'll plough it up and the wildlife's destroyed. It's a very bad scheme. It's meant to stop grain mountains and keep farmers still viable but we're not happy about it.

We're certainly very unhappy in the livestock sector. We've lost a lot of money, with beef in the doldrums. Last year, for the first time in thirty-five years, I didn't rear new calves because I couldn't market them. The BSE crisis completely knocked the market out of our trade. We never had a single case of BSE here but how would we know anyway? BSE doesn't show until an animal is seven years plus, and all my animals, except for Becca out there, are slaughtered much younger. It's been ghastly, the whole business. To see a cow through her pregnancy, and be there when the calf is born, and however many times you see it it's still a wonder; and then to pick that calf up, put it in the trailer, and take it off to the incinerator: what does that do to you? Because that's what so many farmers were facing.

So much about BSE hasn't been proved, but the food merchants have got away with a lot and it's a big bone of contention. One of the problems the farmers had in the olden days was, nothing was put on the animal-food packets. As long as your protein, carbohydrate, fat and fibre content was right, it could be eggshells, could be walnut shells, could be candle grease. We had no way of knowing. That was very wrong. And when one thinks about feeding herbivores on animal protein, I think the food merchants, again, were to blame. The regulations were such that whatever food was being processed probably wasn't heated or treated enough, although we don't actually know whether the BSE infection actually responds to heat. I do sometimes wonder whether organophosphates that were used for warble-fly dressing on cattle perhaps may be more to blame. Warble-flies are flies that attack cattle, and the dressing is poured down the back of the cattle, directly into its backbone. Well, we all know about Gulf War syndrome, and farmers used organophosphates in sheep dips and people have been directly affected by that. David and I have an argument. He'll say, 'Look: how many people are run over on the road each day? How many people have cancer? How many people smoke? And how many people have actually died from BSE?' Well yes, and we eat beef, but if I was the public and worried, I wouldn't eat beef. We've got so many cheap alternatives, I would use chicken.

It's very hard to see a way forward at the minute. I do feel that in the farming community there is this huge feeling of helplessness. I know suicides used to be doctors and vets. Well, I think farmers now are way over that. Farmers are not good communicators. They've lost their local market for a start: now where can you go and talk and have a cup of tea? They often work alone, their pride is at stake, they don't want people to know the humiliation of their circumstances. And I know they're getting subsidies but many of them look at it as handouts and it's against their pride. Some would rather die than sell their farms, and some of them haven't got the option to sell. I think there's also this feeling of, 'What else can I do? This is my life,' and 'my life' means just that.

You see, so often a farm has been handed on, like this farm. Last year we sold the farmyard here for houses, and it was a very hard decision for us, it having been in the family for two hundred years. The only reason we decided to sell it was to generate money to keep the farm going but you still wondered what you were doing. You've got to try and look at it as the phoenix rising from the ashes but I did go through a lot of mixed feelings, and the feeling that I'm left with now is that you have to bend towards the wind to survive. At least the farm is going on, the name is going on. Two of our children, Ralph and Hayley, are farming here, and they're diversifying. Ralph's doing arable. We do thatching straw. Hayley's hoping to do contract rearing of calves and get a tie-in with Aberdeen Angus and Waitrose, and she's doing liveries and school visits up on the Downs. Supposing we had no children, this farm would have become derelict and the whole lot sold off for housing. To me, that is a worse situation than the new houses that we've got out there, and when I go over to see Ralph, when I go to see Hayley, life is going on. It's starting again, it's regenerating.

Those houses are where my field centre used to be, and I grieved over it tremendously. It was where I greeted all my schoolchildren, had them sitting on the floor, had all sorts of posters up. I loved to plaster the walls from top to bottom with pictures and demonstrations, and people were always giving me wonderful presents. If it wasn't a weasel that had got mummified between somebody's bricks, it was a wasps' nest, or a horse's skull. It was smashing, it was just full of goodies, my field centre, and the children loved it. There are twenty-four houses on there now and it's just over one acre. There's a car space for every bedroom, and there's no parking allowed on the road, so that place is a mass of car space. Gardens about the size of my dining room, and they're all instant: the patio, the pot plant, the bit of turf. There's thirteen per cent allowed for open space, and that's it. Where do the children go? Where do the families go? To me, it's horrific. And all the houses, except Gordon's new one, are inward-looking. Gordon's looks out across the fields. His old cottage was pulled down when the land was sold.

I know now, having been rather involved with planning people over the last few years, that they're looking to build houses for another eight thousand people in this area. How can that be done without eroding into the countryside? England is running out of space, we're running out of land, and I don't know what will happen. People want the countryside. I don't know whether we farmers will just become paid custodians of the countryside, or even how farming will survive. I do wonder about this farm. I think the farm of the future is going to be a thousand acres to be viable. My other daughter Emma went to Scotland because land was cheaper. Ralph and Hayley are sure to wonder how they're going to survive here.

David and I went for a meal, to a beautiful restaurant. We sat down to have our meal, David looked at the menu and added it up, what a meal would cost, and he said, 'This is more than a ton of barley,' and he wouldn't eat there. He said, 'We don't generate this sort of money,' so we went to the Little Chef down the road. He just could not come to terms with it. He's right. David's and my life has been a battle with this farm, and if he hadn't been so careful we would never have survived. I'm a little bit more of an ostrich, I don't look too far. My own patch is desperately important to me, and I love my life within it, though I must admit that some of the bigger issues, I really think they're too big. I don't mean that in a selfish way, but they aren't always easy to look at, are they. Farming has had incredible cycles, downs and up. This is a particularly bad one. I'm a great believer in things working out for the best, but when I look at the fact that we're running out of land I can't see beyond it. Maybe England will simply become an airstrip and a housing estate.

Andrew Huddison

Dreaming the Life

We met at my mum and dad's twenty-fifth wedding anniversary and he was doing the bar. You don't expect to meet anybody when you go to the Letcombe Regis Village Hall for a party like that. He kept coming over to me and saying, 'Somebody's bought you a drink and left it at the bar,' and I'd be like, 'Yeah, yeah, thanks.' Just totally over my head that he was trying to make a pass. I never really spoke to him during that evening but apparently he'd seen me in the town, going to the chiropodist in a suit, and he thought I worked there. So he said for a couple of evenings he waited outside at five thirty expecting me to come out, and I never did. And then I happened to bump into him one day in the town and he said how about going for a drink one day, and I thought, I'm not going to assume he's gay, he's just being nice.

We went out for a drink one evening, we came home, hit it off like a house on fire, and that was it, from that first drink. At the end of the first week, we went on holiday to the South of France. When we came back, we rented a room at one of the doctor's houses until we could move into his stable conversion behind it. So you can fall in love at first sight, or on your first date. Instant. From day one.

They were the best three and a half years of my life. People used to say, 'You're always on holiday,' and it was true. I'd started working for Frank Williams and we had a nice lifestyle: we were either in Spain or France or the States. Soon after we met I took Jason out to the Italian Grand Prix with me. We had some woman that came in and cleaned for us, and did our ironing, because I was working full-time for Frank, and Jason was working for his father's firm. Jason was an amazing cook, he could throw anything together. He'd never been to a training college to do it but I believe he now goes to Switzerland and France and chefs in these wonderful châteaux, which I think is fabulous. I never see him now, unfortunately.

I told my parents I was gay when I was sixteen. I asked my friend Ivor Marsh, who was the rector at Letcombe Regis, for advice. He was gay too. I said, 'I want to tell Mum but I just don't know how to go about it. I don't want them to dislike me.' He said, 'Your mum's coming down to me today, so I'll broach the subject.' When I got home that evening Mum was still up. She'd made us some coffee so I wasn't allowed to escape. She said, 'I had a chat with Ivor today and as long as you are happy, that is all that matters.' And it was fine, no problems at all. My dad was very quiet for about a year. He wasn't off with me, and we didn't fall out, he just didn't understand and it took him a while. But now he'll ask questions, and if I refer to anybody who's not gay and say, 'Oh, he must be straight,' he'll go, 'What does this mean?' He'll want to know about the terminologies that we use. And if I'm involved with somebody I always introduce him to my parents. My whole family and the people around here know and I don't seem to have any problems. Frank knows. Frank would always say, 'Well, how's Jason?' as we were on our way to work, which I thought was really nice.

If anybody has had a problem with me, they haven't been brave enough to come and talk to me about it. I normally try to get to know people just as me. A few people have asked me whether I was gay, and I'm quite open about it, though I don't go round saying 'Ooh, by the way, I'm gay.' I think there's a time and a place, and if people don't like it they need the opportunity to be able to walk away from it. And anybody that doesn't like me because of that, then too bad, because what I do after hours and who I sleep with should be totally irrelevant.

Most of my friends are married couples. I've probably got about two or three close gay friends and I choose it to be like that because a lot of the gay people I meet always seem to be into trouble: there's always some drama going on in their lives, which they create themselves, and I prefer my quiet lifestyle. There's no gay community in this town, not insofar as people meet up every Friday for a drink, though there are individuals around. If you want to meet people it's usually pubs or clubs in Oxford or London.

As a teenager, I thought I was the only person in the world who was gay, and I've spoken to a few friends and they all said that they also felt this because they knew nothing else, the world seemed such a big place then. At school I kept it quiet, although there was a teacher who always used to ask me whether I'd brought my knitting to the class, and another one who was a pain in the arse to everybody. He once raised his fist to me in the corridor but I said to him, 'You hit me and you'll be claiming the dole,' and he left me alone after that. It was only after I left school that I'd hear through the grapevine about other people who were gay. One of the teachers even turned out to have been involved with a friend of mine. But it was such a macho school that I think if anybody had found out you were gay, you would have had to have found another school.

I always knew there was something different about me. I went to nursing college in Oxford, and I did go out with a girl there, but I'd see all these nice young studenty types walking up High Street and I'd think, Ooh, he's nice. Then some friends introduced me to a pub in Oxford called the Jolly Farmers. It was near Christmas and we'd only been going a few times, and one night we went in and I got a bit tipsy and I stripped! I actually got a standing ovation for it. The guy who owned the pub said, 'That was so good, can you come back tomorrow, and I'll pay you to do it?' Being a student, I hadn't got much money, I jumped at it. I did it twice. I think he gave me eighty quid or something, which in 1987 was a lot of money. And it was on that second evening that I tripped over somebody in the pub and ended up sitting on his knee, and it was this really nice guy, a post-graduate. He was twenty-seven, I was sixteen or seventeen, and he was my first boyfriend, before Jason.

His name was Jonathan and he used to have a grand piano. He had this beautiful basement flat and I'd go straight there from college on a Wednesday and we'd open a bottle of wine, and he'd play the piano or we'd watch this really stupid French soap. I had such a wonderful time. I'd go to him at the weekends and on Sunday morning we'd lay in bed and we'd have coffee and read the papers. It was nice, and fulfilling, for as long as it lasted. Jonathan knew he was going to London so it seemed pointless getting into something more. And I felt he was in a league far above mine. His life was so civilized, so nice. It was such an olde-worlde type flat, you could hear the birds singing outside, and I thought, Perhaps, one day, I'd like something like this. You always dream.

I was also very close to Ivor Marsh, the rector who told my mum I was gay. When I started working, he used to have every Monday off and he'd collect me and we'd go into London to the nice galleries, the nice films, the nice restaurants. He was very good for me. He actually taught me 'O' level English, privately, and he taught me the best books to read, the best wines to drink, the best restaurants to go to and the best films to see, so I lost a very great friend when he died. Multiple problems he had when he died, I don't think it was just AIDS, he had cancer of the throat too.

I never, ever had a sexual encounter with him. He always wanted to but he didn't do anything for me. I liked his friendship. But I met, through him, a clergyman who I'd been to have supper with a few times, and he accosted me at his house after I don't know how many sherries and paid off my Access card for me, at six hundred quid plus. I'd never, ever do it again. I don't know why it happened and I can't say I'm proud of it at all but it got me out of schtuck at the time. I don't think it was even a night, it was an afternoon, and that was the end of that. I haven't seen him since that incident. It's a pity, because I thought he was a very nice chap and I never wanted anything like that to happen. I was seventeen: he must have been fifty-odd. And even if I meet somebody of my age, I always think, I don't want to spoil it by having some type of sexual happening; because I've had friends, something's happened, and afterwards it's never been the same. But the gay society is such a promiscuous world, unfortunately. Gay men tend to rush into it all in the first six weeks and that's where it goes wrong, because they don't go through that dating process which is when you lay the foundations for a relationship. It's like building a house with no foundations; within a very short period of time it's going to fall down.

I always go on about how I'd like to meet somebody and settle down. Jonathan would have been the perfect type of person. By that I mean I'd love to meet somebody who has money; not because that's what I'm after, I've bought my own house, I can support myself, but I always tend to meet the people who don't have any money and I end up having to support them. It's always me buying dinner, always me arranging things, or I'm the only person who drives, and it puts a great strain on you in a relationship when you're having to give everything all the time, and then you become resentful. I always dreamt I'd find some nice rich man who would give me my own Gold Card, my own Merc., and I could just be Mrs Whoever at home. I've always thought I'd make somebody a perfect wife. I enjoy cooking and entertaining and I've always thought some business-type guy would like somebody at home who could entertain. It's just finding the right person. You picture how you think your life will be, and instead I sit here in this spinster lifestyle, with my chickens, my cat and my dog, in my cottage with the roses outside the front door, and that's all very nice but it does get lonely.

When I left school I did a community care course in Oxford. I never really made it in professional nursing: I wanted to qualify as an RGN but I just had too many distractions, even though I did so many courses I don't think there's an area of nursing I haven't worked in. After working in several London hospitals I was floating around working for various care agencies and I'd got a job lined up with BUPA. However, just before it was supposed to start, Frank Williams phoned up BUPA and said, 'Do you have a nurse I can borrow for one week?' because one of his was going away, and my nurse manager sent me. I arrived at the Williams factory, and I'd been in the building thirty minutes before I realized what they did. It suddenly clicked when I saw the racing cars. So I spent my week there with Frank and on the Friday he said, 'Andrew, is there any chance you could come back and see me tomorrow?' and I said, 'Sure,' and I remember it as if it were yesterday, I sat down on the chair in front of his desk and had my hands between my legs like a little boy at school being told off. He said: 'Andrew, I like your style, I like your attitude. You're clean, you're tidy, I'd like to offer you a job. This is how much I'm going to pay you. These are the benefits you're going to get. If you don't mind working some weekends, when can you start?' I said, 'Monday,' and I've been there since 1990.

I've had some very, very exciting times. In the first two years, I spent a lot of the time with the team, going out to team dinners and functions, and that was amazing because I'd never been to all these countries before. And some of the sights that you saw, the poverty in Brazil and Mexico, I just didn't think that that sort of thing existed any longer. To see it in the flesh from your hotel window: the cardboard shacks, with their bit of tin roofing laid on the top, and people hardly wearing any clothes, or shoes. You had to shut your curtains again, which might seem a terribly selfish thing to do, but it makes you think how lucky you are. When you see things like that you think, I've got nothing to complain about, absolutely nothing.

After a couple of years, I'd had enough of living out of a suitcase every fortnight. Don't get me wrong: it was fabulous. But the third year was like, 'Oh God, not here again,' and it sounds as if I'm being selfish or ungrateful for the opportunity but there was only two of us that looked after Frank. I was the day nurse and Robin was the night nurse, and there was another guy who was supposed to help but who was so unreliable. You'd get your days off, and then suddenly he would ring and say, 'I can't work tomorrow,' and you'd get dragged in again. You'd probably just done a nine-day stretch and be desperate for a day off, or a lie-in, or a change of scenery. It had nothing to do with not wanting to be around Frank, but all work and no play. So I resigned from Williams when this guy had let us down probably two or three times on the trot and I'd got totally fucked off. Suddenly the company car, the petrol allowance, the clothes, the salary meant absolutely nothing at all. I typed out my notice: 'Dear Frank, I wish to terminate my contract of employment with you...' and I thanked him for all the opportunities he'd given me and I said that if ever he was stuck for somebody for a couple of days, give me a ring. I had a phone call the next Monday morning, saying, 'I've got to go to the States. Can you be at the airport with your toothbrush in a couple of hours?' And so we were off again.

It was at that point I became self-employed, and have been ever since. I looked after Frank three days a week; I looked after a chap in Henley, who was a severe stroke victim; I had an HIV client in London; and I looked after a lady with spina bifida in Kingston upon Thames. I worked seven days a week, and two night shifts. Word got around that I could offer a really flexible nursing service. I could make it unique to the client, no odds. More and more people came to me and asked me to work for them. Then I bumped into this lady on my rounds. She was working for a nursing agency who she'd been messed around by, and I said to her, 'If you want to come and work with me, there's work for you tomorrow,' so she teamed up with me. Then social services approached me and asked if we could take on some of their clients, so I went to my accountant, formed a company, got a licence from the Department of Employment, and in our first year we turned over sixty grand, which may not seem a lot but it was considering it was a company that never planned to exist.

It got bigger and bigger and bigger. We were supplying the Nuffield in Oxford, the social services department, BUPA. Towards the end our contracts yielded something like £100,000-plus a year. But again, I was back to working seven days a week, all the hours God sent, and having to put up with all the crap, with people skiving off or saying, 'I haven't been paid,' because *we* hadn't been paid by the social services. We were doing in excess of ten grand a week for them at the time, and one week they sent me a cheque for £16: I said, 'I'm going to frame it.' On another occasion, I had to send a nurse to Oxford to pick up a cheque so we could pay everybody. That's how desperate it got. In the end, I sat at my desk at two o'clock one morning and thought, What am I doing? What am I achieving? I've lost sight of my goals. So I shut the door on the company, packed it in.

The day the company ceased trading I'd had my first lie-in for eighteen months. I used to have the phone going at six o'clock most mornings with a nurse saying, 'I don't feel very well,' and me saying, 'I feel sick too; fucking sick of you lot ringing up and telling me you're not well.' So I'd had a nice lie-in and I wandered into Wantage and just happened to see this house advertised in Adkin's window. I had no intention of buying a house at that time but when I walked in here, saw that fireplace, this stone floor and the Rayburn, I couldn't help myself, I just said, 'I'll buy it. I'll offer you the full market value and I'll confirm that in writing to you tomorrow.' It was mad. My company had just ceased trading and I'm offering to buy a house. I rang my bank manager and he came and had a look at it and said, 'It's lovely, Andrew. I'm quite happy to give you a mortgage,' and then we went and had a pie and a pint in the pub at the top of the road.

Now all I need is someone to share it with. I thought of going to the extremes of putting a thing in *The Times* or the *Telegraph*: '29-year-old professional, self-supporting, idyllic house in the country, looking for...' I thought of joining an agency. There's one called Gay Dinner Out in London, for people that have busy professional lives and find it difficult to meet people because they don't like going to pubs and clubs: this agency arranges smart dinner parties at restaurants, or a night out at the theatre, and they try and put you with people you're going to match with. I thought I ought to join that, and then I may be heading in the right direction for finding somebody.

When I find the right person, I will be very loyal to him. I'm the sort of person who will give somebody two hundred per cent but loyalty is important and if people ever abuse that, I always say, 'No offence, sausage, but it's your loss, not mine. I'll still carry on with my nice lifestyle, with my little cottage and my animals. You won't get a second go.' Because when you share such an intimate thing with an individual, it's special, it's not just something you give out.

I have a picture of a broken fence in my bedroom, and I explain it like this: the grass on one side of that fence is light green and the grass on the other side is dark green. I've been seeing someone recently and I don't quite trust him, and two things I pointed out to him the other night. I said, 'People always think the grass is greener and this picture here is a constant reminder that it is not.' I said, 'If you want to ruin what possibly could be with a one-night stand, you go and do it, but I won't let you make a fool of me.' Somebody else lived here for a while, it didn't work out, and I said, 'You listen to me. If you go behind my back, I will have a really bad job trying to explain to the judge how you fell down these stairs with a rolling-pin stuck out the back of your head.' I'm not like that at all, I was making a point, but if I give everything I have, I expect a little bit of respect and appreciation. Coming from a small community, and a family one, I've always been brought up with great traditional values, and playing around's not one of them.

I've felt pretty lonely recently. The end of last year was bad. Dark mornings and afternoons, and I couldn't get out of bed, and I just felt so heavy in my head all the time. My gran died a couple of years ago and I'd always been very close to her. She lived nearby and I spent an awful lot of time with her. When she died I felt really depressed. There was an extra big gap in my life and I think I was looking for something to fill it. I wasn't a big socialite but I started going out to clubs in London more often. One night I was in a gay club in Brixton called the Fridge and I got chatting to this guy. He wasn't somebody I was attracted to but he was a very kind chap and he said, 'On a Sunday after the Fridge, about ten or fifteen people come back to mine, and we sit drinking all afternoon and then we have a big roast dinner. If you want to come any time, let me know.'

So I went along and I met all these what I thought were nice people, and we went to the Fridge every week, and then I got a bit involved in the drug scene. These people would be taking Es and speed and stuff, and unfortunately I got entangled, every weekend I was taking E and speed. E is not physically addictive but it is mentally addictive and I got to the point where I thought that if I didn't have any speed or E I wasn't going to have a good time. I was away from here every Friday night until Sunday afternoon, and then I'd drive back, full of drugs, put my electric blanket on, have my food, drink my hot milk, take my tablets, have my bath with aromatherapy oils in it, and get into bed and sleep.

It must have been nearly a year I lived like that. And on Christmas Day 1996 I could pull my trousers over my hips with them done up, because that's how much weight I'd lost. Frank had asked a couple of people if I was all right because my eyes had gone back into my head, my cheeks had sunk, all my bones stuck out. Every weekend I was dancing fifteen, twenty hours at a stretch, going from one club to another. I totally wore myself out. So I haven't taken drugs for ages and I don't think I'll take them again. I think I lost the plot a bit at that time, but getting drawn into these groups, it happens without you seeing it happen. I'm resentful of that time now. It's like if you go out with somebody and it all ends in tears, you think, Bloody hell, I've wasted my time seeing them. That's how I felt about that little drugs era in my life.

Now my life's very quiet. Now I always say to people: 'How many people do you come across like me, who go to bed at ten o'clock and get up at six o'clock to let the chickens out?' People think that if you're gay you don't have family values, but I do. Most people don't have the family-orientated, quiet country lifestyle that I've put myself into. If I wasn't me, I'd be looking for somebody like me; somebody in a different bracket, not a run-of-the-mill ordinary gay person that frequented a pub every Tuesday and Friday, but somebody who's got more about them, who's got interests. So many people don't have any interests. They have no depth. I'm studying 'A' level Law at the moment because it's always interested me. I love classical music. I love operas. I enjoy reading. I've got an array of books: I buy books for reference. I suddenly think, Ooh, I must plant that rose, and I get my little rose book out to see what I'm supposed to be doing. I'm only working three days a week for Frank, and people say, 'Don't you get bored?' *Bored*?! There's so many things to do in my four days off I don't have time to fit them all in.

I've always got dreams. If I had the money I'd like to buy the cottage next door. I'd have an archway through there into the kitchen, and French doors going into the sitting room on the other side. The other house I'd do up, and put adverts in *The Times* and the *Telegraph* and have people from London come and rent it out for weekends. It would be nice, old-fashioned, white linen. A couple of pints of milk in the fridge, a nice, flamboyant country flower arrangement on the sideboard, and they'd come down, have a lovely time, and then you'd clean up and make the beds ready for the next person to come.

Having worked my nuts off for the past few years, it's nice to have a break and think about what I want. Whilst everybody else was out enjoying themselves in their twenties I was always working. Now I'm hanging about, taking a year out, or two. I'm doing a charity cycle ride in Cuba in the new year, raising money for the National Deaf Children's Society. I'm happy with Frank but I met the nephew to the Sultan of Brunei, and his PA has offered me a job, if I want one, so if Frank said he didn't need me any more I could ring up the Sultan's nephew and I could have a job.

I sometimes think it would be nice to catch up with Jason, have a chat. I've always said about it, and perhaps it's covering myself, that the grass was greener, or perhaps we just grew up. We were quite young when we got together: it's young to commit yourself to somebody at nineteen, twenty. And I always had so much ambition. I always wanted to *do* something, or *be* somebody, and he didn't, or at the time I got that impression and I felt it as a restriction. Perhaps I should be grateful for the time that we shared together and accept that that was all it was going to be. But it would be nice to catch up with him because since that time ... I mean, I've had relationships with people, and lived with them, or been with them for a year or so, but I don't ever remember having such a relationship with anybody else as I did with him. The depth of it. We lived out of each other's pockets. We did everything together. We thought the same, we liked the same things. It was like living as one person.

When we broke up, it was the time I was really busy with Frank and I got so lost in doing all of that that I don't think I really gave it much thought. But afterwards I wondered whether I'd done the right thing. I don't know if I can say I still regret splitting up but if I have to be true about my feelings, I suppose I could say I might do; I think I do. I'm not going to say that I *definitely* do because if he doesn't miss me it makes me look weak. But if he turned up and said, 'Why don't we do this all over again?' I'd probably say, 'You're on.' I'd probably jump at the opportunity. I have thought about writing to him but I'm worried that I might get laughed at, or he might just chuck it in the bin.

My trouble is I worry too much about what people think. I've always tried to do things that appear right, just on the basis of worrying what people might think if I did something else, and I guess it doesn't make me myself, does it. Jason's parents live locally and I think I once saw him driving his mother's car, and in that split second, my heart turned over. When I first moved here, he did come and say hello and spent five or ten minutes and then left, but I don't ever see him round the town, which I think is really strange, this being such a small place.

Bernard Humphries

Meeting Jack

I could've stayed at the Wantage Engineering Company all through the war. It was a reserved occupation because we were doing war work, but somehow, it might sound silly, I felt it was my duty to volunteer and fight for my country, that was my feelings then. All my mates had gone. So I applied to join the RAF and they asked me what I wanted to do. I said, 'I want to fly. I don't think I've got the qualifications to be a pilot or observer, but I think I could be an air gunner.' I felt pretty confident that I could pass the exams for that without too much trouble. The answer I received was, 'I'm sorry, we've got enough air crew, we badly need more ground staff. Would you consider that?' I said, 'No. If I can't fly, I'm not joining.' I was a bit headstrong in those days.

So I went back to work and about a month later I couldn't settle down: 'I think I'll join the navy.' So I applied and passed the medical. Then I had some papers through, the big brown envelope came through the door, Mother looked at it and she went into a flood of tears: 'He's joined up, he's going to join up!' My father said, 'What's all this about?' I said, 'I'm volunteering for the navy.' 'Whatever for?' he said. 'You've got a good job.' 'I feel I want to do more, I want to fight for my country. I'm up there, we're making armaments, it's true, but it's not really me, I want to do something else.' I wanted to travel, actually,

I wanted to see a bit of the world, that was partly it. He said, 'Well, it's up to you, if that's what you want to do, you go ahead and do it. You've got my blessing.'

I went to do my training at Great Malvern, and that was inoculations and square bashing. Then I got moved to Warrington, that was more square bashing, and they called some of us out to take the class of about fifty men. We had to shout the orders to the other men and tell them what to do. Well, to my surprise, because I was a very quiet chap, I kept myself to myself pretty much, when I got in front of those fifty men I could give them good precise orders and I enjoyed the result of it. They must have thought I was pretty good because they said, 'We need you. You're just the chap we want to train these lads as they come into the navy,' but I couldn't really see myself in Warrington for the rest of the war, however long that might be, shouting at young blokes who have just left their mums, and they're homesick. I couldn't bring myself to do that. I liked the discipline of it. I liked to get a gang of rookies into a fighting force, it seemed as though you were doing something, but I said no. I turned it down.

I then thought about flying again, I was interested in aircraft, so I decided to join the Fleet Air Arm, thinking I might have a chance to fly, which I did. I left the navy, joined the Fleet Air Arm, did six months' training at Henlow in Bedfordshire. I was courting Cissie then, and I used to come home every weekend. I changed the date on my pass every weekend until I rubbed a hole in it. I was really awful, breaking the rules all the way.

In the navy, we called our best suit our Number Ones, so I put my Number Ones on, overalls over the top, went into the mess and had tea. Then I took my overalls off and left the mess without trouble because we had a lot of dispersal camps at Henlow and you had to go through the main gate to get to them. Then it was down the road to the station at Henlow; into the train for King's Cross; I'd cross the lines at King's Cross to what was called the open platform, where they knew you'd had to surrender your ticket on the train, which I hadn't done, of course. There'd be two military policemen on the open platform, no ticket collector, so I had to watch them pretty carefully. When their backs were turned I went past them and whipped out my pay book to get through the barrier. If you were in the services, your pay book sometimes had a railway warrant in it, and there were so many people travelling in those days that they didn't have time to stop everybody.

Then it was over to Paddington, and on the train for Didcot. There was an old boy who used to collect the tickets at Didcot station and I used to give him two bob. Waiting at Didcot were the American lorries, because there was an American air base down here. I used to nip into one of the lorries. 'Can I have a lift?' 'Yeah, man, jump in.' In I got, in the dark, blackout, nearly home again. The American lorries went through Wantage marketplace, they didn't stop, and I just jumped out the back. I was young and agile then.

I got caught once in six months. Saturday mornings, we had fire drill, and they called everybody's name out. When it got to my name somebody would say 'Yes' for me, and the time I was caught they were a bit too fly, I suppose, and the petty officer must have guessed. When I got back to Henlow there were a couple of pickets on the camp gates: 'Humphries! Come on. Close arrest. You've had it.' I got jankers, it's a punishment in the navy. I had two weeks in the cookhouse, the idea being that every night you had to wash up dirty, greasy dishes. And every night for two weeks I went to the cookhouse and the Wrens used to cook me a lovely meal.

I finished my training at Henlow and went up to Scotland and waited for a foreign draft, where they assign you to a squadron to go abroad. So I'm up at HMS *Waxwing* at Dunfermline in Scotland, in the snow, in Nissen huts, bitterly cold, waiting to get a foreign draft any time, and my father wrote and told me my brother had joined the navy. I couldn't believe it. You had to be eighteen to join up, my brother was just turned seventeen. When I joined the navy, apparently he thought, If he can do it, I can. I didn't know anything about this until my father wrote and told me because I hadn't been home for six months. I thought about my brother and I thought, Well, he'll make it. My brother had nine lives. I could go on for ever about the scrapes he got into, the accidents he had.

Time went on and I was still training: firefighting, grenade courses, rifle shooting, really just something to do while we were waiting to form a squadron. And it got around to Christmas '43, and no hope of leave. Morale was pretty low. We all wanted to go home for Christmas but they wouldn't let us. I had a letter from my father and he told me my brother had been killed. He'd joined a ship as an Ordinary Seaman, they'd gone across the Atlantic to America with a convoy. He was on a corvette, which is an armed escort ship; corvettes sailed alongside frigates and destroyers. My brother's corvette came back to England, escorting a convoy. They sailed up the Clyde, and it was a very cold, foggy December afternoon, and he was ordered to lower the starboard accommodation ladder – that's a metal ladder that runs right down the side of the ship – because they were about to dock in the Clyde. He went and undid all the chains and the bolts, and the whole thing collapsed, taking him with it. We never did know what actually happened but I think he must have got caught up in the chains, and he went down into the water with it. The captain wrote to my father and said, 'We lowered a boat, we put an aircraft up, but there was no trace of him.'

So that was it, my brother was drowned. Well, of course this upset me, and I thought, Whatever's that done to my mother, this news? I applied to see the captain, I told him what had happened, showed him the letter and asked to go home. He said, 'Permission refused. You're waiting for a foreign draft and this is wartime. No chance.' I thought to myself, I don't know about that. I was very upset for my mother. So I applied to see the padre. Showed him the letter, told him everything. He said, 'I'm very sorry, but if the captain says no, I can't overrule him.' I said, 'Thank you very much,' picked up my case, put my hat on, and off I went, I deserted.

This is what I thought: I've got to see my mother. Here am I, going abroad, for how many years I've no idea. I shall never settle down if I don't see what things are like at home. I got on the train, no ticket again, all the way from Scotland, down to King's Cross, down to Didcot, home. My mother had had a heart attack when she got the news, she was under sedation. I spent the weekend at home. I knew I was in trouble from the moment I walked out so I thought I might as well spend a couple of days here. I didn't intend deserting, nothing of the kind, I wouldn't have done that, but I felt I could not leave the country without seeing my mother. Cissie and I were engaged that weekend, January 4th 1944.

When I got back to Edinburgh station, there they were, waiting for me, an armed guard. They moved in, fixed bayonets, close arrest. 'Name?' 'Humphries. FX 524247, sir.' 'Right, you've had it.' I knew I had. I was marched back to camp. It was January, I had my greatcoat on, I had my ditty case, that little case that a sailor has with all their gear in it. I had a cake that Cissie's mum had made. I marched into the Regulating Office, and the chief petty officer there, he *hated* deserters; so did I, I really did, I wouldn't tolerate a deserter, but in my opinion I was no deserter. But he *hated* deserters so he made me stand to attention, holding my case, for four hours. I don't know to this day how I did it. I was tired, I was hungry, I was apprehensive about what punishment I was going to get, and I just stood there for four hours without batting an eyelid.

People were walking round me in the office. One hour went by, then another, then another, and I thought, How long is this going to go on for? I suppose it'll go on until my knees buckle and I just drop. After four hours, the chief petty officer said, 'You're going to see the captain.' 'Yes, sir.' So I'm marched in to see the captain: Captain Cunningham, nice fellow he was, very nice chap. Off caps, stand to attention, give your name and number. 'Now then,' he says, 'what's all this about?' I said, 'Well, sir, I came in to see you a few days ago and asked permission to go home to see my mother.' 'Oh, yes, your brother was drowned.' 'Yes, sir.' 'Mmm, very unfortunate. Well, your foreign draft has not come through yet, which is fortunate for you, because had it come through you would have been a deserter, and I could have had you shot.' Which is absolutely true, he could. 'But,' he said, 'under the circumstances, I'm going to just forget the whole thing. I think you've had enough trauma for the last few days.'

The very next morning, my foreign draft came through. I've never felt so lucky in all my life. We moved off to Inverness, in the snow, two trains pulling us, and they had to get another one because the snow was absolutely terrible. At Inverness we had to get on a huge vessel, it was as black as ink, the only light was a tiny little light in the side of this huge ship, which turned out to be the *Louis Pasteur*, a French liner which had been commandeered for British troop movements and troop carrying. We didn't know where we were going, didn't know whether we were going east or west, or wherever. Then the captain gave us a talk. He said, 'Now you're on board, I can tell you where you're going. You're off to America.'

By this time, 1944, the war was so fierce that every aerodrome in the country was operational and there wasn't one left to do any training on. If there was, they were being bombed, so it was decided that the training would have to be done abroad, and our squadron did some of that training. The trainee observers came over from England, they were trained by us in America, and when they knew their job we flew on to an aircraft carrier and came home in convoy. As soon as we got home, off we went again and did the same thing. That's how I spent most of the war, backwards and forwards between Britain and America.

The first trip over to America we had dreadful, dreadful weather. I'd never been on a ship before so I thought it was normal, until I saw people kneeling and praying by the wheelhouse on deck. The first trip back was worse. We had to travel in convoy because of the German U-boats. We were in the middle of the convoy, merchantmen all round us, corvettes all round the outside of them, and we crossed the Atlantic as fast as the slowest ship would go. We had a terrible, terrible crossing. We had submarine scares, we had merchantmen going down all over the place, it was quite heartbreaking. And not only that, all the grain and everything that we were depending on in England had gone to the bottom of the ocean, and lives lost.

In America, unlike England in those days with the blackouts and rationing, it was a fairyland! The lights of Broadway, the skyscrapers, it was absolutely wonderful. I was stationed in New York for quite a long time, at Pier 92, and the first time I went out into New York I just walked and walked. I couldn't believe the skyscrapers. To say that now, it doesn't seem very much, but in those days we had nothing like it. I went up to the top of the Empire State Building, and I looked down and I saw the *Queen Mary* in dock, and she looked like a little matchbox. It was absolutely wonderful.

We were treated wonderfully well over there. When we had time off, if we wanted to go somewhere, all we had to do was go to the Union Jack Club on Fifth Avenue, and see what tickets were available. If we wanted to go to a show we could queue for tickets; if we wanted to go and meet people and have a meal with them, we could get meal tickets; all free. I got tickets one day to go with a mate to Madison Square Gardens, to see Woody Herman and his band, which was very popular, and we had front-row seats: there were American colonels, captains and lieutenants behind us. They gave us the *best* seats in the house, unlike in this country. If the Americans wanted to go to Wantage cinema, they'd be given some free tickets and they stood at the back.

I eventually went to Trinidad for nine months. I loved it there. Loved it. I landed on my twenty-first birthday, I was white then, it wasn't long before I was red. During my time in Trinidad, I had a week's leave due to me. I was in Piarco, which is in the north of Trinidad near the capital, Port of Spain, and I decided to travel down to the south of the island to have a look at the oil fields. I particularly wanted to see the Trinidad Asphalt Lake, which was world famous; that's where most of our asphalt comes from for the roads, even today. I left my camp with a week's leave pass, and another chap was walking out. 'Hello,' he said, 'what are you doing?' I said, 'I don't know really, I thought I would get on a jitney' – that's a bus – 'and go down to San Fernando. What are you doing?' 'Dunno. I think I'll come with you.' I said, 'OK.'

We introduced ourselves. Bernard Humphries. Jack Crooks. How d'you do. We got on the jitney and we started off down the island. We'd gone for some miles when a huge storm started, and I shall never forget it as long as I live. The wind got up to gale force, and a column of rain that was about a quarter of a mile wide and went right up into the sky came across the island, and we thought we were going to be in the middle of it. If we had been, that would have been the end of us. But it passed about half a mile away from us and it went right across the island and disappeared. That's just in passing, but it was the most wonderful sight I'd ever seen. We went down to San Fernando, got off the bus, and wondered what to do next. Jack said, 'Well, we'll have to find somewhere to stay for the week. Let's go to the Social Club in town.' We went there and asked if we could stay there for a week and they said, 'Yeah, sure.' They welcomed us really, because they didn't see many British sailors.

That evening, they had a party and a dance, and an Indian family came in, and we got talking to this chap, and he was such a nice chap; Eric. He told us that he had a clothing firm in San Fernando, and he introduced us to his wife and his daughter and two younger sons, real nice kids, and we got on really well together. He asked what we were doing and we said, 'We don't really know,' so he said, 'We're just about to go down to the beach,' which wasn't very far away, it being a small island. He said, 'We've decided to have a holiday and we're going to our bungalow on the beach. Would you like to come?' Wouldn't we! Of course we would.

He took us home, we had our supper. The next morning, he brought his old lorry, and we loaded the furniture on to it, and we loaded the cooker on to it, and we loaded everything on to it. Great excitement, the kids were excited, going on holiday, and we were really enjoying it. Eric said, 'Have we got everything, Momma?' She said, 'Oh yes. No! We haven't got the bath! We must get the bath!' So they rushed back and got a tin bath, which they put on the top of all the furniture and the pots and pans, and we were ready. 'Oh, we've forgotten the geese! We must take the geese!' So they got the geese, two geese, he tied some string round their necks and he slung them over this bath; one was hanging one side and one the other. I said, 'That's cruel, Eric!' 'No, we've done it before. They've got strong necks, they'll be all right.' And they were.

We went to their bungalow on the beach. Oh, it was wonderful. We started to unpack everything and Eric said, 'Right, Jack, you help the kids with the furniture. Bernard's coming with me.' 'Where are we going, Eric?' 'Ah, you'll see.' We tore along the beach in the lorry, it seemed for miles, and we went to a fish shop. Eric said a few words to the proprietor, and we waited for a little while, and then he said to me, 'There's some sacks under the passenger seat. Get the sacks from under the seat.' So we got the sacks out and Eric said, 'Lay them on the floor.' We laid them on the floor, and they brought a huge block of ice, we put it on the sacks, we wrapped it up, put it on the back of the lorry, and back we went. 'Momma!' said Eric. 'We've got the ice!' No fridge, you see, no electric or anything, just an ice box. We put the ice in, and d'you know that lasted a week in there. Eric put the fish in the ice box, and the meat. Everything.

We had a most wonderful week there. Jane, the daughter, she was a nice kid. She used to come in every night, and she would make sure we were wrapped round with the mosquito nets. She said, 'Daddy said I've got to make sure there are no holes in the mosquito nets, otherwise you're going to get bitten,' and she used to tuck in the mosquito nets. And one day Jack and I were out swimming in the sea, we were a long way out, we were both good swimmers, and we were really enjoying ourselves: we had a ball or something, and we were throwing this ball to each other; the kids were there and we were all having a good time. Suddenly Eric started swimming towards us with his hand up in the air. 'Jack! Bernard! Jack!' We thought, Something's gone wrong: 'Whatever's the matter, Eric?' He said, 'I've brought you something to eat. You must be hungry.' We were right out in the sea, and he gave Jack a huge piece of meat, and he gave me a piece too, and I'm swimming, and I said, 'What is it, Eric?' and he said, 'Toroughbred rat.' 'Oh!' I said. 'Eric, I can't eat rat. I'm sorry, Eric, I can't eat rat.' And he *laughed!* It was a chicken leg. He'd cooked a chicken, and he'd torn both legs off and brought one for Jack and one for me. I shall never forget it: 'Toroughbred rat.' It was a wonderful week.

We had our leave, we went back to Piarco, and I left Piarco when the war ended, VE Day. Jack and I said goodbye to each other, Jack went his way, I went mine, thinking, Well, that's it, we'll never see each other again. I sent a telegram to Cissie to say, 'When I get home, we'll get married. The war is over and now we can start our life.' But d'you know, the war is the most exciting thing that ever happened to me. Nothing else has come close to it for excitement.

The Christmas before last, a letter came through the door, and I opened it, and who should it be from but Jack Crooks. After forty-eight years! He lives in Hull, and his wife Ann said to him, 'We must get this room decorated, Jack.' So he said, 'OK, I'll call a decorator in.' The decorator said, 'I want everything moved. I can't decorate this room unless everything comes out.' So Jack said to Ann, 'Well, if we've got to take all the furniture out, let's make a good job of it and clear the drawers and sort everything out.' Lo and behold, he's clearing a drawer out when he finds a photograph of me and him in Trinidad, and I'd put my address on the back.

Jack said, 'I wonder if Bernard's still alive and kicking? Do you think I dare write to him?' Ann said, 'Well, why don't you take a chance?' He said, 'I don't want to upset anybody. Supposing he's been married and his widow gets a letter?' 'Do it,' said his wife. He did. The letter went to the chap who now lives in my parents' house, he brought it down to me, and that was the start of me and Jack getting together again. I wrote back to him, and then last August we arranged to meet. He suggested we met at Leicester service station, because that's about halfway down for him and up for me. My son Roger came with me. Roger was so pleased to meet him, he liked him straightaway, and Jack liked Roger. Roger took photographs of us and we had a lovely day. We correspond now and we're going to meet again.

Roger and I, we got there first, because Jack was held up in the traffic. Jack had told me what car he was driving and we sat in Leicester service station with the road running underneath, and we watched the road coming down from the north. We watched: 'Is that him?' 'No.' Is that him?' 'No.' 'Is that him?' 'That's him! That's Jack!' We saw him get in, park, and by then we were down the stairs. He's a Yorkshireman, Jack, they're very friendly, so he immediately started talking to somebody, and I walked up to him, and when he saw me, he just ... oh, he just hugged me! He's a big bloke, much bigger than me, and I said, 'This is my son,' and it was really wonderful. And we went to get a cup of tea, and we sat there, talking about our lives and everything, and when I looked at my watch, seven and a half hours had gone by.

Geoff Rice

Part One: Devastation

I still wonder why she married me. She was an English teacher in a grammar school when I met her, and she must have been pretty good because when she'd been there about three years they promoted her to Head of English, very young. She was always very quiet and she never said very much, but she knew where she was going, which makes me wonder what she saw in me. My background was poor and I left school when I was fourteen: Mary was a headmaster's daughter with a degree.

She was lovely. She was the best part of the partnership, without a doubt. She gave a great deal. She was unselfish. She was very gentle; never, never raised her voice. I can't remember ever having a disagreement with her. She knew what she wanted, but she was never aggressive in any sort of way, and if she saw that there was something that I was determined on, she would find a way of accommodating it. We never had any ... 'aggro' they say nowadays. We had a very peaceful life together. I was very lucky, I don't think many men have what I had.

We both had a very heavy cold, and mine cleared up, and she was left with a pain in the chest, and that was basically when it started. Very much to my surprise, because neither of us went to the doctor if we could avoid it, she went to the doctor. It turned out that she hadn't seen him for eleven years. The doctor said that it was pleurisy and gave her an antibiotic, which she didn't respond to. So he sent her for an X-ray, and then said he couldn't understand what the problem was, and he sent her to the chest unit in Oxford. They said she'd had a very slight heart attack, and they'd like to keep her in until they were certain that she was stable. They started her off on the medication they normally give heart people, and she recovered extremely well. Four weeks on, the consultant cut her medication and said that six weeks later she could go back to being an ordinary woman again. He thought she probably ought to keep taking aspirin for the rest of her life, and forget the rest.

Within three or four days she had another attack. We took her into the hospital and she never came home, and I still don't understand what happened. I'm not angry about it, just hurt. I think that if they had put their finger on what was wrong she might still be alive. She'd never had chest pains before, nothing, not a whisker. Her father died of a very similar thing but he was very ill. She wasn't. Her blood pressure was normal, she had no cholesterol problems, she'd never smoked, we had a healthy diet, we got plenty of exercise, she was bang on the right weight for her height. I'm sure it's easy to make mistakes like that with chest pains, but right up to the time she had that cold she was healthy, vigorous. She was physically better than I was. We used to go walking across the Ridgeway. She'd ride her bicycle up the hill to this house and she never got off. I found it difficult to believe that she had this problem. We certainly never got the message that she was possibly going to die. Her last weekend, the family all came to the hospital and she was as perky as you would like, you'd never think she was ill. Incredible. Then they did a by-pass operation and she never came round.

I am aware now that for several weeks afterwards I was suffering the symptoms of shock. Initially, you've got all these things that you've got to do, and I did them myself. You've got to go to the registrar and register the death and get the certificates, and then you've got all the nitty-gritty of the will and bank accounts. There's all the legal people you've got to write to. I tried to cover as much ground as I could, to stop them still writing to her, because I found it very hurtful to collect the post and find things addressed to her. There was the funeral to organize. The undertakers, they ask you awkward questions, they want you to choose the coffin and you don't really want to do that. 'What colour shall we put her in? Do you want us to take her rings off?' Oh dear, oh dear. I coped with all that without too much trouble simply because I don't think I was there, not really, I was half numb from the shock. You're in limbo. The enormity of the thing that's happened doesn't hit you, I don't think, until after the funeral when everybody's gone away and then you're suddenly alone. That was the worst, the very worst time.

It's very difficult to focus on what happens to you when something like this happens. Now, when I've got someone to talk to I'm all right, although I'm not sure I really need someone to talk to as such, I just need somebody here some of the time. If I'd just got someone around, I would feel a lot better. That's the worst thing to cope with: you're suddenly confronted with being alone, and you've got no one to talk to, no one to share things with, no one to touch ... to love. The world suddenly becomes very cold and unfriendly. The one thing I wanted to do when it first happened, I wanted to go with her, desperately. I didn't want to go on by myself. But I'm a Christian and faith is all about hope, isn't it, and I hope I shall be able to find her again. I had more difficulty than she did with faith. Her belief was very much more inside, I think. She knew where she was going.

Several people said to me afterwards, 'Oh, do come and have a meal with us,' but I didn't want to. I avoided company at first because I felt insecure. In the early days, it was extremely easy to set me off in tears, and all sorts of unlikely things will set you off, and I didn't want to break down in public. I have tried since then to become a lot more sociable, I've gone and sought the company of people. You sit here and get screwed up and think, I can't stand this any longer, and my reaction is to go and find somebody to talk to, about anything. That relieves the problem a bit. I sometimes go down to my neighbours and have a coffee, and we just sit and talk; and there's no end of people in town that I know. If I go down the street, I'll almost always find someone I can talk to, even just for a few minutes.

I've found my car absolutely invaluable. Almost straightaway the place where I could, not get away from it, not relax exactly, but where I could partly forget it, was in the car. I've found that, oddly, very helpful. I think it's because you have to concentrate on driving, and your mind can't wander off. To start with, my mind was constantly wandering off, and the hospital was a bad experience, I've always thought that the last thing I would want was to have someone like that die in hospital. I wanted to hold her. I wanted to have her, to hold her, and they just took her away and I couldn't get at her. I probably made a mistake when she was in the recovery unit, when to all intents and purposes she was dead, they were keeping her alive on a machine: I went to see her, and I don't think I should have done that because I've got that image in my mind, you know. That image was one of the things that kept coming back to me, and it was one of the things I could keep away in the car.

I've tried talking to other widowers but I haven't been very successful. They all want to tell you what to do, I find, and I've felt very strongly that their problem isn't the same as mine. It's a very personal thing, and whilst the bare facts are the same, the actual effect it has on people varies quite widely. Most people that I've talked to seem to think the way out of the problem is to join clubs and societies and get a lot of social activity, and I'm not very good at that kind of thing. I play in a band and they have been very good, one or two of them. One girl in particular I did find very helpful. She was pregnant and about to produce as Mary died, and I sort of identified with her as new life replacing old, and she's been very nice, she comes over sometimes, brings the baby. She was like a daughter for a little while. It's funny what you fasten on to, not in a calculated way, but you suddenly find yourself identifying with somebody or something that you wouldn't have expected.

The only thing you can do is to help yourself, really, when it comes to it. It affects everybody differently simply because the relationship between two people is very personal, and what happened to us through our long life together was different from what happened to anybody else. We were a very self-sufficient couple, had no close friends at all, and I think we were sufficiently different that it worked. She was academic and I was practical. We always had a slightly different view of things, which we exchanged. We had our little retreat here, and she sat over there and I sat over here, we often sat for hours and didn't speak to each other, but we had a near perfect understanding. I retired, then she retired, and we had almost eleven years when we did literally everything together.

Mary had a great influence on me. When we married, I was immature and brash. I played football, and I swore. I'm an entirely different sort of person than I would have been if I hadn't bumped into her, I'm quite sure of that. She was always calm. She had a civilizing influence. She wasn't demonstrative, she didn't embrace the children, she didn't do a lot of kissing and slopping, but they knew she loved them. To some extent, she was the same with me. We did it in private. We didn't go down the street arm in arm, but she was absolutely the only woman I ever touched, and I know I was the only man she ever touched, and that's something I treasure. I think you lose a great deal if you have a lot of partners. Perhaps I shouldn't say that. But when we got married we didn't know anything about the mechanics of sex at all and it didn't make any difference.

After Mary died I thought, Who can I go and talk to about where she's gone? I find it difficult to talk to the vicar. He didn't come and see me when Mary died, I felt it took him some time to get up here. I think that it's a mutual thing: he thinks I'm an awkward customer, and he's probably right. So I went to see a nun from the convent instead, Sister Jane Monica, and she said, 'Mary's watching you, you know, she's all around you,' and I can't see that somehow. She's certainly all around me with all the associations and everything, but her spirit? I don't know.

That is one of the problems, perhaps, that a man has in this situation that a woman doesn't have, in that everything I've had to handle has associations. I had quite a problem getting to grips in the kitchen because everything in there was hers, it all had her fingerprints on it. You keep finding things. She was a great one at writing little notes, everywhere there's little notes she wrote. Sometimes you get a little joy out of these little notes, and then sometimes it has the other effect.

And then there's this house. We've never lived anywhere else, which is something of a difficulty for me now because I'm a bit isolated. That's a dilemma, because I don't really want to destroy this, it would be very difficult for me to move. There's so much here which ... well, it's us. On the other hand, what would happen if I slipped up on the ice and broke my leg? I'm independent, I don't like the idea of having to fall back on the neighbours, my daughter Eleanor's a very long way away, and she'd be the person who'd want to pick up the pieces.

It's difficult to see forward in my situation at the moment. I'm not doing anything very positive, not in terms of future, anyway. All I'm doing, really, is feeding myself, keeping myself clean, keeping my house clean. You tend to get very self-centred, you're doing everything for yourself, and I don't like that very much. Neither do I seem to want to get tied down. If you start doing something regular, you quickly get yourself into a routine which you can't break very well. Up to now, I have found that I need to get away, and I've got myself organized so that I'm going to Malta this coming week, for a fortnight; I may well have some French visitors in April; I'm going to Brittany in May. June I'm going to Germany. July, a German family I know are coming to stay here. August, I'm going to France with my daughter and her family, and the end of September I'm going to Germany again with friends.

March the 8th Mary died, so we're pushing up towards a year. The longest year of my life. In the short term, I'm trying to keep myself sane. The long-term future ... I can't see the long-term future at the moment. It does look bleak, and I'm not really sure how it can get any less bleak, not really. I don't know. I've thought, several times, that I need to do something positive to make the future look less bleak.

Joe Stokes

Introducing the Squid

The less you mess around with fish, the better. All the majority of my customers do with fish is put it in the microwave. Me personally, what I like to do is get a bit of skate, put it in the oven in tinfoil with black pepper and butter and it's done. It only takes ten minutes. Have it with bread and butter. Beautiful.

My favourite fish is skate. Skate, rock, tuna or swordfish. I like fish without bones, myself. Skate's got bones but they're flat bones through the middle so you can just scrape the meat off, turn it over, do the other side. And they're not splintery bones either, they're very soft bones, you can eat the bones on skate. Rock's the same, that's only got one bone through the middle. And tuna and swordfish is all filleted, so there's no problem with that.

I can't handle bones. I mean, I love smoked fish as well, it ain't too bad, but the black bream and the bass and snappers, they've got quite a few bones, little bones, and they don't appeal. I eat them but not if I can help it. Like when people come to the stall and they say, 'Oh, what are them red snappers like?' I say, 'Look, they're beautiful fish. If you can handle bones, try them. If you can't handle bones, don't have them.' Because it ain't worth sending them home with two fish that's gonna cost them six, seven quid, and they're gonna get a load of bones in their mouth and throw it all away. I'd rather them have something like a couple of nice lemon soles, and know that they're gonna enjoy them. I want my customers to be happy.

The most popular fish, without a doubt, is cod. Always has been. You've always got your fresh cod fillet, then your haddock fillet, plaice fillets, your herrings, your mackerel, your rainbow trout, all your smoked fish; kippers, haddock. Salmon's probably one of the most staple fish out the lot, especially through the summer. In the summer, I have all whole salmon up here and a big show of salmon steaks and fillets; salmon, trout and snappers, things like that for barbecuing. See, that's another thing: people now, they stick everything on the barbecue, and fish is ideal because it barbecues really well. And then you've got a little bit of shellfish and that, different stuff to what people used to eat. Before I come here, they'd never seen squid in Wantage. Didn't know what it was. But so many people go abroad now, especially younger people, and we eat different fish, we see them in Portugal and places like that. Black bream, sea bass, fresh swordfish: that's very popular, swordfish is. It's expensive, £5.95 a pound, but that's all filleted, and that's fresh, not frozen. The frozen is cheaper but it's different. That sort of fish, you've gotta have it fresh because otherwise it slaughters it. It's sacrilege to freeze anything like that.

This is the only outdoor market I do now. I used to work five, six days a week outdoors. Now I work here once a week, and I've got a market in Watford where I'm at three days a week: Tuesday, Friday, Saturday. On a Thursday I do a bit of wholesale, which is quite a short day for me, it's only about thirteen hours. The rest of the week I get up at half two, leave my house by quarter to three, go to Billingsgate, buy my fish. By the time I've loaded up it's usually about quarter to six, drive to my stall in Watford, or over here to Wantage, unload, set up the stall, work all day, do my deliveries and whatever. I get home about quarter past six, have a bath and do the takings. Normally finish about half seven.

This stall's a bit different from Watford. For here I get a lot of salmon, sea bass, mussels, cultivated oysters sometimes. I can buy wild mussels but the Norfolk mussels are so much better, really nice.

They've still got barnacles on them but they're not overcleaned. The majority of mussels are. Clean black-shelled mussels, they've usually got no flavour to them because they're so purified. And look, here's an uncoloured smoked cod. That's what they look like natural, without any added colour, when they come off the smoking rails. I sell the fillets like that but most popular is the bright yellow. In Birmingham they sell it orange, because that's what people have been brought up to eat. These are good too, these little sea bass. A nice way of doing them is just to grill them with a little bit of lemon and butter; or steam them with ginger and spring onion's nice. They're nice, sea bass, beautiful.

My sister and brother-in-law, they started up in the fish trade in Aylesbury sixteen years ago, and I worked for them. I left school when I was about thirteen. We had a mutual agreement with the School Board that I was never gonna take an exam because I always used to work, and I've never took no exams. The only thing I was good at at school was maths and PE: it's the size of me; I used to throw the shot and that, for all the counties, when I was younger.

I worked for my sister until I was about seventeen, then I come here with my brother-in-law. He started this market on a Wednesday, must have been about twelve years ago. The last two and a half years it's been me on my own because my brother-in-law and sister, they sold up and went to South Africa; they'd had enough, really. They've got a lovely big place out there. My brother-in-law game-fishes now. He takes people out fishing. He's got one of these big boats, I think it's fifty foot, a marlin, whatever they call them, with all the rods hanging out the back and that, goes tuna fishing, shark fishing. Beautiful boat. I'd like to go out there, and it ain't gonna cost me nothing because it's only the air fare and that's it, but it's having the time off. I very rarely have holidays. Christmas is terrible. Sitting around doing bugger all, isn't it. I have a week off at Christmas and that does me. It's no good for my wife, though, there ain't no family life, that's the trouble. I'm always working.

Here you are, this is a fish you wanna see. It's called espada, 'the silver sabre', from Lisbon. Very, very deep-water fish. Like my wife, these are, ugly and vicious! English people don't like this fish, it's not the fish they know. There you go, six nice espadas, nine and a half kilo. They're £55 altogether. They're for Luis. Luis's from the fish and chip shop down the road, Luis and Gillian. They're good customers of mine. Look, nice bit of haddock roe over here, as well. They're lovely. Oh, the flavour of them's beautiful! You can shallow fry them or you can just put them in a colander and blanch them with a kettle of water, and then eat them as they are. That's all you gotta do.

I don't think I'll retire as quick as my brother-in-law and sister did, because he retired at thirty-five and I just really enjoy work, I always have done. I feel guilty if I'm not at work. I don't know why, I just do. And I'm not being funny, but this is not like a boring job where you just go to one office all the time, sit there, look at a computer. I'm supposed to be getting a computer soon but I don't think I want to, really. I don't really need one. My son Luke, he's coming up nine years old, he could tell you anything about computers, anything you want. Even my daughter, Sanchez, she's only coming up five and she knows how to turn one on and do a few keys and whatever. They have to now. If they don't know about computers, they ain't gonna know about nothing.

Of course, you work hard, the money's good. Our turnover last year — that's this stall, my little bit of wholesale that I do, and my other stall — was roughly £365,000. It soon goes. I've got to buy the fish, pay the bills and the bloody tax man. Still, for a one-man band this is a very good market. It's amazing, though; the feller who buys for Harrods — he's a coloured feller, actually — he's up in Billingsgate and he buys off exactly the same people I buy off. He buys the same cod as I buy, I'm £2.95 a pound and I wouldn't be surprised if they ain't £5.80 a pound with it in Harrods. £18 a pound they charge for turbot: I charge £5.50, £6.50 maximum, depending what it cost me to buy.

I wouldn't wanna work somewhere like that. I don't know all my customers' first names, though I know quite a few, but I could tell you who are my customers and who ain't in Wantage if they was all in a big field. I like Wantage. As long as there's fish to sell, I shall be here, because I think the customers really would miss this stall as much as I'd miss Wantage. It's the sort of place I'd like to live later on in life. I like the surrounding areas. I like the Downs, and I like everything to do with the racehorses and that: I serve quite a few trainers here. I serve a lot of lords and ladies, too, and obviously they speak different English to what I speak but I get on very well with them. Very nice people. I couldn't say that there's one customer that I don't like serving here.

So I'd like to live here, but only if I could retire, which I don't think I ever will be able to, but everyone's gotta have a little dream, haven't they. My ideal dream would be to own my own racing stud. I'd love all that. My wife loves Watford, because that's where she was born and bred, and all her family live round Watford. Where we are is very quiet. Where we live, it's not massive gardens or anything, but we face out on to a country park, well, it's green belt, fields and that, which is nice. But I'd like to be here or somewhere like it. I'd have to win the lottery first. It's the same old thing, isn't it, it always boils down to money. Everything in this life boils down to money, doesn't it, I'm afraid. You can be the nicest person in the world, but if you've got no money you can't do nothing and nobody wants you.

Thomas Loyd

Link in a Chain

It was always rather put to me that it wasn't an absolute requirement of life that I was going to be here, but it was more than strongly hinted that this was what was expected of me. Without that proviso, I might well have gone off and done other things. As it was, having left school, I travelled a bit, went to Cirencester Agriculture College, and then based myself here at Lockinge. I did do other things elsewhere but more or less most of my life has been based on the estate.

Actually, I suppose I used it to my advantage. To be honest, it rather encouraged a degree – not of laziness, that's the wrong word, but it certainly made me feel that this was my destiny. It meant that there were times when I felt I hadn't got the time to get stuck into other things, and one's always got some regrets about not doing other things. I mean, I never even thought about a City career, I never thought about anything else, properly. I played around with a video-production company for a bit, and latterly I set up a record company, but I did that very much knowing that I had this to come back to and that records were just another thing to do.

I was twenty-one when I came back to the estate and I got married in 1984, when I was twenty-five, and after that I was pretty heavily involved with the farm here. I mean, there was a very good management team, and they could and did do very well without me being around, but it was still pretty much a full-time job. The farm I'm referring to is the 'in-hand' farm here: you appreciate that the estate's got three or four let farms, but the 'in-hand' farm is what we farm ourselves, which is two and a half thousand acres of mixed arable and dairy, with pigs. There is still a very good management team but it's smaller now. In the beginning, I had an arable manager under me, and a livestock manager, and the estate manager was still very involved. My uncle used to say, 'Too many chiefs and not enough Indians': whether that was a correct assessment or not, I'm not sure, but there certainly were plenty of us involved.

The estate overall is seven thousand acres. Lockinge and Ardington are the main villages but we've got cottages and a let farm in Farnborough, likewise in West Ilsley, and some cottages in East Ilsley, so we have our influence; the evil empire still stretches over several villages! In very round terms, there are a hundred houses, of which fifty are owned by the Lockinge Trust, and another fifty by the Village Housing Charitable Trust. Those houses are principally for retired people but as you can appreciate, we don't have fifty retired farm workers at any given time so they get let to 'people in necessitous circumstances', which doesn't necessarily mean people who are down on their luck so much as people who need to live in the village because they work here. And if houses are sold, the money's not mine. It's held in trust so that I, and my children after me, will be controlled. I always used to wonder why was it ever done like that. Was it to prevent a mad son flogging everything and spending it all on cocaine, or was it for tax reasons? It's a bit of both, is the answer. This country is full of people in my position; well, not full of people in my position, but most of the landed estates in this country would be held under trust in one way or the other.

I like to think that when I took over the running of the estate from my father I was sort of in charge, but it was much more me learning, and it was a very good way of learning. It had moments of being really quite hard work. But while I certainly drove the odd tractor and combine and what have you, I couldn't claim to be a farmer who's as technically knowledgeable, say, as Joanna Castle down the road: she's particularly knowledgeable about her livestock. With a fairly large farming set-up, whoever is the manager at any time gets stuck in at a practical level because they are day-to-day farming people, and I can't claim to have been that. I made the mistake, actually, of calling myself 'farm manager' to begin with. I should actually have just been bolder about it and said, 'I am the farmer. This is my property. I'm very lucky,' but I tended to always rather hide behind the term 'farm manager'. It was probably dreadful insecurity.

I think a lot of people in my position, at my age, might have done the same thing. I think it comes with age, actually, an ability to stand up and say, 'Actually I am very lucky. I have got this.' And so when I say, 'I was running the farm,' I suppose what I was doing was showing a healthy active interest in the farming business; directing it, certainly, but very much relying on others for management skills. And where I was involved heavily with the stocking of the livestock and the cropping and all the rest of it, I had my hand held. I can't claim otherwise. I wouldn't wish to make it sound like I'm a whizz-kid farmer. I'm a very lucky farm and estate owner.

One of the reasons I moved sideways was that I felt I needed to get to know about the other aspects of running the estate, like our property letting, particularly industrial and office development lettings, which are hugely important parts of the business. In the 1970s, my father and the then estate manager, John Haigh, recognized that in order to keep the village communities alive we needed to do something more than just allow our desire, and market forces, to keep things going. The most logical thing to do would have been to sell the estate houses off as they became vacant, or to let them at the market rate to whoever was available, but we thought if we did that we'd just get weekenders. As you appreciate, we're very near to London and could so easily become dormitory villages. So we thought by introducing industry into the villages we would attract people who wanted to work here; and if they worked here their social life would also be here, they'd use the pub, the church, the school, and centre their whole world around here.

It's been very successful. We concentrated on attracting craft industries to start with, and looking back on it, we were glad we did. I mean, it would have been such a huge leap of faith to have gone from a whole lot of tumbledown farm buildings to the high-tech offices that we now have, so it had to be a natural progression, really. We've still got some of those original people with us. We still have a potter and a furniture restorer. We've still got a picture-framer. The people who have arrived since have tended to be more office based but not exclusively so. We've got a car-repair business, panel beaters. We're just doing up some offices at the moment for a firm of head-hunters, and we've got a marketing consultant down at Home Farm who rents quite a considerable space off us.

I don't say I'm a cutting-edge type of person, and I haven't done anything very radical, but I've tried to plan ahead. There's certainly huge pressure on more housing. We know that and we've identified the need for possibly eleven or twelve new houses only, in the next ten years, and that must be quite a relief to the planners, that we're not talking to Barrett Homes. I think Joanna and David Castle were very brave with their development, because you're never going to get thanked for allowing people to build houses on your land. You're going to get attacked. But, you know, blood's thicker than water, and ultimately your family, your very survival, depends on realizing your assets, and that's particularly true for farmers right now.

The other classic one is selling a painting. You suddenly realize that there's a painting hanging on the wall which is just too valuable to hang on the wall any more and you either, as we have done with several paintings, lend them to a gallery, or you say, 'Better sold.' And you do feel you're letting down family. You're not so much letting down local people, because you're not actually blighting their landscape, but you feel you're letting down your forebears, which is unhealthy because I'd like to think if I've bought works of art and my children don't like them, or my grandchildren don't like them, I don't want them to get strung up about it. If I was to sell a painting and spend all the money on a Ferrari, that's rather a different matter. I think one's got to be responsible, in respect of the memory of those who went before me, and in respect of those that come after me. But sometimes, when we're redeploying family and estate assets generally, I think of Lord and Lady Wantage looking down on us and I'd like to think they'd be saying, 'Why are they getting so strung up about it? If they no longer want it, or need it, don't worry about it!'

My artistic taste goes all over the place at the moment. At the moment, I like modern hard-hitting sculpture, and I've got some Elizabeth Frinks. I sometimes struggle with modern hard-hitting paintings, to be really honest. It's such a big term isn't it, 'modern art', and sometimes I think, Do I like this because it's clever to like it or do I *really* like it? Or do I like it because it's a pretty picture and pretty colours and nice patterns even if I don't know what it's supposed to be? And I think there's nothing wrong with that. You can look at a beautiful Turner, or a beautiful Constable, or a beautiful Patrick Heron, or a beautiful Ben Nicholson, and you may come away with exactly the same feeling; so what's the difference, in a way? If, at the end of the day, the person who looks at the painting has the same feel-good feeling from it, then that work of art has done its trick. So I'm very sort of open-minded about art. I struggle with some of the avant-garde stuff: I can't see myself ever having a pickled shark in the drawing room. But I enjoy collecting paintings and sculpture, because we have the Loyd Collection of Paintings here, and it's quite nice to keep that going, and keep it contemporary.

I'm a great believer in that sort of art being seen by lots of people, actually. I'd like to have the Frinks further away from the house, but I can't, for insurance reasons. I really passionately believe people ought to have access to art in everyday life, which they're missing now. They used to. If you think about it, way back when art was purely telling a story, most typically the Bible story, art was hanging in churches, and more people went to churches and saw these things. Now you have to make a conscious effort to go to an art gallery, or you might be lucky enough to have it yourself in your own house, but people don't come across art in their everyday lives like they used to. I don't know how you get round that. I mean, do we hang paintings in McDonald's? And service stations? Probably not. I don't know how you do it, but I think there's a great challenge out there to introduce art into everyday lives: I certainly try to make the art I own accessible to the community here.

As well as redeploying assets, I've tried to be aware of how people's working patterns have changed, and I've tried to respond to that. I've certainly encouraged teleworking here. You can now think globally in your work, which you can do from home on your computer and telephone wires, and then – and it's a rather cosy feeling – you can go off and buy a cake from Mrs Muggins down the road. I think that is a definite trend. It satisfies one's desire to be big and buzzy and dealing with the whole world but at the same time it keeps your roots and your feet on the ground, and I suppose we've attracted people here on that basis without ever quite defining it so philosophically. We've defined it in terms of this being a nice place to work: we've got this beautiful countryside, easy parking, all the practical things as well as quality of life.

I do feel proud of it. There are about four hundred people living in the villages and I think there's about three hundred full-time jobs, including the estate employees and some people who commute in. It's put a completely different slant on the village community because hopefully we've moved away from some feudal feeling, if ever that really did exist in my lifetime, to one where people feel they belong. I think the self-conscious feeling of wanting to call myself a farm manager and not a lucky landowner was partly due to my feeling, 'Gosh, people don't really want Lockinge referred to as an estate because they run their own businesses here, they live here, and they are their own bosses. They might be renting a house off us, or a business off us, but they don't particularly want to be forever reminded that it's an estate.' And I've rather changed that now. I think people *do* want a feeling of belonging. After all, when you say you live at Lockinge or

Ardington that is as much a corporate identity as Coca-Cola, maybe. It's a feeling of belonging, not being owned by someone, and I think I might have got it very wrong in the past, I think I rather misinterpreted what people would like from a community. I think if people like living in a community, then that community has got to have a name.

The names Lockinge and Ardington are synonymous with the estate, but I like to think they're also synonymous with quality. Lockinge and Ardington are villages that are well kept. We don't always win the Best-Kept Village Competition, which we did a couple of years ago in Ardington, but they are well looked after, the properties are well maintained. The village facilities are still here. There is a good pub serving good food. There's a shop. There's a post office. Everything's happening here. The Loyd Lindsay Room is a conference hall. It's nice to think that people can exist now without leaving the villages. You don't *have* to go off to do your shopping elsewhere, and if you want to meet people, there are people here and it's a great place to live.

A lot of the estate's success is down to my father. He's always been incredibly far-sighted, so when the new estate manager, Julian Sayers, took over two years ago, we decided to look ahead by setting up a new ten-year plan. That was done with a huge amount of consultation with people in the villages. We encouraged their consideration and we jolly well got it. People set up groups, and put in a lot of hours, and came up with some very interesting ideas which we fed together in a plan, and last week we presented it to the district council with a view to them maybe including it in *their* next ten-year plan. That happened because people wanted to do it. There wasn't the feeling that there's no point getting involved because the estate's going to do it anyway, which would have been very depressing to hear. It was: 'Maybe they really mean it. Maybe it really is our community. Maybe we really can shape it.' And I think we've proved that because we've accepted their ideas and put them forward, not as our own but as everyone's.

Now there's a great feeling of community, more than I would ever have imagined we'd have felt at the turn of this new century, and I hope people feel less and less apart from us as a family. I hope so.

I mean, there's bound to be difference. There's always going to be an 'us and them' thing in this country, be it through inherited wealth, in our case, or through people who have made it on their own, but I think class is quite unhealthy. I think it will always be there but I think it's getting less. I think that class has been eroded by what people wear. We all tend to wear the same things now, which is very good, and clothes used to tell you a lot about someone, and they don't now. And a lot of it, I always think, comes down to social life. I think what I do in my social life is probably not a million miles removed from what other people do, and I feel that probably has done more, and will continue to do more, to erode this feeling of 'us and them' throughout society than almost anything else.

We are now in the height of 'the Season'. It was Ascot last week. I certainly didn't go to it, I really can't stand it. And I'm not saying I'm a complete Blair-babe, New Britain or whatever, but there are certain things that I can't really be doing with, and I think they are being eroded; or maybe the people doing them are taking themselves less seriously. I don't think you should mock and sneer at people, and if people choose to enjoy themselves spending money, that's up to them, but I think they should be able to laugh at themselves while they do it. I think people take themselves too seriously generally. But when I walk round the village, people don't doff their cap so much nowadays as they might have done in the past, and I've always been known by my Christian name. It sounds ridiculous to make that point but it wasn't that long ago when that wouldn't have been the case. And the younger people who have come into the village more recently would be less inclined to automatically call my father Mr Loyd, so that's a sign that generally people are becoming less formal.

Having said all of that, I've been doing this now for goodness knows how many years and a lot of that time has been spent thinking, My goodness! How do I describe myself? How do we describe this business? What are we? It's a very difficult one. To call oneself 'a landowner' isn't great. It doesn't imply a job, it implies privilege. I can't describe myself as 'a farmer' as such, but if I start describing myself as someone who manages a country estate – or a rural business unit, to use the modern euphemism – I trip over my words. It's unfortunate, there is no easy generic term that describes what I do without implying something that's very outdated or very privileged.

I used to be very embarrassed about that. I mean, I don't deny that I am very privileged but it would be nice to have a job description that would reflect the work and the responsibility. I always joke; I say I think it's easier if you're a duke, because no one really questions a duke, but there's no similar word for me that I can fall back on. I wish someone would help me out on that. When I was doing the record company, for example, I found it fascinated people at a dinner party, and I was only a backer, basically. We only ever made one record and that never got released, but it was much easier to describe, and for people to relate to.

I did rather enjoy the record business, actually. I rather liked the lifestyle. I always say that if I was a complete workaholic, if you want to work all the hours God gives, and you want to be based in Oxfordshire, then combine agriculture with a record company and you have got guaranteed twenty-four-hour-a-day work. You get up early here, and no one in your record business is going to be awake until lunchtime, and they won't make any sense until teatime, by which time you've finished on the farm. Get on a train, nip up to London, and work through until it's time to start work again on the farm the next morning. If you're a complete workaholic, those are the two best trades you could combine! Possibly I'll have a go at something else again, but not here, because I'd do the villages a disservice if I carried out all my experiments here. The other reason for doing things elsewhere is that if you make a monkey of things here it's forever going to haunt you.

I've two daughters and a son, and obviously I think about it a lot, as to what I see them doing in the future. I would expect it should be my son only who runs the estate, and if one of my daughters wanted to do so it would be a problem, but I see no reason why all three couldn't be at least supported by it. I mean, my daughters aren't going to be cut off without a penny, but in terms of who has overall responsibility here, it would be my son, if indeed overall responsibility is something that is needed then. It might not be. It's possible that by then the estate will no longer need a chinless wonder cruising around with his flat cap on.

In fact, I don't feel this estate needs a figurehead so much even now. There are things which one person has to make a decision on, and that's what I'm here to do. I mean, you can't have a gathering of village elders to decide whether a certain bit of grass should be cut. But by the time my son takes over, it'll be easier for him to dip in and out of this place without feeling he's letting it down. I think that my father certainly felt that he sort of let the place down if he wasn't here. I feel it less. I don't think my constant presence is expected any more, or maybe people have got used to the fact that I do occasionally disappear off to London and do other things. After all, my son could be checking on the place via a modem in San Francisco, so there's no reason why a place like Lockinge couldn't be partially run like that, in the same way everyone else runs other businesses.

Most of the time I love it here. There are times when I look at the list of things I should be doing, or things that are worrying me, and I think, Would it not be wonderful to be teleworking in a nice village, where I'm known, and I know everyone else, but I'm not responsible? But then I think it's wonderful to have this feeling of responsibility. There's nothing burdensome about it most of the time, just occasionally it gets too much and one longs for a simpler life. It's certainly very cosy. I can't pretend otherwise. It's extremely cosy, and I'm sure those that haven't got it would see it as nothing but a plus. You may at times resent it, you may fight against it, but I think if, literally from the cradle, you have instilled in you this feeling of responsibility, then you are likely to do a good job. You can be destined, if you like, to run a family business of any sort: you could be a family of brewers; you could have inherited a title that means you're going to sit in the House of Lords. I mean, there are those that fritter away all the family cash, but if you've always had that sense of responsibility drummed into you, there is generally this British attitude: 'Right. This is my destiny. I'm jolly well going to do it properly.'

I feel much more a link in a chain now that I've got my own children. There are occasions, as I see my son growing up, when I think to myself: Thomas, be careful of that. But I also feel that while the chain itself isn't weakening, the level of responsibility is definitely changing, because there are less people directly dependent on my sanity than there would have been dependent on my father's sanity, or indeed my grandfather's, and I think that's bound to have an effect in my son's lifetime, and my grandchildren's. I hope they'll feel a sense of belonging if they choose to stay here and do this, but I imagine they should feel less put upon, less watched over the whole time, less scrutinized for good behaviour, which I'd like to think I don't pay much attention to, even though I do; because we all do, we all care what people think of us, desperately.

It's got much easier for me here recently, since I met my girlfriend. My marriage broke up, and although it was quite amicable, it made a difference because this isn't a job for a bachelor, really. It's hard work and it's easier if you can go home and there's someone to talk to about things, who understands the pressures of the place. There were some difficult times in that respect. For a while it was sort of a bit lonely, if you know what I mean.

Vic Brown

Harnessed

I was born early in the morning, in a heatwave, a terrible heatwave, Father told me. And when Mother went into labour, very early in the morning, he had to ride his bike two miles to the next village to knock up the doctor, who had to knock up his son to go up the field and catch the pony, harness it and put it in the trap. Well, Father cycled back like mad to say the doctor's coming and he beat him to it. Then the doctor arrived and delivered these two little babies. The other one was dead. He thought I wouldn't last five minutes: I was only two pounds four ounces, and weakly.

'Let's see what we've got here,' he said. 'Well, well, it's trying to breathe.' So they got a shoebox and put some cotton wool in it and laid me in that. And he said, 'Don't try and bathe it, just wipe it over with cotton wool. And feed it when it cries. But don't get to love it too much because it won't last seven days.' When I lasted seven days, he said, 'Seven weeks.' And when it was seven weeks, he said, 'Seven years.' And he kept on saying I wasn't going to last much longer till the day he died.

We lived in this little country cottage with just oil lamps and candles. It was a very rural life. Although we'd moved to Wantage by then, I remember when Beulah and I were courting and she first came to supper my mother produced rook and lamb-tail pie. Every spring, the farmers shot the rooks and cut the lambs' tails to stop the maggots getting underneath, and then they made them into pies. They used to just use the breast of the rook, the back was too bitter to eat. The lambs' tails looked a bit stringy but they were very tasty. I tried shaving them with a razor once, to save skinning them, but it blunted the razor.

My family were blacksmiths. Blacksmiths weren't well off in money but they were fairly well off in kind. The blacksmith wouldn't feel poverty to the extent that a town labourer would because he had access to milk, he had access to rabbits. Often a pig was shared between two families: you fed it on two lots of scraps and then when it was slaughtered you had half the pig each. Every bit was used. You cured the bacon, you had the pork and you made brawn and chitterlings – that's the intestines. They weren't terribly nice to look at but it was tasty and it was a meal. And if you worked for a big farmer like Mr Loyd you had a brace of pheasants when he went shooting. We always had firewood delivered too, from the estate. And because they were working on the land, when the war came blacksmiths didn't have to go in the army if they didn't want to.

I came to this town when I was seventeen, one year before the war started. I'm not local: I come from the village of Compton, twelve and a quarter miles away. And honestly, it might as well have been another country here, because I'd never even visited Wantage before. My father was Compton born and bred. There's a picture up there on the wall, of his father and his mother and all their twelve sons, on one photograph. All twelve of them fought in the Great War and my dad had a lucky escape. My granddad had sciatica, and the authorities said that the old man could have one son back to work as a blacksmith, to keep the agricultural horses going. My dad was in France and two days before Passchendaele, when they were establishing the Machine-Gun Corps to be the front-runners and probably get killed, my dad's name was called out and they told him he was coming back to England to shoe horses. He had to walk home. He walked all through Ypres when it was being shelled and all the way to Calais. He walked right across France. His mates were all killed at Passchendaele.

I didn't want to be a blacksmith. I wanted to be a doctor. But my trouble was, I was a weakling, and on the doctor's advice I didn't go to school in the winter. In the winter I was kept in one temperature. I was allowed downstairs but I didn't go out. The doctor thought if I did I'd get rheumatic fever. I grew tall but I was very thin and weedy. There was nothing of me. Also on that doctor's advice, although I wore short trousers, he made me wear long socks that covered my knees: 'You must never let his knees be bare.' Oh, the agony I went through as a boy with long girls' socks on! I used to roll them down when no one was looking and then get a good hiding for it. And my dad was the old-fashioned type, so that although I got nearly six foot he still wouldn't let me wear long trousers. He said, 'When he's a man and is earning his own money, he can wear a man's trousers. Until then, if he's living at my expense, he'll wear boys' trousers.'

In the winter, I read and read and read. I read a lot of history and I knew *Treasure Island* and such books cover to cover. My mum was a book-keeper, and my auntie who lodged with us was a book-keeper, so I was very good at arithmetic too. My mother moved heaven and earth to get me well educated. She even talked Father into letting me stay at school until I was fifteen. But then a big racehorse trainer came to the village with a lot of horses, and Father said he needed a boy and he wasn't going to employ anybody else when he'd already got one. So I had to become a blacksmith's boy.

That was dirty hard work, shoeing. It was always done in the morning, about half-past six, when the horses were still half asleep and tired before they went to work, so they'd lean into you, treat you like a fourth leg. They often had diseases, they were very itchy, so you had to be careful where you put your hands, otherwise you made the horse jump. And you didn't want to do that, especially when you were shoeing the back legs, because if the horse jumped suddenly its knee would come up into your ribs and break them. There was no electric light, and in those days they didn't clean the horses or care for them like they did later, so the hairs and that'd be all muddy from the day before. You'd have to go in the stable with a bit of candle for light and then you had to find the clinches, which is the bit that keeps the shoe on, knock the clinches off, get the shoe off and all, and the old horse leaning on you more and more and more. And Father's saying, 'Come on, boy, he'll be tired in a minute, get it off...' Oh, it was agony. My dad said when I could shoe a horse I could have five shillings. And then I did shoe a horse, it was the milkman's horse, and he said, 'Yeah, but that one had very good feet. That don't really count.' But I'm making him sound hard: he was very gentle and very good to me. He gave me half a crown a week pocket money, and my keep. I never wanted for anything.

If a horse was on the land a shoe would last a long time. But on the roads, three weeks and that would do it. My dad did all the racehorses and I used to have to catch them and hold them, but no trainer would let anybody unqualified touch them. Have you ever heard of pricking a horse? Horses' hooves have something like a fingernail around them that's ever so thick but which gets thinner as it comes up towards the pastern, which is the bit between the fetlock and the hoof. Now, the nail you use to put the shoe on is curved, pointed, and when you put him in, and you start driving, you hear a very firm sound. If he starts going a bit dead-sounding, you pull him out quick, because if he goes in and out again too far, he touches the flesh inside. And that's called 'pricking'. And if, when you pull the nail out, there's a spurt of blood, you're in terrible trouble because you've made the horse lame. If it's a racehorse, you're sacked, just like that! So no one ever, knowingly, would let you have a go at shoeing a racehorse. You had to do it secretly, till you got qualified.

My dad got pleurisy very badly and the doctor said, 'Another winter'll kill you.' So my dad got out of the blacksmithing business altogether. The man who delivered the paraffin to Compton also delivered in Wantage, and he mentioned to Father that the saddler in Wantage wanted to move up to Furzewick Farm and start farming. Everyone knew a war was coming and so the saddler wanted to sell the shop quick. So Father and he, they clinched a deal, and Father bought the business. He employed this old army staff sergeant, who was a real expert old boy, and it was he who taught me how to mend the harnesses. So I was now a learner again and back to half a crown a week until I could make a set of harness. And I never did get beyond the half a crown.

A year after I became the saddler, the Second World War broke out. I had joined the Territorial Army, largely as a social thing because as a new boy to the town I didn't know anyone, and when the war began I was called up and sent to Ireland. There was thousands and thousands of troops in Ireland because they thought the Germans would land there and then come across to England. They also thought they might land seaplanes on Loch Nough, so we actually had a boat out there looking for them every night and I worked on the boat, but the only time I was actually shot at was by eel poachers.

I was in Ireland three years, and then the army staff sergeant from Wantage who had taught me how to mend harnesses, went blind and they couldn't find anyone else in the town who could mend harnesses. It was main harvest time and they couldn't get tractor fuel or spares, so they were desperate: they'd found there were six hundred and forty farm horses in the area idle simply because they had no harness to wear, so I was discharged from the army, transferred to Reserves and came home to wade through all the harnesses.

I never did catch up, there was so much of it. Mountains of harnesses there were, waiting to be mended. They were stored in an old stable and it was full to the roof. I used to work night and day to try and get it done but I couldn't do it on my own and there was nobody who could help: the agricultural harness had become a bit of a dying art, even then. They were plough harnesses, mainly; thill, trace and pole harnesses. The thill is the carthorse harness, the one for the shafts of the cart. The trace is the one in front, for the chains that pull to help, and the two work in tandem. Then there's a pole harness, when you have one each side of a pole, and that is basically the same as a thill, except that it has a bigger collar and there is a strap through the collar to hold the pole up. I also made pannier harnesses for donkeys. The pheasants from a shoot were carried in those. I remember Sir Ralph Glyn didn't like wheels on his land, he only liked horses' and donkeys' feet, because wheels were made of iron and pressed the ground down, so I did a lot for him.

I had a year of that and then I was called up again by the army and I didn't even know where we were going. We got on a troop train, got to Liverpool, got on a boat, and I still didn't know where we were going until the boat set sail and they said, 'You're going to India.' It was a terrible shock. Until I went to Ireland, I'd never really been anywhere.

India was quite an experience. The train journeys were tough because we were in the low-class carriages with hard bench seats, and we were in them ten days at a time sometimes. And then there was the trip to Malaya, on the tank-landing ship, with thirty-five of us, three hundred and sixty Sikhs, and only twenty berths. I did get to see some sights, though. We went down to Delhi for the VE-Day celebrations and fired some blanks for the celebrations with the field guns, and while we were there we did some sightseeing. Then when we were in the train afterwards we stopped in the middle of the night, it was moonlight, and the officer said, 'This train's here for two hours. If anybody wants to get up, you can go and see the Taj Mahal.' And only six of us bothered. The average remark was, 'Who wants to be woken up to go and see a bloody memorial?'

In spite of being away from the army for a year I'd become qualified as an army surveyor. I was one of the ones who told the guns which way to point, basically. You have to be expert with maps and good at trigonometry and working out ranges and triangulation and that sort of thing. We were also doing battle inoculation for Gurkha troops, where you fire live shells over their heads to get them used to it. We used to spend all night doing sums. Those days, there was no computers, we used paper and pencil and a lantern, and you worked all night with log tables and prepared a gun programme sheet for each gun to fire a creeping barrage in the morning, at dawn. And when the firing started, we got put in a truck and sent up with the Gurkhas, to advance with them; so if we made any mistakes with our sums, and the shots fell short, it was us that got killed. It made you do your sums right.

Our basic purpose was to invade Malaya, to force the Japs out as they came down through Burma. My wife was expecting a baby back in England, which was a bit of a worry because I thought I'd never get out alive. Beulah and I'd got married before I left, in the midst of it all. With all the surveying work, and jumping into the sea with all my equipment on, and practising for diving off ships, it was so stressful my hair fell out. We nearly all went bald on that job. We were sure we were going to be wiped out in the initial landing, which we would have been if the atomic bomb hadn't been dropped on the Japanese while we were on our way to Malaya. It meant that when we got there the Japanese were more or less surrendering and we had a fairly easy invasion.

The Japanese had done some really evil things. We didn't object to their fighting, they were good, courageous fighters, and that's war, isn't it. But it's what they did to the civilian population I couldn't stomach. People who listened to our radio had their heads cut off and put on the street corner, to warn other people not to do it. One man heard something, and repeated it, so they sewed his face up with a load of bootlace and a sacking needle. They did things like that all the time, and it was ordinary soldiers that did that, they weren't Gestapo or anything.

I couldn't get over that it was ordinary Japanese men who'd do these things. There was all this face-slapping. There were three grades of private and they had stars on their hats: one, two, three. And the one who only had one star couldn't hit anybody but everybody could hit him. And if they flinched when they were slapped they got terribly badly punished. Their discipline to their own men was savage. They put them in tin cages in the sun, like a hen coop, for any misdemeanours, and they often died from the heat.

I came across a chap in Singapore, when we were waiting for a boat home, a Chinaman, and he was a widower. His wife had been expecting, but there was a Japanese sentry in the town where they had been and the Japanese had a rule that civilians had to cross the road when they came to a sentry, stand opposite him, bow to him, and then go further along and cross the road again. They mustn't cross near him, and they must bow. And because this man's wife was expecting she couldn't bow very low. So this Japanese sentry crossed the road with his bayonet, killed her through the stomach and went back to his post. Because she hadn't bowed low enough he just stabbed her.

It affected my attitude towards the Japanese for ever. Beulah and I went to Paris last year: we went on a boat on the Seine and there was a party of Japanese, all young, except the one in charge. And they were affable nice young people, you couldn't object to them at all, they were just teenagers having a good time. But the one in charge was a Japanese officer type, black suit, briefcase, and we didn't get off the boat quick enough for him. It was a wide gangplank, there was plenty of room to get by, and he said to me, sharp, just like a colonel: 'Would you move aside! People are trying to disembark!' I said, 'You just watch it, Tojo!' And I honestly could have shot him. I could have shot him.

I know it wasn't this generation, it was two generations back, so I have to tell myself that perhaps this generation's different, and I try to feel forgiving because what's the point of harbouring anger. But that chap really got to me. He was just the sort you saw strutting about in *Tenko*. Arrogant. Beastly. They said it was war but ... I don't know. I don't understand it. And yet, when I got into the regimental office as a deputy clerk, in Ipoh, we had a Japanese colonel there for interpreter, because when we rounded the Japanese soldiers up we had to be able to tell them what to do, and he was the nicest chap. What he was like before he surrendered I don't know, but he spoke perfect English and I couldn't fault him. So I would treat every Jap as I found him but I do feel, Be careful with them.

Maybe it's just that the Oriental outlook is different to ours. And though I never came across this business of hara-kiri, where they impale themselves on their own swords rather than surrender, the men wouldn't lay down their arms until they'd seen their officers do it.

When we captured them we used to find a suitable place, with a bit of a hillock, and put the Union Jack up, and a couple of 25-pounders, and then fire a couple of blanks to overawe them a bit. Their officers had to come up two by two, bow low, and lay their ceremonial swords down; and some of these swords had been in their families for generations but they still had to part with them. They hated it. And when they'd all come and made a great pile of them, they were led away, and the men were so dejected after that they'd just hand over everything they'd got.

We even used to make them turn their nappies out. They didn't wear underpants, they wore nappies, and they hadn't got any pockets, the men, and they weren't allowed any personal possessions, not even a photograph of a girlfriend. But they used to keep photographs in their nappies and we found out, so then we even made them take their nappies off and turn them out. We took their watches off them too, anything they'd got. They'd stole them in the first place. And that was the only punishment that they had, except we made them all walk to Singapore to catch the boat home and that was four hundred and sixty miles from Ipoh. We made them walk it barefoot. If we met them walking along in groups, and they'd found any shoes, we used to stop them and take them off them. It was agreed that that would be their punishment. They weren't tortured and they weren't hurried, they could take as long as they liked, but they had to live off the land on the way, on bananas and that, that they found growing, because they'd done the same to the civilian population: they'd starved them. They'd made that walk hard for themselves too: they'd previously blown up all the bridges along the way.

You'd think it would be a great relief to get back to the harnesses after all that but it wasn't. It was a relief to be back with Beulah and our daughter but the work was so, so boring. So boring! I was travelling and travelling and travelling, and seeing new sights all the time, and then suddenly there I was sitting on a stool at a bench, just sewing, doing the same thing over and over again. I started smoking a pipe in India for the first time, to keep the midges away at night, because it's the only way of getting any peace. Well, I smoked and smoked when I was doing that harness-making, it was so dull. I've never smoked so much in my life.

I no longer dreamed of being a doctor. I had a wife and family to look after so I accepted my lot. It was inevitable. There was no point thinking about things that weren't possible. I became an ambulanceman in 1957, then a civil defence instructor, and I got a first-class pass. I later did the Institute of Ambulance Officers exam, which meant doing Anatomy and Physiology up to 'A' level standard. I don't think I saw the job as a substitute for what I really wanted but it's probably fair to say that if I were a youngster now I'd do it differently. You can do so much now. Then you just accepted what was what.

Stewart Lees

The Lost Toss

I was walking down the corridor in the Radcliffe Infirmary in Oxford with a colleague, and we were stopped by one of the consultants who said, 'You two want to go into general practice, don't you?' We said, 'Yes.' And he said, 'Well, there are two vacancies coming up, one in Wantage, and one in Bicester. Which of you wants to go where?' I said Bicester because I knew Bicester and I didn't know Wantage at all. My colleague said he wanted Bicester as well, so we tossed for it and I lost.

There were between twenty and thirty other people going for the job. There were a lot of people wanting to get into general practice at the time because there were large numbers of doctors who'd served in the medical services in the war, who wanted to get into civilian practice, as well as students who'd just qualified, like myself, who'd been called up for armed service during the war.

At that time, the top job in medicine was considered to be a consultant in a teaching hospital, without a shadow of a doubt. London considered itself to have the top teaching hospitals, so to be a London consultant was considered the very top of the tree. Edinburgh wouldn't, for one moment, have accepted that, because they're very, very patriotically certain that they produce the best medicine in Britain, in Edinburgh, but this was true for England and Wales. Now the provincial teaching hospitals, Oxford, Cambridge, Nottingham,

Manchester, are as highly or more highly regarded, but when I qualified there was a very strong hierarchy: London consultants first; then all other consultants in all other teaching hospitals; then consultants in non-teaching hospitals like Hereford, Shrewsbury or Winchester; and then general practice, which was regarded by many consultants as a dustbin towards which the less able would gravitate. This was not the view which was held by my colleagues and me: we didn't want to go into consultant work. We wanted to be our own masters, rather than spending years in a hospital as registrars working for other people. I think perhaps we'd already had enough of being ordered around in the services. We wanted to run our own show.

There were three of us in the practice here, I was the junior partner, and the workload was enormous. The NHS had come in in 1948, two years before I joined the practice, and an enormous backlog of people turned up who hadn't been able to afford to see the doctor before the NHS was introduced. The old National Health Insurance only covered those who were in work and it didn't cover their families, so general practice became extremely busy. Our surgery was a small building, crowded, where I personally would see an average of sixty to seventy patients a day: forty to fifty at the surgery and around twenty home visits. And if you had an epidemic of influenza or winter illness it would go up much higher. There was no appointment system at the time, so it was first come, first served, and patients sometimes spilled out on to the pavement outside. Morning surgery started at eight, then as soon as you'd finished morning surgery you would rush out and start some visits, grab a ten-minute lunch at home, and go on visiting through the afternoon, before evening surgery began.

This went on for years: a thirteen-hour day, in which I usually drove fifty miles on top of the surgeries, very often followed by night duty; and there was no rota system for night duty, because the senior partner didn't like a rota. If a message came through to the surgery, it was put through by the surgery housekeeper, Mrs Dowse, to the senior partner. He'd find out from Mrs Dowse who it was and then he would say, 'Well, give that to Dr Lees.' He decided his seniority entitled him to do the minimum of night visits but he would go and see those whom he went fox-hunting with, always. You had a half-day off each week but you were on call at weekends. There was one period when both partners were off sick and I was called out every night for a fortnight, some nights two or three times. No GP now would do that. Nearly all have night rotas, or their night calls are done by an outside agency. I'm sure from the patient's point of view the ideal doctor is the singlehanded one who is always there, day and night, but it's a killer.

I set out to alter things. I got an appointment system arranged, because I thought it was grossly unfair for patients to wait three hours sometimes to see a doctor. I finally persuaded my partners to have a rota system for nights, and we had a switchboard put in so that the practice phone could be switched through to our homes when we were on night duty and on call at weekends. The partners' wives answered the phone at home when it was switched through, which meant that they couldn't leave the house when we were on duty at weekends. It would be unthinkable now to expect a GP's wife or husband to do that, but then it was accepted without question.

When I came here, very much in favour of the NHS, there was still an aura of private practice for the big houses and the richer people round the county and I was adamant I wouldn't have them as private patients. One of the reasons why I have always been ferociously opposed to private practice is for funding reasons, because if you don't have all social and economic classes using the NHS, quite apart from the matter of equality, you don't have it properly monitored. Politicians are apt to say that the NHS is 'a bottomless pit' as far as funding is concerned. The phrase was, as far as I know, introduced by Enoch Powell, and I think it's one of the most damaging things ever to have been said of the NHS. I don't believe it's a bottomless pit at all. It's a fairly deep pit, but it's not bottomless; but it's become accepted by many, many doctors and administrators that it is, and it's been used as an excuse for not increasing health expenditure. Health expenditure in the UK is the lowest of the developed countries. The NHS is a very inexpensive method of providing health, but it's been starved of funds and is still underfunded. It's always behind, and never quite catching up, and a relatively small and painless increase in tax could make a hell of a difference. But then out comes the bottomless pit argument.

Since the NHS was introduced, there have been three phases to general practice in Britain. The first phase, from 1948 to about the mid-sixties, was the phase of stagnation, in which general practice did very little to improve itself, disputes with governments were over levels of pay, and were often bitter and protracted, and the status of the GP in the eyes of other members of the profession stayed low. I think it's fair to say, however, that GPs were highly regarded by the local population in towns all over Britain, probably more so than the other professions. It's certainly true that our patients had a touching amount of faith in us.

The second phase of general practice saw a huge rise in income, the growth of fully funded health centres with much more equipment and organization, and the establishment of vocational training for general practice. When I qualified, there was virtually no training for general practice. You took the hospital training and adapted it as best you could. As a medical student, the most you hoped for was that you would be attached to a general practice for a week, and it was a hard-fought battle to get that. Now GP training takes three years, and it's transformed general practice. So that second phase was the time when the majority of the best medical students opted for general practice instead of going into consultant medicine. It lasted until the late eighties and is now being referred to as 'the happy years'.

The third phase was the Thatcher reforms, so called, and the idea of having fund-holding practices caught on, which turned general practices into large companies with a lot of accountancy and managerial work. Since then morale has sunk, very considerably. Now, even in the best practices, it's very difficult to attract one or two people. The Thatcherite revolution has been disastrous for general practice and I've no idea what the future holds either. I was in practice until 1980 and there were no financial barriers at all. Any treatment we wanted to give, we could give. We were continually exhorted to be economical, because it was NHS money, but it was an open cheque. Any patient, regardless of their status or their income, was entitled to any form of treatment that we wanted.

Fund-holding came in as a reaction against the open cheque and the inability to control expenditure in general practice, which accounts for about 93 per cent of contact between patients and doctors. One of the advantages of fund-holding was that before it came in GPs had no power to persuade or compel hospitals to undertake an operation for a patient, except by appealing to their humanity. Once fund-holding came in, and GPs were paying hospitals directly for operations, GPs could shop around and, in the jargon of the day, it empowered GPs, because hospitals were the providers and they were the purchasers.

However, the non-fund-holding practices were in the old position: money for their patients' operations was being provided by the local health authority, and local health authorities tended to run out of money more rapidly than the fund-holding GPs. You then had the anomalous position of two people in the same street needing a hip replacement, and Patient A, with a fund-holding practice, gets into hospital, and the hospital of his or her choice, within a month, while Patient B, with the non-fund-holding practice, can't get an operation because the local health authority says, 'We have no funds left for this financial year.'

The policy of fund-holding forced a lot of practices who didn't approve of it into swimming with the tide in the interests of their patients. And what is worse is that it was introduced by that bastard Kenneth Clarke, who had no grasp of, and no interest in, the complexity of the issues. As far as the Tories were concerned, the whole thing was based not on clear thinking but on political dogma; that competition is good and anything which produces competition lowers prices, and if it's good for business it's good for the NHS, which is a total non sequitur because health matters are not business matters. If you get ill and need something done, you need it badly and usually quickly.

Yet despite enormous advances in medical science and huge

improvements in general practice, nowadays it's fashionable to be anti-medical science, and anti-medical treatment, and anti-doctor. I've been very interested in some of my friends who claim they couldn't possibly afford to belong to a private patient's plan, and yet an astounding number will spend twenty or thirty quid going to an alternative practitioner. If they get headaches, or pressures in the top of the head, or a feeling of being tired, or a bad back, or aches around the shoulders, they will go to the chiropractor, or the homeopath, or the aromatherapist. They have no use at all for the NHS, and they will spend a lot of money. And if you spend a lot of money, and you get some drops, and your back gets better, which backs do anyhow, you will swear by them.

It is wholly and totally illogical, and yet these people have a very clear, although unconscious, classification of where they go for treatment of various ills. They select alternative medical treatment for the chronic, minor, disabling things. But homeopaths, and chiropractors, and aromatherapists, who probably would be furious to be lumped together, these people are utter nonsense in purely medical, scientific terms. They certainly provide a niche in terms of time: I think most people go to them with long-standing feelings of uneasiness, unhappiness, being generally unwell, and they find somebody who is going to listen to them for thirty minutes, provide sympathy, and then provide something physical. But where alternative practice becomes dangerous, and one becomes very unhappy, is when therapy is offered for cancers, and patients are dissuaded from getting radiotherapy, or chemotherapy, which is genuinely effective. Then I think it verges on the criminal.

Chiropractors probably get up my nose the most. They certainly used to believe that most diseases were caused by displacement of the vertebrae in the spine. I remember one telling me that this was the cause of heart and lung trouble, that there was a certain thoracic vertebra that got out of place and you could manipulate it back. Sometimes they'd say, 'There was a vertebra turned right round, and I turned it back again.' Well, anyone who's done any anatomy at all knows that the one thing you can't do is shove vertebrae around. So it's difficult to take terribly seriously systems of medicine which appear to be based on this kind of balls. Many people these days have a quite irrational hatred or fear of science: the word science means knowledge, knowledge acquired systematically, formulated knowledge, and yet lots of people adopt instead an approach to medical problems of almost religious fervour and dogmatism.

I question my friends about this. I say, 'If you woke up in the middle of the night, and had a sudden agonizing pain, would you wait and go to your chiropractor?' 'Oh no, I'd get my GP.' 'OK. If you fractured an arm?' 'I'd go to Casualty.' It tickles me that many young people, particularly people in their twenties to their forties, are often highly critical of the health service, and of medical science in general. They think a lot of it is intrusive, and reductionist, and male-dominated; that it does more harm than good; that doctors give you too many drugs, and they operate too readily. But if they're really ill, they will go for conventional NHS treatment like a shot.

Before the National Health Service was introduced, hospitals were for the poor. The middle and upper classes went to private nursing homes. Hospitals were essentially places where the poor were treated in large numbers, and there was a very authoritarian attitude towards patients, which has since changed beyond all recognition. It's a small example, but one of the most conspicuous changes came about in 1950 in Amersham Hospital in Buckinghamshire. Until 1950, parents were not allowed to visit their children in hospitals more than once a week, because it was said that it made the children cry, and children's wards were very regimented. They were often run by fairly heartless, disciplinarian spinsters, and children would sit mute and immobilized, in a state of institutionalized pessimism. Then a marvellous man called Dermod MacCarthy, who was running the children's ward at Amersham Hospital, introduced open visiting on the wards.

I remember the Amersham children's ward well. It was untidy. That was the nice thing about it; the children were allowed to play with toys. They could have their mummy and their daddy, and of course they cried when they went, because they wanted to go home, but that was a good thing, not a bad thing. And because of this marvellous man, Dermod MacCarthy, who received a lot of *bitter* opposition, the practice permeated nationally, so that open visiting became acceptable within all wards in hospitals. Once that happened, hospitals lost their rather military, disciplinary atmosphere and there was much more consideration and kindness towards patients.

Dermod MacCarthy was part of the change in attitudes surrounding health care in Britain in the latter half of this century, and the Conservatives went to extraordinary lengths to damage the NHS, the doctor–patient relationship, and the high standard of care that hospitals offered. People don't *want* to go to their doctor, and don't *want* to go to hospitals. They don't want to be ill. There are very few people who misuse the system. Most of us don't go near a doctor unless we're forced to. When we do, I think we should have the right to get our treatment quickly and free at the point of cost. It's not easy, particularly with an ageing population taking up quite a large amount of money, but it's perfectly possible. We are living longer, so there are more people contracting and dying of cancer, but if we all lived long enough, we'd all get cancer, because malignant changes in cells tend to increase with increasing age. But there has been, in the last fifty years, an enormous reduction in deaths from most infective diseases such as chronic bronchitis, lung infections, emphysema, tuberculosis, poliomyelitis and scarlet fever. Infant and maternal mortality have come down really spectacularly. Babies are getting bigger. Children are growing taller: they're having fewer episodes of illness. And deaths or disability from illness are increasingly uncommon in youth and middle age. Heart disease is decreasing. People are healthier.

For me, the most exciting part of general practice was diagnosis. You never knew what was coming through the door next. You would see case after case of very simple sore throats and earaches and colds and flus and rheumatisms, and then somebody would come in with something that was clearly serious, and the challenge was how to deal with that when you were running at such a pace. You also got to know a lot of people, you got to know their ways, and you got very fond of them. I took on responsibility in the practice for a lot of the obstetric care, and I got up to delivering about a hundred babies a year. It meant you had complete continuity of care because you saw your patient from the time you diagnosed pregnancy to delivery, which you almost always attended. It was a very, very satisfying part of general practice. Mostly you're dealing with sickness and illness, but obstetrics is very optimistic. Things can occasionally go wrong, and when they do you've got to move like lightning, particularly with post-partum haemorrhage, but mostly it's sheer joy, and I delivered quite a lot of women whose mothers I had delivered before.

When I left general practice to do research I found, walking around the town, that the people who'd stop me to talk were nearly always mothers I'd delivered. They were always profoundly grateful when you'd done absolutely nothing. They never forgot you and they considered the event a bond between you. And this is one of the paradoxes of being a GP. If you had a patient who had a highly complicated, life-threatening illness, and you steered them through it, they would very rarely refer to it because it was a horrible experience. Equally, if you had a breaking up of a marriage, and you helped in some way to stop it, patients would never refer to it and they wouldn't say thank you. But if you deliver a baby, you get a degree of gratitude that's far more than you deserve and it goes on for years. When it happens, as occasionally it still does, I feel a real surge of nostalgia for my time in general practice.

It was a wonderful job and I loved it, and it would have been perfect had there not always been lack of time, and ultimately lack of energy, to cope with the numbers. There was this constant, constant, constant pressure. When I changed from general practice to research, I can't tell you how much of a luxury it was to be able to make my own timetable, and to do things completely thoroughly; to be able to say, 'I'm going to look into this hunch of mine, and I can take all day, or a week, or a fortnight, doing nothing else but that.' I mean, general practice would have been a pearl of a job if you could have done that.

It would have been a pearl of a job if you saw ten or twelve people a day. But it was fifty to sixty a day, plus going to bed knowing that the telephone will probably ring on one in every three nights for the next thirty to forty years.

Celia Teare

A Job for Life

The media is full of medicine. People come in, with an article they've read, because they think it sounds like something that they would benefit from, and you have to unpick that with them at the same time as keeping your mind open to possibilities. Sometimes people want alternative medicine, and I think, often, that alternative medicine's absolutely the right approach; an osteopath or a chiropractitioner can help where we can't. If people want to consult a homeopathic physician, I don't object, but the practising of alternative therapies in general is wide open to abuse. Quite often patients will come and they will tell you, very firmly, that they want your opinion about their health, and they don't want to interfere but they don't want any of your treatments, and they don't believe in antibiotics.

What I find worrying about society as a whole, really, is this belief that if you go to the right practitioner, or you take the right thing, somehow you're guaranteed perfect health. Health promotion was put firmly on our doorstep in the new NHS government contract in 1990, and the implication was that if we measured everybody's height and weight, and told them to stop smoking, we could make a big difference to the health of the nation. Obviously GPs have a role in promoting health, but people do have responsibility themselves for their own destinies, and we are none of us immortal. People do get ill, diseases do strike. You can't buy health and I think some people think you can.

I'm pleased that there's been a wave of protest against primary care being offered in supermarkets or on railway stations, which is something that both Conservative and Labour governments have suggested; that doctors could offer primary care to people as they do their weekly shop. It will simply undermine the whole system of general practice in this country, which has been described as 'the jewel in the crown of the health service'; a jewel that politicians seem very busy trying to crush. However, there has still been a great shift in patients' expectations. An awful lot of what we do is acute 'here and now', and a lot of the time patients are just going to whoever they can see that day because it's convenient, so the individual, personal care has been eroded to some extent. Our list is about eleven thousand eight hundred people, and our neighbouring practice is a bit less, but there's been a transfer of care from hospitals to general practice, and GPs are being asked to do more while at the hospital end the technology has wildly expanded.

You do feel trapped by your own lack of time as a result. You always feel that you haven't done the job completely, but you're never bored, ever, and your interest isn't just fired by something new and rare. Managing common problems such as heart failure can be an enormous challenge and worry. There's a lot of new pharmacology, and often you don't feel that you know enough about the drugs you're using, so you're learning as you go along. It's a surprise, after all this time, to find how often that happens. You'd think surely after twenty years you'd know what to do in most situations, but every patient is unique and the variables are always different. And by and large, we work with very intelligent people who are part of the debate about what treatment you're going to give, and what the choices are, so a large part of our work is spent explaining. In the past, patients might have said, 'You're the doctor, you know best,' but I'm not used to hearing that any more. Patients are much more informed: they want to know what, why and how.

Perhaps one of the most difficult things about being in general practice in the last twenty years is that there have been so many changes in the NHS. The present government has taken fund-holding away, and that's fine, but you set up a lot of systems, and you employ staff, and you work very hard to get something going which you didn't want in the first place, and then you're told that it isn't going to be any more. I think this is why new doctors are not looking to come into general practice. I think they see us working very hard, with a lot of externally imposed change and regulations, and if you've been conscientious and wanted to offer a very excellent service, it's hard to take. It almost undermines your professionalism, which you don't take on lightly. We've become very vulnerable in that sense, in a way that GPs never were before.

The other reason why young doctors aren't wanting to go into practice is the nights and weekends. The newer generation of GPs don't want to do all night and work all day the next day. It's very interesting looking at the *British Medical Journal*'s adverts for jobs: almost invariably they say, 'Out-of-hours covered by deputizing', or 'Out-of-hours co-operative in the area'. Nobody's saying, 'We do all our own night calls.' We stopped doing all our out-of-hours work on our own in 1997. We now pay a commercial organization which employs receptionists and doctors and drivers, and personally I think that will happen everywhere in the future. All of us have got very mixed feelings about it, but culturally it's just what's happened. It hasn't happened because doctors wanted it, or because patients wanted it; it's evolved. The out-of-hours work soared when the Patient's Charter came in, because the Charter stipulated that you should be able to have access to your GP at any time of the day or night, but nobody thought about who was going to provide that care, and there was no more resource put into primary care to offer night-time surgeries, you just had to spread what you'd already got.

It's been quite a big shift for us in this practice, because it appears that we don't care any more, that you can be ill in the night and your doctor won't come. We had a long time working out what we would do about night calls, and what would be safe and acceptable to our patients. That kind of questioning is painful and challenging, and you feel that it's undermining the philosophical nice vibes about looking after the community, as if you're saying, 'I want to look after this community but I don't want to do it in the night.' That doesn't sit comfortably with me but you also become critical as time goes on. In the old days, people really only called the doctor out when there was dire need. These days, people seem to feel much more as if everything's somebody else's responsibility. People cannot contain worry for a night, with a child with a fever, or a pain in the tummy, or whatever, they can't hold on to it very long. They have to tell somebody and have some help, so a GP working all day and the next day has to get up four or five times in the night to visit patients, whereas if someone rings on a busy Monday morning at nine o'clock, and you say, 'There isn't an appointment until this evening at five o'clock,' they say, 'Fine. Thank you very much,' and are content to wait eight hours to be seen.

The GP's role has changed in lots of ways, and all of them are to do with resources, whether human or financial. For example, once you bring funding so close to home that you're buying an operation for somebody, and the budget's running out, and it's either them or someone else, then you're no longer the advocate for all your patients. Competition trickles down to patient level, which doesn't sit comfortably with me, and yet somebody had to be accountable somewhere because the NHS bill is too big. I don't think you ever could have enough money to run the NHS, because all the time techniques are improving, with costs soaring, and the sort of things on offer just to investigate a simple symptom mean you as a GP have to make quite difficult decisions about whether or not to pursue something, expensively, to the bitter end. There are lots of decisions like that that we never had in the past. And when you send people for expensive investigations, expensive treatments, you might never know in the end whether the decision can be justified financially.

Somebody said to me, ages ago, that if you stayed in a job more than five years that was a mistake, because you would be stale and not giving your best. And I thought about that, and I thought, It's nothing to do with being in the same job for five years. Jobs change. My job's changed, not at the core but bits round it, and as long as you can change with it, being in one place to do it is actually a security. I've done twenty years, I've done two-thirds of my life's work here. I feel I belong here now, and that derives from feeling that I have a commitment to the people here through the practice. This was exactly the sort of area I wanted to end up in, because it's a community that's defined, it's got an edge round it. I came here first as a locum and I thought it was the most wonderful practice that I could ever have found. It was exactly what I wanted.

There was a huge cross-section of people here when I came, from the old country families and people who had never gone away from their village, ever, to very sophisticated people commuting to London, and I liked the variety. It's not overly top heavy with wealthy families: there are plenty of people struggling with poverty and the chronic ill-health that comes with that. It's privileged compared with lots of places, with access to good leisure and education, but there's a broad spread. I also felt it was a stable community, where there were families where you would know three or four generations, and there's such a lot, in medicine, that is intuitively based on your knowledge of a family. It's an ideal community to work with, and although it's a little bit more woolly around the edges now, it still is very defined. You can embrace the place but it's not so small that it's claustrophobic.

It wasn't easy coming here as a single person. It was a completely new feeling to me to settle anywhere, I'd been very nomadic ever since leaving home at eighteen, so by twenty-eight I wasn't sure what settling somewhere meant, you know, what you did. Did you join things, or go to functions? The work was very busy, but it was difficult, really, wondering how to settle, and feeling a bit exposed, a bit public, for the first time. Working in hospitals, your persona is very private, but it's quite a shock to find the people you're looking after you're also bumping into in the bank and the shops, and you feel a little bit exposed.

I had a need to make friends, but I found it difficult to make friends with the patients because you're very conscious that there is this professional role; you're privy to a lot of very private information about your patients, but you don't give back the same, so it's a very skewed relationship. I'm here because of a commitment to the community but it kind of stops short at my private life. I will give my all, you know: I do, at work, but at home I want to preserve my space. It was much easier once I met my husband. Apart from anything else, just having somebody's support made a huge difference. I don't think I was very good at being single. I didn't buy a house as a single person, I was renting. It was only once I was married that I felt I could put down roots and say, 'I belong here, and I want to be part of this community.'

Once I'd made the decision to join this practice, I envisaged that that would be it for my working life but, as I said, there's a huge swing against general practice at the moment. Now there is a sense that the GP should provide a service and go home at five o'clock. Quite a lot of the younger doctors have that approach, that general practice is not so much a whole way of life. I think it's sad, because I don't think it is just any job, at its best it's wonderful. You're in a very privileged position with people, you're allowed to be very close to them at the most important times in their human experience. I think you have to treat that with some awe.

Pat Elliot

Body and Soul Matters

I'm divorced and I dealt with our divorce myself and the thing that struck me about it was how easy it was. It was a question of filling in the appropriate form, and then it's given to the court, it goes through a couple of stages, and that's it. I know that's not the case for many people, many people have solicitors involved and difficult settlements, and arguments over the children, but the process itself is amazingly easy. I had been in the relationship with my ex-husband for twenty-five years, and I thought, Is that all that it takes to just wipe that away? I mean, that's obviously not what it took to wipe it away because it was a gradual thing over many years but the final act was amazingly simple and I am not so sure that's a good idea.

I suppose our failure as a society is partly what makes a business like mine successful. Families have become so fragmented. When the wider family lived in closer proximity there was a built-in network of support for all the generations, which isn't there now because people are dotted all over the place. And because people feel unsupported they come here, because a lot of what they get here is support. Our society still doesn't touch people very easily and if you are busy building a career, or coping with a divorce, or moving to a new area, you put up an enormous brick wall around you just to cope. So to be able to come here and say, 'I want to be touched for an hour, please, without any strings attached, without any sexual connotation, without any expectation of any other type of relationship,' is very important. Also, people who are bereaved are very much more on their own these days because of this dissipation of the wider family, and touch is the one thing shortly after bereavement that you really, really miss; that close proximity of your partner that may have been there for years and years.

A lot of people in their seventies and eighties come here. I think often people don't realize how long it takes to get through the grieving process, and this sort of work can help: you can lend support, lend an ear, as well as touching. With aromatherapy, some of the oils are good for relieving grief anxiety and insomnia. However, certain oils will suit certain people and certain conditions, and those same oils will not suit somebody else. It's a very individual thing. The oils work through absorption through the skin and through smell. The fastest way into the system is through smell because the nerve routes in the nose are closest to the limbic system in the brain, so they get absorbed into the bloodstream very quickly through the nasal mucosa. That's where aromatherapy gets its name from. The other way oils get absorbed is through the skin, and the good thing about that method is that it acts as a slow-release system, so the effect of the oil can last for three, four or five days.

Aromatherapy is regarded as a load of rubbish less so now than it used to be. The only thing I have a problem with is that it's called aromatherapy whether the oil is used indiscriminately by beauty therapists or by trained practitioners like us. There is a huge body of people out there who feel that it's daft, and that's fine. What I am concerned with is widening the field of people that don't feel that, and encouraging the ones that have found benefit to spread the word. And in economic terms, complementary therapy can actually save the health service quite a lot of money because the amount of intervention with drugs gets less if you use complementary therapy, and in cases like insomnia, depression and stress-related illness, there are sound economic reasons for using complementary therapy.

I use the word 'complementary' advisedly because it isn't an alternative to allopathic medicine, there is a place for both things. I wouldn't come to a herbalist if I had appendicitis or a broken leg, but for chronic illness or disease or discomfort, then something like this is ideal. At the moment, there are great pressures on people in all types of work and I think a lot of it came about during the eighties, when Margaret Thatcher was in, and people decided that it was good to run companies with very few staff. That put huge pressure on people who were still working, on people that were made redundant, and on the unemployed. It created a lot of stress. And I think the word 'stress' has become devalued, but stress is what we see a lot of. All of us need some stress to get us through life or we don't get anything done. But if someone is suffering at work, or through lack of it, if they are suffering difficulties with relationships, or are ill, that can cause physical or mental stress. The body is like a jigsaw puzzle and what stress does to the individual is change the body's ability to deal with things, and it all has a knock-on effect which, if it's not dealt with, may cause headaches, digestive problems, backaches, and at the other extreme, strokes and heart attacks.

There are also great pressures on families these days. I think the feminist movement didn't actually do women many favours, at the end of the day. I think women felt that it was the right thing to do, to disregard their feminine qualities and try to become like men in their jobs instead of offering the different qualities that they had and proving they could do the job just as well in a different way and retain their feminine qualities at the same time. So women now are caught in the trap of thinking that they've got to have careers, and then they find that they still want families but they can't devote as much time to the family; and being a mother, which is actually the most important job in the world, has been tremendously devalued. I think it's changing now, but during the eighties it was hard for women and hard for families. The pressure in the commercial environment also meant that men were away from home for longer, were a lot more involved with their jobs, were bringing their jobs and all the stress that goes with that home with them. It was a terrible time for family life.

Because modern women are working, they feel the lack of support more. I'm not necessarily an advocate of people always being at home, but in the days when women were at home it was assumed that it was their responsibility to bring up the children, and now it's assumed that it is their responsibility to bring up the children, look after the house *and* go out and have a career at the same time. It's no longer good enough just to have a job, you've got to have a *career*, and there's a huge distinction between jobs and careers. Lots of women have had to take part-time jobs because there aren't full-time jobs around, and they end up with this half-life at work and at home. So I think you have to be very aware, very capable, to survive at the moment in our society, and some people don't have the gift so they don't survive: the pressures are actually too great for them.

I think there are a lot of people who are unhappy deep down, who must wonder what life's all about, who feel very empty sometimes. And I think people change when they realize that quality of life, of body and soul, matters; that there is more to life than attaining more and more status symbols, albeit the mobile phone or the latest car. Our whole society seems at times to revolve around the self. It's this self-worship all the time, and yes, OK, you do have to be aware of yourself and at ease with yourself but you also have to look outside of that in order to have a solid relationship with someone else. As a Christian, I try and encourage the good in people and help them to see the good in themselves again. If you can get them to stop being quite so introspective, and help them begin to feel happier with themselves and to realize their own power, if you can get them to look outwards again, then I believe that has a direct result on how they are in the world.

Catherine Fourcampré-Maye

The Name of the Game

When I was little, my mum was at home and my father worked. These days both parents work, and in the summer holidays there is nothing for that child to do. Nobody gets two months off in the summer, and the children have to be put somewhere, so they come to us at the leisure centre and we have to offer a different service than we did in the past.

The summer holidays, there are a lot of weeks; seven weeks, in fact. It's a long time for children to be left or for people to afford childminding fees. We only charge £9 a day per child and we have them for nine or ten hours a day. But you can't do sports for nine or ten hours, so we do fairly active things first thing, and then they have a more leisurely activity towards lunchtime, because they're getting tired. After lunch, although they're full of beans again because they've had a good break, we know they're going to feel sick if we start running them around, so we tend to do craft activities, and then we give them another good running around and make them quite tired before they go home. This summer, we had one thousand four hundred and sixty-one children, an average of fifty a day. It's not bad but it's not that great. I think we can do better next year.

It's very important that we have diversified in this way. Our overall user figures, this last year, were a hundred and forty-seven thousand people, but we still need more in order to make a profit. People's idea of what leisure is is changing, and we have to respond to that. Nationally, swimming is on the decline, and so is squash. Basketball is on the increase. That's the influence of the States. England is very influenced by North America, and whatever goes well there tends to spill over to England, although things like American football don't work, because of finance and facilities, so your traditional football would always be very popular. That is probably your number one sport in England, is football. That's very strong. The middle classes and above play tennis because it's one of the things you do, but the little boys down the road won't be saying, 'Mum, Mum, can I go and play tennis?' The children that have got less money are always going to play football.

Aerobics is still quite popular here. Aerobics is a figure thing, yet people that are overweight don't tend to come to aerobic classes because they don't want to be seen with the leotard brigade. That's why there's been such a growth of ladies-only activities in the last ten years, because the overweight women, or unfit women, tend to hover around in the ladies-only sports sessions; it's when they start to ease themselves back on the scene with baggy T-shirts and baggy tracksuit bottoms. That's also why line dancing is so popular now, because people can come in with a lot more clothes on and still do some fitness.

Line dancing has come from America. So has the gym. Americans are lazy. They want to do everything in one room and then go back home in their car. To some extent, it's because there's great distances in America, so they drive everywhere, whereas in England we live very close to our facilities. But we still inherited their way of doing things, and you'll find that most of the companies that make machines for the gym are American. We get their gimmicky machines all the time, their rowers and their steppers, plus a lot of pressure from the public to buy them. You mustn't forget, there's market forces out there that are trying to influence you because they want to build a machine to make more money out of you, and they're trying to influence you into persuading me to buy one.

Leisure's big business, a multimillion-dollar market. At the moment, the Americans are trying to push a machine where people can cycle backwards, because they're saying this is a good overall hamstring thing, but I know it's a gimmick. I know it would be fun to have the machine for a while, but I know it's a fad. There are such fads: the step, the slide. The step was introduced as an added tool to make you more out of breath. The trouble is with the step, it's high impact, therefore it causes more damage to your body, so you have to buy better shoes and that's more money, blah, blah, blah. The following year, this same company came out with the slide, and you had to put little fluffy slippers on your shoes, and then you had to slide from side to side doing sets of movements, and the selling point was that you would get your inner thigh muscles fitter. You could, but it was difficult to control so you could become injured. It's all gimmicks, and there'll always be more of them.

I have to succumb to a certain extent because the name of the game is to keep your customer. If you don't keep your customer, they'll go somewhere else and do something else. Things like swimming, there's only so many ways you can swim. You can't really introduce your customer to different elements in a pool. What we need with swimming, probably, is more fun pools, so that it attracts different types of people. But if we had the next Duncan Goodhew tomorrow, I suspect my swimming figures would increase sharply because national success has a great impact on any sport.

There's a lot more awareness on fitness and leisure now, and the benefits of being fit. Before, people weren't very aware of their fitness needs, and the leisure industry didn't target groups with marketing. In the past, leisure centres were not very inviting, and people didn't make any effort to introduce the environment to the local people. Now they do. Now we go out of our way to create childcare facilities, or to set up sessions to say, 'Come and try this,' or 'Have a go at that.' Now it's much more friendly.

I employ a lot of friendly staff here, because the public see them, they don't see me. I'm not friendly myself, I leave that to my staff. In fact, the worst aspect of this job for me, personally, is the people issues. I don't have a lot of patience, and I don't like to pussyfoot around because people feel aggrieved by this or that. I like to steam ahead, and I don't always have the tendency to get people in a nice frame of mind before I do. I tend to lose people as I go along because I'm not very tolerant, which is too bad, but I don't particularly want to work at changing that side of me because I know, deep down, I'll never change myself. That's the way I am.

What I enjoy most is the variety of my job. You can sink yourself into finance one day, personal issues the next day, and setting up a new activity the next, like a triathlon for next summer. It's fun. You can be as creative as you want. But I'm impatient. Because I want us to achieve, I tend to demand a lot. I try to be fairly open to public and customers but I don't like to respond to every whim and whinge that people have, so I can collide with customers sometimes, or my bosses. Maybe that's because I am not English, I'm French, and I have a different upbringing, possibly a different way of living. Culturally, I was educated in a different way. Socially, I know I'm different to most of my English friends. If we have a dinner party, there can be times when there is a stony silence, because I tend to be quite heated about my views and I can launch into a discussion, and there's lots of arms and things, and my voice probably rises, and people can be a bit shell-shocked because traditionally a lot of English people are quite reserved in their discussions and they'll stay on an even keel, or be polite enough not to ruffle feathers.

Some people are attracted to me because of that. Some are not. At work, I can make nightmares for myself because of my personality. I think it's because I don't conform in my attitudes towards other people, whereas the English are very hierarchical. I mean, there is a tendency, in England, to mix with likes. I don't often see different types of people who have no money, or little education, mixing with those who are middle class, which is not something I have been used to in France. I wouldn't like to say this is the French way, that we don't care about social status; I don't think that's true, but I don't care about it myself.

But in England, it's a lot more structured about who's who. I mean, you have a book, *Who's Who in England*, isn't it? Well, we don't have a French equivalent. I think people in France are more interested about who you are than how much money you earn, which in England seems to be the other way.

The other thing about the English is that they're very set in their ways. I find that with the customers here. They don't seem to be wanting an awful lot of change. They tend to be a bit frightened by some of the things that I have done. I've brought an awful lot of changes with me, and comments were made to me like, 'Why change it? If it's not broken, why do you want to change it?' My attitude is different. If it's not broken, that doesn't mean to say it is never going to break. Strengthening it will make it different before it breaks, it will make it more interesting. And in the leisure industry, you have to change with the times. You cannot stay still.

People love change once they are used to it, children particularly. Children are different these days. They are more sophisticated and we have to compete with a lot more in leisure now. You know, you've got McDonald's doing parties, you're not just a leisure centre doing children's parties, there's a lot more competition, there's choices. The television is a choice; and so many computers in everybody's life now. Yes, traditionally we were a sports centre, and maybe we should be talking about sports, but sports has become leisure, and maybe leisure will become something else too. Maybe computers will come into children's activities eventually. You don't know. My own gut feeling is that in ten years' time children's activities will incorporate computer games: we will have in the leisure centre, probably, a bank of computers where children will play against each other. Virtual reality games will come to leisure centres. And when that happens we can't stay where we are and say, 'Right, children, we'll do badminton today.' Kids might not want to do that in the future. So we have to go with them, within reason, because we can't forget how we change as human beings.

Sarah Wakeley

Bringing Up Baby

When you're young you think money doesn't matter but it does in the end. It certainly does when you've got kids; especially now, when they're asking for more things and they're getting into difficulties at school because we haven't got a computer and they're the only child in the class who hasn't got a computer. They keep saying, 'At school, we were supposed to do this on the computer, and we were supposed to use a CD-ROM to research it.' Computers are £1,000, some of them. It is an enormous outlay. I don't know how so many people afford to have them. But in this area, especially on the estates, everybody has a computer, everybody has those Toyotas, those Range Rover things; those are the scene now. I mean, they're so ridiculous, aren't they, and they drive them down from the estates, masses of jungle truck, these great desert things. It's stupid.

The middle class, middle earners around here are obsessed with keeping up with the Joneses. They have to have the dinner parties, they have to have the Jeep, they have to have the holidays abroad, they have to have the great careers. I'm one of a very small crowd who stay at home with the children. Most of the middle-class mums I know work, but until mine all go to school I feel that I want to be here. I think every mother ought to stay at home unless it's absolutely essential. I do. I think it's terribly, terribly important, and there's definitely a tremendous difference between the children who have stayed at home with their mother or father and those children who are childminded even three days a week. I think it probably isn't so bad in extended family situations, where you've got a grandmother or somebody who's going to step in, but these day nurseries I can't bear. There's loads of day nurseries round here. There's one nearby which is from birth to two, poor little devils. I think that speaks for itself, what kind of area this is.

I walk past a large day nursery when I'm taking my children to school, and somebody's always dropping off a toddler screaming its head off, going, 'Mummy, Mummy, I want you,' and the mothers are just going, 'Yes yes, come on,' and looking at their watches and saying, 'Oh God, I'm going to be late for a meeting,' and the child is just dumped off at the nursery. Well, to me, why have them? I'm sorry, it really gets under my skin. Why have the kids if you're going to dump them in a nursery and let somebody else bring them up, feed them, watch their first steps? There's something wrong somewhere and I think that's pressure from society. People aren't content any more to stay at home and have nothing and look after the kids. They want to have the children *and* they want a paid job, *and* they want to be able to holiday abroad, *and* they want all the material things that money can give us. I think that's terribly sad. I think there's going to be a generation of children who are going to have tremendous psychological hang-ups because they've been dumped. They're going to think it's normal to have a baby and give it to somebody else to look after. In this nursery they've got a window which they've now blacked in, but you used to see these ranks of cots just waiting for babies to be dumped down in. It's like an army. I can't bear it.

I've always wanted lots of children and I suppose I've been privileged to have been able to bring up all mine. I've spent fifteen years with little kids and absolutely loved it, but you get to a stage where it's time to do something else, and now Tom's at a private school I need to get work. When you start down this wretched path of private education, it's a real killer. Tom's fees are horrendous. They're something like £1,750 a term, excluding the £200 for the bus, which brings it up to about £2,000 a term, and that's a hell of a lot of money. *And* that excludes outings and all the rest. It really is a sacrifice for us, but if we did ever get the money to send the others we'd both be willing to because it gives them so many more opportunities.

I think private education's wrong. I think it's wrong because it is elitist and I think everybody should have the chance, but when Tom was at the junior school he was very shy, very introverted. He worked very hard and we believed that by sending him to the local state school he would probably be a first-class victim for bullying. A single-sex education, in a small school, was what we wanted for him and what we'd like for all of them because it's a really nice school. And OK, I know bullying happens in private, state, whatever schools, but he's in small classes, he's made lots of friends, he's blossomed, he's a much more outgoing person in himself. What I would like is for all the state schools in the country to offer what the private schools offer, then no one would ever think of sending children to private schools. The local secondary school, I don't like the way it's on three sites, I don't like the way the children seem to be in the town all the time instead of in school, I don't like their huge classes. There's lots of things I don't like about it, and until it improves a lot I don't think I would send the others there.

So yeah, it would be great to have more money, and we'll need it if we're going to send the others to private school, but I'd still rather be in when they come home from school than be out earning money. Then if they're worried about something you can say, 'Don't worry, we'll sort it out.' To have a child coming home from school who hasn't got somebody to talk to, or has to go into a kids' club or something, what happens to those problems? The parent comes home late, tired, and the child's going to bottle them up. And I think it's a much more worrying world to bring kids up in than, say, my parents brought us up in. We didn't have things like BSE. We didn't worry about the environment. I think that's what I'm most worried about now: I think we grew up in a cleaner world and that worries me for the children, and their children, because we're just wrecking the planet, and unless we do something pretty quick I think there's going to be devastation.

When I was young you worried about getting pregnant but that was about it. We didn't worry about AIDS. We were brought up in the seventies in a fairly free sexual way and there was never any fear. Maybe I was naive, I don't know. I didn't even know about homosexuals until I went to college, whereas my kids all know. I mean, I didn't know about drugs at all until I was at college, whereas Sam knows about them already, and he's eight. Tom knows that if he goes to a party he must be very careful what he drinks in case someone spikes it. I would never, ever have thought about that at thirteen. I think it's really frightening.

Frances Wallis

Franklin's Mother

I had been having quite a lot of women's problems and in the end I went to hospital for an operation and I was in for four days. My husband George and I didn't have a car but George's twin sister, Freda, did, and George was going to phone me at the hospital and see that I was ready to come out, and then phone Freda to fetch me. It was early January, really cold and foggy, and he was going to make the phone calls, come home and light the fire, and get the house ready for me.

Well, he spoke to the hospital, phoned his sister, and then as he was going back to his workshop he collapsed. The young lad who was working with him got the first aid but he was unconscious by this time. They weren't quite sure what had happened, whether he had had a stroke or what. He was just fifty. The medical officer at work said, 'Take him to the hospital, but if he dies on the way you will have to bring him back because they don't accept dead bodies.'

Freda and her husband Ray were on their way to fetch me while this was happening, and when they arrived the hospital staff asked them to go down to Casualty and identify someone with the same name and from the same address as me, that had been brought in unconscious. So poor Freda and Ray went to see George, who was still unconscious, and they came up to me and said, 'We can't take you home yet because George isn't very well, they've had to bring him in here; he's had a nasty turn.' This went on until about seven in the evening, and then the sister came in and said that he had died without regaining consciousness, that he had had a massive cerebral haemorrhage.

You could imagine what that was like. He was hale and hearty the night before and he had nothing wrong with him. He was a bit overweight and I remember he had had a check-up with the doctor, but it was a terrible shock. And then to have the same thing happen with our son Franklin at exactly the same age. For George to go and then Franklin to go too, both at the age of fifty. Doctor Lees said to me after George died, 'Take it a day at a time, that's the only way you can face it,' and it was.

George's friends from work were good. One of the men from along the road, he said, 'If you have any trouble with the boys, don't be afraid to ask.' Their old headmaster was absolutely wonderful. Even though the boys had left school he came about ten o'clock one night and just sat and talked. He said he realized losing a young man is not so easy, you expect people to die when they are older, but he said, 'Look what a dull place heaven would be if it was all old people there.'

The only thing I could think when George died was that God was there and he was going to help me. I just don't know how people manage if they haven't got a faith to hold on to. Because when it comes like that and you are not prepared it is dreadful. Funnily enough, thankfulness comes through as well. Although you are devastated, you are thankful that they didn't suffer. George was two years older than me, so I think perhaps if he had still been alive he would have been crippled with arthritis or suffering in some way and I am so thankful that he is free from that. It's the same with Franklin, though it was terrible at the time to face it, to lose a son who was still so young, who was such an extrovert, who did enjoy life so much.

I felt extremely different about their two deaths. With George I felt absolutely alone after he had died and gone. We weren't a very demonstrative family but there was always that solid something in the background, and in a funny sort of way he relied on me much more than I relied on him; he always said I was the strong one. But I did feel and still do feel that I am not a complete person, that there is something missing, as if there is only half of me operating. It's funny, isn't it, still now after all this time. It's thirty-odd years but I still think when things happen, Oh, I must tell George about that. I do it with Franklin too. Oh, I must tell Franklin I heard that tune on the radio. We were very close, Franklin and I. After George died, for a while he was the only one at home with me, and he did a lot for me.

A husband and child are different. I think when Franklin died I felt more possessive than anything. At the time I could see how terrible my daughter-in-law, Carol, was feeling and I knew exactly how she felt but I couldn't say that to her because in the same circumstances no two people do feel exactly the same. What I *really* wanted to say was, 'He was mine before ever he was yours,' and I felt that was wrong. I was angry with myself for feeling like that. But in a way it was such a natural feeling because I couldn't help thinking back to when he was young. He was such a lovely baby, he was beautiful.

It was a great strain on me and Carol. I felt she was resenting me. I felt that all the time she was thinking, 'Why couldn't *she* have gone? She has had all these years: why not her?' I suppose it would be the natural thing to think. We did find it very difficult the first two or three months and we couldn't really communicate much. His daughters were fine. I remember one of them saying to me, 'Oh, Nan, you're so strong. How can you be so strong?' And I said, 'Well, I've got a faith.' But Carol was all the time saying, 'Don't tell me there is a God. How can there be a God?' She was annoyed with me about that. That was really hard and I thought, Well, if there isn't a God, what are you going to rely on? It was a difficult time. But it worked out. She comes now and tells me all sorts of things.

There was never anyone after George. I had various offers but I was so busy with the family and with my nursing job that I never really felt I wanted to. I felt as if my life was full with other things. And maybe I didn't want anyone else, I don't know. Marriage is by no means made in heaven, we had our ups and downs, and even though I don't think romance quite came up to what I expected, what with the books I had read and everything, on the other hand there was a lot of kindness and consideration. George was the kindest and most considerate of men and he tried to do his best. Kindness and consideration come into marriage far more. When the glamour has gone off you have still got that.

I'm eighty-five now. I still do my things, I go swimming twice a week. It keeps me busy. Ever since George died, and then Franklin, I've always just taken one day at a time. Another of my friends has just lost her husband and I said the same thing to her as was said to me, I said 'Take it one day at a time,' because it helps. You go to bed at night and think, 'I have got through today: tomorrow can't be any worse.' That makes me sound unhappy. I'm not. I enjoy life very much. Most evenings, I go to bed grateful for the day and looking forward to the next, wondering what tomorrow will bring.

Lisa Wallis

Franklin's Daughter

She's great, my gran. She used to live in this house, and when she moved into the centre of town, my husband Mark and I moved in here. And I always remember, because Gran's always been open-minded, when I was little, if I'd had an argument I could come and sit in here and sulk and she wouldn't even ask me what was wrong; you know, just to have somebody else there was lovely.

I definitely think to have a stable family life's the most important thing to any human, really. It's something I want to give my children, because if you've got that then you'll be OK. And it's lovely now, for the girls, that Gran's there still. They love her. She's eighty-five and she still goes swimming in the mornings, she loves it. And sometimes she goes in the evenings, she gets a fancy for a swim, and off she goes, bless her. But she did say to me the other day, 'If you come and I'm not here, do come and have a look inside, won't you.' I said, 'Well, yeah, of course, Nan, if you want me to.' She said, 'Because I might have popped off.' She said: 'Sometimes I sit in my chair and I think, OK then, that'll do, I'll be happy to go now.' That must be so nice to feel like that, that you've done everything. And I can't say I'm looking forward to dying but I'm not frightened of it. I don't, obviously, want to leave the children and the people that are here, but I think it'll be great because you can let go; you can just let go.

My dad died when I was twenty-six. He just went out and didn't come back. I think he knew. He must have known. He'd been for like an MOT with private health care a couple of months before, and I don't think he felt ill. He went out for a bike ride with his friend, they used to bike out Denchworth way and up to White Horse Hill and back down, once a week, and he just fell over and that was it.

A neighbour phoned and told us what had happened, and the first thing I thought was, Oh, I wish I'd been there. Thinking of it now, I think that would have been awful, because I don't think you'd ever forget that, would you, but that's how I felt at the time: I wish I'd been there. Looking back, it was almost as if we knew we were going to lose him early, I don't know why. He always packed so much in all the time. He never slept, you know, he would go out playing with his band and that, he'd be out until three in the morning and be back up at six to work. In the early sixties, before we were born, he lived in France with the Beatles and the Stones and played in their backing bands. We've got some great pictures of him, singing and playing. He'd done so much. He always used to say, 'I've done everything I want to,' so he was happy.

We knew the kind of funeral that we wanted, because he'd told us what kind of funeral he wanted. He wanted to be buried, and he wanted a jazz band, and he wanted everybody in summer clothes, and he wanted everyone to walk. Luckily it was in the summer, so that's what we did. It's quite difficult to get a jazz band to play at a funeral but I found one and, in fact, everyone was dancing. It sounds quite blasphemous really, doesn't it, but we danced to the cemetery. I think some of the older ones were a bit horrified but my gran just fitted in with everybody else, which is really good because she's religious and it wasn't very religious, and it must have been awful for her, losing her son.

I feel quite cheated by his death, still after six years. Especially for my children, and for my sister Zoe's children too. Especially when ... I don't know, this sounds kind of bitter, but Mark's father ... I just feel my dad should be here, which isn't a very nice way of thinking, but you can't help it sometimes. And when we drove over to my parents' house the night Dad died, Mark said to me, 'It shouldn't have been him.'

Dad always had an answer about anything, you know, even if it was wrong. But if he didn't know, he'd find out for you, and there's not many people like that around, is there. I'm sorry, I knew I'd cry; it's just ... that's the main thing I miss, not being able to talk to him. Obviously he wouldn't be able to help in all my problems, a lot of things parents can't do anything about, but just to talk to him ... I can still do that, of course, and he can't answer me back, can he, he just has to listen to me all the time now. But he was always there and he was just like us. He could be your dad, he could be a grown-up dad, or you could go out for a drink with him. He was whatever you wanted him to be, really. He's special.

When I was fifteen, my first boyfriend, Allen, he died. That was a shock: he was only sixteen, and people didn't die. God, it was awful. He was run over by a hit-and-run driver and everyone knew who it was, it was the gypsies, but nothing ever came of it. But I think I learnt from Allen's death that death is not that bad: being left behind is awful but death is not that bad. I don't know really why I feel that but when Dad died, years after Allen, a friend of ours came to see us and she had a little boy, and he was about six, and he said to his mum, 'Why are they all crying?' She explained what had happened and he said, 'But he'll be happy now.' And that made me think that if a child can see that, then there must be something in it. We put a lot of obstacles in the way, and think of ourselves a lot when someone dies, and when you go to a funeral it's very sad because you see the family and you think, 'You poor things,' and you know the people are often crying for themselves and for the family that's left. But I think death is going to be a nice place to go. I *hope* it's a nice place to go, wherever it is.

It's been shocking to face death, really. But I don't think we deal with death very well, and if one of the older relations dies in the family I always take the girls to the funeral because I think that's important. I know when I went to Allen's funeral, I just couldn't cope with it. It was my first funeral, I didn't know what was going to happen. I'd never seen a dead body. And they brought a coffin in, and there was a dead person in there, Allen, and how do you cope with that? So I think it's important for the girls to know about death and to be around death. It's kind of morbid but death's a big part of life, isn't it. We're all going to go there sometime.

I don't believe that death's just nowhere: I don't because then you can't accept people just going, can you. And things that happen tell you that maybe they're still around. Maybe it's just your imagination, but things happen, funny things. I can smell Dad's smelly feet, and things go missing and then turn up, and I'm sure it's him. Mark's often said, 'Do you think it might be your dad?' I drove to Oxford, actually, not long after he died, and it was a horrible night, and something grabbed my hand on the steering-wheel. Now, I don't know what it was, and I don't know why but I looked in the wing mirror, and I saw Dad's face. I was obviously thinking of him. But I'm petrified of hitting an animal, and it pulled me away from a fox that was in the road, and I probably would have crashed otherwise. It's things like that. And if I've got a problem, I'll talk to Dad.

I'm sure Allen's around too. Mark and Allen were very good friends. Mark and I had a little cottage in town, which I lived in with someone called David, who I was engaged to before I married Mark, and who's still a really good friend. Anyway, David moved out and Mark moved in, and the bed would be moved over to the other side of the room when we came home from work. Not tipped over, but pushed over to the other side of the room, and I could understand if it was a wooden floor and you'd pushed it by mistake, but there was carpet. The kitchen was the worst thing. We slept up on the third floor, and you know like if someone comes in when you're in bed and starts making coffee and banging around in the cupboards? Well, it was just like that. And Mark would run as fast as he could, down the stairs, and there'd be no one there. It was very loud and it happened so often we didn't take any notice. It calmed down a bit after a while, but

Mark was convinced it was Allen and I think we both felt that at the time. It did seem that someone was trying to tell you they're around.

I hope Dad's still around. I'm sure he is. I think he thought there was definitely somewhere afterwards. He used to go to acupuncture for his knees, he had stiff knees, and for his weight, and for his smoking: I think he just enjoyed that kind of thing. And his acupuncturist phoned the morning after he'd died, and we hadn't told him but he knew that Dad'd gone, and he said that Dad was a very old spirit because he'd passed straight over, he'd gone straight through.

I don't know if Gran mentioned it but I've got a cancer gene. My mum's had breast cancer twice, and I've got the gene, so I had a double mastectomy and implants last year, and that was partly a decision with Dad: I talked to him about it, and I know that's what he would have wanted. He would have said, 'Do what you want to do.' It really wasn't a decision, it had to be done, but they made me go for counselling before they did the gene test, and I was trying to explain to them that it's not a problem, that it's not going to affect me, or our marriage, or my relationship with my sister, because our family, if you've got something like that, you do as much as you can do for yourself and then carry on, which seems quite logical to me.

You've got a fifty–fifty chance of inheriting it and my sister Zoe didn't get it. But then, you know, you worry about the girls; my daughters, will they get it? You don't know. Hopefully, they'll know more about it by then. I'm not quite sure of the numbers but I think about 87 per cent of breast cancer is caused by this gene, and there's a slightly increased risk of ovarian cancer as well: so that's another surgical procedure I'm going to have to go through sometime, because my cancer gene carries both risks. But there you are: even when I'm old I'll have good boobs, though they don't feel normal, obviously, because they're not.

Mark found it quite difficult, I think; not the surgery, but for me to be so determined to have the operations, because I had to fight the surgeons to make them do it. My surgeon said, 'You know, there's no guarantee. You can still get it.' But I've done all I can, and I can be screened, and I feel fortunate that they found it and I can know that I've got it. You could get angry. I could, quite easily, if I sat down and thought about my life, I could think, It's not fair. But there's no point in being like that, is there. You just think of tomorrow. And backpacking, one day.

I'm thirty-two, and Poppy's eight now, and I've still got kind of itchy feet. I've always wanted to go backpacking, and maybe that's Dad coming through: I'd definitely like to see some of the places he did. Mark and I came together when we were both quite free spirits, and then I had Poppy very quickly, we hadn't been married a year, because I'd had endometriosis and they told me, 'If you want children, have them now.' We did want children but we didn't want them now: we were thinking of going away for a couple of years, so that's something we've never done. We had the children before we'd really had time to think.

It was quite a shock for both of us to be responsible for a baby so soon. And I suppose, since Dad died, in a way Mark's had to be like my dad as well as my husband, because I do try and be happy most of the time but sometimes it's difficult. A lot of people don't see me when I'm angry, and when I'm really ratty, but I've got a very foul temper and not many people know, except for people like poor Mark. He's had to take a lot on with me, I think, because I used to go and do that to Dad, I could go, 'I'm pissed off with this: this just isn't fair,' and he'd say, 'No, it's not,' and Mark has to do that now.

The person I find I have to look after is my mother. Not look after, perhaps, that's not the right thing to say, but I like to make sure she's all right. I suppose I do have to look out for her a bit more now, like phone people up and shout at them; things like that. I've stepped into Dad's shoes there, I think, because they had quite an old-fashioned relationship. Dad did all the book work and paid the bills, and Mum was the housewife, although she did work as well, and when Dad died all the paperwork was left to me to sort out. Dad was always self-employed. He was a panel beater, amongst other things, and the book work for his business was in a terrible mess usually, but when he died it was all up to date. There was little notes about things too, and he had a phone book that he always kept in his briefcase, of all his contacts, and that was left with the paperwork. It was totally out of character, and it's things like that that make you think he knew he was going. Everything was left in its proper place.

Mum's got someone now. He's a friend of the family. We've all known him for years. He's divorced, quite a bit older than Dad and her, and he's lovely. Completely different to my dad but he's great, and he loves the kids too and that's nice. But in a way I think I felt a bit like Gran did about Mum, that I had to look after her and let her get over her grief before I could grieve: because she just wasn't here, she was on another planet for months, really. She didn't make me feel like that but I put myself in that situation, and Mark had to put up with my tempers while the grief was being delayed.

Dad's death was kind of the making of Mark, because Mark hadn't had a stable upbringing, he would always stand back and let other people do things, but he took over all the manly things to do, phoned everybody and told them, which he just wouldn't have done before. He felt he had to look after us, as I felt I had to look after Mum, and he was there behind us all. It was almost as if Dad'd left Mark the responsibility, because Dad'd become a father to Mark, and Mark'd learnt a lot of things from Dad, although he hadn't really known him all that long. And I know I want to give my children what I had. I want to be the one that gives them all the answers, like Dad was to me, like a rock at home that you can hang on to. I want them to know that there's always someone. I want them to know that we're always here, it doesn't matter what they do. So it's almost as if Dad left us all something to do, and to be responsible for. Almost as if he knew he was going, but he left us all in the right place at the right time.

Ian Mould & Tina Jones

The Twilight Zone

TINA: I hated the place.

IAN: Yeah, but then your mum didn't help things, did she. She told Tina, when they was moving to Wantage, that it was such a small little village that it'd get snowed in. 'You get snowed in,' she said.

TINA: Yeah, she said we'd be moving into the country and I pictured a little cottage in the middle of fields. To me, that's what the country is. And Dad said I could have a horse, and I was expecting all sorts of things, and instead I got a housing estate.

IAN: Her mum was still telling everybody they'd get snowed in.

TINA: I used to look out of my bedroom window and see houses. It just wasn't what I expected. And to go from a good girls' grammar school, where you stood up when the teacher walked in, to a secondary school like Segsbury, was dreadful.

IAN: Bedlam Segsbury.

TINA: It was an awful school.

IAN: It was, yeah. Terrible for education. It's supposed to be better now.

TINA: There was no discipline, was there. I mean, you just did whatever you wanted.

IAN: Yeah. Running around being a pain in the arse.

TINA: And there were teachers being abused by pupils. It scared the life out of me, I couldn't cope with it at all. I didn't really enjoy it until I was about fifteen, and by then it was too late because there was no incentive to do well and I gave up.

IAN: I found that with Wantage all in all, though, really.

TINA: No ambition, is there.

IAN: No.

TINA: The ambition is to get married and have children.

IAN: Yeah. I go back to Wantage now, and I'll go into the Swan pub. Like, I've not been in there for years and years and years, and when I go in there I bump into someone who I've not seen for about five years. And he says, 'Hello, Mouldy. I've not seen you for a little while, where you been, then?' I says, 'I moved out years ago.' He says, 'Oh, I thought you was drinking in a different pub.'

TINA: We used to say when we were in Wantage that you could guarantee that you could leave it and then come back in ten years' time, and it'll be the same people, in the same pubs, at the same time, doing exactly the same thing. We used to call it the Twilight Zone because it doesn't move on. I mean, it's nice to go back but I'm glad I'm not living there any more. I'd never go back there to live.

IAN: No, it's a strange place. And it should be a beautiful little place, really, shouldn't it.

TINA: It should be. It's such a strange mixture. Say on a Saturday, everyone's out shopping, and you've got the yobs sitting outside the Bear Hotel, and then you've got the horsewomen in their jodhpurs and their BMWs and their Mercedes coming in to do a bit of shopping, and the St Mary's schoolgirls trotting around. The St Mary's schoolgirls were the worst; terrible snobs. I think they were worse than anybody else there.

IAN: St Mary's girls were easy: a lot of them were old slags. At those point-to-point meetings, I've caught loads of them shagging behind the beer tents.

TINA: Shagging them yourself.

IAN: Only one, only one. Though you'd think St Mary's girls wouldn't look at me, a common Wantage kind of person.

TINA: I was back in Wantage a couple of weeks ago actually. I went to visit my mum. And I saw somebody that had been in Wantage for years and I said to my mum, 'I can never imagine being born somewhere and living your whole life there, and dying in that same place.' I could never imagine that.

IAN: Well, what about Herbie, this guy that I work with? He's got a lovely cottage down in Dorset, and a friend of his, he hasn't been outside the village. The village is only five hundred people but he's never been out of that village in his life, except he's been down to Bridport once. That's the only place that he's ever been in his life, Bridport.

TINA: I can't understand it.

IAN: Well, some people just can't see no further than the end of their nose.

TINA: I suppose if you haven't got a lot of ambition and you're quite happy to be in the same place, and all your friends are there, you just get in a rut. It's just what you want out of your life, isn't it, really. I mean, our life changed because we went to Australia, and after that we just didn't want to come back to Wantage.

IAN: Well, it was putting a strain on us, really, being in Wantage. So much strain. Like, I wanted to be with my mates all the time, and it was unfair, really, on our relationship. I wanted to go out with my mates and Tina wanted me to stay home.

TINA: It's an old drinking place for blokes, Wantage. The whole social life is the pubs, there's nothing else.

IAN: Yeah. And we decided that if we was going to stay together, we was going to have to get out of Wantage. If we'd stayed there we wouldn't be together now, and we wouldn't have our two little boys. It would have dragged us right under.

TINA: And you've changed dramatically since we've left.

IAN: Oh yeah, definitely. Definitely. I'm a lot easier-going now. I used to be fighting all the time. Now I look back at it and get so embarrassed. There was not a weekend that'd go by without me getting into a fight. Stupid, pathetic.

TINA: It was all drink related.

IAN: There's so many pubs, and Wantage is such a small place, with nothing else to do, that people would drink and just end up having a fight. It's sad, it's terrible, it's embarrassing, it's crazy.

TINA: The way Ian's lived, his life could have gone one of two ways, and it's gone OK. But he could be in prison by now.

IAN: Oh yeah, easily.

TINA: I mean, the amount of times with him fighting, it used to scare the life out of me: I was terrified he would hit somebody, they'd fall and crack their head on a kerb, dead. You know, that's manslaughter. A brawl could have ruined his life.

IAN: And I can honestly say, since I've been at Guildford I've not been into a fight. I've not been in any trouble at all, have I.

TINA: No.

IAN: Not at all. It's Wantage, you see, the Wantage culture; drinking, fighting, that's all it is. Have you ever seen that film *The Stepford Wives*? That is like Wantage. The women are meant to leave school, have babies; the men are meant to go to the pub, get drunk and have fights, and that's it.

TINA: Him and Graham Douglas and their friend Steve were terrible. If they weren't drunk and fighting, they'd be getting other people into trouble.

IAN: There was a bloke in my class, Michael Farrar. Graham and Steve and me, we was always getting Michael into trouble. I remember throwing one of those snap-it things, those things that you used to throw on the floor and they'd bang. I threw one of those and Michael Farrar got the blame for it. I was sitting there, innocent, and the teacher looked at Farrar and said, 'Farrar, I saw you do it,' and Farrar said, 'Well, you're fucking lying.' And with this, the teacher grabbed hold of Farrar and frog-marched him to the headmaster. Anyway, we're all bloody unruly now, 'cause we're in a classroom full of no teacher, and we're all throwing things about. This other teacher – Egghead – he walks past and he sees this lot going on, so he walks in and he stands behind the door to quieten us down. Then we see Farrar coming towards the classroom, going like this, rubbing his bum. He walks in, not knowing that Egghead's behind the door, and he goes, 'Do you know, that fucking fat bastard caned me!' And Egghead frog-marches him back there, and he gets it again.

The week after, Steve pushed Farrar out the window. Farrar was having a fag out the classroom window and I said, 'Give us a drag of that, Farrar,' and he said, 'Yeah, in a minute,' and I said, 'No, now,' and he went, 'No, in a minute.' So Steve says, 'I'll sort him,' and he pushed him, like joking about, and Farrar fell out the window. We was expecting him to get up, and he didn't get up, he was on the floor, like bloody twitching about, when the teacher came in. Fag smoke was drifting up through the window so I said, 'Farrar, put the fag out, quickly. *Quickly*, put the fag out!' but he was still lying there. Steve said, 'He's bluffing,' but he wouldn't move. So Steve says, 'Look, Farrar, if you don't move, I'm gonna gob on your fag,' so he spat on his fag, and Farrar still didn't move. The teacher come marching over and said, 'Mouldy. Steve. You've been smoking.' We said, 'No, no, we haven't, sir. We haven't. We've just come in here.' He said, 'You've been smoking, I can smell it.' We said, 'No, no, we've just walked in here. Do you know what, we reckon Farrar's been having a fag out the window and he's fallen out.' So Farrar got dragged up, and after they'd revived him, they caned him.

TINA: It was a terrible school.

IAN: See, that's one of the things about school. School can ruin someone's life.

TINA: Especially when you've got people like you there.

IAN: It's true. I look back now and think, *Why* was I like that? I would never, ever wish that on anybody, some of the stupid things me and Steve done to people. It can ruin people's lives, it can ruin their self-confidence.

TINA: Can you imagine someone doing what you did to people, to your children now? You'd be horrified, wouldn't you.

IAN: Oh yeah, it would break my heart, it really would.

TINA: But you just don't think when you're kids.

IAN: Thank God I got away or God knows how I'd be now. Like the ones who stayed behind, I suppose. And do you know, I can't think of anybody in Wantage who's actually stayed there who's changed. When I go back there, there'll be a big issue over which pub to go to. They'll be like, 'We're not drinking in the Blue Boar any more. No way!' Now that's a big thing to them, but I've got so much to tell them, because I've been doing so much up this way, and all they can talk about is which pub.

TINA: One time, I was still living at home in Wantage and my parents had gone on holiday, so I'd organized a big barbecue, make the most of an empty house. Ian and I'd invited a few people and they wouldn't come because it was a Saturday night. I said, 'Have you got anything else planned?' They said, 'Well, no, but it's a Saturday night. We go to the pub on a Saturday night.'

IAN: They go to the pub.

TINA: I said, 'But you go to the pub every night.' 'Yeah, but we don't like to miss a Saturday.' And they wouldn't do something else socially because it was Saturday night and that was pub time.

IAN: And then when someone actually discovered Oxford, where there's *loads* of pubs, full of different people, it was like the world wasn't flat after Wantage. God, it's sad, remembering.

TINA: All driving back drunk.

IAN: Yes, God, it's disgusting. I lost my licence, and I'd never, ever, *ever* do it now. I'd never.

TINA: Everyone did it, didn't they.

IAN: Yeah.

TINA: All the blokes, anyway.

IAN: You just don't think of the consequences. You don't think that you might hit someone. It's only now that you think, Oh, God, why? Why did we used to be like that? It was lack of direction, I think.

TINA: And I didn't really have much of a social life outside Ian at that time because all my friends had gone off to university, or left Wantage, and I was working in Oxford; so I would come back home, expecting Ian to be around, and he wasn't. There were so many times we'd arrange things. There was one time, I'd got really close with a girl from work, invited her and her husband over because my parents were out for the evening. Big barbecue. I was really chuffed that I was hostessing something, you know, one of my first ones. I got back home and Ian'd been drinking all day. *All day.* And I couldn't even rouse him, he was that drunk.

IAN: So embarrassing.

TINA: I mean, I kicked and punched, I was so angry, and in the end he said, 'I'll go and walk the dog. I'll get sobered up.' So these people came over and halfway through the dinner Ian fell into his.

IAN: Oh, it's embarrassing, thinking back to it.

TINA: This was the norm, this was the norm. I don't know how I stuck it, I really don't.

IAN: I'm glad you did.

TINA: Yeah, I'm glad I did. But I don't know *how* I did.

IAN: So we both decided that it wasn't for us, Wantage.

TINA: I mean, Saturdays, the blokes just went out and drunk all day, from eleven o'clock in the morning. And Sundays, we used to go down the pubs at twelve, finish at three, then we'd be down the Indian by six. And by the time we'd had our meal, the pubs would be open again at seven.

IAN: Isn't it sad, living just by the pub opening times, and there's so many other things to do. We were lucky we got out. I mean, there's a few people in Wantage who have done really well, like my friend Andy. He's just landed this new job, and he's on £1,750 quid a week. A week!

TINA: There's a lot of people that have done well.

IAN: Yeah, but that's only from getting out of the place. Andy's in Oxford now. He'd never, ever have done that in Wantage. Although Graham's done really well, Graham Douglas. I was always surprised he became an estate agent. I always thought Graham was destined to be a professional footballer, because he had such a talent, he could have been. His dad was so annoyed about that, you know, because Graham should have been training and he was going out and bloody drinking with me and Steve. Then all of a sudden Graham met Jane and he changed overnight.

TINA: He seemed to lose it, didn't he, when they split up.

IAN: Yeah, he got very down.

TINA: I mean, it was real sort of intensive relationships in Wantage. Like, it was all dramas when they finished.

IAN: Yeah, but Tina, you think of it as intensive relationships, but in a town like Wantage, when you've got nothing else to talk about, if someone splits up with someone that is the main news.

TINA: It's incestuous.

IAN: Yeah, oh definitely.

TINA: I've got a terrible memory for people in Wantage. Ian's always saying, 'Do you remember him? Do you remember her?' and I can't.

IAN: Do you remember Lynn Ross? I used to go out with her.

TINA: Ian's first love.

IAN: Yeah, we was going to go out to France, I was going to drive her over there, that's what I always said.

TINA: She's up herself, Lynn.

IAN: Oh God, yeah, if she was made of chocolate she'd eat herself. She was so bloody pretentious.

TINA: She hung around with Sharon Rawlings.

IAN: I used to go out with her too. Do you remember Louise Lee?

TINA: Yeah, Louise Lee is imprinted on my brain.

IAN: She used to get her nipples out, show us her nipples. She said, 'Look at that, I've got no tits at all but I've got the longest nipples in the world.'

TINA: There's a lot of people like Louise Lee in Wantage. She's from one of the families that everyone knows. Her grandmother's there, and the aunts and uncles, whole generations have lived there all their lives.

IAN: Yeah, and if you go out to the villages, like Hanney, Hendred, Lockinge, Ardington, Letcombe, Childrey, Uffington, it's even worse.

TINA: That's what my mum used to say when she first moved to Wantage. She was so used to London life and rushing around that she'd go to a shop and she'd be in there half an hour, queuing, waiting for two old grannies to stop their conversation. Now she's one of those old grannies. She's completely into all that now, knows all the ins and outs about everybody.

IAN: That's another thing. You couldn't do anything in Wantage without everybody knowing about it. All the Chinese whispers as well. Like, you can start a rumour, just for the laugh, and say, 'Look, I don't want this to get any further,' and guarantee that later that night you'll hear the same story and it's twenty times worse. And that's another reason I'm glad we moved out.

TINA: Claustrophobic.

IAN: Like, if you've got ambitions, if you want to travel, the attitude in Wantage is, 'Why? You can get a video about it if you want.'

TINA: Yeah, and I think if we hadn't have travelled when we did, we could very well still be there.

IAN: I wouldn't have been there now. No way at all.

TINA: You don't know that.

IAN: I wouldn't have been, Tina, not at all. See, I was always money-motivated, I always wanted to make a lot of money. When I was in Wantage I was earning good money, because it was the eighties, boom-time, and at the age of eighteen I was getting £80 a day. That was a lot for laying bricks. So I was earning brilliant money, but when you're drinking all the time it doesn't go anywhere, not after tax. I was giving my mum twenty quid a week, then by about Wednesday each week I'd be getting a sub off of her: I'd be saying, 'Oh Mum, could you lend me thirty quid?' I was doing such stupid things. I had a nice car. And my bedroom, you should have seen my bedroom. Two videos in there, the telly, a stereo: everything was remote control, I'd paid real big money for everything. There was an aquarium in there too. It was so tacky! There was a fridge full of wine and beers. Oh, and I had a phone: I used to dial 173 or something, and then hold the thing down, it would ring inside the house, my mum used to pick the phone up and I'd say to her, 'Could you bring us some breakfast?'

TINA: We used to order breakfast. I feel awful about that.

IAN: Yeah. And my mum used to trot up with it.

TINA: She did. We were only eighteen and she used to bring up breakfast, and we'd be laying in bed together.

IAN: It was great!

TINA: He used to be allowed to get away with murder.

IAN: I didn't. I was always known as 'Mummy's little lamb chop, boy of the million moo cows.' She still calls me that now, 'Mummy's lamb chop. Hello, lamb chop.'

TINA: Well, you don't get breakfast from her now.

IAN: No, now my mum and dad live in Spain and they've got a plaque on the wall, it says, 'Spending our children's inheritance.' So, like I said, I was definitely money motivated, and that made me want to get out of Wantage because I didn't think you could do well there. We went travelling to Australia for a few months, done Malaysia too, and when we came back we thought, Let's go to Guildford, Guildford's a nice place, bigger, with more opportunities. So we did, and Tina really got back into her work. She started working at Toni & Guy's and she was earning great money, and I started getting a bit lazy because all of a sudden she was overtaking me. You was earning great money, wasn't you, Tina.

TINA: I was.

IAN: So I thought, Well, I don't really need to work this hard now. And I started getting a bit lax and not working on a Monday.

TINA: Went back to your bingeing on a weekend.

IAN: Yeah, but that was before the children.

TINA: It's only quite recently you've changed.

IAN: The last four years.

TINA: That's quite recent. We've been together thirteen.

IAN: I know, but you've forgiven me now.

TINA: See, I had great ambitions, big ambitions. I saw myself as an executive-type person. I don't know how I got into hairdressing, it wasn't a first pick at all. I think it's because at school you were either going to be a cook, a nurse, a hairdresser or a secretary.

IAN: That's what they brainwashed you into thinking.

TINA: I applied for a variety of things, hairdressing and secretarial work, and I thought about going into the police. I really wanted to go into the police force but because of peer pressure I didn't, because everyone had such a low opinion of the police. I still regret that. I thought about it a few years ago, and he, Ian, he really hated the idea.

IAN: I did, yeah. I did.

TINA: He was more concerned about what friends would think.

IAN: See, we've got so many friends round Guildford. We could be at a dinner party. Say there's ten people round the table, and maybe there's five or six people we don't know and we introduce ourselves: 'I'm Ian, I'm a builder. And this is Tina, my partner, she's a police officer.' The conversation would just go dead. They'd think, 'Oh shit, I ain't got no road tax for the car at the moment.' That sounds silly but it does happen like that, Tina. I *know* it's a great job—

TINA: It's something I always wanted to do, Ian, and I think if I'd have gone for it and done it, I would have been really good at it.

IAN: You'd have been a horrible copper! She'd have been a real tyrant. They used to call her Tina the Tyrant at work, all the juniors.

TINA: Yeah, they were pretty scared of me.

IAN: I'm still scared of her now.

TINA: A lot of people are. I suppose it's because I speak my mind; and because I find it really hard to get to know people I'm inclined to be stand-offish until I know them well. I don't know where it's got me, though: my life hasn't gone anywhere near how I planned it because I chose Ian before what I had in mind for myself.

IAN: Yeah, the way it should be!

TINA: And then sometimes I think, Well, what if I hadn't done things because of him? The only reason I went to Australia was because Ian really wanted to go and we were about to split up.

IAN: I was originally going to go to America with Steve, wasn't I. Me and Steve were living together and Steve bought his mum's council flat. At the time you could remortgage at the drop of a hat, so he bought this place, straightaway remortgaged it by ten grand, and said, 'Let's go travelling.' I said, 'I can't, I'm seeing Tina.'

TINA: And Steve said, 'Well, finish with her.'

IAN: Yeah, 'Finish with her. I'll pay for everything.' So I phoned Tina up and said, 'Tina, we're going to have to split up,' and we were getting on brilliantly at the time.

TINA: I was devastated.

IAN: She wanted to know why and I said, ''Cause Steve's taking me to America.'

TINA: Men are so cruel.

IAN: Horrible.

TINA: He didn't go. He stayed with me on the grounds that we were going to go travelling, so we did. And I enjoyed it but I had a really good job at the time, I was doing really well, and I had to give it up.

IAN: Tina could have gone a long way with her work, couldn't you.

TINA: Yeah, I could of. Six years I was there, I was head of department.

IAN: And I was a bit jealous, I think, if I'm honest.

TINA: I think you were.

IAN: I didn't like it that I was earning great money and then suddenly Tina was earning more.

TINA: Did you think I was doing better than you?

IAN: Yeah, I did. Tina was doing really well and I thought, Hold on a minute, this isn't right. There was a bit of jealousy there, definitely.

TINA: But you should have supported me in what I was doing.

IAN: Yeah, I know.

TINA: It's a shame, because I regret leaving there.

IAN: Yeah, you see, I can get a job anywhere; Tina can't. Though she got offered a job in Australia: we could have stayed.

TINA: Yeah. Could of. But by that time we were missing everybody and we just wanted to get home. And I really like Guildford, I'm glad we moved here, but if I could do it again, I would do it differently. Now we've got the boys and that's really cool; and I'm working from home now, so that's OK, but I do find it very stressful doing hairdressing from home because I've got to fit it round everything.

Right now I'm finding things quite hard. I go through the motions of being a mum, and I do love my kids, but I feel that that's not me. I mean, I'm a mother of two children but I don't see myself in the *role* of having two children, I see myself as somebody different. I see myself as a person going out to work and earning money and being independent, and I'm not that person now, and that's what I find very hard because that's what my self-image is. When I was at work, I could say to whoever, 'Go and do that for me, go and do this for me,' and they'd just trot off and do it. Now I'm at home with a three-year-old who I tell to do something and he just turns round and blows raspberries at me. I've always had authority and I don't at home. At work I was respected. At home, I haven't got any sort of authority, or any routine, it's like days just flow into days.

I can see now that I had post-natal depression after my first child and that's affected me. I had no support from Ian at the time, he quite openly says he didn't support me at all. None of my friends had children, I was stuck in the house, had nothing to do apart from looking after this child. I didn't really bond with him at all because he was five weeks early and in special care, and I couldn't wait to get back to work. I was just going through the motions of looking after this baby, changing its nappy, feeding it, putting it to sleep.

IAN: Yeah, but you've gone the other way now.

TINA: I've been the opposite with Jordan. But with George I was in labour all on my own because Ian wasn't there. Ian was out on the piss.

IAN: Do you know what, I really do regret that. That's something in my life that if I could ever change, that would be it.

TINA: He couldn't help it, he didn't know it was going to come that early. I had a four-hour labour, so it was like, push, gone, all of a sudden I had a baby. It was so surreal, it was as though it wasn't me at all. Ian came to see the baby; he went, 'Oh, a baby'; he stayed about fifteen minutes and then he was off down the pub. And when I got out with this baby, it didn't feel like it was *my* baby. It was just *a* baby.

Three months later I went back to work and I was so glad. My first client said to me, 'You must feel awful, leaving your child,' and I felt awful thinking, No, I couldn't wait to get here. I could not wait to leave that baby with somebody else. But the minute I went back to work I was back to myself, and I couldn't wait to get back to my baby.

IAN: Right, you say that now, Tina. But with Jordan, right, it's gone totally the opposite way. Sometimes it happens like that. She's giving such a bad picture of herself but Tina's such a loving mother, she really is.

TINA: I'm intrigued, though, because if you ask women specifically what they feel, a lot feel like I did.

IAN: Yeah, but with little Jordan, right, as soon as he was born Tina couldn't keep her hands off him. And she can't keep her hands off him now, can you, darling. Honestly, she's all the time cuddling him, and there was none of that with George.

TINA: No, I used to feed George, put him down, that was it. Jordan was a different story. Obviously I love George but when I was pregnant with Jordan there was more support from Ian.

IAN: But Tina hasn't alienated George, have you. George is still very special.

TINA: Oh yeah. After a while I thought, How can you love anyone as much as your first child? We always kept saying that, 'We can't imagine having another baby.' But you do and you love them just as much.

IAN: I'll tell you something now. A friend of mine, right, he's a drugs dealer in Guildford, he's probably one of the biggest drugs dealers around Guildford. And he's got five cats, right, five cats. Recently, he's just got this girl pregnant. And I took him down the fish and chip shop. We'd been out for the afternoon and I'd bumped into him, and he said, 'Can you give me a lift down the fish and chip shop?' and I said, 'Yeah, all right, mate.' So we was driving down the fish and chip shop, totally sober, and he said, 'Here, Ian,' he said, 'you've got two children, haven't you.' I said, 'Yeah.' He said, 'Well, you know I'm expecting one.' I said, 'Yeah?' He said, 'Well, can you love a baby as much as you can a cat?' Right? And I said, 'Yeah, yeah, of course you can.' And he said, 'How, though? 'Cause I love my cats and I can't imagine loving anything more than them.' This is a real big-time drugs dealer, and if you mess him about with money he'll get someone to sort you out, and he's saying he can't imagine loving anything more than a cat. He said, 'Explain it to me, then,' and I said, 'You can't explain love.' I said, 'The thing about a child is it's totally dependent on you.' I said, 'You have to do everything for a child because it's totally hopeless. With a cat,' I said, 'as soon as a little kitten's born, it'll go out, it might be able to find its own food, it'll forage. A baby can't.' 'Oh,' he says, 'OK, then.' And that was the last of the conversation.

TINA: Ian's really changed since the children. He's really into them now. Before, he used to go out for a drink on a Saturday lunchtime and come back whenever, whereas now he's always there before the kids go to bed, and weekends are family completely, aren't they.

IAN: I realize time's precious now.

TINA: And the minute these two go to school, I'll be back to work full-time. I don't understand women who don't. I could never imagine being kept by a man.

IAN: Tina still lies to me about money all the time. I give Tina my money every week, and whatever Tina makes I really don't know.

TINA: I control all the finances.

IAN: Before, when Tina used to earn a lot of money, it never used to be a problem. I'd go to the cashpoint and it was just like I had a never-ending money supply. We're putting my money in, and Tina's money in, and I'm like, 'Oh, I'll get a hundred quid out, yeah, great, go down the pub, brilliant.' I'd go the next day and get another hundred quid out and it was just not a problem. Like Utopia. And then all of a sudden you've got the children and there's only one wage packet, and you think, Shit! And Tina's saying to me, 'No, we can't afford that this week. We can't go out for a meal. We've got enough money for nappies until your next cheque clears.' I'm like, 'What's all this "till my next cheque clears" stuff?' Tina has honestly sorted the finances right out. She's a real steadying influence, Tina is. Tina is the big rock, actually, she really is. And I'll tell you something about true love. I loved Tina from the first day I saw her. This is straight up: I could have taken Metalwork or Woodwork in the fifth year at school but I took Home Economics because Tina was in the class.

TINA: We used to be best friends, didn't we.

IAN: We were only friendly, Tina, because I fancied you. That was the only reason. It wasn't like matey matey. There was always an ulterior motive, believe me.

TINA: He was going out with Lisa Wallis then and I was seeing somebody else.

IAN: Yeah, I was really jealous about it.

TINA: And we used to chat. He used to tell me about Lisa and I used to tell him about my boyfriends. And then we got really drunk one night and ended up sleeping together.

IAN: It all went horribly wrong.

TINA: It did. Going from being really good mates to being lovers. We didn't speak for about four months. And then we had a nightmare relationship. We started living together, and Ian used to go out on Friday night with his mates and roll in Monday morning.

IAN: That was terrible.

TINA: And I was thinking, Right, that's it. If you ever do that again, I'm leaving you.

IAN: I was really into my mates.

TINA: The next weekend, he'd do exactly the same, and I didn't leave.

IAN: I was just a man. A man's man. But I regret what I put you through, Tina.

TINA: I regret it myself. My dad used to go absolutely mad at me. 'God, he's just a prat. What are you doing with him? You're just an idiot being with him.' I used to go through such hell, really, for Ian. The only thing that kept me going was that I kept thinking, He's going to come good; it's going to be really good; I know it'll work. And it's taken thirteen years for it to work but it has.

IAN: And now we're going to get married.

TINA: We are.

IAN: It was definitely a misinterpretation, because I said to Tina one night that I'd love to see her in something long and flowing and she interpreted it as a wedding gown. But I meant the River Thames!

TINA: Now we've got the two kids, we know we're definitely staying put in the relationship, and I want to get married because I feel strongly that I'm the only one that hasn't got the same name.

IAN: Yeah, Tina's a Jones.

TINA: It's not that I particularly want to be a Mould.

IAN: No, it's not the kind of name that you'd covet, is it.

TINA: All the time we were living together, it wasn't that important, and we had better things to spend our money on than getting married. We never really thought about it. But now we've got the two children, it's to do with security as well. I don't like being Miss Jones. It gets confusing. And we've been together a long time, plodding on, and now it's like a bit of excitement, getting married.

IAN: We're going to have a great big party.

TINA: Registry office and a massive party, with everybody there. Just go for it.

IAN: And then apply for residency for Australia at the same time because we're still toying with the idea of emigrating.

TINA: Ever since we come back that's all we think about, isn't it. Every few months we talk about it.

IAN: It's such a good standard of living, and I didn't have a bad upbringing in Wantage, but I wouldn't want my children brought up somewhere like there, I really wouldn't. I wouldn't want George and Jordan brought up anywhere in England probably, because by the time they grow up there's going to be guns and everything here, it's going to be really violent. So that's what we want, Australia, or possibly Spain. We'll sell up and go away and in twenty years' time we'll have a big house that I will have built, plenty of money in the bank, and a good lifestyle.

TINA: Living the life of Reilly. Two successful kids.

IAN: Yeah. I want them to be sportsmen.

TINA: I'd like them to be sportsmen too, I don't want them to be in the building trade. And I'm not going to push them to go to university,

I'd be quite happy for them to be in an apprenticeship-type job. I know I didn't stick to my ambitions but I would never push my kids into education.

IAN: Oh, Tina, come on, you can't say that. I'd like them to be educated better than us.

TINA: But I would never want to be a pressurizing mother.

IAN: But they could fall into a real bad trap, especially with me being the father, because in their summer holidays I could give them £30 a day to come and help me, and then they'd think, Hold on a minute, what's the point of bloody educating myself when I can earn this kind of money? And I don't want them to get into that trap. No way at all. They're going to go to college, and they're going to have a great education. They're going to pass all their exams and they're going to go for degrees as well.

TINA: I always remember my dad saying to me, 'If you grow up and sweep the streets I'll be proud of you,' and I think that's such a nice thing for a parent to say rather than, 'You've got to get your "A" levels, you've got to go to university.'

IAN: Well, yeah, but look what happened with me. My parents badgered Peter, my eldest brother, about education, because he was the first son: 'You're going to have a good education. You're going to do well. You will sit at home and do your homework.' Now, Peter is one of the top guys at the atomic research centre in Harwell, he's got a hundred people underneath him, he's earning mega, mega, mega money. But they lapsed off after him and what've they got? They've got my sister Lynn, who works for that Jewish guy, and me.

TINA: You're happy doing what you're doing.

IAN: I'm a bricklayer.

TINA: You're happy doing that. To be honest, Ian, I can't see you being in management, personally.

IAN: Well, no. But there are other things I want from life. There are other things.

Bill Galbraith

Death of a Nation

I grew up in a generation when we were in the middle of a war, and England at that time meant something. We were winning a war with practically no resources, and if you want to see the hand of God, it was certainly in the period 1939–45. Our generation, the first time we could vote was after the war, and we all voted in great expectation of social change and things being better for everybody. We were very happy to pay high income tax if it was providing National Health. When we were living in America we really argued with our friends about the National Health Service. We made some friends there who were medics, and one of them used to give one day a week for poor people, he had no pay for that day, and he thought that was the right way to do it. And we said no, we thought the National Health Service was the best. We used to have heated arguments about it.

I've spent a lot of my life studying particle physics and cosmic radiation. We lived in Wantage for sixteen years, while I was doing particle physics at the Harwell Laboratory. Then I got a Commonwealth Fund Fellowship to Berkeley, California, and I was at Berkeley for a year and a half, then later for another year in the US National Lab at Brookhaven, before coming back to England ultimately to take a Chair in Physics in Sheffield.

Going to California was just great. We were still rationed in Britain at that time and America was the land of plenty: there was petrol, and the sun shone all the time. You didn't need heavy clothes. You had cars, big cars. Everything was available. Everything was possible. After that, when I came back, I was intolerant at first, because when we were in America people would say, 'Let's do it!' They wouldn't stop and think. Whereas when we came back to England and we'd say, 'Let's do so and so,' people would say, 'Oh, you can't do that, it's impossible.' I don't mean professionally, I mean just in day-to-day life.

America was really an eye-opener, a change of life. All countries have their problems but I have a lot of time for America. I like the American way of life, the gung-ho attitude. They get on and do the job. My son's a plant scientist and he has a Chair in America, so we go over there a lot. We love it. There are some very sincere and pleasant people in America, it's television which depicts all the worst aspects of American life. American television is the dregs, as far as I'm concerned. The intellectual content is zero. They used to have things in America, on TV, which they thought were so wonderful because they came from the BBC, but not now.

Now the BBC also panders to the lowest common denominator. Now, TV programmes in England are all rubbish. You'd think from watching them that the whole country is nuts, and everyone is a child molester or a drug addict. That's something else that's changed in my lifetime: the whole attitude of entertainment. I mean, entertainment's not good clean fun any more. Violence, sex, drugs, that's what people want to watch, or that's what they're fed. I can't believe it doesn't have some effect on people, if they think this must be the norm.

The media knocks everything too. Everything. Particularly anything that's considered part of the establishment. The BBC constantly lets down the Christian Church, not directly, but by insinuation. Britain is trying to be a Christian nation in its approach to all these different religions within it, and that's good, but I am annoyed that the BBC treat Christians as if the whole thing is a joke. Our whole ethos, our Parliament and Queen, everything, revolves around the Christian faith, whether you like it or not, but the BBC just throws it into the melting pot with all these others. What are they trying to do? There are enough people trying to make this country pay no attention to religion whatsoever. But the Christian religion is one of the boys as far as the BBC is concerned, and considered fair game for snide jokes and innuendoes, particularly from comedians who should know better. They think it's being smart but it's not an English thing to do. Not as far as I'm concerned, anyway.

Everything's become so unethical in this country since the war. England as we knew it began to die with Heath. It finally died with Thatcher. We were trying our best to be a multicultural society: before Thatcher, there'd been twenty-five years of multicultural society. With her coming in, everyone turned into their own shells. Under Thatcher, England stopped being a receptive pleasant nation. Her attitude towards the miners was absolutely disgusting. Disgusting. That was the watershed, the years when she came in. I'm disappointed with the present Government too, they're a bunch of go-getters; though Prescott's a fine man, Prescott I like.

I can sum up British politics. I'm now seventy-four, and the *first* time my vote counted for anything was last May, when we changed our MP from a Conservative to a Liberal Democrat. Every other election I voted in, it made no difference whatsoever, and there's something wrong with politics when it's like that: people should feel there is merit in voting. I once voted Conservative because Elizabeth and I were so disgusted by the two candidates that she said she'd vote Labour and I'd vote Conservative so the votes wouldn't count. We couldn't not vote. You must vote. And any woman who doesn't vote, after all that women went through to get the vote, I feel is very wrong.

Some people wonder what's the point in voting. I suppose I can see why. I mean, we haven't had a statesman in this country since long before the war. People talk about how great Churchill was but Churchill was a war leader, he wasn't a statesman. He turned everyone upside down. He turned Europe against Britain, Britain against Europe. Winston Churchill didn't really make much of a name for himself as a PM in peacetime. Beveridge, he was a statesman, but they cut his kind to pieces. Ramsay MacDonald went in and out rather rapidly. Baldwin was a gentleman farmer from Shropshire. Chamberlain, oh God. Then Churchill. I'm perhaps a bit unfair on Attlee: Attlee was OK. Still, he wasn't a great figure by any means. Eden was. Compare Eden's stature in the 1930s with the current Foreign Secretary's now, there's just no comparison. Macmillan was blighted by his attitude that Britain had never had it so good. Harold Wilson, a wheeler-dealer. Edward Heath, weak. Callaghan came close to being a statesman but he was too distracted by trying to be a man of the people. Thatcher was overwhelming. Major: what can you say about him? And this present lot, they're not my cup of tea, these guys. They have no gravitas, no statesmanship about them whatsoever, any of them. They're run-of-the-mill politicians. There is not a single statesman left in Britain.

The whole atmosphere of this country has changed. I've felt this more and more over the past forty years. Money is God. I think that there are a lot of people nowadays who get paid far too much money and don't know what to do with it. We were at the theatre the other night in London, and I was amazed, going into the bar there, I was the oldest person in the bar and there were all these young yuppie types drinking gins and tonics and God knows what, and I felt completely alienated walking through them, heading for the loo. Maybe I was too sensitive but I sensed that they thought, 'What's this old codger doing coming through here?' In Derbyshire, we go walking, and you stop and have lunch in a pub after you've walked and you're all the same, you're all in walking boots and trousers whether you're twenty or whether you're eighty.

And d'you know, I didn't see a West Indian or African face in the theatre, and this was supposed to be a social occasion. There's a social divide there, so this idea of England being a multicultural society is pure imagination on behalf of the politicians. England's a very divided society. Elizabeth and I have Asian friends, African friends, some Chinese friends. There are people of all ethnic backgrounds in England, and they're trying to live normal English lives, but what is a normal English life now? There are English people who are trying to live English lives, and even they don't seem to be quite sure what that means any more.

Ralph Cobham

Beauty and the Beast

I'm lucky. Not everybody has a vocation. There was a time when, because of the antecedents in my family, I seriously considered entering the Church. There'd been three generations in the family who had been members of the Church and I was brought up with a very strong churchgoing ethic. In the end I chose a vocation that related to the things I felt most comfortable about, that I'd been trained in, and I chose to use that as the vehicle for trying to make a contribution to society. I'd been brought up to believe that if you'd been privileged you needed to give back, you needed to serve. That, as well as a real love of the countryside, a real love of nature, has driven me.

I live for the outdoors, totally. I'd always wanted to run my own business and I was increasingly attracted by the concept of environmental consultancy and advice, in those days when the environment didn't even register. I began the business by going to visit my brother, who at that stage was making a botanic garden in Tehran for the Shah. We had a fabulous time: Tehran was a very social place when the Shah and others were around. At the end of the fortnight, my wife Sue came home and I stayed on and walked the streets of Tehran, peddling a brochure of environmental and landscape design, planning and related services. Day one produced nothing, day two produced nothing, but by lunchtime on day three I had won enough work to keep six people and myself peripatetically busy in that country for eighteen months. One project led on to another, led on to another, led on to another. We worked in Iran, helping to prepare the master plans for twenty market towns, and were involved with some major irrigation and rural development projects. Out of that came a whole array of commissions in the Middle East, mostly to do with irrigation and the use of waste water, but also the creation of green belts around the city of Kuwait and some cities in Saudi Arabia, out of which I was able to finance some not very remunerative but important work in this country.

I was green before it was fashionable to be green, though today there are huge numbers of people involved. And of course when one talks about the environment and the countryside, one isn't just talking about visual beauty: nor is one just talking about the wildlife component, or the cultural and historic heritage, or the social dimension. You're actually talking about the integration of all of those things. At the same time, you're saying, 'Ah, but this has to be a living and *working* countryside. It can't just be a play place. It can't just be a pretty pastiche. It must have viable, human, open spaces. It must be a place where we generate food but in such a way that enables these other elements to coexist.' The challenge to the environmental management consultant stems from the need to combine all of these ingredients. So I put what I do very crudely: I am a broker, in pursuit of the marriage between beauty and the beast.

Because my work involves so much travelling, I chose, with Sue, to buy this property, recognizing that it was essential that the family and the children should have a rocklike base where people would be happy even if I wasn't here, and a place back to which, when I was abroad, often under fairly extreme conditions, I would feel strongly drawn. Wantage is a very attractive market town, this property is located in a fabulous part of that market town. It's part of a unique green corridor. It was even more of a green oasis when we came than it is now because the orchard land to the north of us had not been developed, but we came here at a fairly dramatic time of change. England was suffering from the beginning of Dutch Elm disease and within six months we lost all the English elms on the southern side of the property, and then very sadly the wych elms on the northern boundary succumbed. I must have spent three years with little else than a chainsaw in my hand, other than a cricket ball for my son, Hugo, or a racquet for playing tennis with my daughter, Mel. We played a lot of tennis; tennis has been a very unifying activity for us as a family.

We chose here because Oxfordshire was, geographically speaking, the perfect place from which to run my business, although there were some family draws. Sue's grandmother had been Mayor of Oxford and it wasn't too far from where I'd been brought up as a boy during the war. I came to look at this house and I fell in love with it. The grounds were in a pretty derelict state and the house needed work but we thought it would be a challenge. Somebody also happened to mention to me that Sir John Betjeman used to live here, which was an added attraction, since we're avid admirers of his poetry. Moving here meant a ten-year plan: twenty-three years on we're doing the last room, for the first time.

Every community is unique. But there are certain characteristics about Wantage that make it very special and which, in part, inform what I do: its physical layout, its greenness, its marketplace, its cultural and religious roots and its heritage. The town has also served, since the war, as a dormitory for people working in one of the centres of applied scientific excellence in this country – Harwell – and so you have in the community a melting pot of science, religious beliefs, commercial, professional and rural practices.

I think there's quite a challenge for market towns to fulfil new functions in the next century, in the computer age. This town is well placed to address in microcosm some of the bigger challenges, some of the bigger issues, forming life on a much greater scale outside. And I ask myself, as our roads are becoming increasingly congested, whether there isn't a case for market towns like Wantage to help with the evolution of new patterns of life in Britain and beyond; a Britain where people will not be getting into a vehicle every day and driving miles to an office but will be able, courtesy of e-mail and the Internet, to work at home. Maybe market towns will provide the business and commercial hubs that will service those people who are working from home, so that the community can become even more vibrant; can become a place where people aren't leaving their homes and leading nine to five or seven to seven lives; where the home becomes a centre of the main breadwinning work. Towns like this can become active players in the search for new, sustainable lifestyles, because one thing is certain: we have to find them.

It would be easy to get depressed about the state of the environment globally but you can't afford, in the activity that I'm engaged in, to be anything but continually, hopefully pressing forward and trying to find new ways of doing things. There are periods when I feel sad. In England, I feel very sad about the way in which some of the road programmes have been undertaken, like the one which carved through Twyford Down. I am still angry that despite containing a Site of Special Scientific Interest, despite containing heritage monuments, despite being part of an Area of Outstanding Natural Beauty, despite all of those central government designations, it was still possible for the Department of Transport to achieve its myopic ends: to drive the road through the middle of Twyford Down instead of paying approximately £80 million extra to put the road in a tunnel. And although that seems a large sum of money, in terms of the length of time over which people would have continued to have enjoyed those three designations, in perpetuity, and in relation to the money that we've spent on the Channel Tunnel – another project I've been involved with – it's peanuts.

What really saddens me is that until recently no direct vehicle existed for the British public to be given a choice: 'Do you wish, or don't you wish, to spend an additional £80 million on putting such a feature in a tunnel?' No, through the democratic process we delegated that responsibility to government, and the government of the day, having looked at the figures – but without the benefit of a formal environmental impact assessment – came to the conclusion we couldn't afford it. There were no ways forward for serious objectors other than to contribute significant sums of money and take the decision to the High Court, which we did, and we pursued it until we were advised by our legal counsel that it wasn't possible to make progress, that we would just be wasting further money. We were going to challenge it further, through Brussels, but it became obvious that politically the scene had been stitched up.

There are countless examples, not just in this country, but internationally, where environmental and cultural interests are in effect raped. But every now and again there are major successes. I can cite one in Botswana, where we lived and where I worked for two years, assisting the preparation of a national conservation strategy. There was a decision taken by the Government of Botswana to create a major reservoir, associated with the southern end of the Okavango Delta, and the organization with which I was working persuaded the Government of Botswana that the economic returns, as well as the other non-quantifiable impacts, did not represent a good investment. To its eternal credit the Government of Botswana made a decision then and there, the day that the report was issued, not to go forward with the project. And I never imagined that the Government, seeing the extent to which it was influenced by inevitable political pressures, would act in such a way, but it did. So there *are* examples of where the green and the seemingly weak, in comparison with the commercial giant, do win.

We have a case here in Wantage, with the Betjeman Memorial Park, which is a supreme example of how it is possible to succeed when a group of like-minded people come together to take on a commercial developer. The Betjeman Park is one and a half acres but its size is not really material. It's important because it's near the centre of town. Like many other towns, Wantage's open space has been located largely at one end. There we have the recreation ground, which is a Victorianesque park with its railings, swings and hurdy-go-rounds and large area of cut grass like a green desert. And mothers with children, old people, all the people of Wantage, if they want some green areas, are forced to walk quite some distance from the market-place before they actually hit a major piece of green. So I'm thrilled that the district council has helped us to purchase the land, because it has meant that a group of us could establish a charity and change the land to public open space, for the people of Wantage and to commemorate Sir John Betjeman. And although dealing with the minutiae is fraught with difficulty, it's worth it to realize that we have actually got something to celebrate the millennium, and we have also enabled Wantage to say thank you to Sir John Betjeman, who gave untold wealth in terms of his evocative verse, some of which relates to Wantage, some of which relates to nostalgia, and some to rather sad features of our urban life. And personally, even though I've been involved in some very extensive projects abroad, this is one which has perhaps given me as much satisfaction as any other. I expect that's because it's close to home, but it does represent a triumph of the small over the large, the green over the commercial giant, conservation over greed; beauty over the beast, for once.

Geoffrey Bailey

Top Dog

Personally I don't like men's moccasins, they're all right, they have a place, but to me they're not nice: I only sell them because there's people that want them. In ladies' shoes, the ones I don't like I don't keep because I have what I call a fashion-based shop, which offers a unique range of shoes. I get all the old women in town wanting wide-fitting interlaced shoes and I say, 'I just can't do it all.' You have to make a market decision and I can't handle Nora Batty stockings and shoes to match, I can't be having that. I have a few pairs quietly downstairs so that if one of the sisters from the convent needs a bit of help, then I'll sort them out with pleasure. I'd rather do that than have a shopful: that's not being disrespectful but I have a different image. I have got friends in the industry who make a living from servicing that sector, but they're the ones I won't do.

There's another big problem in the industry that hit me very hard in the late eighties. Retail price maintenance is illegal, so a supplier cannot require me to sell a shoe at £59.99. As a retailer, I can sell it for what I like. But the supplier wants me to sell it at £59.99, and not only me in Wantage, but me in Warwick and Witney and Wallingford and Warrington and wherever else you like to think of in the United Kingdom. Well, to my mind that's fair if the product is supplied at the same price to everybody, but it isn't. Some suppliers, for example, they supply their own shops and their franchises at one price, then they supply people with three or four shops buying a few thousand pairs a year at another price, and by the time they get down to Geoffrey Bailey, Market Place, Wantage, who just wants a few pairs, well, he's paying more than anybody else. That's not fair, and that's why I don't do them.

For example, I pay a lot for Bally but I quite like the image and it helps me sell my other shoes. Some other brands, they are a disappointment to me. Some brands use the independent sector to launch their merchandise, they put them into a lot of independent shops like mine. We get behind the product and do well with it, and lo and behold, now they sell to multiples and don't have to go trundling around all the villages selling to us lot. People who launch new brands often use the independent sector as a base. Then they walk away from you.

The loyalty thing is largely gone everywhere. Customers too. They come in here and they're all very proud that they've been to Oxford, Reading, Swindon and Newbury, and I say, 'Well, you'll know where to start next time, won't you.' There used to be more loyalty about. People would think, I'll go and see Geoff before I buy a pair of shoes; but they don't now: they'll go in Tesco's and if they see a pair of shoes as they're passing, they'll buy them. I have to accept that that's the case, and I do have a lot of loyal local customers, of course I do, but more and more they're coming from further and further away. A lot of people move away from here, then when they get married and start a family they realize that the shop where they're living is no good, so when they come back to see Mum and Dad they bring the children in to me. So I'm doing some third-generation kids now, which I like, it's quite good fun. As long as they behave, I don't mind: I can't stand free-range kids. After thirty-two back-to-schools, I can't handle them any more. But I've only chucked about three out in all that time because it's not my policy to chuck people out. It's not good business.

The other thing about retailing is that people have this notion that running a shop is easy, and if they can buy a pair of shoes for twenty quid and sell them for forty, well, that's twenty quid in your pocket.

Mary Loudon

But when they come to look at the list of overheads, and the responsibilities that go with it, and the commitment that goes with it, it's a different matter. That's why bored-wife shops don't last very long, where the early-retirement chaps set their wives up in a boutique. They soon get tired of turning up at seven in the morning to clear the Chinese takeaway off the front and tidy it all up and make it look decent; they soon realize that you can't run a shop between half-past nine and half-past three in the afternoon, that there's a lot more to it. I think that's one of the major reasons that independent retail is not so popular now as it was: it's a huge commitment in time, the competition is so much greater, you've got the big multiple stores opening twenty-four hours a day, and they're selling such a broad base of merchandise you can buy shoes anywhere, you don't have to buy them in Geoffrey Bailey's shop.

This is why I have to make my shop something very special, otherwise I won't survive. There's a lot of talk at Chamber of Commerce meetings about, 'Why do you let so many estate agents and charity shops into the town?' It's not a question of letting them in, it's a question of if you're the landlord of a property and you need a return on the property, and they're prepared to pay and nobody else will, you'll take their money. That's what people don't understand; and people who come into retail without doing some enquiring first usually pack up after a year or two.

During the recession I was working six days a week between 8 a.m. and 6 p.m., and then a bit of evenings and a bit of Sunday. Now it's settled here my current routine is five and a half days, working about ten hours a day. It doesn't worry me because I like what I do. I love my job. I get an enormous kick out of buying something cheap and selling it very expensively: I get an *enormous* kick out of that. There's a lot of claptrap talked about wine and stuff like that, but I know what a product's worth and if I see somebody supplying it that doesn't know what it's worth, then I'll buy it and sell it for what it's worth. And yes, I'll make a good profit. I also like to sort out the difficult kids, the ones nobody else can fit. Most of all, I love selling my men's shoes; a proper pair of shoes for a proper bloke, that does me well, that's my favourite bit. I'm more knowledgeable about it than most other shopkeepers. I know a fair amount about the kids' and ladies', but the men's I have a particular authority about. I have my fishing books in here, my trout and salmon books, and they say, 'Oh, are you a fisherman, Geoffrey?' and I say yes, and then you can start talking about fishing and that's nice, I like that.

Those are the greatest thrills. What I don't like are badly behaved children or snobs, those people who think they're the only ones with a right to be served. I try to deal with everyone exactly the same, I try not to have any special deals for anybody. You offer a service for a price and the genuine ones understand that, but the snobs that want special deals because they're buying a pair of shoes for £180, I've not got time for. They don't ask for any discount in Marks & Spencer's; they don't go to Waitrose with their big trolley and say, 'Right, how much do I get off because I've got a big trolley full?' I say to them when they ask me will I wheel and deal, I say, 'If you want discount, what are you going to do for me?' The old farmers come in and they want deals but as soon as I say I want half a cow or something, 'Give me a butchered-up piece of meat and then you can have a bit of discount,' they never do. They all want it for nothing. Well, I won't do it.

The other difficult thing about this job is you never know when you're going to be busy, so you can only really staff it for the average performance of the average day, and it doesn't work like that. You've either got a shop full, or it's empty and there's very little steady business. The beginning of the seasons are the busiest. September, April, May. In the New Year you're into sales and all that rubbish. I rarely buy anything in for the sale, it's all genuine ends of lines. These people that sell lawn-mowers for half the price, what does it mean? Nothing. I'm afraid we don't have to buy in much for the sale because we've got plenty of stuff that hasn't sold to put in it, especially in ladies'. I bought some walking sandals this last summer that I thought were brilliant but they were too stiff. I thought they were magic, and I bought twenty-four pairs and sold three; hopeless, absolutely hopeless, especially when you have to pay up front for pretty well everything you get. Anything I really can't get rid of, I give to my church. And if I know somebody is going to the Far East or Eastern Europe, I say, 'Take them.' Some people from the Baptist Church, they go off to places like Romania and I give them any I've got left. It gives them a little something to take and it clears my shelf off. You can't have shoes sitting around.

I came here as Dad's manager thirty-two years ago, and I've been here ever since. My father's business was founded by his father in 1903, and was inherited by my brother and I as third generation, and we worked together for years until my brother went away. Then I started Geoffrey Bailey Shoes in 1984, on the main market square, number 47, and the rates and rents there were £25,000 a year. In those days you had to pay huge sums for leases and I had to borrow a lot of money. I paid my own family £25,000 for the key to the shop door, which meant our house was up for grabs. It worked very well until 1989, 1990, when things began to get difficult, as indeed they did everywhere. What happens nationally reflects locally, doesn't it, and the recession hit me pretty hard. The reserves that I'd built up, which fortunately I hadn't spent – if I had done, I should have been in real trouble – the reserves all went and I had to do something pretty dramatic.

It was then that I bought the freehold of this building, which is 34 Market Place. It was terribly rundown, ever so dirty, wet and full of rats. The business before, a gift shop, they'd just walked away and the shop was left to rot. It was in a terrible state but we've made it into a very attractive building. It looks lovely now, we've taken all the old paint off the front and put it back to how it was, and I've reflected that image in that I do things in a very traditional way. I wear an apron in the mornings and wash the shop front and ride my old signed bike up and down. You've got to be very individual in the shoe business to get the people in now, and to get them to come back, and that's what I try to offer, an individual service.

The first couple of years here were difficult because I had to get the staffing levels right, but it had the great advantage of being on one floor, unlike my old shop, and I do like all the little nooks and crannies here. The mirrors are very carefully positioned in this place too; they may not look it to you, but from my little office I can see everywhere in the shop, I can see absolutely everything. Since I moved, the shop's a lot more focused than it was. It's focused on style, not fashion: specialist shoes, classic shoes, shoes in half sizes and fittings. I'll sort kids out with a pair of shoes that fit but if they want lemon laces and purple stripes and stuff like that I don't do it and I don't pretend to do it. My children's room is only ten feet by ten feet but I do manage to cram in about nine hundred pairs of children's shoes.

On average, I sell a thousand pairs of men's shoes, two thousand pairs of ladies' and three thousand pairs of children's shoes every year, as well as the odds and sods like handbags and leather goods. At the moment, the commercial highlight of the business is the men's, especially with this sort of clubby atmosphere that I've created in the men's department. I have a range of English shoes which are all sewn and welted, which is a traditional construction at which the English excel. The Americans try and do it, the Spaniards try and do it, but they can't do it like us, they don't make them like us. We make the best welted shoes in the world.

Men are buying better shoes now. The great advantage of the men's market is that it's ageless. The young exec. in the local estate agent's office has an aim in life: to get a decent pair of English welted shoes. I wear them as a boring fifty-odd-year-old, my father wore them, my son wears them: they're ageless, they're classic. I get young lads of twenty in here wanting a first pair to the old gentleman who wants to replace his. I do them between £80 and £180. You can go into lots of shops and find part of that range but you can't go into many and find that broad spread. Those brogues there, they're £180 a pair, and I can still sell them to the travellers: the fair boys will buy those because they know they'll last. Their father and their father and their father before had them, and they'll tell their children, 'That's what you've got to have, a proper pair of shoes.'

A competition was run by *Shoe and Leather News*, the trade magazine for the shoe industry nationwide. There were five divisions in this competition: Best Shoe Retailer within the Clothing Sector, Best Family Retailer, a couple of others, and one called Most Innovative Shoe Retailer. I thought, I'll have a go at that one, because I was serving coffee to all the customers and doing things my way, and when I opened this shop I got special packaging and all that. Well, we won that division, and then and only then there was a winner of the winners, and I come out top dog!

It was very, very exciting: we were Shoe Retailer of the Year! It was absolutely brilliant! There was a wonderful presentation ceremony at the Botanical Gardens in Birmingham, and that chap from the weather forecast, Ian McGaskill, he did the after-dinner speech and gave the prizes. There were about five hundred people there, so it was a big affair, and there was this great big picture of Geoffrey Bailey Shoes on a giant screen; this little shoe shop in Wantage came up all across the back. I think that was probably the best moment I've had in the trade because I was recognized nationwide for what I'd done and I'd beaten all the big boys. A lot of the big boys had entered it, professional people filling in their entry forms and all that stuff, and I just did mine in longhand and we beat them all. That was the highlight. Never to be forgotten. It helped enormously because I got a lot of publicity. I was a bit sad I didn't get on the telly, especially as a carpet-fitter got on Central News the other week because he won the carpet-fitting competition. I won £1,500 too, which I put back into Geoffrey Bailey Shoes. I got taxed on it, which was a bit annoying.

The staff were delighted. I've got a good bunch of staff, all part-time. I had an excellent manager here for eighteen months, he was a gem, he was very special. In fact, he's the only person that I've ever had in here that I could have said, 'You can carry on Geoffrey Bailey's empire,' he was that good. But when he was poached by the police force I hadn't got anybody in-house to follow in his shoes, so we're a team management now; a bit like the Church, team ministry and all that. There's three of the staff and me. We have a bottle of wine and a chat every three months, just to keep the liaison going, and I'm very pleased with it.

I pay my staff more than the major supermarkets and more than they'd earn in most other independents. After all, it's not easy being here on your knees all day, unpacking shoes and being kicked about looking after everybody's requests, and I think you should be rewarded for it. I'm a sharing man. I like the John Lewis Partnership, their philosophy, and I try to follow it in my own little way. If we make profits, I share them with the girls who've done the best work and the most loyal work. I think that's right and fair. A major change in the minimum wage would affect me but it doesn't worry me because I'm pretty certain you won't find anybody in town paying more than me; and I like politics, I love to discuss it, but I think I can be successful under any government.

You don't have to be that clever to sell shoes but it helps my image if you're nice. All I want in my staff is genuinely pleasant people. If they're interested in people and they can turn themselves out decently, that's fine. The rest of it I do, and there's no doubt it's a very self-centred business, centred around Geoffrey Bailey, but if that's who the customers come for I have to be about. The staff understand that, they know that it's historical. It is a bit difficult for them sometimes, especially when customers come in and say, 'No, I want Geoffrey to fit my children's shoes, please,' but then it makes sense when you think that my house, and everything I own, is in these shoeboxes.

I've got three children, and none of them want the business. The girls are twenty-eight and twenty-six, and laddo is twenty-two. I'm quite philosophical about it. If they want it, then I could show them how to make a living out of it. If they don't, I shall just shut it up. I couldn't sell it for what it's worth. I could sell the shoes and the building but there's no such thing as goodwill now. In the past, somebody would pay you for the customer flow that you've generated and that was called goodwill. You used to buy the lease, the fixtures and fittings, and the goodwill of a business. Nowadays, the lease and the goodwill are worth precious little. I said I paid £25,000 to my family in 1984 for the lease: well, I wouldn't pay them a penny today, shop leases aren't worth anything. In fact, a lot of people have been trying to give them away. Businesses like Next, Laura Ashley, Body Shop, places that expanded very quickly in the late eighties, they bought leases left, right and centre and they got locked into twenty-five years. Then suddenly they're not making the money and they want to get out, and nobody will take the lease.

The key to good retail business in this country lies with government policy to out-of-town shopping developments. For a place like this town to work, you have to look at everything within three miles of the town centre. You have to look at the next town and all the surrounding villages, and you have to be able to serve people with all the things they need daily: bread, vegetables, milk, et cetera. That hasn't been easy in this town because for years now there's been only one supermarket, and if that hasn't got the broccoli you want, or the sauce that you particularly like, or the brand of cornflakes that you want, there's nowhere else to go except the post office in an emergency. I've always said that if you can get the food right, customers will stay in that area to try the shoe shop and the record shop and the rug shop and the furniture shop, and the whole community will generate itself again. If you can't get easy access to the food you want, then it won't work. That's why I was so pleased when Sainsbury's came into town. Out-of-town stores, on the other hand, are a killer. You drive your car there and that's it, shopping done. People drive straight home again.

One of the other things I resent is that the local authorities spend a lot of money on what I call fringe activities, whether it be tarting up the Civic Hall or whatever, and then the weeds start growing around the marketplace. The whole town looks very shabby now, and it's affected the general ambience of the place; it's not conducive to good retail business. That's what saddens me most, the shabbiness. People chuck paper on the floor. They never used to, but they chuck paper out of the windows of their cars now.

That's one of my pet hates, I hate the rubbish. After all, the local people like me who've been here a long time and work in the town, we make quite a big contribution to the way the place ticks and the way it looks. Another example: the Christmas lights appear every year and they're a magic bit of Christmas for the kids round here, they love it. But the same people put them up year after year after year after year, and when they've retired, there's nobody happily coming to take it on. It's the same with the flowers in the square: the same people put them up and take them down every year. Multiple chain shop 'managers', and I use that word in the broadest sense, are not so keen to turn up on a Sunday morning at five o'clock and put Christmas lights up as members of the community are prepared to do. Generally, the people that do the work are the people who live here, because this is where we make our living.

The truth is, you've got to be very, very professional to run an independent retail outfit in a small town, much more so than most people realize. And you've got to be better than the opposition, you've got to do something special. I've done my best, I wouldn't say I've done it all, but we have made it work. I am quietly proud of it. It hasn't come easy, but then you don't want everything to, do you?

Stella Church

The Ripple Effect

Eddie was born in 1970 and he was two and three-quarters when we got him. He was tiny. We went to visit him in his then foster home in London and I found it very weird. Bob is easier with people than I am, it takes me a time to relax with people, so Bob sat and read a book to him and I chatted to the foster-mother and the foster-father. When we came away, we couldn't speak. We drove to just outside High Wycombe and stopped for afternoon tea. We got into this café, sat down, ordered tea, and Bob said, 'Well, what do you think?' I think it hit us then. We realized the enormity of it.

Eddie came to us for one visit and the only game he could play was, 'Bang bang, you're dead!', you know, toy guns and that type of thing. And that was all the visiting we had, which I think on reflection was quite wrong. Then we all went to collect him, me and Bob and our two boys, Michael and Andrew. We had a big box of clothes given us for Eddie, no toys. Not a single toy. When we got home, Michael went through the bag with the social worker while I was seeing to the tea and Andrew was playing with Eddie. Michael was only nine but I can remember hearing him say, 'My mum won't have this rubbish in the house. You might as well throw it away, it's dreadful. He can't wear that.'

The idea was that we were long-term foster carers. We were going to see Eddie right through to school and after. That was what we wanted. It was something that would be settled, not only for Eddie, but for us. It was difficult and I can remember crying, wondering how I was going to cope with this little boy who, at three, was still wetting; who didn't know how to play; who, when he arrived, hadn't got a car, hadn't got a teddy, hadn't got anything.

Most children, when they have a bath they splash you, or they splash each other. They make a mess, they enjoy themselves. Eddie just sat in the bath. You bathed him and you pulled him out. And it took me about a week to think, There's something wrong here. So I got Andrew and Michael to have a bath with him and once he realized he could have fun, it was murder! His birthday, he didn't know how to undo a parcel, he'd never had a parcel, and that was quite a shock to Bob and I. I used to cry about it, it was so sad. But once he got the hang of it there was no stopping him. I took him to Geoff Bailey's shoe shop to buy him some new clothes because Geoff sold Ladybird clothes then; and the clothes that we bought for Eddie there were so small, and the shoes so tiny, little kid bootees, the first size, what babies were wearing, virtually. When we took him to the doctor for a medical I said I was worried about his size but the doctor said, 'Just go home and give him lots of love, and he'll grow.' And he did.

Eddie never saw his parents. And though he seemed all right about it, I think on reflection there probably were things that upset him because the facts for him were quite hard. He used to make up stories about his family, who his mum and dad were, that they were Americans, that dream world sort of thing. But Eddie always felt like family to us and I think he felt the same way although it changed for him in his teens. We adopted him when he was twelve and he told me later that he could remember thinking, when he was adopted, It doesn't matter now, I can do what I like and get away with it. He felt, once he was adopted, that we wouldn't ever get rid of him, that we couldn't get rid of him. Up until then, there had always been the possibility of us saying, 'We've had enough.'

The day the adoption came through we bought a tankard and had an inscription put on it and went out for a meal in Oxford and had a celebration. Everybody was pleased. Everybody accepted Eddie as our son, right from the start. In fact, a lot of my aunts and uncles didn't even realize that he wasn't naturally ours. I can remember going to a family wedding, when he was five, and people saying to my mum, 'Oh, I didn't realize Stella and Bob had got three children,' and she never said otherwise, never went into the whys and wherefores.

The trouble started when he was fourteen. Andrew had gone into the air force by then and Michael had left home, and Eddie missed them dreadfully. Oh, what didn't happen to Eddie then: he started drinking; he may have started the drugs then too. He went into the marines when he was sixteen and a half, he desperately wanted to be a marine and although he got in he didn't make it through, he came out when he was about six weeks from graduating. He'd started drinking heavily before he went in and I think not making it really compounded everything for him because he had to come back and face all his friends, and he'd boasted to his friends, you know, about going in the marines. It was a big thing for him, he wanted to prove himself.

Eddie had been away from home, Bob and I had had seven or eight months on our own and enjoyed it and there he was back again; and teenagers are teenagers, they don't consider their parents have a life. It was very hard. He was getting into trouble, getting drunk, coming home drunk, doing stupid things drunk, and it went on and on and on. His first bout of real trouble was when he smashed all the windows at the secondary school. He caused so much damage it wasn't true. He didn't have any particular feeling against the school but his girlfriend lived near it and he was drunk and it was temper, sheer temper. And I always blamed myself for that, in a sense, because I was working at the chemist's and a friend came in and said, 'I've just seen a policeman talking to your Eddie,' and of course when I spoke to Eddie on the phone at his girlfriend's and said, 'What was the policeman talking to you about?', wham, that was it. He just hit the roof and off he went. He got caught too. He was up a tree, the silly bugger. He got fined, put on probation and of course he thought he'd got away with it.

Then there was a riot in Wantage at Christmas. There were police, helicopters, all sorts. And he didn't come home from that so I knew there was something wrong, knew he'd been arrested. He was drinking a lot then, a hell of a lot. He hadn't actually been involved in the trouble but he was accused of inciting trouble and he went to prison for it. He got nine months. I've got to be honest, I was relieved, because he was out of the town and he was out of trouble. I did go with his girlfriend and visit him but Bob wouldn't go. Bob was so angry with him, for everything he'd put both of us through; he was *really* angry with him. His brothers were very angry with him as well. It's like a ripple effect. The ramifications in families are like pebbles in a pool and the hurt and the damage that you can do to one another are like ripples and ripples and ripples.

Having to tell our parents was awful, really hard. More ripples, affecting everyone. They all wrote to him, and my mother-in-law, bless her heart, she was so sweet, she sent him money and never held it against him at all. He found that very hard. My mother had died not long before, so she didn't know. It was an awful, awful time: my mother had died; my old gentleman that I home-helped for, and was very fond of, Len, he died too. My cousin Kath died. And my friend Linda Slade, she was very ill and dying. I will always remember the day Eddie went to prison because I was going to visit Linda in hospital with a friend, Betty, and we didn't know what was wrong with Linda then. I said to Betty, 'I'll come with you but can you take me home first, and then I'll know if he's been sentenced or not,' because Eddie hadn't wanted us to be in court with him. And he wasn't at home so I knew he'd been sentenced.

So we went to the hospital, which seemed surreal and weird, and Linda met us in the ward entrance: 'I've got cancer of the stomach, I'm not expected to live.' What do you say, you know? Betty and I came away from there, and went and had a meal in Brown's, of all the places; it was noisy, it was loud, and we didn't know what to say to one another. We talked about everything but Eddie. I couldn't. Then Betty dropped me here and Bob came in from work, he was four to midnight shift so it was quite late, and we sat up until about three o'clock in the morning, crying. The loss. It was dreadful. The loss of a son ... Linda ... my mother ... Kath ... Len. It still makes me cry now. But the support we had here was wonderful. I had to tell my boss about Eddie and he said, 'If anybody says anything to you, you're to tell me and I'll deal with it.' People from church were lovely, neighbours, friends, everybody. Nobody said anything to us, nasty, and I know they must have been talking, because it's natural, you do.

My doctor could see that I needed to talk to somebody who was impartial and he put me in touch with a counsellor. The counsellor was smashing, she made me look at Eddie in a different light. *He* drank, *he* took drugs, *he* did it, nobody made him do it. I was feeling that I'd failed him, and also, by this time, Michael had told me how unhappy he'd been at school as a teenager, and I hadn't even noticed Michael, I'd been so concerned about Eddie's adoption at the time. So I felt I'd failed all round as a parent.

The decision we made about Eddie was that we wouldn't have him back home to live because he had physically threatened me when he was drunk, and it frightened me. I don't cope very well with drunk people and drink. That was a hard decision and we had to tell him that. Eddie came out of prison a fortnight before we were going on holiday to Portugal. I know it sounds awful but I was hoping they were going to keep him until we came back, but they didn't so he had to go into digs. His probation officer didn't believe that we would refuse to have him home but we knew that he'd got to stand on his own two feet. The trouble is, he didn't, and to this day I don't know whether we took the right decision. But we took it and we stuck with it.

Bob had been saving up for a new telescope. He'd got a Long John bottle in his wardrobe. I didn't know, because you have private things in your marriage, and Bob's wardrobe was his, and mine was mine, and I didn't go there unless I said, 'Can I go and put something in your wardrobe?' And he said to me, a couple of days after we'd come back from Portugal, 'Have you moved anything in my wardrobe?' I said,

'No, I don't go to your wardrobe, unless I say.' He said, 'Well, there's something missing.' He didn't tell me what it was but it was the Long John bottle, and it was about eighty quid in there.

I didn't want to believe that it was Eddie but it was Eddie. I can see now that there were all sorts of other things too. When they're on drugs, they can't make eye contact, and they're twitchy, it's kind of weird, they're on the move all the time. But I didn't know that then. Eddie didn't talk, he didn't come and spend time with us. He wouldn't let us touch him. All the affection had gone. And then he stole from us again.

We'd decided to retire. We both packed up work and we were planning to go to Australia and New Zealand to see family. Because I'm always open about things, I've always had money lying around, and I still did it, even though I knew that Eddie was stealing from us when he came here. I wasn't changing my lifestyle for him. It was his problem, in a sense. Anyway, Bob had a new cheque card and he hadn't destroyed his old one: the old one is still valid for about three weeks and Eddie had taken that and he'd used it. We didn't know until we had a letter from the bank asking us if we wanted our overdraft extended. Well, we never used our overdraft, we didn't know what they were talking about. So we went and got a readout, and there it was, all this money going missing. Even then I thought a card had been duplicated. I didn't want to believe. But Bob knew. And as we came out of the bank, we met Eddie. I said, 'Eddie, you'll never guess what's happened. Somebody's stolen money out of our bank account. I don't believe it! How do they know our number?' I just didn't believe that Eddie would do that.

We didn't see him again, from that day, for a very long time. He never came near. I think he was stunned. Bob was acuter than me, so we went to the police station. The police couldn't do anything because I thought that someone else had got our card, and Bob thought he'd got rid of his card. There was £1,200 missing, which is a heck of a lot of money. Three weeks later we got a phone call from the bank manager: 'Mrs Church, the card turned up in Weymouth, Dorset. Can you and your husband come and see me, please?' They had a video. Eddie had gone from Lloyds Bank in Wantage, across to Barclays, then into Abingdon, in one day, and taken out the maximum that you can. The next day he'd gone to Didcot and to Oxford, drawing out all this money and spending it on drugs.

Bob said, 'I'm going to prosecute. The buck has got to stop, it's got to finish somewhere.' The bank manager said to him, 'It's your decision but we're right behind you if you do.' So, back to the police station. They were always very nice because they knew Eddie and they knew us. I said to one of the policemen, 'Could I see the video, please?' He said, 'You can but your husband can't, because he's prosecuting.' So I was taken into another room and shown. He said, 'Even before we unscrambled it, we knew it was Eddie. We could tell from his walk.' And there he was.

Bob was so angry. He said things like, 'Well, I'm glad he's not my flesh and blood,' which cut me to the core because I felt he was. He didn't talk about it a lot to me, he talked about it to friends. He was just so hurt, I think. He said, 'It's going to be bad but I will do it because it's got to stop. He can't go on like this.' I was all for cancelling our holiday to Australia but the policeman said, 'You must go.' Eddie was twenty-two, and I can remember thinking, when they shut the door of the aeroplane, That bugger can't get at us any more; and I put him out of my mind. That sounds hard. I did think about him in Sydney, I sent him a postcard, but he was so out of it, he was in so deep, I couldn't reach him. Later he described it as being in the deepest pit he'd ever been in. And he did a stupid thing while we were away. He broke his bail conditions and robbed the fish and chip shop, and the hairdressers, and got caught. Why they ever gave him bail conditions in the first place I don't know, but they did.

We came back and six months went by before we saw Eddie. We wrote to his solicitor and asked did Eddie want any contact with us. He was still on bail and in hospital by now because he'd been so ill from the drugs. The solicitor was, rightly, very wary of me. Who was this mother, now on the scene, who wasn't on the scene before? But I didn't go into explanations. It wasn't for him to judge us. The solicitor said that Eddie would get in touch with us. By this time he was due to be sent to the Ley Community, which is a drug and alcohol rehabilitation unit, instead of prison, and he was very fortunate to get in there.

They were marvellous, the people that worked with him there, absolutely marvellous. I don't know what drugs he was taking before; everything, I think. He wrote to us, and the letter was full of apologies and really quite a hard letter to read. Bob wrote back and Eddie wrote back to that: 'Bloody hell! I never expected Dad to write to me, ever again, after what I'd done to him.' It was strange that he felt he'd done it to his dad and not to me. Still, the communication started up again. Then he wanted a visit. At the Ley Community things like visits are done on trust. It's their whole philosophy. There's a line, and if the people inside step over that line, they're in trouble.

We were sitting in this room, waiting for Eddie, and Bob said, 'Here he comes.' I said, 'That's not Eddie,' but it was. He'd got long hair all tied back in a ponytail and I just didn't recognize him, he'd changed so much. We were all very tearful. He came in with his partner, because they're paired, so Bob and this other lad were talking, and Eddie and I were talking, and it all poured out of him. It was like a big confession. And I can remember saying to him, 'Fine, you've done all that, you've said all that, but it doesn't make it right. There's a lot of work to be done before we're ever back on a good footing,' because the trust had gone. He'd abused his home. I said to him, 'Was it because we wouldn't have you back here to live?' and he said, 'No, that was the best thing you could have done for me. It would have been far worse if you hadn't.'

A lot of it was the marines, the fact that he'd failed, that he hadn't achieved what he'd hoped to achieve in a very tough environment. But it wasn't just that. When Eddie was seventeen his best friend, Paul, died from a drug-related problem and Eddie was devastated by that. He'd been friends with Paul since they were four, and he felt he'd let him down somehow when he died. Then when Eddie was eighteen, my cousin Kath died and left a substantial sum of money to each of our boys. Eddie went out of control. He says now if he hadn't had that money he probably would never have got into such hard drugs, because they were expensive, but he was showing off. Look at me, the big spender. By then, Eddie knew he had let us all down and he kept letting us all down. Not just Bob and I, but his brothers, and his grandparents. He felt a real need to prove himself and it just got worse. He said, 'You get to the point, Mum, where you're in the pit and you think, Might as well carry on: I can't make it any worse than it already is.'

I firmly believe in good and evil. I think there are genuinely bad people, who have no compunction about doing what they do, and I knew Eddie wasn't like that. I used to pray that, no matter how low he got, God would be there for him because I couldn't deal with it. I was completely out of my depth and so was Bob. People would say things like, 'You don't deserve it,' but whether you deserve things or not, as a parent that's what you get. That's the downside of being a mum and dad, that you get the bad as well as the good; you get the flak, the 'It's all your fault.' I think the secret is to say, 'Yes, some things are my fault but they're not all my fault,' and to stand up for yourself as a parent.

Eddie came out with a lot. What he told me shook me rigid; I couldn't even begin to cope with it. The people he'd stolen from and abused! He said he knew it was wrong, that it was totally down to him. He said he knew there was a right way and a wrong way and he chose the wrong way. And in the Ley Community he had to stand up and say this in front of a group of people who gave him no quarter at all because they'd been there. Some were hard-core prisoners, so he got away with nothing. No reasons. No excuses. No pretence. You accept what you've done and then you put it to one side, put it away.

It was hard for Eddie to face us when he came out, and very hard for him to come back here because a lot of our friends were hurt for us and didn't want to see him. But he faced it, he did it. It was tough for him meeting his brothers again. Michael was extremely good with him; he gave him no quarter either. Andrew is far more emotional, bit like me; he's a tough RAF bloke but he found it very hard. The partner that Eddie was in the Ley Community with got caught with drugs so he was out, and that shook Eddie. I think that was the turning point in some ways, because he said to me, 'He's let me down. Now I know how you and Dad felt.'

When Eddie came out he had to make a life for himself, so he went to live in Oxford. His probation officer was a chap called Mike, who was working very well with him, and Mike got him on a phone-in programme about drugs on Radio Oxford. There were people like a retired army major, a clergyman, a doctor, social workers, the presenter, Eddie and the probation officer. And one of the points that Eddie made was that he didn't blame his parents; what happened to him was him, it was his fault. And a guy rang in and said, 'That's a load of nonsense. Your parents have got to take some of the blame,' and Eddie said, 'No. I chose to do drugs. My parents didn't tell me to do drugs or drink.' And he so impressed people by his attitude, and his response, that the probation officer started the ball rolling for Eddie to apply for a place on Operation Raleigh, which he got. That was a real break-through for him. It's quite hard to get on to, and he had about two and a half months to raise nearly £1,000. He was quite lucky, he didn't have to raise the whole money because we helped. The church was marvellous, we had a coffee morning here. His brothers contributed, our friends contributed. He went to Zimbabwe and helped to build a school, and did a conservation thing to do with hippopotamus. He had a wonderful time.

He hasn't found it easy since. He hasn't got any qualifications. He's now down in Brighton, doing a part-time course in social studies and sciences. I'm hoping he sticks at it. He's staying with his brother at the moment and that's not going to be a permanent arrangement, he's looking for somewhere to live, but he still gets a bit panicky: the drugs have made him very nervous about being in enclosed spaces, and travelling, and being with lots of people. He's not brilliant, but he's OK.

He had to do a lot of work with Bob. I think mums tend to

forgive easier than fathers. He now has a good relationship with Bob, though he still tends to take us for granted, which we all do, with our parents. I have a different relationship with him now, a closer relationship. He's very affectionate, much easier to be around than he was, though he's still hard work and I can't be around him for days on end. I think that's probably the drugs, what they did to him. He says he'll never touch them again, says he never wants to get that low again. He says the only way out was either death or up. That's how low he was. He said, 'If I'd have gone to prison it would have been death in the end.' It's changed us too. When we were on holiday in New Zealand, we were sitting in the bus station and I said to Bob, 'That girl's on drugs.' I could never have done that before.

So Eddie comes here now and it's home. One or two of the neighbours round here were very standoffish towards him but he took that on board. His godmother, who is Margaret next door, has been great. She just talks to him. One of my neighbours who he'd been very abusive to, she's OK, but the relationship will never be the same. Never. But she's suffering a bit herself, with her youngest son, so she might have a little understanding later on. We're still close but I would never ask her to do anything for me again. It was made clear to me that she wouldn't do anything for me again because of Eddie and what he'd said to her when he was drunk. Fair enough. And if you have a relationship with a friend after that sort of thing, if it can still be sustained, it's OK. Another friend invited us for Christmas dinner and said, 'But you can't bring Eddie.' She said it was because they were so hurt for me and Bob and I said, 'Fine, I take that on board, but I'm not going to leave him,' so they relented. Eddie went round there himself before Christmas and spoke to them, and they told him what they thought, and Eddie took it on, and that was it. And she said, 'I will never talk about it again,' and we haven't. I don't know what was said, I didn't ask. I didn't want to know.

After Eddie had begun to settle down, Andrew's marriage broke up. The day we found out was one of the worst days of our life. It was the ripples again. I missed my mother dreadfully then because I couldn't talk to anybody and I could have talked to my mother. It's those times in life when you really do miss your parents. You want to have somebody bigger than you, and we're that generation now, Bob and I.

It never stops, being a parent. In fact, it gets worse, I think, as you get older. When they're little, you're in charge of them to a certain degree. When they're adults you have to step back and let people make their own mistakes. But all three boys are very affectionate and they get on well, which I'm pleased about. And although the bad things have rippled through our family, in a sense I'm glad because it shows they care, and you haven't completely failed if you have caring children. I just hope whatever Andrew's looking for, he finds, and Eddie too, because they're the future.

Paul Kirkland

Something Out of the Ordinary

Constable, Sergeant, Inspector, Chief Inspector, Superintendent, Assistant Chief Constable, Chief Constable, and then God. Nowadays, to get to the rank of inspector, you've got to have a reasonable head on your shoulders, operationally and academically. I'm thirty-four, and there are very few that get this kind of post at this age, and so I'm very pleased to have got it. Very pleased to have got it indeed.

Of course, it's not like a routine nine to five office job, it's totally and utterly unpredictable. It's something out of the ordinary. The police service has gone through some incredible changes over the last five to six years. If you asked the routine bobby on the beat, five years ago, 'What are the real priorities that we should be focused on?' then I very much doubt if he or she could've told you. But what we've got now is a much more business-focused service.

I'll give you an example. Up until 1994, the Thames Valley Police, which is an organization with a budget of about £207 million, never had a business plan. The Police and Magistrates Courts Act of 1994 came along, and enshrined in that legislation was a need to produce a costed policing plan. It was to give the Home Secretary and the local community some idea of what the force classes as its priorities, and how it's going to achieve that. So we were thrust from a culture where we didn't have too much of an identity, I would say, into a performance and achievement culture, which is where we are now. And I personally feel that it's the healthiest piece of change that the police service has ever gone through, because at the end of the day we are a public service, and the public needs to know what its money is being spent on, and when that money is spent, what the results are. Additionally, they need to know that what we're spending their money on is what they want, and is going to make a real difference to the quality of life.

It's hard work to get that process right, and I was keen, when I took command here, that we'd get that process right. In the past, a package of policing was delivered to the community of Wantage that whoever was in the chair here would put together. But you could never be sure that you'd hit the mark in terms of what the staff and community thought were important, so we were a little more creative last year. We had a community planning day in the Civic Hall, where we invited a complete cross-section of members of the community and about seventy-five per cent of my staff, and we worked together for a whole day, looking at seven key priorities that the force had focused on, and putting a local slant on them.

From all the ideas that came out of that day, I put together this year's policing plan. I was perfectly honest with people that I couldn't achieve something that was beyond my resources, but where possible I would weave into that plan everything I could that would make it truly local. That was the first time that it's been done in this force, at this level; and I'll stick my neck out here and say that I don't think it's yet been done anywhere in the country at this level. I have a policing plan that reflects local need, my staff have had a major input, and so have the community. So there's your closeness, there's your ownership, and we're in the process of making that work.

Of the seven priorities that the force look at, the first one is to make ourselves more accessible to people and match our services to their needs. The second is to reduce the fear of crime and improve safety. The third is to help communities fight crime; the fourth to reduce the level of robbery and burglary by twenty per cent by the year 2002; the fifth to protect our communities from drug-related crime; the sixth to deliver a high-quality, value-for-money service; and the seventh to ensure that our staff are equipped to do their jobs.

One thing that came out of that meeting was for community bobbies to prepare quarterly articles for the parish newsletters. This way, the community could have a feel for what the levels of crime are, because we find that people's perception of the level of crime is actually far higher than what reality suggests; and that's true more or less everywhere, believe it or not.

Another idea that came out of that meeting was to explore the concept of video production promoting local police services, for inclusion in the local library, and for general public use. We're developing a leaflet for circulation within the local community that will provide information on local policing. We deliver presentations to the Wantage sixth-form students on subjects that they want to hear about. We proactively go out into the community and set up community police surgeries. We take exhibition units out on the road. We've also negotiated with the *Wantage and Grove Herald* to put in a policing supplement twice a year, and we achieved one in May this year, a twelve-page colour supplement that went in the newspaper. We have a good relationship with the local paper. I think I counted half a dozen stories in last week's *Herald* that had a police involvement, so it's a symbiotic relationship, really: they need to satisfy us and we need to satisfy them.

At the moment, the bulk of crime in the town centre is criminal damage. Most of that happens on a Friday and Saturday night. Last year there were a hundred and one criminal damage offences, which, in terms of raw value, was about £60,000-worth of damage. Think about the impact that has on the traders, because it's mostly their windows that get put in. Think of what it does to the community's perception of how safe it is in the town centre at night. So we've put together an operation recently where we have increased foot-beat officers, put highly visible patrols on the street at key times and in key places to prevent crime happening. The very early indications are a reduction in the amount of criminal damage compared to the same time last year, and I'd expect, when we look at the year-end results, that we'll see an overall decrease. As a policing operation it has cost us £1,300 in terms of overtime but that's a lot less than £60,000.

The beauty of sector-policing is that you've got local police officers working with local people to solve local problems, and that's the key to policing success. But I've got to be sure that the money I'm putting into it is going to yield a product and I have to make sure my staff have the support in order to do the job, and win, and make an impact. I'm also accountable to the community, and I passionately believe in that. They've got to be able to see that what they're getting is what they want, and that it's good value for money. Within our force, policing costs about 28p a day for every member of the community. I think that's pretty good value.

For me to be able to manage Wantage Police Sector properly and effectively, there needs to be a sufficient spread of resources, and it's a bit of a sensitive issue. How many police officers do you think are policing Wantage at the moment? And Wantage actually means Wantage, its neighbouring town, Grove, and twenty villages. There's four officers on at the moment, and that's normal. If there always seems to be a lot of policemen in the town, it's because we target our resources carefully. I have five sergeants at this station, four community bobbies, and nineteen constables. That's our very minimum. I've got sufficient to be able to deal with most things and the first-tier response will always be your local police, but if there's an incident that is so major, like a huge rave on the Ridgeway, that we can't deal with without other resources, then we call them in.

Our crime profile is fairly low, and I'm very proud of that. Over the last three years we've reduced crime by thirty per cent, which is huge. The bulk crime here is car crime: theft of cars and theft from motor vehicles. Then it's criminal damage. Then burglary of people's homes and of commercial premises. Violent crime is way down the bottom; it's one of the lowest crimes we've got, and it can mean anything from assault, robbery, and sexual offences to public order offences. Last year we had a total of fifty-eight recorded violent offences and we detected ninety-eight per cent of them. We had two robberies, one of which was armed, and both were detected. But normally, violent crime in this community is fisticuffs when the pubs turn out, a domestic dispute, or behaviour which warrants an arrest for a public order offence: it could be a group fighting, or a group having a stand-off, threatening each other with words, or with bats and stuff. That would be classified as a violent crime. But the chances of walking out in Wantage and getting attacked by somebody you don't know, and being totally unprovoked, is literally zero. It really is literally zero.

Having said that, although serious crime is more confined to urban areas, Wantage has had a handful of murders. There was a young woman whose body was found in the brook over twenty years ago. There was the young man who shot his ex-girlfriend and her new boyfriend, and then himself, in Lockinge village. That was about ten years ago now. And two years ago a young woman was murdered during a disturbance in a local pub. A man was convicted of her murder and sentenced to life imprisonment but the premature loss of such a young life touched all of us here, it touched the whole community. It was an appalling tragedy, terrible.

We deal with quite a few suicides. They use all kinds of methods: hanging, trains, carbon-monoxide poisoning, overdose, shotgun in the mouth. We had one just off the patch the other day, a guy tried to cut his head off with a chainsaw. I've never known one like that. It initially came in as, 'Somebody's had their throat cut.' He actually used a chainsaw. The son had found him in the garage. Awful. Awful.

What we do have more of here in Wantage is an involvement with the misuse of drugs, whether it's the drugs you think of immediately when someone says 'drugs', or whether it's alcohol. Last financial year we had nine hundred and fifty-two recorded crimes, which represented a fourteen per cent reduction on the year before, which was better than the area average, the force average, and the national average. We detected one in three of those. I would suggest that there is an inextricable link between the commission of crime and drug abuse.

I'll give you a very vivid example of that. Last year we ran a bulk drugs enforcement operation called Operation Western, and that involved gathering intelligence on local people that we knew were involved in the supply or misuse of drugs. And on a Friday in July last year, simultaneously, we raided twelve addresses in Wantage and Grove. Made eleven arrests, seized cannabis, heroin, cocaine, amphetamines. A number of people were charged with offences as a result of that operation. And it was very interesting to note the impact that that had on crime, because for the first three weeks afterwards, the reported crime on our patch dropped sixty-five per cent.

I have to say that those who are involved in the supply of drugs are the kind of criminal that I probably dislike the most because they have such an impact on society. They cause me the most problems, and they cause the public the most distress. Fifty per cent of crime, I would say, is committed by a hard core of about five per cent of your offenders, but if you focus yourself on the offender as opposed to the offence, that can yield some tremendous results. With drugs, if I had to give you a profile of the offenders who are likely to come through the custody unit, I'd say they would be males, between sixteen and twenty-four; they probably haven't had a particularly good upbringing, they won't have a particularly good educational profile, they'll be unemployed, and would be likely to have been unemployed for some time.

That's the kind of profile you'd expect, and that's what came through the back door when we had Operation Western. And that's not a local picture, it's a national picture; we're no different to any other town of a similar size. But if you look at the social and economic profile of the town compared to an inner city, there's a vast difference. We haven't got the unemployment issues, the housing issues, the social and economic decay that would have an impact on the rate of offending or drug misuse. But the availability of drugs is far more than it ever used to be and that's probably because the criminal element has got a lot more organized.

There's a number of arguments in terms of legalizing certain kinds of drugs. You could legalize some drugs and cut out the clandestine element of the misuse, which impacts on health issues; the dirtiness of needles or what have you. But if you look at some of the evidence in other countries where cannabis has been legalized, it hasn't solved the problem that they thought it might, because if you legalize the drug, you have outlets that are licensed to sell it, and you end up with criminal diversification. The criminal element will creep into those areas of supply, and that's where the danger comes in, and I don't think you'd ever eradicate that.

There's a lot of pros and cons, but I don't favour legalization. The current thinking with the misuse of drugs is that enforcement alone just won't solve the problem, you've got to look at education and rehabilitation for the offender, and I would certainly like to think that with a juvenile there are options open to us and the courts to try and rehabilitate as part of a sentence, because a prison sentence won't solve the problem. Statistically, prison doesn't work, it doesn't reduce the rate of re-offending. My own view is that we should look at why the offending is happening in the first place. That's why it's important to tackle this issue early, and that means getting to kids when they're young, by involving the police in a structured schools programme, with a professional approach to drugs education and substance misuse, and that includes alcohol. Alcohol is just as bad. It causes society all sorts of problems. Drink-driving is one: you've got a potential murderer behind the wheel of a car. It's a serious threat, it's a serious offence, and it's a recordable offence. I wouldn't say that it's predominantly youngsters either, you do get that business and management element going out for lunch and maybe having one that they shouldn't have. That misuse of alcohol can have a big impact on people's lives.

We have a pub watch here in Wantage which thirty-two of the licensees on the patch have signed up to. That's most of them. And we work very closely with the licensees, dealing with those customers that are violent, or who try to drive when pickled. We've had a number of occasions when a licensee's made an effort to get car keys off a customer and not been successful. So the first thing they do is pick up the phone to us, and we pick up the offender. But just as with drugs, instilling values is a cultural thing, and I think if you can get it right when children are young, then you're going to make a difference.

Until this year, we had a superb community bobby, Pete Butler, whose job it was to go into the schools and talk to children about these issues. Pete died in April. He was only fifty-two and he was tremendously popular. The community was devastated by his death. He used to do conjuring tricks for the children, and they used to call him PC Pete. I'll never forget the day of his funeral: hundreds of people lined the streets to pay their last respects to him. There were men, women and children in tears. It had a profound effect on me, and on all of us here.

Pete represented all that community policing stands for. I don't think I have ever known a man loved and respected by so many on both sides of the line. It's bobbies like Pete who generate creative relationships between the police and the general public, but these things take time. They don't happen fast. If you look at *The Bill*, for example, everything is happening all of the time, and there's never a dull moment. Look at real-life policing, and dare I use the phrase, but it isn't that sexy. Historically, we've also had a negative image, and that's because the training in terms of conflict management, public order management, simply hasn't been there. You've had situations where officers have been confronted with large-scale disorder and with no management of their involvement. The red mist has come down, and all of a sudden you've got somebody on camera apparently thumping a member of the public, or hitting him with a truncheon. That is an awful image, and once you get tarred with that image, it's difficult to shake it.

Now I think that we're making some pretty good inroads to demonstrate to the country, to the community, that we're more professional in what we want to achieve. But the reality is that there will always be major public order situations we have to deal with, and some of our tactics involve a quick, early resolution, which means a very rapid intervention. That's got to happen, and I'm pretty sure that the vast majority of the public would want us to do that. But because professionalism in the service is far higher than what it was, the decision-making is much more sound, the judgement is sound.

If I went into Wantage today and there was a public order incident, my job is not to get in and roll around the floor and make the arrests, it's to stand back and manage it; to make judgements on whether we need to stand off. Do we need a balanced and measured response, or do we need to call in other resources? There are loads of factors that go into making that decision, and you have to make those decisions quite quickly. Sometimes you get it right, sometimes you get it wrong, but that is the nature of the job. Those incidents are not always that predictable. But historically, we never used to go on camera to say, 'This is why that happened, and the professional operational judgements were absolutely right.' Now, you see senior officers going on camera and giving those views, and that puts the balance there.

We've changed. The service is not into its macho, crime-busting role any more; officers with big boots and skinhead haircuts charging into a problem and cracking a few heads. Thames Valley has adopted a 'problem-solving' policing style, and most British police forces are looking at that too. And what 'problem-solving' acknowledges is that we can't solve crime, or reduce the fear of crime, unless we work with the community. That means getting close to them and looking at other agencies that have got an influence, like local authorities, housing, local education, leisure facilities. That's where we hope to forge some pretty powerful strategic partnerships, and that's where you get away from the police service's sexy image.

I was eighteen when I joined the police. It was wanting to put something back into society that really drew me towards the profession, doing something that I could feel would make a difference, have an impact. It had an impact on me. Believe me, the learning curve is very steep and very rapid when you join the police service, in terms of the sheer amount of things that you're exposed to: suicides, domestic disputes, drug misuse, general social problems, death, very bad car accidents. I drove through Hungerford on the day of the shootings, twenty minutes before the shooting started, and I got involved with the

Wiltshire end of the operation. The lady who was shot in the back in Savernake Forest; it was our little group that went in. And watching the story unfold and listening to it on news bulletins, we couldn't believe the scale of that disaster. That had quite a profound effect on me. It really galvanized in my mind the whole issue of firearms. I don't see why people should have handguns or rifles or automatic weapons in the home at all, I really don't. I'm frightened of firearms, I absolutely hate them. I'm called upon quite regularly to manage firearms incidents and the pressure on you to get it right is enormous.

You grow up very quickly in this job. The training period is about two years, you're sworn in straightaway, and you could be with your tutor out on the streets within about fifteen weeks of joining. As a constable of nineteen years of age, with six months' service, I'd get sent to a domestic dispute involving people old enough to be my parents, and I'd be expected to try and give some suitable advice. I thought it unusual that more often than not people would actually listen to what I was saying. The odd one would come out with the quite proper view that you're probably wet behind the ears, and who are you to give me advice? Nowadays, we are no longer trying to recruit people at a young age. We don't like to take people much before their mid-twenties, so those that come in have got a little bit of experience of life.

At the moment, Thames Valley is struggling to attract the right calibre of recruits, and we're running about two hundred short in the force. We've got the lowest police officer to population ratio in the country, so we're spread quite thinly. That's worrying. I dread to think what hours I do. My average week is about sixty hours, some of which is on call, and the way we police here, Wantage is mine: when I go home, nobody else sits in that chair, I've got twenty-four-hour responsibility, and because of pagers and mobile phones, twenty-four-hour contactability and accountability.

I enjoy it, I get a lot of satisfaction from the role. This is a good place to be professionally, and from the point of view that it's my home town, it's good for me, good for the staff, good for the community. I like to see what we're achieving out there, I like to see the development of staff here, and the feedback we're getting from the community because, on balance, I think we're getting it right. And that's a good motivator for me, because if we're getting it right, then we can continue making it better and better. It's just harnessing the energy. I know it's here, it's just bringing it together and tapping into it that has to be done, and that's exactly what we try to do. Nothing very magical about that.

When I left school I had seven 'O' levels and at the age of thirty I realized that, educationally, I needed other things if I was going to progress. And I was put in a position where I had to decide: do I stay with the academic qualifications that I've got or do I better them? I decided to better them. Over the last five years I've got two professional, nationally recognized management qualifications, and a Bachelor of Science Honours Degree in Policing, from Portsmouth. That was all distance learning, I cracked it in three years, and that's at the same time as managing this job and a family. So the ambition is there, the drive is there, the energy is there, and I see Wantage as a stepping stone, really, to something else.

Eileen Sykes

Band Aid

There's no difference between brass and silver bands, it's just a posher
name really, Wantage Silver Band. It sounds nicer than Wantage Brass
Band. We are a brass band, really: our instruments are silver-plated or
lacquered but they're all brass underneath. And I'm not a snob but I
prefer it being called Wantage Silver Band to Wantage Brass Band. It
just sounds better.

What's so nice about the band is that it's amateur and people can
join if they want to. People don't need to be lonely in Wantage. I'm
sure other towns are the same. Nobody need sit at home doing nothing.
Most towns in England have a band, especially in the north of England,
and there are band contests all over. The regional finals are in London
usually. Next year they'll be in the Albert Hall, and I want us to aim
for that because I've always wanted to play in the Albert Hall, it's the
one thing I've always wanted to do. But we're only a little town band
and the standard is very high and the competition is very fierce.

We've played at a lot of contests. We've been to a contest in the
Isle of Man; Pontins used to arrange concerts; we used to go to Brean
Sands near Weston-super-Mare every Easter, and Prestatyn in October.
We've been abroad but not for contests: we've been to our twin towns
in Germany and France, and to Belgium for a hot-air balloon festival.

Every year in March we go to the Saddleworth Contest. We go up there in a coach, we change in a lay-by, and then we go to a village, pile out of the coach, and play. We march along the road, and then we play a set piece or a set choice of marches in an arena, and we're judged. Then we all get back in the coach and set off for the next village, and do the same. I think there's about seventeen places you can go to – we did five last year – and we take in a pint or two, and fish and chips, and we get back here about four in the morning. It's unique. It's one of the highlights of the band year. People up north can be outspoken and occasionally they've said, 'Oh, you're not too bad for a southern band,' but generally they're very encouraging, you get a wonderful clap, and they'll say, 'Wantage? Where's that?'

It's lovely being in the band. You can do as much or little as you want. You meet people, and there's always something going on. There's the Lord Mayor's Procession in Oxford next month. We get asked to do a lot of things like that but the town always comes first. You see, that's what we're frightened of, people booking us further afield and then Wantage town coming and saying, 'We need you here.' It would be a shame if we weren't around because it's very much a town band, that's the most important thing. It's nice to do contests and things like that, but our good players come and go and we're meant to be here to do the town concerts and carolling and fêtes.

We got a Lottery grant last year, £67,000, so we kitted out the A Band and the Youth Band with new instruments. That's the nice thing about a band, the fact that if people haven't got enough money to buy an instrument they are given a good one anyway. I have my own because I play the E-flat cornet and my husband bought me a new one for our twenty-fifth wedding anniversary. The E-flat cornet is over £1,000 now. But with the Lottery grant, when we all had a new instrument, an identical new cornet arrived for the soprano player in the A Band, and that's me, so I've got the new one and I'm lending my own to somebody in the B Band.

We've got nice new uniforms too. They're purple, and at first we had V-neck tabards which were made of velour because it was cheap, with a little slit down the side, and the men's had buttons down. I wasn't very keen on them and some people laughed at them. Now we've got these smart uniforms, purple jackets, cost over £100 each, properly made, and we have our band emblem on them, a laurel wreath, with WSB in the middle.

There are about a hundred and thirty of us and four separate bands within Wantage Silver Band: A Band, B Band, Youth Band and Beginners. Every December we separate and rearrange all the bands and become Holly, Mistletoe, Tinsel and Crackers, and every night all through December there's at least one band out. We play the carols for the town, we collect, and we give a percentage each year to a charity. This year we gave to the day centre, to an ambulance defibrillator, to a play group that has been rehoused. We can make £3,000 at Christmas but it's a lot of hard work. You go out on a very cold, miserable evening, round the streets, and you might get about £40, and you think: I could have put £10 in and stayed at home. But if you don't go people miss you, they like to hear the band. On Christmas morning we go round the almshouses and old people's places. We don't collect then: it's a service to the community. We also do private parties and the Rotary, the Round Table, rugby clubs, occasional weddings and funerals. Recently a fellow died who was in the British Legion and was quite a good friend of the band, so we played at his funeral.

One of the weirdest things we do is the Palm Sunday March for the parish church, where we walk behind the donkey and the vicar at the front. You wouldn't think that would be weird, but it is because they actually march to hymns and it's quite difficult, marching to hymns. 'Onward, Christian Soldiers' is all right, but some of them, they're three beats in a bar, so that's pretty weird. We've also done bandograms, which started by accident. A man called Major Debenham was the president of the band; he was quite fierce, actually, he used to frighten me, to be honest. A little group went to play 'Happy Birthday' at his eightieth birthday party and somebody suggested we should do it for others, so we advertised bandograms and we've had a few now. I remember we played 'Wonderful' for a fellow's eightieth birthday, and he had his bow tie on, and he came out and had a photograph with the band. It was quite moving, he thought it was so wonderful.

Every year I wonder whether to carry on. I keep saying this is probably my last year. I've really struggled this last couple of years because I've had problems at home. My mum lives with us. She's ninety this summer, she's not got a very good memory, and she has to have help getting out of a chair even. Most of the time she doesn't know where she is, though sometimes she does, which makes it harder. If she was the same every day it'd be so much easier to cope with than her being very sensible one day and not the next.

It means somebody's got to be in all the time because we've got her, and we've got Alan's dad too. I can't just nip out, I always have to make arrangements. Nurses come and help with Alan's dad, and my mum's all right if you're around, but it's been an awful strain the last couple of years, and my dad's not very well either. My mum has now been with us nearly twenty years, Alan's dad's been with us for three years, and my dad's been in the nursing home for five years. They rang up the other day and said did I want to collect for Help the Aged: I said, 'I've got them all here.'

It's had an effect on everything, looking after them all. When my dad had a heart attack and then cancer, and my mum couldn't look after him, it put me in an awful position. I already had two parents here. They did take him in at the nursing home, and that helped, but then my mum started deteriorating. Now she goes to the day centre every day, they send an ambulance. It's wonderful. People complain about the social services but they've been really very good to us here. I know it's been very fraught having her at home but people do their best. My dad's costs at the nursing home are £212 a month, and Mum's £48 a week. And people complain! I don't know how people can complain. I think it's a wonderful service.

I can tell you, though, I'm about ready for a break. We're going to Australia a week on Friday, for two weeks. I had to get my mum into the nursing home for two weeks while we go. I can't tell you what a relief it is. And the trouble is, if I'd have given up doing the band, then I wouldn't have had an outlet, and these problems would be more so because I'd have been with them all the time, rather than escaping. It's nice to go out and do something completely different.

Madeleine 'Kim' Brown

Battles and Barbecues

I still had my head in the packing crates when the Division Commissioner of the Guides was on the doorstep saying, 'You will be District Commissioner, won't you?' And then the County Commissioner came to see me, and I remember her looking at me and saying, 'Forget about being cosmopolitan. This is a quiet country area, and the Guide Leaders have been Guides and Brownies here and they have *roots!*' And it was true, they'd known each other from the cradle. I was an army wife. We moved to Wantage when my husband resigned his commission, and I was very much an outsider. But because of Guiding I was welcomed in. I was accepted immediately.

Guiding's part of my life. I was a Guide during the war, when I went to grammar school on the Wirral, and I've been doing it ever since. We Guides had quite a lot to do with the farming round the Wirral because labour was scarce, they had a few Italian prisoners of war but mostly it was us. We went to help with the forestry. We helped build a village hall. We went potato picking and harvesting: we had a week off school to go potato picking because it was so vital. The feeling of Guiding was and is a tremendous passport. It doesn't matter where you go, if there are Guides or Scouts – and I was a Scout too, because I ran a Cub pack at the army school in Detmold, Germany – you have an instant link, an instant rapport. There are no formal introductions, you're in, that's it.

Through guiding, we got to know a man here called Dick Squires. Dick was a country doctor, and Dick had seen a lot of old farm buildings falling into disrepair and was very sad about them. Dick at the time lived in a rented farm called Tulwick, and he had begun by rescuing derelict farm machinery. He wanted to conserve what he could see fast disappearing, and after the farm machinery, which he used to store in the barn at Tulwick, he got interested in old barns.

A lot of the big barns around here were late 1800s and they no longer had a use, partly because they were in such a bad state, and partly because the downland above the town was no longer arable. Wartime, the downland was used a lot for corn and a lot of the sheep pastures were ploughed up, but the concentration of growth up there had dwindled and the barns weren't needed any more, so they were neglected, and Dick began to rescue them. Luckily in town we have Terry Carr, who is a master builder who specializes in old barns, so Dick co-opted him to come and help, and they got backing from the district council, and between them they restored Lain's Barn, a couple of miles out of town, as a community centre.

The very first people to help at Lain's Barn, once Dick had the go-ahead to restore it, was a big group, a very smelly group in the end, of Venture Scouts and Ranger Guides, who went and bagged up all the concentrated goodness out of the stockyard. And this supermuck, as Dick called it, was put into fertilizer sacks which Dick had scrounged from goodness knows where and transported back to people's gardens. There was an incessant, smelly, smoky bonfire the whole weekend, and bags and bags and bags of supermuck. And every time Dick went off on his practice rounds, he put supermuck in his trailer and sold it at 50p a bag, and I think he rather bulldozed his patients into having it. That money from the supermuck was the first funding that we got for Lain's Barn.

Lain's Barn is now run by a trust, and the district council underwrite it, as they do the museum. They have their own catering trust now, but the Guides used to go and staff the catering, we did the serving and clearing and laying-up for all sorts of functions from

Morris dances to weddings to conferences to craft fairs. Dick's wife, Kirsty, did a lot of the cooking, and Dick did the meat carving, very expertly. We had a lot of fun down there but it was hard work and the facilities were not modern, and in the end authority descended and made them strip out the kitchen and rebuild it, but to begin with it was rather like Guide camping, you improvised.

From Lain's Barn came the fund-raising for the museum, and eventually fund-raising again for the Court Hill Centre, which is the youth hostel up on the Downs. The hostel site was a quarry which the town had used in Victorian times to take chalk from, to make the roads down into town more passable. After that, it was in-filled with a lot of rubbish. Dick Squires's original idea was just a simple bunk-house, with some sort of rescued farm building being the basis of it, and the planning people tore their hair out because he kept being offered derelict barns to incorporate into it, and in the end we had five barns built into it, not just one, and a stable block.

We had an awful lot of voluntary help. We had particular help from a scheme which found out-of-work people something to do, and they came and helped for short periods, and then they were more able to find jobs elsewhere. That particular group worked up there right through the most bitter winter of all, 1983, when they were putting up the oldest barn, which was the foundation of the big Common Room. They had to stop digging drains because the ground was frozen solid for well over three weeks, and they couldn't do any cementing for the same reason. They came looking like Russian spies, with balaclavas and coats up to the tops of their heads. Most of the timbering was finished that year, and by spring 1984 it was finished enough to try it out as a hostel just after Easter. In the summer, David Bellamy came and formally opened it, which was a great occasion.

At that point, the YHA came in as our tenants. But the main idea of having a hostel up there was so that local people would enjoy the Ridgeway and the wildlife. We have a lot of school groups come, and they use it as a base to go out and inspect things and thoroughly enjoy themselves in the wood. We have a lot of overseas people. We have many who are walking the Ridgeway. We have people who are interested in the area and just want a base for a few days. We have people who come to the holiday flat attached to the hostel, to stay for the whole week. It's a real mixture. The hostel sleeps up to sixty and it has camping as well, so now there's a full-time warden living there with his wife.

Because we were down to bare chalk when we started, we left the site alone from the planting point of view for a couple of years. The Field Club put in some shrubs and trees but very little else because we wanted to see what would come back of the natural habitation. There were no animals, no butterflies, no birds, no plants for a couple of years, and then gradually they began to come back. By that time, I was responsible for the planting, and the Guides used to come and help quite a lot, and young people doing their Duke of Edinburgh's Award helped, and gradually we put in native hedges.

Now the grounds have acquired hundreds of bulbs, so we have a lot of spring colour. There's a big primrose bank, there are bluebells in the wood. We have kept the banks of the car park as natural as we can. We've deliberately planted things like teasels for the finches and asters for butterflies. We've had young people help with tree planting, shrub clearing, or bonfiring, and doing surveys of what is growing there. We had some schoolgirls who were doing their Gold Duke of Edinburgh's Award, and they came and did a very intensive flower survey. I take out the thistles, because it's not fun for the schoolchildren or the campers, but we've now got fruiting hawthorns and brambles and spindleberry, and so many, many birds now live there. We've had nightingales come back; they're getting scarce. We have field birds and woodland birds. We have an ongoing battle with the rabbits, who eat all our wallflowers, and they're doing quite a lot of damage in the wood with the young trees, which means that all the young trees have to be in protective tubes. There are muntjac deer, fallow deer occasion-ally. Hares in the fields below us. We know there have been hedgehogs and foxes occasionally. There is a badger sett in the field below us, so they may well come up into the wood eventually because there's some soft earth there.

A lot of local people use the wood, people who walk their dogs and like somewhere peaceful, because the grounds are always open. Anyone can come and sit at the picnic tables and have their meals looking at the views, and they can come and use the barbecues if they like. And a lot of people from the town, who didn't really know it existed in the beginning, have now found it and come up and enjoy it in the evenings. There are functions there too. The hostel has a licence for weddings, and people can book it for conferences, and quite often we have had business people there for two or three days at a time. It takes them well away from everything else and they can concentrate on what they're doing. It has so many uses, it's a very great community asset.

Last weekend it was filled by an association of people called the Children of Albion. They came in medieval costume, down to the last goblet. They put up banners to obliterate all our modern information and they acted out all sorts of situations. I was up there last weekend, working in the wood, my husband had a group of Duke of Edinburgh leaders who were doing their leadership training, and some other innocents came up to camp; and we found these Children of Albion all over the place, dressed authentically, beards, ladies in flowing dresses, and they were doing all sorts of interesting things, starting off with rape and pillage. The campers were agog at all this. The Children of Albion were telling the campers later, 'Oh, it's extremely interesting. We had a wedding with the mingling of blood and we had ritual jumping over the fire.' Goodness knows what they hadn't had. There had been battles in the woodland. The whole thing had been master-minded over the last year; it takes them a whole year to dream this up. No set scripts, it just happens. It is meant to be an experience. It certainly was for our campers.

I think, for everyone, the opportunity to go out of doors if you want to is the important thing. It doesn't really matter what you do when you get there. I do a lot of gardening at home and at the hostel, and the hostel has been tremendously important to my husband and myself because if we feel too constricted by the ongoing traffic, which has built up so much since we came to live here, then we can escape up there to fresh air and get on with the work that needs doing. It is always a pleasure. Gardening has been, for both of us, a tremendous source of interest. Our first impression of this area was how lovely the soil was, because it was greensand, it was fruit-growing country, very fertile, and we had the contrast of the chalk Downs above us. We felt this was a lovely place to be.

The other thing that endears us to this area is that the sense of community here is probably better than we've ever known anywhere else. It's lovely, and I think the way we live here is the way that most English people really would like to live. Our community is about the right size for a community to feel as if they are a community but it's big enough for everything you want. It has good schools, it has good sports facilities. It has just about every conceivable club and interest you can think of, from bee-keeping to model-making to photography, music, art. It has a good evening-class range. And of course it has the great outdoors. When we came here we wanted to be somewhere where, rather like an army garrison, you have contacts and an instant appreciation of what is there. From our point of view, it's just the right place. I'm glad we stayed. Thirty years ago, we didn't think we would.

Margaret Bateman

Something Really Crazy

I don't know what it was about Mexico. I never felt good about myself in those years before I went there, I had a lot of bad feelings about my own inadequacies, and suddenly, in Mexico, I seemed to be all right. Everything and everybody seemed to be accepting of me, somehow, and it gave me ... I suppose it gave me myself. Right from the beginning it made me feel right about myself.

I've lived in this area for twenty-four years and coming here was very, very hard indeed. I came here from Mexico when my first marriage broke up, not because I wanted to be in this area at all but because my family is from near here and I wanted my children to be near my family. It was the right decision, but I personally had wanted to stay in Mexico for the rest of my life because as soon as I went to Mexico, it was my home. It was *my* place, the place *I* wanted to be. I always loved it. Always absolutely loved that place. And because it was so vibrant, and so full of people of all nationalities, I found it very, very hard to settle down in England again. I was absolutely madly in love with that country and it took me a very long time to get over leaving it: England felt so provincial, I pined for Mexico.

Before I came here, my first husband and I were in Brussels for a while, and Brussels was so cold and unfriendly after Mexico that there were ways in which England was a comfort. To light the Rayburn for the first time in the autumn, and see the combines and the tractors with their lights on in the fields, in August, in the evenings; things like that, that were special about here, made me cope better with not being in Mexico any more.

I still dream about Mexico sometimes. I was twenty-four when I went there, so maybe it was just my age, but I do know that suddenly I was right away from everybody, and I felt free for the first time. I wouldn't want to go back because it's going to be very different now and I want just to remember it. I still sometimes long for it but I probably long for me then, for my youth or something.

I find Wantage difficult to live in. I found it very difficult when all four children were young because I'm a single parent, and I was very poverty-stricken indeed, and I used to say that I wanted to go into the Market Place and scream my head off because I found the place so boring and so right-wing and so narrow-minded. I found it very hard to take, being in Wantage, and I suppose that it's only different now because I can get out of it more. There were years when I never went to London, there were years when I almost never went anywhere at all, where I hardly ever left the place, and it did nearly drive me mad. I found it very frustrating because I came across so many opinions that were so different from my own, political opinions, opinions about what matters in life; and I found it a very snobbish place, still do.

In all the years I've been here, I don't think attitudes have changed very much. They're very pedestrian and prosaic and without a spark of real intellectual excitement. People are certainly spoiled and complacent. And I couldn't really express that, because people would have hated me if I had, they would have said, 'Who does she think she is? Where does she want to be? So let her go there!' So I didn't say anything except to friends, and I've got some wonderful friends here, but it took me several years before I found some really like-minded people: most of them have been through the drama groups I've been involved with since I came here.

The most difficult to be around are some of the County set. They come in to the shop where I work and some of them are vile. Maybe I should be more tolerant towards them but they drive me crazy. It's their arrogance. It really makes me see red. I get the impression they don't really know what life is like outside a pretty small market town in Middle England. They don't know how hard life can be for so many millions of people, but I suppose that's what happens if you live in a protected environment all your life.

What is really pathetic is the ordinary people in the town being affected by that in their own lives, and thinking it's a good thing to be a bit snobbish, and earning enough money to move to a smart part of Wantage, thinking that it's better than the part of Wantage they grew up in. That sort of thing perpetuates itself in a small town and becomes very claustrophobic. Certainly the real things that go on in the world outside seem very distant from most people here. What's real to them, and I hate to say this, is being able to afford to buy their shoes at Geoffrey Bailey's shoe shop, because that is very important to a lot of the people here, being able to afford shoes at a smart shop like that.

I think those kinds of people are really, really sad. I find it pathetic that they should be so influenced by the social dinosaurs that they're on the way to being dinosaurs themselves while they are still young. I think they are the people who ought to bugger off out of here and get themselves some sort of life. I mean, it's all right coming to Wantage after living in other places, and seeing it for what it is, and just making what life you can here, but if you've lived here all your life, and you're really influenced by the class consciousness in the place, that's just sad.

There are things about here, once you are able to enjoy them because you're able to get out, that are absolutely lovely. There was one particular evening, when I was first living in a cottage out at Wood Hill Farm; it was a Saturday evening, I was going to a barbecue for the drama group in the Chairwoman's paddock, and as I walked along the footpath by the brook, the church clock struck nine and a hymn tune was played. And for some reason, I'll never forget that feeling, I'll never forget that moment. It was summer, it was a lovely evening, there was nobody about, and this town, at that moment, was beautiful. And something of that feeling about Wantage has never gone away, no matter how infuriated I've been with it, no matter how frustrated.

All the same, people who've lived in more exciting places would never want to come here. In Wantage, what is there, really? What goes on? The Machine Knitting Society. When I look through *What's On In Wantage* every month I think, There must be something this month, and I look to see if there's anything about to happen here and there never is. I suppose I'm unfair because I'm not an artist, and there are quite a lot of art groups and photographic groups; I'm not a musician, and there is a lot, musically, that happens in Wantage; and of course there's the drama and theatre here. But apart from that, there's nothing.

I just want something. I'm waiting for something outrageous to happen in Wantage. I'm waiting for something really, really exciting and wonderful, something really crazy, to happen, and it never does. There have been eccentrics who have lived in Wantage in the past, like John Betjeman. There's still Dick Squires. There was old Jessie Gibbs, whose poltergeist followed her everywhere: Jessie used to have a pink wig which she wore for special occasions. But even the eccentrics in Wantage have never really livened the place up very much, somehow. Maybe one day somebody will turn up who is going to take the place by storm, but I doubt it. They're not going to want to bother with here, are they; they're going to want to be in the places where things are happening.

Betty Mitchell

Waiting for Julie

I'm looking out the window for Julie. Julie's my nurse and she comes to visit me at home. I've suffered from depressions for years, you see, that's why she's coming. I got so low I took an overdose in the end.

Jim couldn't put up with me. He couldn't. So the doctor told him to go out and leave me. I never forgave him, the doctor. Of course, Jim went out. He went out every day to the day centre. I was sitting in that room through there one day when the doctor came to see me and he said, 'There is nothing wrong with you mentally. You should feel lucky. You haven't got arthritis.' Well, I have got it now. Anyway, I thought that was very unkind and I changed my doctor.

I've got a bit of depression at the moment because Jim is such a handful. He sits there and he don't speak, all evening he just goes to sleep. I have to do everything for him in the mornings. I pay £15 a week for somebody to come in and dress him but everything else I do and I'm frightened to death he'll fall. He fell a week ago, you see, in the bathroom. Now he goes out and my depressions come and go. I had this breakdown because I was left all day. I don't know if you've ever had it but it's terrible, depression, and people think you're making it up because they can't see what's wrong with you. I take depression tablets but they stop me sleeping. I'm afraid to go out now, I'm so tired. I hate going out. I take my walking stick, I go as far as the town, and that's enough.

Is that Julie? It's six weeks since Julie has been. I used to go to the day hospital but I can't leave Jim. I didn't used to get home until five and Jim was home from the day centre by then and I can't leave him on his own. I used to have to go at twenty past eight in the morning and that was awkward because I can't rush around in the mornings. I used to get so tired because they made you do exercises and cookery and all sorts. I was worn out when I got home.

When I took an overdose I was taken into the hospital. I took the pills and went to bed. I was still there when Jim was brought home from the day centre. They couldn't get in to me and they had to break in. It was a spur of the moment thing, I just couldn't cope any more. The daughters were very angry with me, all of them. They're good now, but nobody knows unless they've had it what a dreadful thing depression is, and there's so many people who've got it and nobody realizes.

I was in the Warneford Hospital for five weeks. I didn't like it because there were people there a lot worse than me. One man used to walk about with nothing on and I said, 'Oh, for goodness' sake, David, go and put your pyjamas on.' I used to get up early to have a bath and get out of the ward because the other patients would start banging on the bedrails and the nurses used to come streaming down, and lights would come flooding, you know, and you couldn't sleep.

The neighbours didn't want to know me afterwards. I felt very much on my own. The nurses, like Julie, they were very understanding. Julie is wonderful. Jim is very affectionate, but Jim's depressed too now because he can't walk and that. He can't come to terms with it, you see. 'I wish my legs would get better,' he says, but he sits too long. I think he should walk more but he don't like it if I say anything and I've got to watch him, you see, all the time.

I find it difficult getting old because I used to do such a lot of voluntary work; the hospital, Age Concern. I used to go and visit people, nine people every week, on my bike. I used to do the church flowers. I belonged to the Mothers' Union. If you're active it's all right, but if you're not it's terrible. The mornings are the worst now, they're dreadful, I find it hard to get up. I just feel terrible. I'm getting so tired and weary. I used to sob my heart out in the bath sometimes. It's a terrible thing and you can't shake it off and it's yourself that's got to do it, really. Oh, good, here she comes, Julie. I thought she wasn't coming.

Maria White

Getting On With It

It was funny, but the first word I spoke was 'Ipswich', and that's quite a complicated word to say. At the time, my brother's wife was with me and saying that she wondered who Swindon Robins were riding that Saturday, and I just said, 'Ipswich.'

I was seventeen. Kept having headaches and being sick. The doctors just said I had migraines. Went shopping with my Mum, Christmas shopping, and I kept losing my sight on and off, and we went to the hospital. They sent me to the eye hospital, and they took me in to have a shunt. It's something they do to relieve pressure from the brain. But that didn't work. I come out Christmas Day, was home for a week, went back in and had the tumour out.

I was in a coma for forty-eight days. Can't remember directly after the coma, but I can remember I had a bed on the floor, because I kept falling out. Afterwards, I couldn't speak or walk. Couldn't see. I wasn't frightened. Don't think I was. Loads of people said it must have been awful, but I didn't really take much notice. I just wanted to get better.

I had to learn to speak again. Not communicating, it was a bit frustrating. But there was an elderly lady, Barbara, from the League of Friends, who used to come in every day and read to me, and she's still a really good friend. She's in her eighties now. I love speedway, so she read me speedway magazines, and Mills and Boon books. Can't remember them now. I know that she couldn't pronounce some of the foreign names, and I used to laugh.

When I come out of hospital, they wanted to send me to a college, but there weren't any near. So the first place that I went was Birmingham, Queen Alexandra College, and I was there for three years, in a wheelchair. That was a college for the blind, but there weren't many totally blind, most were partially sighted, and only two of us were in wheelchairs. Then I went to Hereward in Coventry, which was for disabled, and did a computer course for a year. They hadn't had blind people there before doing computers.

My sight went completely. The doctors didn't know if it would come back. It hasn't. Think the nerve was damaged. No one's suggested anything can be done. I must have had the brain tumour for quite a while at school, because it was that big. The surgeon said that if he could have seen how big it was, on the scan, he wouldn't have operated.

I've always had a good memory, and that weren't affected, so it didn't really take that long to learn Braille. I just visualized the dots. I don't read books in Braille. They take too long, and you've forgot what you've read, so I get my books on tape. I like mostly murder mystery. Have you read *The Horse Whisperer*? Long! I like the television. I like court programmes, because they explain it all. I also like *Frost*. *Morse* I like. And I like *Taggart*, but that is very visual.

I had to go to a lot of speech therapy. I went to it at Rivermead Hospital, and I went to it at college in Birmingham too. At first it was just making sounds and I found it stupid, a bit frustrating. But it's more annoying when you have to speak to someone you don't know, and they don't really listen, so they don't hear you properly. It took quite a time to speak again. Must have been about three years, I think. I don't exactly know. Now my speech is very slow.

I did a lot of physio in hospital, too. I was in hospital for seven months first, and then eleven months. Then there was two months when I went for two days a week. Now, walking, it's all right with someone's arm. It's probably as good as it's going to be. I walk with my fiancé, Derek. I have a stick, but I usually leave it folded up because

I hold Derek's arm. It's better now I'm not in a wheelchair. When I went to college I used to be really shy, and people used to just leave me places because I was in my wheelchair. That's why I wanted to get out of my chair. So I learned to speak up.

To start with, after the operation, I needed twenty-four-hour care, and my parents looked after me. They didn't get any help. Because Mum couldn't drive, friends brought her to the hospital. Some friends were very helpful and kind. But other friends, I think they didn't want to know. Then when I left college and come home, there weren't any groups for us disabled people. So Paul, my social worker, and a few disabled, started having meetings. At that time, I didn't know hardly anyone disabled, so I helped start Open Access, a group in Wantage, and I first met Derek there in '91. Gradually we saw more of each other, and in '94 I started going out with him. Then November '97, we got engaged. I say November because that's when our party was, but we were on a horse-riding holiday in August and that's when he asked me. The ring had to be specially made, so it isn't sticking up in the way of things.

Started horse-riding when I was at Rivermead Hospital. Then when I went to college, I could only go in the holidays. So for four years I didn't go much. But now, I go every Tuesday. When I first started, I used to have someone leading and someone walking each side of me, and now I just have someone leading. Usually our group likes to go for walks, and once a year we ride along the Downs from Court Hill Youth Hostel to the Red Barn, though I don't know where the Red Barn is. It's quite a few miles from the youth hostel, because we ride there, have a picnic, and ride back, and it takes all day and I get a sore bum. Brandy, my horse, he's known for getting spooked a lot. He doesn't bolt, he just, like, jumps; gives a little jump. But I'm used to him, so I just hold on.

I said how I helped set up the disabled group, Open Access, in Wantage. Well, I was also a founder member of a group of disabled people in Faringdon. Me and Derek do the treasury for that group. Derek does the writing and I help him with this and that. I'm the secretary. It gives us things to think about. And every other Monday afternoon I go to the Stroke Club, although I've not had a stroke, but they do craft things, making things, and our craft group had ended, so they asked me if I would like to join. It's mainly older people, that's the one problem: me and Derek are usually the youngest people there, and we don't like just socializing with old and disabled. That's partly why me and Derek didn't get together before, because so many people were on about we *should* get together because we're both disabled.

People I meet, who don't know me, some of them are really nice, and a few, they don't take much notice. We go to a country and western dance once a fortnight, me and Derek, and usually we go and speak to the band after, and most of them are really nice. But you get the odd one that don't really want to speak. Yet I don't know if it's because I'm blind, or what. I just think, Well, they're not worth knowing.

My family treat me the same. Just as Maria. I am the same, except I'm not so shy as I was. If anything, it's more me that goes and does things with my friends: Derek wouldn't say he's got many friends now because when he was ill they just didn't want to know. And because he's that much older he's not met as many new people. He had a brain haemorrhage when he was thirty. He's thirty-nine now.

Derek sees outlines. He can't focus very well. Derek used to build kitchen cabinets and that, but because he can't see the really small things, like millimetres, it put him off. I think he would like to work, but there's nothing round here, and to get anywhere for him to work, it would cost too much.

I get Severe Disablement Allowance because I've never worked, and Income Support. That's about £75 a week. And because I'm on Income Support I get my prescriptions free automatically. Derek gets a bit more because he's on Incapacity Benefit, but then he has to keep on filling in forms to get his prescriptions free. If he did work, his benefit would be cut and he wouldn't have enough to live on.

Being disabled has changed my life. I wouldn't have done as much as I have otherwise, I don't think. My friend Theresa, she's married, lives in the same village she grew up in, has two children, and that's all she's done. I've been to Denmark, been to Germany, been to Belgium, been to Greece. Me and Derek went to Greece last year. I think my mum weren't too sure, about the rough roads and that. We're going to Belgium again in July, because friends of ours over there are getting married.

Sometimes I get a bit emotional. I've never got angry, not really. Just got on with life. I was speaking to Samantha, a friend of mine from school, on the phone the other day. And she said to me that I was always like that at school. Didn't worry about things, just got on with it.

Henrietta Knight

Ups and Downs

Horses are a bit like a drug, they get in your system. I've always had ponies, always ridden, and everywhere I've ever gone — holidays abroad, train journeys through the country — I've always looked into the fields to see what horses are there.

I always said I'd never get married because I was perfectly happy to live here with my horses and have my own existence, and then along came Terry Biddlecombe. Terry used to be a jockey, and a very good jockey, a champion jockey in his day, and we met at a show I was judging at Malvern. He'd been married twice before, he'd lived in Australia, he'd been an alcoholic and sorted himself out, and when he came back to England he said he'd come and help me here at the training yard, and he's stayed here ever since. We finally got married and it's worked very, very well. We're completely different but we both have the same love of horses and racing. The end goal is the same.

We have sixty horses here and you need a lot of staff to look after them. There are about twenty lads who come in daily, and they look after three or four horses each, and work long hours, but Terry and I feed the horses every morning at quarter to six. We see every horse, feel all their legs, their bumps and lumps, their hot and cold spots, and we can tell if a horse is just not himself. I don't know how some people train two hundred horses and know them all individually.

Fitness and condition is what training horses is all about. You want to make sure that their muscles are all as fully developed as they can be, so each horse gets ridden out or exercised in some form for about an hour a day; not very long, when you think they're stabled for the other twenty-three hours. They go for hacks, and they go on a thing called a horse-walking machine, where they walk round and round in a circle in an enclosure. They're fairly stupid animals, horses, and they're quite happy just to plod round and round in a circle. We obviously train them with jumps, because with steeplechase training you want to give horses as much jump education as possible so they're not intimidated by obstacles over three miles, but we rarely put them in fields. Sometimes we put them in the paddock for fresh air with an old horse who is a sort of nanny to them and doesn't gallop round, because they do a lot of injuries to themselves if you put them in a field: they crash into the fences, and injuries are expensive.

We have a set daily rate per horse, which at the moment is £30, though it's about to go up. On top of that we charge for the shoeing, which is now very expensive, it's about £40 per set of shoes. We have the blacksmith in the yard nearly every day: shoes on, shoes off. In the old days, you took the horses to the forge and they got lovely hot shoes which were moulded to the horse's hooves. Now the shoes are brought to us cold, and you have to fit the hoof to the shoe. A horse is shod with general working shoes once a month approximately, but they race in aluminium shoes because aluminium is light. The general working shoes, which have to go over these roads round the villages, are steel. So the day before the races you put the aluminium shoes on, and then you whip them off again the day after. It doesn't do the foot a lot of good because you have a lot of little nail holes, and if you get the shoes changed so much that the wall of the hoof breaks up, sometimes the shoes won't stay on properly.

On top of the shoes, the owners also have to pay what's called a gallop fee, which is about £45 a month. The gallop fee pays for the rent of David Gandolfo's training track, and for our small all-weather track here. By 'all-weather' I mean it's a track that's been dug out, drained with stone, and then had a synthetic substance put on the top so that we can gallop when it's wet. Our track is only four furlongs, and there are eight furlongs in a mile, so it's half a mile. Some of the tracks are longer but it's a question of cost. To do a four-furlong track cost me £50,000, and I did it eight years ago by borrowing the money from various owners and reducing their weekly training fees in order to pay it back. It's very expensive to maintain. The horse-walking machine was much cheaper. It was only £12,000.

The owners also have to pay race registration fees, and they have to pay for a jockey to ride the horse in a race, which is a flat fee of £90, though obviously the very successful jockeys get paid a lot more in other ways. Certain yards have what they call 'retained jockeys', where they give a jockey x thousand pounds a year to be there to ride the horses. Other jockeys, like Richard Dunwoody, are retained by owners. Richard's with a very rich man called Robert Ogden, who's got horses dotted all over the country with different trainers, and Richard and he have an agreement this season that Richard rides all his horses, and Richard would be paid a fair bit for that.

All in all, to keep a horse in training in a yard like this one costs about £1,000 a month. So we tell owners who are going into racehorse ownership that they have to think of spending £12,000 a year to train a horse alone, and that's after buying the horse itself. A reasonable horse to go hurdling or steeplechasing costs anything from £8,000 to £80,000; top whack for a jumper would probably be about £200,000. And there's very, very small rewards, because in the jumping game the prize money is very bad. If the owners break even, they're lucky. We did have two or three horses in the yard which actually made a profit last year, but on the whole it's a luxury sport. In the flat-racing world owners can make money, but there's a big division between jumps and flat. The Arabs have really got control of the flat and it's done as a business and a pedigree breeding industry.

We've had several years that have been at a loss and people don't understand it, but the outgoings are huge. Sixty horses at £1,000 a month each is a lot of money but my wage bill for a month is £20,000.

Trainers are expected to provide all the saddles and tack for horses, all the rugs to keep them warm, and a rug can cost £80. A day-to-day riding-out saddle would be about £200 to £300. The bridles cost over £100. But even the lads in the yard think we must be terribly rich because we live in a nice house. They've no idea what the overheads are just to keep the whole thing on the road: the insurances, the cost of hay, the cost of the oats and the food, the blacksmith's bills, the vet's bills.

We don't own this house, anyway. It belongs to the Lockinge Estate. The estate belonged to my grandfather, my uncle inherited it from him, and it's now run by my cousin, Thomas Loyd. In fact, if this house wasn't a tenanted farm, and I had to pay rent for the stables, I couldn't do it because I'm quite extravagant, I like high standards. I have a brilliant secretary here, Christine Douglas-Home, whose father trained a Grand National winner and a Derby winner, and I couldn't run this place without her because I'm a very bad businesswoman. I'm OK when it's buying or selling horses, I know their value, but not the day-to-day running of things. Christine says I'm far too extravagant, she says I've got to economize. I always think a horse wants a warmer rug, and therefore go and buy it. I use the old attic upstairs to store a lot of the saddlery, and Terry says if he sees me going off to a horse show again and buying another bridle or bit, he's going to murder me. He says there's enough bits in the loft to last most people a lifetime and more. But I can't resist, if there's a saddlery store somewhere, buying something new.

That's why it's very important to win enough money in the year to get a little bit back. As a trainer, you get about five or six per cent of the prize money for the yard, and you get it for first, second or third place. Last season, the total prize money won in this yard, before our percentage, was £287,000. The season before, we were better, we were £300,000. The season before that, £314,000. I remember we had a very bad season in 1991–92, there was only £53,000: we were hit by a virus that year. So far this season we're up to about £120,000. We haven't hit form yet. We've had a few winners but not enough. The average win is pathetic, anyway. The Cheltenham Gold Cup last year was worth £148,000 to the winner and the Grand National was worth £212,000, but those are the two biggest steeplechase races. A little race will get less than £2,000 for the owner, and when you think what he's paid to keep the horse, and race it that day, and what risks are involved in a race, it's pathetic.

The Mecca of racing is Cheltenham. We've been lucky enough to win one of the races at Cheltenham last year and the year before, but I don't like the National, it frightens me. Terry likes it because he used to ride in it, but I'm very bad at watching all the horses run. The National's four and a half miles, and it's been modified a lot, but a lot of people won't risk their horses in it as it's considered dangerous. I think the fences are probably perfectly fair in terms of height, and the safety limit is forty horses now, but you still get five or six very good horses, a bunch of middling ones, and a bunch of rubbish at the bottom, and it's the rubbish at the bottom that causes the problems in the race: it's the speed, numbers and overcrowding, and the horses panic. The National's like a lot of bad drivers going around Hyde Park Corner in the rush hour and getting in the way of the good ones.

You're also very lucky if you have a good horse. I've got a very good little French horse in the yard at the moment called Edredon Bleu, he cost around £80,000. He was quite useless for the first season and he didn't win a race. Last year he won four, including one at Cheltenham, and this year he's won two. Horses like that don't just appear. Also, certain horses race better on different sorts of ground. If it's a very wet season, and you've got a horse that prefers a firmer surface, you can't run it: it's not going to show its true form because it's got a longer stride and wants a sounder surface. If you have a horse that has rather a short stride and brings its knees up more, it rather likes the mud. Last winter was not very wet, it favoured all the dry-ground horses, so the trainers stocked up with them. This year a lot of those horses are standing in their trainers' yards, not racing, because it's been exceptionally wet this year, and the weather means it's not their ground.

Obviously, all the successful trainers are highly competitive. There's plenty of rivalries in racing and I'm not a very good loser, I hate losing races. Over the years I've been training, we've been lucky enough to have been in the top twenty every year in the training list, out of around five hundred trainers; though of those five hundred trainers there's probably four hundred licensed trainers like me, and the others are 'permit trainers', amateur people who can only train their own family horses. The top professional trainer at the moment is a man called Martin Pipe, who has his horses down in Wellington in Somerset. Pipe's been the leading trainer now for the last ten years, I should think. He has a vast number of winners and wins a lot of big races, but he has so many horses they're in and out quite fast, and then the next lot come in. I mean, I wouldn't want to knock Mr Pipe because he's very skilled and very successful, but he has a totally different approach to us here.

In the *Racing Post*, which is incidentally run by the Arabs now, they do statistics every day of the top jump trainers in Britain. Martin Pipe, so far this season, he's already won £562,000. He's had ninety-three winners and he's leading. Then there's a man called Paul Nicholls, down near Shepton Mallet; David Nicholson, near Stow-on-the-Wold; Mary Reveley, who trains up in the north; Philip Hobbs on Exmoor; a very successful new girl trainer called Venetia Williams, who won the Hennessy Gold Cup and a King George; Nigel Twiston-Davies from Stow-on-the-Wold; Nicky Henderson at Lambourn; Tim Easterby from Yorkshire; Sue Smith, who's married to an ex-show jumper called Harvey Smith; the Sherwoods in Lambourn; there was Mrs Pitman in Lambourn before she retired. Those are today's leading trainers and I'm about fifteenth on that list. I've run a hundred and thirty-six races this season and I've won thirteen and got a huge number of seconds, so we're way behind. This time last year we'd won about twenty-five.

We've had a lot of bad luck. Recently, one horse ran very badly in two races. Couldn't understand why. It was a very good horse galloping at home. We thought maybe he'd got a breathing problem, because he kept fading at the last bit. He had blood tests, he had the back people looking at him, the muscle people. No one could find anything wrong. They were going to send him to Bristol University, to put him on a treadmill and test his intake of oxygen, but instead they sent him to the vet to have a bone scan and he'd got a fracture of one of his cervical vertebrae. It was pressing on part of the spinal cord and that's why he was getting behind.

We had another one the other day: the jockey pulled him up between two hurdles and said, 'The horse feels a bit wobbly,' and it was lame when it stopped. It had broken its pelvis. Then we had one last year which was rather sick, a lovely lovely horse, Terry's and my favourite, called Wild West Wind, a beautiful young horse: he won four races and we thought he'd got a bit of colic. Went out to feed him in the morning and he was dead in the stable. He had a massive heart attack and a burst ulcer.

It's like *Emergency Ward 10* in a racing yard. There's always something going wrong with horses. Breathing problems are common. A lot of horses are what's termed in the racing world as 'bleeders'; they break blood vessels when they race, and at the end of a race you'll see blood streaming out of their noses. There also seems to be a major problem with viruses now. I wonder whether it's all to do with modern farming using a lot more chemicals, but horses are getting much sicker than they ever did in the old days. Terry rode a large variety of horses in the past and he never remembers horses being as sick as they are now. Whether it's summer or winter, the yards seem to be hit by a different virus, and most of them hit the respiratory system. I think perhaps vets have overdone it with antibiotics, and the horses' immune systems have gone.

So many things go wrong, I sometimes wonder why we do it. But the worst thing about being a trainer, much worse than all the worry, is going to the races. I hate going to the races. It's such a waste of time because you have to drive so far, and I'm not all that sociable, but the owners expect it. Today is a good day because there's no racing. Yesterday we went to a meeting near Chichester, and that's three and a half hours in the car when you could be doing something else. In the winter, the racing can start as early as eleven thirty, and if you've got to get to somewhere like Leicester or Bangor it's a hell of a sweat to get through Birmingham and all those ghastly places. Terry drives, or my assistant, Caro, drives, and I do all my book work in the car, and I telephone the owners. Terry says he dreads the day when I have a fax machine in the car, but it will come because I can't afford not to be doing things.

Training the owners is as difficult as training the horses, especially as a lot of the owners nowadays know nothing about horses; they've probably just thought it would be fun to have a racehorse. When you start talking to them, they say the most ridiculous things. And when you go to the races, they don't know where to stand, and where to see the horse, and you have to explain everything to them. It's the usual thing to stand with your owners and watch the race, but they're quite used to me now: I very seldom stand with them. I prefer to stand on my own, or with Terry. Very often I watch the race on the television because you can see more.

A huge cross-section of people are owners these days. There's the old-fashioned country people who have had horses all their lives, bred them maybe. There's the young business people who don't know a lot about horses but they've got a lot of extra money to throw around. We've got several members of the Jockey Club. We've got a lot of people who have horses in syndicates, the people who are from every sort of background in little jobs, and they've just got a little share of a horse. We've got about six or seven different syndicates here. Some of them have got twelve people in them, some of them have got a hundred and fifty, and obviously we try and accommodate the owners, especially the syndicate owners, so that they can all get to see their horse if possible, but we try and choose the right race. You'd never enter a horse in the Gold Cup, say, if it was way out of its ability. I mean, it's rather embarrassing if it goes round a jump behind everything else. There's a horse in this country at the moment called Quixall Crossett, it's fourteen years old and it's now become a national hero because it's run ninety-five times and never won a race, and it just keeps on going. The owner is a permit trainer and he puts it in because he says it enjoys the exercise.

I could categorize my owners in the same way that I could categorize the horses. You get owners that are very bad losers, and then they blame you, they blame the jockey, they say you haven't trained the horse properly. We haven't got too many of those owners left because I tell ones like that: 'If you don't like it here, go somewhere else.' Quite a few of them have taken their horses away, and we've had horses from other yards too. It happens, backwards and forwards. Then some of the owners want horses that are what I call social runners. They're the worst: those are the owners we hate. They only want the horse to run at a big meeting because they like socializing with the people that go to that meeting. We like every horse to run with a chance of being in the first four, and if it hasn't then it's a waste of a race, because there's probably not more than six or seven races in any one horse in any one season. And if you wear it out against horses it's never able to beat, you probably dishearten it. We don't train for social reasons. We train on the merit of the horse.

I've often said to owners: 'You are the most awkward owner I've got, and I've put you very low down the list at the moment,' and I laugh at them. You can only say that to ones you know quite well. That's where Terry comes in so useful, he's very good with the owners. It doesn't matter what he says to them. He's got a fairly dirty mind, Terry, he's always laughing, always joking, and he's brilliant with them. If things go wrong he always raises their spirits, and he's very good with the jockeys because having been a jockey himself he can help them. He's got a very good eye for how the horses should look and how the riders should ride.

Of course, there are moments when horses have not been ridden quite like I wanted them to be ridden, and I've taken it up with the jockeys, and they've always had some excuse: the horse was off colour, or it didn't feel right, or it was making a gurgling noise in its throat. There are so many excuses which are produced. But even though people are always on about all these jockeys they keep arresting, because they say that they're fixing races, no one's ever offered me a backhander. I do know people who have been offered them and turned them down, and fixing's always been a thing in all of the Dick Francis books, but it's not so easy to do it in steeplechasing because you've got jumps in the way.

There is definitely a certain amount of doping that's done, but the jockeys are pretty shrewd and they know when the horse is cantering down to the start if they feel peculiar. A couple of horses were withdrawn from races the day before last, they'd been doped. There have been quite a number of jockeys and trainers who have been banned for short spells recently, for not letting horses run on their merits, but wherever there's gambling there will be some skulduggery, and the Jockey Club has tightened up tremendously on keeping the game straight, so that the punters get a fair crack of the whip. You get corruption in all the sports. Racing is no exception.

Racing's the ninth biggest industry in this country and I suppose it's a way of life for me now, but quite frequently I ask myself why we do it. You have so many downs, and the ups are so few in comparison. When you get a winner, and everything's gone right, it's incredibly exciting, especially at a big meeting. There's nothing like it, the excitement of it. Yesterday we won a race with a mare we'd chosen in Ireland, and out of three runs she's had two wins and a second. That was a high. Then the next race, we had a horse that's been here a long time, a lovely horse, he's won fifteen races and he looked, yesterday, as though he was going to win again. He was doing really well and then a horse fell in front of him, rolled over, crashed into him and knocked the jockey off. It was so disappointing. And then we ran another horse in the last race that we thought would run quite well and it didn't do any good at all. Didn't like the mud.

So I'm going to give up when I'm sixty, I've decided, because I've had enough of driving the length and breadth of the country, and worrying. We'll give up training other people's horses and maybe buy and sell a few of our own. We've got three or four already but they take up boxes which could be taking horses at £30 a day, so they're not really economical. And then I think I'll have a sale of all my tack, because most of the tack sales are either when trainers have given up completely or died, and I think I might cash in on mine before I die.

Margaret Hoddinott

The Invisible Lady Wantage

Mother had two brothers in the Berkshire Yeomanry, and the yeomanry was moving from Wantage to Churn, which is on the Ridgeway just by Blewbury. There was always a big army camp up there and my grandfather took me up to the main road to see these two uncles go by on their horses. Roads weren't tarmacked in those days and they always had piles of flint at their edges, to mend a hole if there was one; and I can remember, vividly, standing on a pile of flint and waving a flag to my uncles as they went by. It's my first vivid memory, the outbreak of the First World War. All three of my mother's brothers went, and the one I liked best, Uncle Norman, was killed at Gallipoli. My father, being a farmer, didn't have to go.

My father worked as a tenant farmer for Lord Wantage, four miles out of town on the Lockinge Estate. My grandfather came to the area in the 1870s when Lord and Lady Wantage were married. The Lockinge Estate comes from Lady Wantage's side: her father, Lord Overston, gave it to them as a wedding present. It was fifty-eight thousand acres and neither Lord nor Lady Wantage knew the first thing about farming; Lord Wantage had only ever been in the army.

My father had a thousand acres from the Ridgeway down to Wantage Station; the farm was six miles long and two fields wide. Everything was done by shire horses in those days and he employed about twenty men. My father never actually worked with the men. I don't ever remember him ploughing a field or anything like that, he just went out at seven every morning and told the men what to do. He did go to the market sometimes. Every Wednesday was market day, and eggs and chickens were taken from the farm to be sold at market. The market filled the whole of the square. There were pens of cattle and sheep being sold but my father sold all his cattle and sheep to the butcher in Wantage. They used to be driven along the road to the butcher's own slaughterhouse behind the shop.

Father was always travelling. He had the farm to look after and he was a county councillor, a rural district councillor, a guardian at the workhouse and an alderman. To begin with, he went everywhere on a pony, and then a pony and trap, and then I can remember one morning, it was during the war, about 1916, at breakfast he said, 'Now, I want one of you to come into Wantage on the back of my bike because you'll have to ride it home. I've bought a car.' So I went. In those days, bicycles had a step that somebody could stand on and the back wheel had a bit which took one foot, and you held on to the rider. I went into Wantage with him like that and he bought the car, drove around the marketplace twice and the man who sold it to him, Cyril Kent, said, 'That's all right, then, you can drive home now.' So he did, and I rode the bike home. They didn't have any driving tests then. That's all the driving he did before he had a car.

Later on, he had a bad accident, one of his shire horses knocked him down and stepped on his left hand, and from then on it was almost useless, he found it very difficult to do the gears and the brake on the car. So from the time we could reach the wheel and understand what we were told to do, we used to sit beside him and change the gears. We all drove as soon as we could reach the pedal, because from the main road to the station was a private road and you didn't have to have a licence, and from East Lockinge Manor up to the Ridgeway was a private road, and we had a private road all through West Lockinge too. We used to drive him all over the estate by the time we were about twelve or thirteen.

It was such a carefree life. Every Friday, we used to come in to Wantage shopping. My mother would drive in in the pony and trap and we would put the trap up at the Bear Hotel. I think it was a shilling, and they would unharness the pony and put it into a stable, and we would go off and do our shopping. You never paid, you had a bill sent to the house. My father had a bill at the end of the month or end of the quarter. And you *never* carried a parcel, you wouldn't dream of it: it was wrapped up and when you got back to the Bear, there it was in the trap. Shopping was very, very easy in those days, and very different. You went into a shop and you were given a chair. You sat at the counter. I can't *imagine* now going into a shop and sitting down and saying, 'I want a reel of cotton,' and them getting it for you, and then you saying you wanted a yard of elastic, and them going to get it for you while you stayed in the chair. I often think of it now when I go in. The other day I had to go all around Waitrose, and I thought, Isn't this awful! I don't know where anything is. I wish I were back in the days when I could just go in, sit at the counter and say, 'A pound of sugar, a pound of butter,' and have it all delivered. That was wonderful.

And in those days, if we wanted some meat, we just used to get on the phone at eight o'clock in the morning and say, 'A shoulder of lamb,' or 'Rib of beef,' and within half an hour it would be out at Lockinge, a boy on a bicycle would deliver it in time to cook it for lunch. It always arrived on time; you didn't even think about it not coming, you knew it would. There was also a grocer's shop in Ardington village, and they came up once a week, took an order, and delivered it the next day.

There was very little stress then. The place was empty. And when I did start to drive a car into Wantage, I never had to lock it, nobody would ever have stolen anything. There weren't many families with cars, so when you drove into Wantage you hardly ever met anything, and you just parked when you got there. My father parked in front of Cyril Kent's shop always; all his life he had the same parking place.

The manners of the people were very much better too. People were very courteous and much more formal, very formal, especially on the estate. I miss the formality. I often think of it. You were always very properly dressed, and when we went to church on Sundays we never went without a hat and gloves. The first time I went to church without a hat or gloves was only a few years ago. It was a long time before I could bring myself to go to church without a hat and when I did it felt very wrong.

They were lovely, those times. We lived at West Lockinge Farm, where Henrietta Knight now lives and trains her racehorses. I was the second of five children and we always had our own rooms. There were six bedrooms and there was what we called the nursery end; a great big nursery with two rooms off it which we used as bedrooms later. Then there were six attics, two of which were used as bedrooms. We always had two maids living in, a woman came every day to clean, and an odd-job man came. He cleaned all the shoes every morning and filled all the coal boxes; we had no electric light. He did a bit of gardening and he was also a groom, and when we first went to kindergarten, and later to school, he drove us into Wantage in the pony and trap. We also had a nursemaid who took us out for walks and played with us in the nursery, and we had a governess until I was five.

The Wantages never had any family, which very much upset Lady Wantage, so we used to go to Lockinge House quite a bit for her. She would have loved a family and so she asked my mother if we would go and play in the garden at least once a week. We felt so restricted there because there were so many rules: don't step on a flower bed; don't fall in the lake; don't pull up a plant; don't do this; don't do that; but we always did go every week and play in the garden. She never played with us. She never came outside. We never ever saw her, not once, but evidently she saw us because if we didn't go, sure enough a footman would come around and ask if anybody was ill and why hadn't we gone. So she obviously watched from the window. It's so sad and she was so very nice, she really loved children. I have got several presents and books that I had from her at Christmas time.

My parents didn't think girls should work and we weren't expected to help out as children. When I first left school we helped with the hens and learned to cook but that was all. I was always very fond of gardening and I did quite a bit in the garden but mostly Helen and I went out an awful lot. I know one week we went to a dance maybe every night. We used to go dancing in Shrivenham, ice-skating in Oxford, and we belonged to a hockey club at Faringdon. We went all over the place playing hockey once a week in the winter. We had our own tennis court at Lockinge and in the summer we had tennis parties every week and went to other people's houses for theirs, and for cards parties. All the big farms had their own tennis courts and in the middle of the week it would be ladies' tennis, and at the weekend it would be mixed. Sometimes we would go to someone else's house in the morning and have lunch, play tennis all afternoon, have tea and play tennis again in the evening, have supper, and then play cards until midnight.

Besides the tennis court, we had another lawn where we played croquet, and another bit where we played clock golf, so when we had a party we would have a lot going on. There was a big hall in the house and sometimes we had dances in the winter; we could have thirty people dance to a gramophone. There was no question that we should be doing anything else: for us girls, life was either going out or having parties at home. The Second World War changed all that, of course.

Rachel Peskowiecz

Change of Scene

Hector and I are pretty seriously into parties. We live in Brixton and there are a lot of parties here, lots of things going on at various clubs. South London is very good for that sort of thing. We go out most weekends, Friday and Saturday nights, with the odd couple of months' break in between, where we might go out maybe once, because you do have to have a break from it. We tend to go to places where they play acid-techno and trance, and it's very much a community feeling. It's really lovely to be able to go to a club and see, maybe, forty or fifty people that you know who are almost like a family, and you see them very regularly throughout the year. Some of them you see outside of the party scene as well, which is extra nice, because then you really do get to know people properly.

Socially, it's a real mixture. Age range is anywhere from fifteen to fifty-five or sixty, which is quite a spread. Drugs are a big part of the scene insofar as a lot of people are doing an awful lot of substances a lot of the time, but I think that once you're into that mind-set you don't need to take the drugs necessarily to be able to go to a party and pick up on that vibe. And the techno and trance scene in London is extremely vibrant, there's a lot of good things going on, people networking, setting up little businesses together. There's an awful lot of positive energy that comes out of it, and the atmosphere is so good that you can pick up on that alone. If you go clubbing when you're completely straight, you might not have quite enough energy to last the course necessarily, but in the end the positive things don't have much to do with drugs. They're self-generating within that scene.

There are a lot of different drugs on the scene. LSD is particularly popular, as it was in the sixties, but it's mostly Ecstasy. The whole Ecstasy thing is about making contact with people, about being fluffy, about being open, letting your barriers down. It's so completely different to alcohol in its effects. You don't see people getting aggressive and you don't have any of the related alcohol problems. I mean, you do have other problems where people are having depressions midweek because they've overindulged at the weekend, but actually while people are on Es the whole vibe is completely different. If you go to a party where people are taking Es, and everyone's on a similar trip, and the music's good, then there's nothing like it.

I would say to anyone who disapproves, or is afraid of it, do a bit more reading. Talk to people who are actually on the scene. Talk to the older ones, particularly, who've been doing it for a long time, and maybe go to a party and see what's going on. It might be a bit of a culture shock, and it might be quite a difficult thing to do, but it might change your perception of what the scene's about. Of course there might be health problems later. There is not yet enough information on the long-term effects of using E, and people do die occasionally. But the percentage of people who actually take E, and the percentage of people who kill themselves doing it, is minuscule. There are millions of people taking the drug. If you compare that to alcohol-related deaths, then surely that tells you something. So really, to have an opinion, I think you've got to go and have a look, see for yourself, talk to people, and then decide what you think.

For proper facts about E, people need to look them up. There's a very good site on the Internet called *ecstasy.org*. It's worth checking out. The effects of E are very empathetic, very warm, you really get into the music that you're listening to and it makes you relate to people in a very non-judgemental way. You're much more open socially. There are a lot of people using speed, which makes you a lot less warm and fluffy. I used to use speed. I did get very badly into it while I was at university, but it's psychologically addictive, physically it's extremely bad for you, and any long-term speed abuse doesn't do much for your personality either. It makes you very aggressive, very violent, and gives you very bad come-downs, whereas with occasional use of Ecstasy you don't get so many of those negative effects. You might get a bit of depression, and your memory might not be as good, but it doesn't cause the aggression that speed and coke do. There is a difference.

The other thing that's making a bit of a comeback is acid, which is hallucinogenic. It lasts for a few hours, depending on how much you take. It also enables you to get into the music, and it's not something that you get particularly empathetic on but you do get amazing visuals and sound distortion, and that sort of stuff. If you can imagine a very large room full of people, maybe a thousand people, all on different substances, then it's a world away to what's happening at parties where people are drinking. It's a completely different sort of energy. That's not to say that, necessarily, mass drug consumption is a good thing, but it's no worse than people drinking alcohol. It's a different state of mind. It's a different trip.

If you look at people, if you look at the way that children aspire to go to pubs, and to drink alcohol, and they're told that it's a good thing, and the kid's bought a pint by his dad, that doesn't necessarily mean that after alcohol they're going to move on to harder drugs. In fact, if you were to use that argument, I'd say that nicotine is probably the gateway drug. I also believe that, with cannabis, a lot of people just smoke and don't do any other drugs. Taking cannabis doesn't necessarily mean that you're going to move on to taking Es, and if you take Es it doesn't necessarily mean that you're going to move on to harder drugs, and I don't think there are any statistics to prove that that's a correct argument. It just doesn't happen.

There are some people who will get addicted to anything, playing fruit machines, glue, whatever, but if you think about how many people are doing various drugs in the UK, and then think of how many people are using heroin, if it was the norm to move on to harder drugs you'd have a much bigger heroin problem than you have now. It doesn't really work like that. I've never been offered heroin. I wouldn't even know where to go and buy it. It isn't a social drug, and it's not a drug of choice on that scene, just as people don't use crack on the scene either.

The glue that holds the scene together is not drugs. It's the friendships that people make, and they tend to be friendships which you might not normally be able to make as quickly if you weren't using drugs, because your barriers come down and you talk to people in more depth, perhaps. Or you just have an experience with them on the dancefloor that doesn't require anything at all, it's simply about being exactly on the same level, so you have a connection. And if you have a lot of people making a lot of connections in large groups, then you have something that's quite closely knit. People do seem more tolerant and more able to give other people mental space, in a way. It's almost as if anything's acceptable but in a very organic sort of way. It's lovely. It's good.

I've always been quite honest with my mother about my life. I smoke in front of her, and I've told her about various trips that I've done, and she always says, 'Oh well, be careful, won't you.' She rings me up every now and again when she's read something in the papers. I've spoken to her on the phone before, quite caned, and she has picked me up on it occasionally, so she doesn't approve of it but she's a little bit more well informed about it now than she used to be, and more open to it. She says, 'This is your life. You decide how you want to live it.' Which I appreciate.

Being in London, particularly Brixton, is absolutely the best place to do this sort of thing from. I couldn't have this lifestyle in a small town. There are such dominant values there, always this big need to conform, and if you're in the least bit different then you aren't in. Socially and mentally, there's nothing there for me. I always had the feeling when I lived in Wantage that I was waiting to get out, that I was going to go, but there was never any question of me staying there, so that kind of made it bearable.

We moved to Wantage when I was thirteen. Before Wantage we lived in Wembley, North London, which is an armpit. I really, really disliked being there, and I much preferred being in the country. But I felt restricted in Wantage for a lot of reasons, including the fact that my parents weren't English. Because my background was Jewish it was different to anything else in Wantage, so I always sort of looked at Wantage as a place where it was quite nice to grow up because it was in the country and it was quite safe, and I had a few good friends, and it was really quite uncomplicated. Small-town Middle England. It's a bit of a cliché, but that's very much the way it was. And I always knew that the minute that I was able to leave, I'd go and see something that wasn't, effectively, village life.

My parents came to England as immigrants from Eastern Europe after the war. My father was a toolmaker and my mother didn't work once we came to Wantage. She did work before that and it was always quite menial. She worked in a glass factory in Wembley, owned by a friend of ours, because she came to England without any set of definite skills. She did odd jobs for people. Biscuit packing once. She was quite well educated. Her main interest was playing the piano; she studied at the conservatoire at home. But when they came to England they didn't have enough money for things like pianos and her music fell by the wayside. I think if they'd had the money then she might have carried on.

We always spoke the mother tongue at home. My father also spoke to me in German when I was quite small, and my aunt did as well. Certainly my mother never spoke to me in English, apart from if I had school friends round: her English wasn't good then and it still isn't wonderful now. She always seemed quite grateful that she and my father were able to come to England but I think not speaking English was a way of setting herself apart from other people. I would have been apart whether I'd wanted to be or not. I felt different at school because my background wasn't English, but it was also kind of drummed into me by my parents that it was quite good to hang on to your own culture, you know, to be Jewish, and education was an important part of that. I have one brother, he's eighteen years older than I am, and he's a university professor. He was always the academic one. I was always the one that really had to work. It would have been unthinkable for me to have done anything but go to university: it was expected from a very, very young age. And seeing as life was a bit of a struggle for my parents I thought I should knuckle down and do what they expected.

When we moved to Wantage we got a television. It was a cause for great excitement at the time. Up until then I'd been brought up to read and do other things. My parents were very much into going to see ballets, and sending children to music and dance lessons, and they always took that sort of stuff for granted because those things were quite normal where they grew up, whereas in England it's a very English middle-class thing to do. So although they weren't at any point and by any stretch of the imagination part of the English middle-class scene in England, they wouldn't fit in a million years, their aspirations were actually very similar, ironically enough, which as a child I didn't really appreciate because I wanted what other kids had around me, and that wasn't ballet lessons. They were also very much more into saving up and wanting you going on a foreign holiday, as opposed to somewhere in England, which I think was almost a shame because it would have been quite nice to know a little bit more about the country where you were brought up.

Leaving Wantage was quite an eye-opener for me. I had a year out before university, when I went to Israel, and then I read Psychology at Manchester, and I had an amazing time socially. Certainly in Wantage I was extremely straight, although I had some fairly experimental friends. Obviously I was living with my parents, so there wasn't much scope for me to experiment, and I lived there with the knowledge that very soon I'd leave, and then I could go and find out what other people were doing to enjoy themselves. In Manchester I got very much into the punk/Goth scene, and discovered various substances along the way which were much, much more fun than alcohol, and that's the way that I introduced myself to a whole different kind of lifestyle. As you can imagine, Manchester is a world away from a little place in Oxfordshire, it was a completely different mind-set. I mean, I'd never seen parties in Wantage like I'd seen in Manchester. It was wonderful. It was amazing. It was a great time. My parents took the change in me really quite well. I mean, they didn't really like it when I shaved my head, but they didn't have a massive problem with it, and they'd seen the sixties come and go, so they were actually quite mellow about it. Looking Goth was how I enjoyed looking and a way of saying, 'This is me,' as opposed to having to be something in Wantage.

My father died when I was twenty-one. He died at home, of lung cancer, and it was quite hard just seeing someone's personality change so much in a matter of months. It was a growing-up process, I suppose. It was difficult but it was unavoidable. Eventually it's going to happen, it just happened earlier for me than for most people. I don't think you ever stop missing people but I feel more for my mother, in a way, than I do for myself. My parents were married for years and years, very happily, and the most difficult thing was seeing how my mother would cope on her own. It did take a while, it took maybe five years until she had built up a life of her own, but she did that very successfully, to my complete delight. It's good to see. She's always on the go, which is great, because I think that's what keeps her quite young in her head. I'm very close to my mother, extremely close.

Actually, the funny thing is that despite my lifestyle, which is very different from theirs, I still recognize quite a lot of my parents' attitudes in myself. It's not despite myself, it's just that some of them are still there, and the older I get the more obvious it is. And I don't think it's necessary to be only one way and not another. You can have a whole mixture of yous, if you like, making up the whole, and what I do with my life now is added to a very, very solid base. I've got my education. I feel stable. Hector and I got married seven years ago, when I was twenty-five, so pretty young by today's standards, and he and I started doing some work on the Internet nearly five years ago. I now have an Internet company, and so does he, and the companies are doing OK. The plan is to sell them in four or five years' time and stop work for good. Why work? The only reason that we're doing it is to make the money, then we can do whatever we want for the rest of our lives, with any luck.

The plan is to travel. I'm completely aware that I've seen such a tiny slice of the world and I *must* be quite limited in my outlook because of that. To see the rest of the world, see how other people live, what their lives are made of, what else there is, is just the ultimate in freedom for both of us. I've seen a bit of Europe, a bit of the Middle East. Hector has seen a bit of America, knows France quite well. That just leaves the rest of the world. There's a lot out there, so wherever the journey takes us is fine. That's the plan, anyway.

I've never felt any great draw towards England. I've never felt as if I belong in England, or to England. I wouldn't say I was Eastern European either. Culturally I'm much more Jewish than I am Eastern European, though not in any religious way. And if I distilled it down, wanting to travel would probably come down to feeling quite limited in my cultural attitudes, in what I know about people and their motivations. In England, I think you only see a very narrow cross-section of lifestyles. Places like Manchester and Brixton are very multicultural but that's not quite the same. I don't think you can really understand what makes people tick unless you can immerse yourself, to some extent, in their culture, and see how very different it is to what we've got here. I'm in a very, very fortunate position that there is a possibility of our being able to do that. It is a luxury. But having said that, Hector works very hard for it, and I've put in a fair bit of work myself, and if we don't achieve that, then fine. There'll always be time to travel. But the ideal is to do it for as long as we want without any financial constraints, or time constraints either. Oh, and that's the other thing, no children to restrict us. We've no parenting instincts, none at all. People say it might just hit me. Unlikely. I could get run over tomorrow too.

Geoff Rice

Part Two: Four Years Forward

I wanted a more positive kind of approach. I didn't really think it out, I didn't look at all the things that might happen when I got here. My primary motivation was to get away from Wantage. It was hurting me, because of all the associations. People always looked at me as Mary's husband, which I found difficult. I also got a fair bit of pity, which I didn't want.

I didn't really consider that coming to Norfolk I was coming back to my roots: it was something that hit me later, that I had actually come back almost to my birthplace. That didn't really figure quite so strongly as the terrible urge I had to get away. I have returned to Wantage a few times, and I don't like doing it. I get a sort of leaden feeling as I approach it and a clear sense of relief as I leave; and I am very reluctant to visit the cemetery. Mind you, I am a person who can turn my back on a situation which I've been in for a long time, and forget it. I turned my back on work when I retired, I just left it. The only thing I wouldn't have been able to turn my back on was Mary.

I don't think Mary would have done what I did. I tried to persuade her, when we both retired, to move back to East Anglia. At the time, her mother was ailing, and we were shuttling backwards and forwards from Oxfordshire to Suffolk, and I tried very hard to persuade her that we could save ourselves an awful lot of energy and petrol money and everything else, and go and make a new start at that point. I'm probably glad we didn't, because I wouldn't have landed here, and I think I've been very lucky in that I've landed in the right place. Of course, I also came here to be near my daughter, Eleanor: I came to her for comfort, and she's lovely, she's super, absolutely super.

I've found it very easy to make friends. I have put a fair bit of effort in, but this is a very friendly little town, and I've got an advantage. My vowel sounds come over as very Norfolk and no one has ever asked me where I come from, I'm accepted as a native without any question. I think that's been an asset. I've also been extremely lucky with my neighbours. I've got two lovely families, one next door, and one next door but one, who are very open, and they've accepted me as a neighbour and treat me as a part of their little community. One family's got three girls, and they are extremely friendly, they come and see me sometimes. I take the middle one to a violin lesson sometimes, and that kind of thing, which is very nice. I like children. I would just hate to be in a row of senior citizens.

I was getting worried at Wantage about being selfish, in that I was concentrating almost the whole of my efforts on my own house, my own food. There was no one there that I could do things for. Having come here, I'm not being so selfish. I've got my grandsons I do things for, my daughter I do things for, my neighbours I do things for. When you're on your own, it's very easy to become self-centred, and I think that's very dangerous. I think it leads to depression. I think the evidence is quite clear that quite a lot of elderly people get into that kind of problem, don't they. One of the things I regret was how I behaved when I found myself on my own. Hugh, my younger son, I think he was very hurt at the time, and I was so tied up I could not think outside my problem, and he needed comfort, I'm quite sure he did. He was much closer to his mother than the other two: they'd both been away from home a lot longer than Hugh. But I chat to him about her and it's all right now, there are no problems.

The other thing that worried me at Wantage was that the house at Wantage was Mary's house, really. Everything was where she put it.

Most of the plants in the garden were where she planted them. I was very reluctant to change things afterwards. Here, this is my house, everything is where I put it. Whilst she is in my mind here, I think of her as a guest, whereas she was a resident at Wantage. This house has been very important for me in trying to re-establish my own individual identity, and looking back I think it's clearly the most important thing I've done.

The only thing that I haven't achieved so far, and I don't think I'm going to, perhaps, is I haven't found anyone to love, and I badly need somebody. I mean, I've found love in all sorts of other places. I think I mentioned my German friends before. Their eldest daughter, who's fourteen, I am very firmly attached to her. She is very lovely, she's very kind, she's very, very caring, and she and I are great friends. And since I've been here, I've got quite close to Eleanor's eldest son, who responds to me. I think that's the thing: I think you need somebody who responds to you. If you show affection, you need somebody who spots what you're offering them.

I don't think necessarily I'm looking for love in terms of a wife so much as someone to share things with; someone to share thoughts with, someone to talk to, someone to do things for. I think that's one of the key things that I now miss. Obviously, I miss Mary a great deal, but I miss the little things we did for each other. The thinking about each other, you know, anticipating what the other person's needs might be. It probably sounds a bit queer, but I'm not sure that I could take another woman. We didn't mess about when we were youngsters: Mary was my only woman, and I was her only man, and that still gives me considerable satisfaction, that we had that. I have got on quite friendly terms with one or two ladies, but it's felt a bit like *Blind Date* and I've drawn back. You have to be very fortunate to just cross paths with somebody. I've thought about joining a dating club. I might try it, just to see what kind of person I find. I did send for some details quite a while before I left Wantage but it was too early. It was too early, definitely. I'm very much more relaxed now.

When I'm alone, I find myself thinking about her. That's not grief, somehow. Grief does occur. I went to my mother-in-law's hundredth birthday this last week, and that was grief nearly all the time. I loved the old lady, she was very good to me years ago, before Mary and I married. She was one of those original engines of determination, always beavering about doing something for somebody else, a very unselfish person, and now she is helpless. I don't think she had a clue what was going on at her birthday party. She opened her eyes once or twice but I don't think she knew what was going on.

It's very distressing to see her like that, and I spent most of the weekend thinking about things we did when we were younger, and I did have quite a serious session of grief. I didn't cry. I've got over that now, crying. No, I just ... You know what a snail looks like when you put salt on it? You feel a bit like that, you know, you sort of curl up inside. I'll tell you one thing that I did feel this weekend: I did think how glad I was that Mary didn't end like that, in a nursing home, despite the fact that she got cut short when she was really going quite well. It would have been very much worse for me, I think, if I'd had to go to a home and see her humiliated. Humiliated is not the right word, is it, but you know what I mean. It must just be so awful to be helpless.

It's sharpened up my religious belief quite a lot, all this. I was sort of meandering along, the way people do. Now, I'm very much more regular in my worship, and I think about what I believe a great deal more. I've been going to discussion groups and making my voice heard, which is another thing that I've done here which I always found difficult at Wantage. The Wantage system has always been very priest orientated, and you never get a word in. There, I never found any satisfactory way of expressing my opinions. I was brought up as a Methodist, and when I was a teenager I decided that I would follow in the family tradition and become a local preacher. But the war sort of tore that in half, and I was drafted in the RAF, and I never did it. But I've always had the urge to say my piece and I've found the opportunity here. That's part of what I mean when I talk about going back to my roots.

The other thing that worried me about staying in Wantage was, it was increasingly becoming a sort of dormitory, and the community seemed to me to be suffering. The community here is very strong. Most people work locally and certainly don't travel any further than Norwich, and Norwich is a place with a very strong community. That's another thing that I've got back: my Norwich. I'm very strongly biased in favour of Norwich, I think it's England's nicest provincial city. It's got lots of history, and it's really nice, it's very friendly. I get a great buzz from going to Norwich on the bus. I usually go on a Friday and have my lunch and poke about and find things that I hadn't seen for years. I get a great buzz from that.

Another thing I've gone back to is football. I've got a season ticket at Norwich City, and I take the youngest of Eleanor's boys with me, and we go to all the home matches. Football's something I'd completely given up, it wasn't Mary's thing, and I've gone back to being a fanatic. I'm seventy-three and there's a limit to how many more years you can look forward to getting in your car and buzzing off and doing things like that, but I've still got my independence, so I feel very lucky. And I'm a very much more outwardly friendly person than I was. Before, I didn't have to have friends because Mary and I were very complete. If Mary had been here, we wouldn't have made friends with all the people I've made friends with, definitely.

I'm into the fifth year without Mary. When I'm watching my grandsons play football, or driving the car, my mind is occupied, but sometimes something happens to spark off a memory and you start thinking about her. Things like her little notes from the kitchen, which I found very painful, they're not a problem any more. They're all still in existence and I use them quite happily. The odd twinges I get are mostly when I dive into books of photographs, particularly when I find one I didn't know was there, which seems rather odd. I dug into one the other day, with photographs of a French town which we went to twenty years ago, and I found a picture of her that I had completely forgotten I'd got. She jumped off the picture at me.

That kind of thing doesn't happen very often now and when it does I can usually cope with it quite well. I think that faced with the problem you have to try to push it gently far enough into the background so that you can comfortably live with it. My sister-in-law is very fond of saying to me, 'Oh well, of course, you've got all your memories,' and I find memories are rather negative, you know, you're looking back. I think it's dangerous to look back. I very much prefer looking forward.

Jamal Uddin

Good Life

I came this country when I was age of twelve. My father came this country first, 1952. My father came very young and very poor. My granddad was a very, very rich person, and suddenly when my granddad die, he die age about forty-five, suddenly all our everything ends, and everything gone. My uncles, my dad, they sell out everything, then they become a very poor peoples, penniless.

My father came this country and he really work hard. He was working from seven o'clock in the morning till twelve o'clock at night. He work first in a restaurant and very big hotels in London. It's amazing thing that even with all my uncles, my father is only person working, only person looking after such a big family. My father said, 'I was ill but I was working. I was ill but I know if I stay in bed one week, my children, my wife and my brothers, they will be starving.' And slowly, slowly, my father send money back home to our family to survive. Gradually, my mother buy some lands, and everything is getting better and better and better, and 1983 my father invite my brothers and sisters and my mother to come to this country. So it's much better in our family now: now we are the best in the village back home. We have enough money and enough food and enough land, and my father become a very respectable person in our society and in our village.

In 1989, my father die. Suddenly, he had a heart attack. He was so young when he die, I didn't believe it. He's only fifty-four. It's too young. And he was a very, very nice person, very sharp-minded. My father was a very honest person. He was the best person probably I have around in my life, my dad. He really loved me so much. He always would tell me what is wrong, what is right. Lots of people in this country, they go to drugs, things like this, so he just tell me clearly: 'Anything you do, think about where you come from.' My dad was a great person, and we are lucky that we have a great dad. He give good education and good jobs. Everyone happy. No one say anything wrong to my dad or my mum. They did best they can, and they did it right, so I am very proud that I born in this family, and proud that I am born back home, in Bangladesh.

I was very upset when my dad die. I didn't see him. I was here, and he's dying in Bangladesh. When he's first in this country, my father was looking after his brothers and sisters, he was looking after everyone, because everyone is very poor. In 1960 he's *one* person looking after about forty people. It's amazing. Can you believe it? I mean, it's *one* person. In that time, if anything happen to him, everyone finish; everyone *finish*. My dad write letters to my mum, from this country, he said, 'I'm sending this money, give to my oldest brothers,' and whatever he do, he do for everybody's best. My father send money to my uncles, to build a house, to buy lands, to give money for education for us, and that makes us great back home. And this is the reason that my father loved England.

He loved this country. He said people are very honest in this country. They're very polite, he always told me that. They look after each other, there are much more human rights in this country, they understand each other. It's like my father said, 'If you do anything good, you'll get good. But if you are wrong person, and you do anything stupid, then you never get good things. Only you get something better in life later if you do something good now. If you really work hard, if you believe in yourself, you can make something for yourself in England: then one of the days, you become a great person in Bangladesh.' And that's how I live.

He give me so much, my dad. He is the person give me all these angles. He show me everything: how to talk to people; always look after the old people; always speak to person if he's older than you, and whenever you talk to them, you talk to them nicely, quietly, try to understand them. I love him so much. And my mum also. She's a great lady. She really survive. I'm really honoured that I born in this family, because my mum, she really brave lady. She's got a lot of kids, and she don't have the money to survive, and end of the day she stay in my father's house and she look after us. My mum said always to me, 'Husband and wife is most important thing in this world, because if you trust each other, and if you love each other, you can make anything you want.' My mum was married, she told me, when she was sixteen years old, and they really work hard, my mum and dad. And for what? For us, you know. They give us best choice. Now I can buy anything I want, although when I spend some money I think about why my mum and dad worked so hard to make us happy.

We all married now, my brothers and sisters, and all arranged married. I have been married in 1994. I had a choice. My whole family give me a choice that I could marry someone if I know her, but I said, 'No, I didn't see anyone. All I want is your choice,' because my family will never choose anything bad for me. So they said, 'OK, you have to go back home to get married,' and I was a bit shaking because it is arranged, and I'm brought up this country feeling something different, feeling I don't know this person, how can I get married to unknown person?

They looked out about six girls, so it's like a blind date. One of them, her father was a contractor, and he have his own business, she is a nice lady. I spoke to her about ten minute, and she don't talk to me much, so I joke around to her, say I've been in jails and everything, and would she marry me? And she said, 'I don't think my parents will bring anyone like this in our house.' So I left it. 'Nice talking to you,' you know. Then I went off to see another lady, three days later, and she was a very nice lady, the lady I am getting married in the end. She's wonderful.

I went to her house, and her mother was very, very bright, my mother-in-law. She spoke to me, 'What do you do? What house? What sort of business you have? What are you doing back home? What education you have? What education in Bangladesh?' All this, she give me a question, and I gave the right answers, and they give me about twenty minutes to speak to my wife, and I said to her, 'Will you marry me if I tell you truth in everything?' She said, 'If you tell me the truth.'

She tell me a little bit of her life story and I tell her all this: 'I have four brothers and three sisters, and I come with lovely family. Can you cope with this? Because you'll be a very youngest daughter-in-law in our family to my mum, and my mum, she had a very hard life, and I want someone to look after her. I like you, but I don't want to marry someone that she only like me. She have to be a right person to look after my family.' She said, 'We have a large family as well.' So I said, 'Look, one more thing. Do you like me? And do you have any other comment that you tell me? I don't want to know anything about your previous life, but if you love someone else, you just tell me, and I'll say to your parents that I didn't like you.'

She said, 'Thank you very much. I like you, how you talk. And I am very pleased about the way you talk to me, I do appreciate, but in our society it is not that I find someone else for myself. This is not the way we brought up. If you think that, you come to wrong family. And if you think like that, you might find in England there is a girl there for you.' I said, 'OK, you sure you like me? I like you. You're my first lady.' I said, 'This is my life: my father is die 1989, and if you look after my family, then after I'm married, don't say to me that I didn't tell you.' I said, 'I'm from different society but I'm same culture. My mum had a really hard life, and she give so much for us, and I want to give return to her. I want to make her life best, but once I'm married, probably I go to my work, and who is at home? You. You need to look after my mum.' So she said, 'You do like me?' And I said, 'Yes, I like you.' Then she says, 'OK,' and we are married after fifteen days. She is first woman in my life. I was twenty-four years and she was only nineteen. My wife is a great lady. Rukshana is her name. And now I have one daughter, one son. My daughter is three years old, my son one and a half years old.

This arranged marriage, wife and husband respect each other very much. Love marriage doesn't last long usually; this I find out. My two friend has been in love marriage, and they've been divorced in this country, and plus, I can see this in other English peoples. Listen, in this society, the love and marriage is a joke. Why is a joke? Tell me what's the joke! Joke is: husband and wife, they don't *trust* each other. This is the biggest problem. And the love, yeah, it last six, seven, eight month, then it disappear. The older English people, their marriage long-lasting because they love each other so much, twenty years, thirty years, forty years. But the young married, I think they destroy everything.

Marriage is very important. When your marriage is not working, your mind is not working, you crack yourself, you know. In this country, the husband and wife they asking all the time, where have you been, what you do, where are you going, you know, things like this. When I'm busy in here, I'll go once a week near home. My wife is perfect for me, she's the perfect one for me. She never ever tell me, 'Why don't you come house? This is not life. You need your children, you need me.' She never did once question.

I'm a very happy person. In this world, so much unlucky people, they don't get the right partner, and I can see with my friends and everyone how they are having a terrible time with their wife or husbands. But I'm such a lucky person, honestly, with my wife. I'm happy. If you go home, and your husband or wife really upset with you, you really miserable yourself: this whole day is finished. I know, I work with my friend, and he been divorced. Every time he go to his house, his wife says something to him, and he says something to his wife, and I am the middle person. I understand his wife, and I am understanding him. I met his wife every week, and I met him every day, I talked to him after we finished work, I said, 'Look, Sam, don't do that, don't do this, this is your life, man. Think about your wife. She loves you.' And I tell her also, 'He loves you.' I try my best to make their life, but at the end of the time they've been divorced.

For me and my wife, what's important is ourself and our children. We want a good life, but we have to make something for a better life first. I am working long distance, but one day we can make enough money we can work near to each other. I want to make my children life best as possible. My daughter is very, very sharp. She's very, very nice. I want to make her something good, get her good education, make her life good. I'll give the education to my daughter because in this society, and this world, everyone need a defence, you know. Used to be, Muslim girls they don't need to work, but in this world you never know what happen to you tomorrow. It's getting crazy and crazy. So I want to give my daughter good education, and then if anything happen to her in her life, then she could stand by herself.

What I want money for, I want the money for my children to make theirself. But in this society, the money is very important for luxury. Luxury is very important; this all the day is important to the English. Love in marriage, and in family, *this* is what is important, but in this society, they don't think about the love, I can't believe it. They destroy everything, you know. Why? Why they do it? They're crazy. They're not respect each other and not really happy. They show each other happy, but they're not happy. It's important to your life to have the marriage and the children. Yeah, you need the fun, but you need the family, you need it in your life. You can't stay young in your life, you get old one day.

My wife in Bangladesh now. I have house here but I'm looking for another house for us all to be in, then she will stay here most of the time. But I'm thinking I'll settle back home in future, because we have enough money we can go back home and relax. Our problem in Bangladesh is job. The job is very important and back home there is no job; there is probably two thousand peoples wanting one job. Even if you are very educated then you won't get it. So only these people like myself in this country have the jobs and everything. When I came first in this country, I only intend to have good life, good wife, good house, lovely childrens and to look after my brothers and sisters, Mum and Dad, everyone. My dad said, 'If you are one person looking after three person, you have a hard time, but one day from them you'll get something. Probably they might not help you out because they're poor. But they will give you lots of love for your inside.'

The first job in hotels, my father earn £7 a week. It's so hard life he had, it's amazing how he cope with this. From when I start working, from when I was seventeen, I never, ever keep money to myself. Every week I go home, I give to my dad or my mother. And this money, they never spend that money. I didn't know that. They keep it for me, and one day after six years they said, 'OK, this is £15,000 for you.' Yeah? 'This is for your business, do whatever you like.' And they know I never do anything bad, so they try me. They test me with some money.

I said, 'OK, what shall I do with it?' I didn't know what to do. So my mum said, 'OK, we'll transfer this money to back home, buy something for you.' And she transferred this money to my father's place, and they buy some land for us; for me, for my other brothers and everything, because in our society, whatever a person earn, it's for everyone. It's not for one person. You are earning just for yourself, no. You will be equal with everyone, even if you are young or old, no matter. Even if you don't work, it doesn't matter. Everyone equal. In some families, the people fight about money. But in our family, it's very, very different, because my father always wanted us to stay together.

1996, I came here, to Prince of India in Wantage. I was working in this restaurant in Thame six years, the Thame Tandoori. The persons who own that place are wonderful people. They became very close friend of mine and when I tell them I want to do something for myself, they said, 'OK, maybe we open a restaurant or something, maybe we become partners.' So we become partners, and I run this place.

I come here, I change most things. Now is getting better, day by day. I love this place but it's very funny town, actually, I find out. You can't rely on the business. Every day, up and down. Sometime is good, sometime is bad. One day you are very busy, next minute you are very quiet. And the people in here, very nice, I'm not complaining, but the people are very old character, they're not changing much. They're very old fashioned, traditional, and there's not much money in Wantage, it's not rich people here. This town look like it's lots of money, but I find out it's not. You can't predict like in some other places. Tonight, you might get twenty people, you might get fifty people. I'm in this trade twelve years, and wherever I work before I know exactly how much I'm going to do in this day. But here, you can't tell anything.

It's not a happy town. If someone come here they'll say, 'ghost town', because it's very old character. It's OK for very old people, but for young people, I don't think so, they're not happy. Even the middle-class people, middle age, they don't like this place: there's not much about it. And people are not friendly much, it's like they don't know you. You know what I'm saying? Like I work here three years but I cannot go closer to make a good relationship with customer. I don't want to go to their house, no, but I work in Thame, I work in Folkestone, I work in Sheffield, and in two months in those places you can make lots of friend, customer as a friend. In Wantage, three years, I not make much customers as friends.

I don't know if something wrong with me or something wrong with the people! My English is not perfect because it's my third language, but I like talking to people, I want to make them friend. I went to schools in this country and I haven't ever had a problem because I am from Bangladesh. Honestly, I never had a problem. And even in my working life, twelve years, I never had any problem with any customer. The only trouble I had with people in this country is the people that drink over the limit. This is a big problem, because people once they drink, they lose control. That's why our religion say 'Don't drink.' I never ever touch a drink, not even sip.

A long time ago, Muslim people drink. But one day, one of the person, he went to drink and he came to his house, and suddenly he rapes his daughter because he didn't know what he doing. From that day, is our religion not to drink. Some people, like middle-aged people, they drink, they understand. They can take theirself. This is OK. I think so. But the young people when they drink, you can't control them. Oh, they use so bad language to me, but you know, this is not racism, I think. This is not racism, this is drink.

I took one of the person one day, I said, 'Look, you've been drinking too much,' and he use me so much bad language. He make me a lot of bad promises. I said, 'Look, you don't know what you're doing in these promises you make me.' And he said, 'Why you come this country? You go back to your country.' So I said, 'OK, I'm going tomorrow.' I said, 'You happy? I'm going tomorrow. I'm going to phone someone, you know, give me a passport, I go home. I'm going to get my ticket tomorrow, and I'm going home.' So he said, 'Are you sure you're going tomorrow?' I said, 'Yes, sir, I am, certainly I'm going home. Don't worry, I'll never ever live here because it's very bad place.' He said, 'What do you say? Bad place? Why you telling me bad place this?' I said, 'It's a bad place because you don't like me. That's why I'm telling you bad place. That's what I'm telling the people when I go home.' He said, 'No, this is good place but you are to go out of it.' And suddenly he gone. Next morning he came and he take me apology. He know what he talks, and he said, 'I'm sorry, what I did last night. It was very bad.'

But I don't blame everyone. I mean, in this world, even if you go in our country, people is mixed. There is good and bad people in this world. Some people, when they see some coloured people, they become racism. But the Muslim people really soft-hearted. Generally, if you have Muslim friends they give you good friendships and they give you good times, they give you respect, they give you love, everything. There is no doubt about it. People think of Muslims and they think of Saddam Hussein, that we're crazy religious people. But Saddam Hussein, he's a different character. He's a dictator. He can make anything he want. Mainly, Muslim people, they don't want to give you the hard times, they want to be your friend.

My dad used to say how it was so nice in this country; people love each other, they look after each other, they look after any problem that you can tell them. But day by day it gets worse and worse and worse. You can see these murders; the teenager, Stephen Lawrence, is so bad. He was a nice person and things like this happen. They frighten yourself; you don't want to go anywhere. You don't want to involve with night-lifes, go to London, or go Oxford, in case these things happen with you. It's so bad. Why people do this? Why? All the human beings the same. I mean, I feel guilty myself sometimes, you know, because we have such nice society here, so why they do violence? No one has any problem. If they go to our country, or another country, it's different. Think about Kosova, things like this, people starving, they're dying for food, medicines, everything. Then think about this country: you don't have any problem in this country, no floods, no heat, no anything. Yeah? So people should be very happy in this country, they have so much good thing. I mean, they should be proud theirself: 'We have a great nation.' But they do stupid things and it's really bad.

I blame the parents in this country. There is no respect from the younger people. I mean, teenage people smoking underage, eleven years old, smoking in here, I can't believe it myself. This is amazing to me. In Bangladesh is completely different. Even teenage people smoking, this is all under the table, because of respect for older people. Here, this is a different society. Teenage here think they're very respectable smoking in front of someone. I think it's terrible. I really hate it. It's a horrible thing. And drugs: in this country, it's getting really worse over drugs. In every corner, the children's in drugs. I seen it in Wantage every Friday, Saturday night. I don't know why their parents doesn't say anything to them. I mean, why they not saying 'You must be home at nine o'clock'? Why they not saying this? But now, English people, their daughter giving them a lecture that she not coming home, she going with her boyfriend until midnight.

The English don't respect family now. It used to be English as a large family. Now the people they don't like much children. They want a simple life, simple family, very small family. They used to be very respectable family in this country, long time ago. My father told me they're very, very nice people, very honest people in this country. They look after each other, they look after each other parents. But there's been a lot of change. Now people live a long way from their families. Why? Family is important. My parents, they give me good food, good education, good behaviour. If they don't give me that, I might be somewhere in very bad place. So I should remember my parents, you know. I should look after them. This is the important bits in life. And if children doesn't look after parents, they're not children; they're very bad people, I think.

I don't understand in England: they have the big houses, three bedrooms, four bedrooms, and the father work, the mother work, the grandparents live far away and the children they have nanny. Why they have nanny? Why? Why not the grandparents live in the house? I don't understand. When people get old, they need their children around them. You know what I'm saying? When they get really old, they have the childmind, they don't feed theirself, or they're not feeling well or feeling bad, they *need* their children. They need them so they can be happy. They can play with the grandchildren. They can do lots of things. But if you leave your parents, they got empty hand. Money is not important. Money is *not* important. Money can make today, tomorrow is finished. Money never stay. But parents is important, you should look after the parents.

I really love Bangladesh for the family life. The reason I'm saying why the society there is different is because in this country everyone is very miserable. The people here, everyone busy, everyone busy theirself, you know. They're thinking only money and money and money, nothing else. I don't blame them, but back home, if people work hard from nine o'clock till five o'clock, they'll still come to see you. The older family, they'll give you lots of respect, they'll look after you. They give you lots of love. So I will go home to Bangladesh and I will be safe, I think. When I die, I'll die peacefully. I'll be looked after well. In this country, who going to look after me? You know, you have to phone your councils, or you have to phone the pension office, things like this. It's amazing. There's so much you have to do in this country, so much headache.

So it's better to get the wage here, then you need to leave this country. I'm not saying I don't like this country. I love this country. That's how I am who I am. That's why my name spread back home, from this country, and all my family there is become respected because of this country. I can't say anything bad to this country, but I belong to Bangladesh. Honestly, I love this country, because the politics are very good. You don't have any headache or problem about politics. In our country, you know, so much headache about politics, so much corruption. But retirement is better in Bangladesh. It's good life. Once you retired there, you do a little bit gardening, lovely weather, you can exist there, it's nice. Easy, you know.

So this is how things is in my life: I have good job, good wife, good children, good family. I'm very happy person. I love this country. And one day I go back to Bangladesh.

Acknowledgements

I would like to thank everyone who appears in this book, not only for their time and hospitality, but for their faith and generosity in allowing me to work freely with their secrets and lives in order to write this collection of stories. I would especially like to thank my husband, Andrew St George; my agent, Georgina Capel; my parents, Jean and Irvine Loudon; my transcriber, Marion Haberhauer; and my editor, Georgina Morley. I would also like to thank, below, both those people whose stories I couldn't include in the final book, but who gave up their time for me and made me welcome in their homes, and those others who offered particular assistance, suggestions and encouragement:

Clare Alexander, June Alexander, Phoebe Atkins, Pauline Ballard, Beulah Brown, Robert Caskie, Bernard and Gladys Collins, Carol Dunwoody, Tom Elder, Elizabeth Galbraith, Karen Geary, Kathleen Hawkey, Ian Hermon, Paul and Frankie Hexter, Margaret Highcock, Michael Jones, Barbara Keep, Michael Loudon, Maisie Lovell, Len and Ivy Lyne, Brian MacArthur, Chris Manners, Pauline Merne, John Miller, Jim Mitchell, Stephanie Mullin, Jackie Primrose, Mary Rousseau, Beryl Stoter, Jeremy Trevathan, Paulette Tucker, Felix Velarde and Fay Weldon.